AMERICAN
STREET GANGS

Tim Delaney
State University of New York at Oswego

PEARSON
Prentice
Hall

Upper Saddle River, New Jersey 07458

Library of Congress Cataloging-in-Publication Data
Delaney, Tim.
　American street gangs / Tim Delaney.
　　p. cm.
　Includes bibliographical references and index.
　ISBN 1-13-171079-6 (paperback)
　　1. Gangs—United States. 2. Juvenile delinquency—United States. I. Title.

HV6439.U5D45 2005
302.3′4—dc22

2005048735

Executive Editor: Frank Mortimer, Jr.
Assistant Editor: Mayda Bosco
Editorial Assistant: Kelly Krug
Production Management: GGS Book Services, Atlantic Highlands
Production Editor: Trish Finley
Director of Manufacturing and Production: Bruce Johnson
Managing Editor: Mary Carnis
Production Liaison: Barbara Marttine Cappuccio
Manufacturing Manager: Ilene Sanford
Manufacturing Buyer: Cathleen Petersen
Senior Design Coordinator: Miguel Ortiz
Illustrator of Graffiti Art (Chapter 6): Rebecca Jerrett
Cover Designer: Carey Davies
Cover Image: © Royalty-Free/Corbis
Printer/Binder: R. R. Donnelley & Sons

Pearson Education LTD
Pearson Education Singapore, Pte. Ltd
Pearson Education, Canada, Ltd
Pearson Education–Japan
Pearson Education Australia PTY, Limited
Pearson Education North Asia Ltd
Pearson Educación de Mexico, S.A. de C.V.
Pearson Education Malaysia, Pte. Ltd

10 9 8 7 6 5 4 3 2 1
ISBN: 0-13-171079-6

CONTENTS

Chapter 5 Gang Structure and Process

Chapter 6 Street Gangs: Local, Regional, and Super-Sized

Chapter 7 Female Gangs and Gang Members

Chapter 8 Criminal Activities of Street Gangs

Chapter 9 Gang Prevention, Suppression, and Treatment

PREFACE

The very mention of the words *street gangs* and *gang members* conjures images of violence and intimidation. The lives of the citizens who live in gang-infested neighborhoods are constantly interrupted by the terror and intimidation that often go hand in hand with gangs. Community leaders and social activists work hard to keep youths out of gangs, and law enforcement officials perform their societal duty of arresting and incarcerating gangbangers. But the attitudes of people who live their lives safely away from street gangs is that of indifference. Most people's knowledge of street gangs is correlated to the manner and degree of involvement with gang members. *American Street Gangs* provides a comprehensive review of all the critical elements relevant to gang life. It is designed to provide the necessary background material on gangs so that the reader has a clear idea of the cultural and structural components of gang activity. Gangs have become such a major phenomenon that their existence has become institutionalized—that is, they are now a permanent fixture of American society—and students as well as many members of the general population have an increasing desire to know about street gangs.

The study of street gangs presents many obstacles, beginning with the fact that there is no agreed-upon definition of what a street gang is. Street gangs, as we know them today, have existed since the early 1800s, beginning with the Forty Thieves in New York City circa 1826. Gangs were limited primarily to the urban cities of the North and Midwest until the mid-1900s, when gangs began to expand to the cities of the West. By the 1980s, Los Angeles, the city of angels, had become known as the city of gangs. Today, there are more than 700,000 gang members in the United States, and they can be found in the suburbs, rural areas, prisons, and on Native-American reservations.

The primary goals of *American Street Gangs* is to provide a clear and comprehensive review of critical issues related to gang life; examine and assess the major theories and socioeconomic reasons why gangs exist; provide a description of all types of gangs, including small, regional, and super-sized (nations); analyze law enforcement techniques to combat the growing problem of gangs and diversion efforts to keep youths out of the gang; reveal private information about gangs in an attempt to better understand gangs; and increase the reader's general knowledge of gangs, especially the socio-psychological aspects of individual and group behavior.

My own interest in gangs grew in earnest during my years as a field supervisor for a major chain of convenience stores in Los Angeles and the surrounding areas. As a field supervisor with stores in gang areas, I often came face-to-face with gang members on a daily basis. One of my most interesting recollections of these regular conversations with gang members is that while my company believed that they "owned" the property that the store was located on, rival gangs often felt like they "owned" that turf. Although my company had the law on its side, the store personnel who had to work in these stores often realized who had the real power—those on the streets. Maintaining the safety of my employees often involved bulletproof cashier enclosures (which does not make the average customer feel too good about shopping there!) and various techniques of minimizing potentially deadly confrontations. During my years of living in Los Angeles, I observed many gang-related incidents, poverty-stricken neighborhoods, and general mayhem. (This is not to suggest that I am knocking Los Angeles, as it is my favorite city in the world.) When I moved back to New York State, I began to study gangs sociologically, including interviewing gang members in Buffalo. Some of the information that I learned about Buffalo gangs is shared in this book.

ACKNOWLEDGMENTS

There are a number of people who assisted in one way or another in the publication of this book. Special thanks go to Tim Madigan, who proofread the first draft. A special acknowledgment goes to Rebecca Jerrett, my research assistant. Rebecca retrieved numerous books and articles and also served as the illustrator of the gang graffiti found in Chapter 6.

I would also like to acknowledge the work of my two research assistants Sara Dapson and Gary Holland, who assisted me in the making of the Instructor's Manual.

My thanks also go to the following people who reviewed the text and provided additional insight and helpful ideas: Professor John Anderson, CA State University, Fullerton, CA; Professor Steven Cureton, University of North Carolina, Greensboro, NC; Professor Jonathan E. Cella, Central Texas College, Killeen, TX; and Professor Morris Jenkins, University of Toledo, Toledo, Ohio. Special thanks to all the people at Prentice Hall, including Frank Mortimer and Mayda Bosco, and to the staff at GGS Book Services for their assistance in the final editing process and production.

And, of course, to Christina.

ABOUT THE AUTHOR

Dr. Tim Delaney, assistant professor of sociology at the State University of New York at Oswego, holds a B.S. degree in sociology from the State University of New York at Brockport; a M.A. degree in sociology from California State University at Dominguez Hills; and a Ph.D. in sociology from the University of Nevada at Las Vegas.

Delaney is the author of *Classical Social Theory: Investigation and Application* (2004) and *Contemporary Social Theory: Investigation and Application* (2005). He has also published numerous book reviews and journal and encyclopedia articles.

Tim Delaney has presented nearly 40 papers at regional, national, and international professional conferences, including papers that were presented to the Russian Academy of Sciences during international conferences at both St. Petersburg (1999) and Moscow (2001). Delaney maintains membership in ten professional associations and has served two terms as president of the New York State Sociological Association. Delaney is listed in *Who's Who in America* and is a charter member of the "Wall of Tolerance."

CHAPTER ONE

What Is a Gang?

People have formed groups throughout human history, for social interaction plays an important role in an individual's life. Individuals want to feel as though they are a part of a group, community, or general society and want to experience a sense of unity with their fellows. Consequently, by joining together in groups, individuals become a part of a whole. They become a unique person within the group and at the same time acquire a distinctive identity as a result of group membership (Lee 1993). This is especially true with primary groups, which Cooley (1909) described as those characterized by intimate, face-to-face association and cooperation. Members of a primary group share a sense of "we-ness," involving the sort of sympathy and mutual identification for which "we" is a natural expression. The "we" feeling helps to create a community characterized by group loyalty. Community implies shared interests, characteristics, or association, as in the expression "community of interest" (Foster 1990). Nisbet (1969) described a community as a fusion of feeling and thought, of tradition and commitment, of membership, and of psychological strength.

Loyalty to the group among its members is a trademark of human behavior (along with most species found on Earth). Among the most common types of groups is the *ethnic group*. An ethnic group, from a sociological point of view, offers communality in language, a series of customs and symbols, rituals, and appearance (Roosens 1999). Although ethnic grouping and identification remain popular today, there exist many alternatives for group formation. Among these choices is joining a gang. The gang offers many of the same membership advantages that were motivated by ethnic clubs (e.g., rituals, beliefs and outlooks on society and community, a sense of extended family, norm expectation, and anomie and alienation reduction). Through such associations as gang membership, individuals develop a sense of self. Gang membership (a primary group) helps to fill the void resulting from whatever is missing in the lives of so many troubled youths, young adults, and life-long gangsters.

DELINQUENCY AND GANGS

The concern over delinquency and gangs stems from the reality that most individuals first join a gang in their youth and that the largest numbers of gang members are juveniles. *Delinquency* itself refers to violations of juvenile law by juveniles. "Broadly considered, juvenile delinquency could mean any type of behavior by those socially defined as juveniles that violates the norms (standards of proper behavior) set by the controlling group. From this viewpoint, juveniles could be considered delinquent if they adopted modes of hairstyle, dress, or action that were opposed to the standards set by those in authority. In a narrower sense, juvenile delinquency is defined as any action

1

by someone designated a juvenile (nonadult) that would make such a young person subject to action by the juvenile court" (Kratcoski and Kratcoski 1996, 2). Delinquent offenses range from minor offenses—such as drinking, making prank phone calls, and truancy—to more serious violations, such as murder and robbery. There is no set standard for what ages are considered juvenile, although a majority of states consider persons as juvenile until they reach the age of 18, at which point they legally become an adult. Children under the age of 7 are not held accountable for any criminal acts they may commit (Champion 2004). As Trojanowicz, Morash, and Schram (2001, 4) explain, "delinquent behavior is prohibited by law and is carried out by youths approximately up to the age of eighteen. The exact lower and upper age limits differ from state to state, but age ten has been recommended by experts as the most logical cutoff point for children who are old enough to understand that their behavior is wrong."

More than 2 million youths are arrested yearly (in the United States) for juvenile violations (Siegel, Welsh, and Senna 2003). Only about 6% of juvenile crime is violent, but one in five offenders of violent crimes is under the age of 18. Although most juvenile law violations are minor, some offenders are extremely dangerous and violent and are involved in multiple serious criminal acts; these are referred to as *lifestyle*, *repeat*, or *chronic delinquent offenders* (Siegel, Welsh, and Senna 2003).

The Development of a Juvenile Status

It is important to note that the juvenile status—identifying persons based on age categories—is a historically new distinction.

> The treatment of children as a distinct social group with special needs and behavior is, in historical terms, a relatively new concept. It is only for the past 350 years or so that any mechanism existed to care for even the neediest children, including those left orphaned and destitute. . . . In Europe, during the Middle Ages (A.D. 700 to A.D. 1500), the concept of childhood as we know it today did not exist. In the paternalistic family of the time, the father was the final authority on all family matters and exercised complete control over the social, economic, and physical well-being of his wife and children. Children who did not obey were subject to severe punishment, even death (Siegel, Welsh, and Senna 2003, 11).

Young children were expected to obey the rules of the family and seldom did formal law interfere with the punishment of violators. "In biblical times, Roman law vested parents with the almost exclusive responsibility for disciplining their offspring. One's age was the crucial determinant of whether youths were subject to parental discipline or to the more severe penalties invoked for adult law violators . . . the age of 7 was used in Roman times to separate infants from those older children who were accountable to the law for their actions. During the Middle Ages, English common law established under the monarchy adhered to the same standard" (Champion 2004, 7). Children of medieval times faced an abrupt passage into adulthood. As soon as they were physically able to perform work tasks, they were expected to do so. There was no "childhood" status and certainly no distinction of "life as a teenager." Education and leisure pursuits were luxuries reserved for children of the elites. Children age 7 and older were expected to be productive members of the family and society. Attitudes toward children were most likely shaped by the grim demographic realities (i.e., high infant mortality rate, high death rates, short life expectancies) that may have forced the adults to regard the young with indifference. Children were often ignored and abandoned during medieval times.

In colonial America, the family remained as the source and primary means of social control of children. Children who violated the law were sent back to their families for punishment. Because of the agrarian lifestyle during the colonial era, children were relatively valuable as a cheap form of labor. Colonial children were not pampered. In part because the concept of "original sin" (a religious belief that a child is born "flawed") was prevalent during this primitive time, violent punishment was common, especially caning and other forms of public beatings. However, "ever since the colonial period, society has gradually taken authority away from the family and given it to the state for correcting the behavior of children. The house of refuge, the first juvenile institution, was proposed as a better solution than the family in the early nineteenth century. At the end of the nineteenth century, the juvenile court was created to save wayward children by assuming parental responsibility and care. This court was based on the legal concept of *parens patriae*, a medieval English doctrine that sanctioned the right of the crown to intervene in natural family relations" (Bartollas and Miller 2001, 5). The term *juvenile delinquency* was first coined in 1818 by the Society for the Prevention of Pauperism and was initially used to describe the disapproved activities of neglected immigrant children who roamed the streets of New York City (*Encyclopedia Americana* 1998, 248). Citizens were growing concerned about abandoned children and wanted the government to do something about it.

In the past three centuries the role of the state in the control and discipline of children has increased and the role of the once-central father has dramatically decreased. After the formation of houses of refuge (created by the "child-saving movement") came the creation of reform schools, which were established to supervise unruly juveniles. Thus, America was going through an ideological and cultural change in its attitude toward strategies of social control of children during the nineteenth century. The first juvenile court was established in Cook County, Illinois, in 1899. Progressive reformers hoped to find more "beneficial" ways of dealing with juvenile delinquency, such as forming agencies that helped to keep children off the streets and provide them with a place to go after school and before their parents returned home from work. Community-based private agencies such as Hull House, established in Chicago by Jane Addams in 1889, provided an opportunity of something to do for immigrant children who would otherwise be unsupervised while their parents worked long hours.

It is also important to recognize the role of economics on family life. The economic shift from the agrarian lifestyle to one based on the industrial model had a dramatic effect on family life. With the rise of industrialization, most adults were now primarily working in factories. Child-labor laws prohibited children from working in such places. With this economic shift, children now had something that few children had ever had before—free time. In the past, children had always been too busy working to have free time, but all this changed with industrialization. Improvements in medicine ensured that children lived longer (lower mortality rates) and faced fewer life-threatening diseases, and the overall perception of children began to change. Parents began to pay closer attention to the individual personalities of their offspring, and society as a whole became more sympathetic to the plight of children. Thus, in the eighteenth and nineteenth centuries a separate stage of human development became recognized— childhood. *Childhood* was now viewed as unique phase of life, and children were seen as needing both protection and education (Thornton and Voigt 1992). Compulsory education provided control over young people's lives and helped to change their status identification from that of a small adult to that of a *child*.

After the passage of compulsory school attendance, truancy laws were established as a means of keeping children in school, but equally important, they were a means of keeping children off the streets where they might commit delinquent behavior (Champion 2004). Sports participation became another tool used by social control agents to occupy the free time of children. For example, in 1929, store owners in Philadelphia banded together to solve a common problem of "teenagers with nothing to do" who were committing acts of violence and vandalism, by instituting a youth football league (Powell 2003, 4). In fact, from the latter half of the nineteenth century people in both Europe and North America have used sports participation in a controlled environment as a means to organize children's lives, especially so that boys and girls would develop into productive adults in the rapidly expanding capitalist economy. "Sport activities were organized for young boys in schools, on playgrounds, and in church groups. The organizers hoped that sports, especially team sports, would teach boys from working-class families how to cooperate and work together. They also hoped that sports would turn boys in middle- and upper-class families into strong, assertive, competitive men by providing them with experiences to counterbalance what they thought were 'feminized' values learned at home. At the same time, girls were provided with activities that would teach them to be good mothers and homemakers" (Coakley 2001, 110). Until the 1970s, girls had been generally discouraged from participating in sports and were instead taught domestic skills. It should come as no surprise that as women have increasingly made headway in the corporate world, the importance and value of sports have been taught to young girls and that their sports participation levels have never been higher.

As the role, and perception, of children changed in society, the judicial system changed with it. "Special courts were subsequently established to adjudicate juvenile matters. The technical language describing inappropriate youthful conduct or misbehaviors was greatly expanded and refined. These new courts were also vested with the authority to appoint probation officers and other persons considered suitable to manage juvenile offenders and enforce new juvenile codes" (Champion 2004, 19). Thus, where historically children over age 7 were held criminally accountable for their actions (subject to the authority of the father and punishment from the family), this was no longer the case. "The creation of juvenile delinquency as a special category for children offenders can be understood only in relation to the discovery of childhood as a separate stage of life" (Thornton and Voigt 1992, 1).

The development of a *juvenile status* (the category of childhood) and the changing role of the family, especially the role of the father, throughout the past few centuries have had a dramatic effect on juveniles. The traditional importance of a strong father figure in the family, especially for the purpose of disciplining children and assuring their conformity to society's expectations, has nearly vanished. The link between this and the disappearance of the father from many contemporary households may be attributed, at least in part, to the taking away of his authority in the family by the state.

> There is little reason to believe that the 300-year-old legacy of *taking authority away from the family* is likely to change in the near future. Even if the state were receptive to relinquishing some of its power (all indicators point to the fact that the state wants to increase rather than decrease its power over citizens), the American family is under greater pressure than ever before. Its mounting problems include high rates of divorce and single-parent families, alarming rates of abuse and neglect of children, problems with drug and alcohol abuse among both parents and children, and increasing numbers of out-of-wedlock births (Bartollas and Miller 2001, 5).

The lack of a strong male presence in the family is critical to the examination of gang behavior, especially for male gang members. Taking personal responsibility for one's own behavior and correcting the social injustices that often contribute to one's decision to join a gang remain two other vital components to the study of gangs.

The Organization of Delinquency

Delinquents may be categorized in various ways, ranging from *loners* to *formal organizations*, but many organize as *peers* (Best and Luckenbill 1994). *Loners*, as the name should imply, do not associate with other delinquents. They commit their criminal behaviors by themselves. Examples of loner delinquency include most murderers, rapists, check forgers, embezzlers, amateur shoplifters, pedophiles, and art forgers (Best and Luckenbill 1994). The loner prefers to commit deviant behavior without the company of others. "Loners choose deviance because they face situations where respectable courses of action are unattractive, not because they want to rebel against their socialization. For example, a loner may decide to commit a deviant act because the costs of breaking a norm seem less than the costs of respectable conduct" (Best and Luckenbill 1994, 16). Since most delinquent acts involve two or more youths (Erickson 1971) and gang membership implies group activity, the loner is of little interest in the study of gangs.

There are two forms of *colleagues*: legal and illegal. Legal forms of colleagues include teachers and other professionals who share some similar work function. Illegal colleagues perform deviant acts such as pool hustling and computer hacking. "The relationship between deviant colleagues involves limited contact. Like loners, colleagues perform their deviant acts alone. But unlike loners, colleagues associate with one another when they are not engaged in deviance. . . . While loners devise their own deviant techniques and justifications, deviant colleagues build a body of shared knowledge through their contacts. This knowledge is called a *subculture* because it exists as specialized knowledge within the larger culture" (Best and Luckenbill 1994, 24).

Gang members, although possessing a subculture similar to that of colleagues, act as *peers*. "Deviant peers are distinguished from colleagues by their shared participation in deviance. While colleagues carry out their deviant operation alone, peers commit deviant acts in one another's presence. . . . Peer groups can emerge under various conditions. In contemporary society, illicit markets and youth roles have features which encourage deviants to organize as peers" (Best and Luckenbill 1994, 32–33). Peer groups often form social clubs and adopt a name for themselves. This is also true for gangs.

Some youths will engage in juvenile delinquency. Among the most dangerous and predatory juveniles are *gang members*. Not all juvenile delinquents are gang members and not all gang members are juveniles.

DEFINITION OF A GANG

When people hear the terms *gang* and *gang member* a certain image comes to mind. Most people believe that they understand what these words mean. But defining the term *gang* is not as simple as one might think. In fact, there is no single definition, although every definition includes some mention of the word *group*. Consequently, defining a "gang" is problematic. For example, is a group of young people hanging out together a gang? What if this group is hanging outside a convenience store talking loud and acting proud? What if this group creates a name for itself, starts identifying members with specific clothing, and uses secret hand signals and handshakes and intimidating nicknames such as "killer" and "assassin"? But the group just described could actually be a sports team! Add to this description the commission of a number of deviant acts and fraternities and sororities would also fit this profile.

The word *gang* has not always implied criminal activity. In early English usage *gang* referred to a walking or a journey (Klein 1995). A 1975 *Random House College Dictionary* definition of *gang* utilized positive or neutral connotations, such as a "group or band"; "a group of persons who gather together for social reasons"; and "a group of persons working together" (Sheldon, Tracy, and Brown 2001). In 1989, *The New Merriam-Webster Dictionary* defined *gang* as "a set of implements or devices arranged to operate together"; "a group of persons working or associated together"; "a group of young criminals or young delinquents." In the past, some prisons punished prisoners by making them participate in physical labor as part of a "chain gang."

Since most crimes or acts of delinquency committed by juveniles are done in groups, it is important to distinguish between groups and gangs. For example, in Indianapolis "many of the groups of known, chronic offenders that law enforcement encounters are not part of a well-structured nationally or regionally organized gang but rather local cliques or crews of offenders who are well known to law enforcement. Many of these groups have names and colors, but their membership is fluid, and many are not territorial" (McGarrell and Chermak 2003, 85). Consequently, law enforcement in Indianapolis uses the term *chronic offender* as an integral component of determining whether a particular group of delinquents is a gang or not.

Other definitions of gangs emphasize the importance of territoriality (protecting "turf"). For example, Decker and Van Winkle (1996) described St. Louis gangs as loosely confederated groups of youths often bound together by neighborhood ties or associational characteristics. Most gangs do claim turf. However, as Curry and Decker (2003) explained, there is some controversy about the use of turf as a criterion for a definition of a gang. "Many contemporary gangs do claim some territory as their own, either because it is where the gang began or where most of the members live. However, some gangs, particularly Asian gangs, do not claim turf, but meet all of the other criteria of a gang. For this reason, most definitions of a gang do not include turf, though most gangs claim turf" (Curry and Decker 2003, 5).

Most gangs display visible symbols of allegiance, such as hand signals, specialized language, colors (especially related to clothing), and claiming a name for themselves. Spergel and Curry (1990) emphasize that the gang is primarily concerned with issues of status, prestige, and turf protection, along with the importance of colors, special dress, signs, and symbols.

The fact that dictionaries, gang researchers, and gang members themselves cannot agree on the definition of a "gang" is not nearly as important as the fact that law enforcement agencies across the United States do not have a common definition. Consequently, accurate tracking of gang-related statistics is often difficult. When the Office of Juvenile Justice and Delinquency Prevention (OJJDP) conducted its National Youth Gang Survey (1996) of nearly 5,000 law enforcement agencies, it used the definition of a gang as "a group of youths or young adults in your jurisdiction that you or other responsible persons in your agency or community are willing to identify or classify as a 'gang'" (Shelden et al. 2001). Who are the "responsible" persons that determine which group of deviants are labeled a gang and which ones are not? Motorcycle gangs, hate groups, and other "gangs" usually associated with adult members are excluded from the OJJDP statistics.

In 2000, the OJJDP identified a number of criteria that must be met in order to classify a group as a youth gang:

- The group must have more than two members. Gangs always have more than two members.

- Group members must fall within a limited age range, generally acknowledged as ages 12 to 24.

- Members must share some sense of identity. This is generally accomplished by naming the gang (often referring to a specific geographic location in the name) and/or using symbols or colors to claim gang affiliation. Hand signals, graffiti, specific clothing styles, bandannas, and hats are among the common symbols of gang loyalty.

- Youth gangs require some permanence. Gangs are different from transient youth groups in that they show stability over time, generally lasting a year or more. Historically, youth gangs have also been associated with a particular geographical area or turf.

- Involvement in criminal activity is a central element of youth gangs. While some disagreement surrounds this criterion, it is important to differentiate gangs from noncriminal youth groups such as school and church clubs, which also meet all of the preceding criteria (Esbensen 2000, 2–3).

The California Penal Code (Section 186.22) defines a street gang as "any ongoing organization, association, or group of three or more persons whether formal or informal . . . having a common name or common identifying sign or symbol, and whose members individually or collectively engage in or have engaged in a pattern of criminal activity." Albuquerque, New Mexico, state penal code (Section 11-9-4) defines a street gang as "any ongoing organization, association in fact, or group of three or more persons, whether formally or informally organized, or any sub-group thereof, having as one of its primary activities the commission of one or more criminal acts or illegal acts, which has an identifiable name or identifying sign or symbol, and whose members individually or collectively engage in or have engaged in a pattern of criminal gang activity for a one-year period." The state of Alabama (Section 13A-6-26) defines a street gang as "any combination, confederation, alliance, network, conspiracy, understanding, or other similar arrangement in law or in fact, of three or more persons that, through its membership or through the agency of any member, engages in a course or pattern of criminal activity." The state of Florida defines a gang (Section 874.03) as "a formal or informal ongoing organization, association, or group that has as one of its primary activities the commission of criminal or delinquent acts, and that consists of three or more persons who have a common name or common identifying signs, colors, or symbols and have two or more members who, individually or collectively, engage in or have engaged in a pattern of criminal street gang activity." The Chicago Police Department defines a street gang as an association of individuals who exhibit the following characteristics: a gang name, recognizable symbols, claim a geographical territory, have a regular meeting pattern, and are involved in continuous criminality (Block and Block 1993). In all cases, a criminal street gang member is a person who meets the legal definition of any particular jurisdiction.

It is important to note once again that the definition an agency uses affects the numbers that measure gangs, gang members, gang-related criminal activities, gang crimes, and so forth. It is also important to realize that gangs are not solely criminal organizations. Most of the time gang members simply "hang out" or engage in other nondelinquent behaviors (watching television, going on dates, etc.).

For the purposes of this book, I use a definition that incorporates the ideas of many other researchers along with ideas influenced by personal observations. A street gang is a group of individuals whose core members interact with one another at a high frequency rate. They possess a group name, generally wear certain types of clothing, can generally be identified by specific colors, are most likely to claim a neighborhood or turf (or marketplace), and often engage in criminal or other delinquent behavior. Gang members are known as **gangbangers** or **gangsters**. Participating in gang activity is referred to as **gangbanging** behavior. Criminal **gang activity** refers specifically to gang-based crime. The term *gang-related crime* is applied if either the criminal or the victim is a gang member.

GENERAL DESCRIPTION OF GANGS AND GANG MEMBERS

Once again, conjure up an image of a gang member. Is your assessment accurate? Are gang members mostly inner-city minority males who love to fight, wear certain clothing, have tattoos, wear bling-bling, and sell drugs? In many cases, the answer is "yes" to all of these stereotypical images of gangs. In other cases, gang members look much different from the stereotypical image most people have of gangs. The fact is there are a wide variety of gangs and gang members. Some of them are unique; others neatly fit the general "profile" of how one thinks a gang member looks. This section is a brief review of some of the general descriptions of gangs and gang members.

One of the most basic questions regarding gangs is, where do they come from? The simplest answer is based on the fact that ties of friendship link gang members to one another and the fact that many gang members knew each other before joining the gang. Researchers call this type of gang formation *spontaneous*. "A characteristic which may be regarded as typical of all gangs, as distinguished from more formal groups, is its spontaneous and unplanned origin" (Thrasher 1963/1927, 40). As with nongang members, young children grow up together and play and go to school together. When they enter adolescence, some may decide to give themselves a name and become a club, or a gang. There is a much greater likelihood of this occurring if there are already older gang members in the neighborhood. The youths may look up to and admire the existing gang members. Through imitation they quickly learn the subcultural values of gang members. Gang members are peer groups bound by informal ties and generally identified by a group name and distinctive clothing. For example, the Crips, a Los Angeles-based *super gang* (discussed in greater detail in Chapter 6), are associated with the color blue and wear blue bandannas, or handkerchiefs. The primary rival of the Crips is the Bloods. The Bloods are associated with the color red. The bandanna (or "do-rag") is symbolically equal to a national flag; it is to be protected at all times and is never to be lost in battle.

Interaction among gang members varies with the size and complexity of the gang. In larger gangs it is common for interaction to be limited to immediate cliques (a close-knit group). Hard-core members associate with one another almost exclusively while peripheral members may associate with people outside the gang along with other gang members. On important occasions such as a gang-sponsored dance or fight with a rival gang, the entire gang may mobilize collectively. The collective mobilization of the entire gang increases group cohesiveness (Klein 1995). However, day-to-day activities typically involve "traveling cliques" or close friends within the gang who are on patrol of their turf or involved in some criminal activity (e.g., selling drugs, robbery, and auto theft). The gang is dependent on shared activities; they are its lifeblood. As with any group, if the members of the gang stop associating with one another, it risks dissolution. Gangs are not created for the sole purpose of engaging in criminal behavior; instead, it becomes one of the activities that the members carry out as peers.

Social interaction among gang members allows for the transmission of subcultural beliefs and attitudes. Younger gang members learn such values not only from older gang members, they are a product of the surrounding adult culture as well. Thus, gang members from lower economic social classes tend to take on the values of the greater community, where such traits as toughness, street smarts, and excitement are dominant core values. For this reason, many gang members act, dress, and attempt to look tough. They often possess arrogant and defiant attitudes. Above all, they value their reputation of being tough and aggressive. They must never "punk out." For male gang members, ideals of manhood and masculinity are central aspects of their personality. Gang members are defined culturally and vary according to ethnicity and social class (Schneider 1999).

People in lower socioeconomic classes possess limited resources, and the items that they do possess they are expected to defend. Thus, the importance of toughness comes into play. The limited possession of material objects adds to the importance of protecting home territory, or turf. Members of the outside community may wonder why anyone would risk death to protect a ghettolike neighborhood, but economically poor gang members view turf as their top possession. Material goods like gold chains, diamond earrings, and large finger rings (bling-bling) are items that lower-class gang members highly desire. Visible tattoos that reflect a gang member's allegiance are symbolic of loyalty to the group. Thus, expensive jewelry and tattoos are often signs of gang membership (*Youth Gangs and Juvenile Violence* 2003).

Clothing is an integral aspect of gang membership. Beyond the obvious distinction of red bandannas for Bloods and blue bandannas for Crips, a wide variety of posse paraphernalia is associated with specific gangs. Melissa Roth (1998) compiled the following list of gang wear:

- **Duke University Sweatshirt:** *DUKE* means *Disciples Utilizing Knowledge Everyday* if you belong to the Gangster Disciples, a Chicago-based gang. They were once known as Satan's Disciples, therefore members of this gang identify with the Duke University mascot, the Blue Devil.

- **North Carolina University Jersey:** Crips claim the Tarheels sky-blue gear as their own—plus *N.C.* can stand for *Neighborhood of Crips*. Duke and North Carolina may be conference rivals in sports, but their uniforms are worn by gangland allies.

- **Playboy Hat:** The playboy icon is worn by the Vice Lords, sworn enemies of the Gangster Disciples. But if the rabbit's right ear is flopped down, the wearer may be from the Simon City Royals, a gang linked with the Disciples.

- **Bomber Jacket:** Asian gangs are less likely to advertise the fact that they are gang members, but the Blood Red Dragons may wear this red-hued garb evoking both China and blood.

- **CK Jeans:** Calvin Klein's monogram is interpreted as *Crip Killers*. The stand-alone CK logo is considered too dangerous to wear in some Los Angeles neighborhoods.

- **Star of David:** Gangster Disciples wear the Jewish Star of David as a tribute to their leader, David Barksdale, who died in the 1970s. Barksdale, a gentile, wore the medallion because of its namesake (David)—and because he considered himself a star.

- **Louis Vuitton Hat:** An emblem of status and wealth, Louis Vuitton's intertwined logo stands for the mighty Vice Lords to those who choose to read the initials backwards. Gang members often tailor the logo by marking it up with their colors.

These are just a few examples of gang-related clothing. Examples of graffiti and other gang clothing will be discussed in Chapter 6.

Stereotypes of Gangs

The image many people have of a gang member is greatly influenced by the media. A large segment of the population remains relatively removed from the daily problems that gangs represent in certain communities. The information that people have on gangs is usually limited to that provided in newspaper articles and news reports. Often, the journalistic slant relies on many stereotypes regarding gangs and gang behavior. As a result, many people believe that the "typical gang member is male, lives in the inner city, and is a member of a racial or ethnic minority" (Esbensen 2000, 3). Joan Moore (1993, 28–29) provides the best summary of the gang stereotypes:

1. They are composed of males (no females) who are violent, addicted to drugs and alcohol, sexually hyperactive, unpredictable, and confrontational. The reality is that gang members, among many exceptions, can be female, organized, and against the use or sale of drugs.

2. They are either all African-American or all Hispanic. Although it is true that currently over eighty percent of gang members are either Black or Hispanic, they come from all races. An interesting point about gangs in regard to race and ethnicity is the fact that gangs tend to be homogenous in nature, even if they live in a heterogeneous neighborhood. That is, gangs are seldom a mix of any racial or ethnic groups; they are one race or ethnic group.

3. They thrive in inner-city neighborhoods where they dominate, intimidate, and prey upon innocent citizens. Once again, there is a strong basis of truth to this stereotype, in that the largest number of gang members are found in the inner city; but the fact is, gangs can be found anywhere and everywhere. They exist in small rural towns, the suburbs, beach cities, and Native American reservations.

4. They are heavily into drugs, especially crack cocaine. Compared to other youths, gang members proportionately are more likely to use drugs. Some gangs do control drug markets, while other gangs forbid the use of drugs. The crack cocaine "epidemic" has disappeared, and law enforcement's fears were not realized. "Crack appealed mainly to hard-core drug users. The number of crack users began falling not long after surveys began counting them . . . what is less well known is that most crack users are white" (Ivins 2003, C11).

5. "A gang is a gang is a gang"—in other words, they are all alike. Gangs vary a great deal (e.g., Straight Edge).

6. There is no good in gangs; it is all bad (a corollary to this is that anyone who would want to join a gang must be stupid or crazy). Youths join gangs for a variety of reasons, some complicated, some obvious.

7. Gangs are basically criminal enterprises and youths start gangs in order to collectively commit crimes. Felix Padilla (1992) wrote a classic ethnographic book using this very subject as his title, *The Gang as an American Enterprise*, so there clearly is some basis of truth to this stereotypical perception. On the other hand, many gangs are loosely structured and come nowhere near resembling an organized, criminal enterprise.

8. The "West Side Story" image of aggressive, rebellious, but nice kids has been replaced in recent years by the "gangster" image of a very disciplined criminal organization complete with "soldiers." It is difficult to image why Hollywood made a romanticized gang movie like "West Side Story" in the first place. (Note: It was a successful Broadway play first and represented a modern version of "Romeo and Juliet.") Gangsters dancing while fighting (and with mere switchblades) is certainly far from reality.

The significance of stereotypes is that they shape the definitions of gangs and therefore determine policies structured to deal with gangs. Often, crimes committed by juveniles become "labeled" by the police as "gang-related." On the other hand, many newspapers do not describe specific crimes as gang-related when those involved in research in this area know that such incidents are gang-related. To repeat: The media does indeed shape the audience perception of gangs.

STATISTICS: COUNTING GANGS AND GANG MEMBERS

Gangs are everywhere. They exist in all 50 American states, in all socioeconomic classes, and in all racial and ethnic groups. For some citizens, the problems presented by gangs are a daily nightmare. For others, their knowledge of gangs is based on secondhand reports. The first line of defense in combating street gangs is law enforcement agencies. The manner in which they deal with and apprehend suspected gang members is based on agency policy. Agency policy is dictated by the definitions used to describe gangs and gang-related crimes. For example, in Syracuse, New York, the Police Department denied for years that there were gangs in the city (see Chapter 6 for a further discussion of Syracuse gangs). In 2002, Police Chief Dennis DuVal and other city officials acknowledged that there were gangs in Syracuse and consequently created a gang task force to eliminate them (Sieh 2003).

As stated earlier, there is no single, agreed-upon definition of gangs among the various law enforcement agencies across the United States. Consequently, coming up with accurate statistics on the number of gangs and gang members is relatively difficult. Gang researchers and law enforcement agencies often work together and share information on this subject. Since 1995, perhaps the most cited (and reputable) source for statistics on gangs comes from the Office of Juvenile Justice and Delinquency Prevention (OJJDP) fact sheet published by the U.S. Department of Justice as part of its annual youth gang survey, which it sends to law enforcement agencies throughout the United States. In 2002, 2,563 surveys were mailed and 2,182 (85%) law enforcement agencies responded. The OJJDP (2004) reported that there were approximately 731,500 gang members and 21,500 gangs active in the United States in 2002. It would be safe to say that in 2004 there are at least three-quarters of a million gang members. (Imagine if all these gangs united into one super gang!) According to the OJJDP (2004, 1):

> All cities with a population of 250,000 or more reported youth gang problems in 2002, as did 87 percent of cities with a population between 100,000 and 249,999. Thirty-eight percent of responding suburban county agencies, 27 percent of responding smaller city agencies, and 12 percent of responding rural county agencies also reported youth gang problems in 2002. . . . Based on survey results, it is estimated that, in 2002, youth gangs were active in more than 2,300 cities with a population of 2,500 or more and in more than 550 jurisdictions served by county law enforcement agencies.

As the statistics clearly indicate, gangs are a problem in many jurisdictions, including smaller towns and rural areas. However, the OJJDP (2004) reported that larger cities and suburban counties accounted for approximately 85% of the total estimated gang members in 2002.

A number of studies of individual cities with gang problems can be found in Decker's *Policing Gangs and Youth Violence* (2003). According to a Metro Gang Task Force report in Marion County (Indianapolis), there were a confirmed 80 gangs with 1,746 confirmed gangs members in 1995. These figures were believed to represent just one-quarter of the actual number of gang members operating within the county. The Task Force found that 56% of the gang members were African-American, and over 40% were white. Just 1% of the confirmed gang members were Hispanic. The U.S. Department of Justice conducted a more extensive study 1 year later and found that the number of confirmed gang sets increased from 80 to 198 and the number of confirmed gang members increased from 1,746 to 2,422, a 40% increase (McGarrell and Chermak 2003). In the nation's third-largest city, Chicago, the National Youth Gang Center (1997) found that there were 33,000 gang members in 1995, the third-highest total of any jurisdiction in the country, behind Los Angeles County and the city of Los Angeles. The Chicago Police Department estimated that there were 132 Chicago-based street gangs (Coldren and Higgins 2003). In 1995, the St. Louis Metropolitan Police Department estimated that there were 280 gangs with approximately 3,500 members in the city of St. Louis. One-half of the gang members were estimated to be 17 years old or younger, and "those 25 or older constituted less than 20 percent of all gang members. The desire to make money and gain respect and being intimidated to join were the primary reasons individuals were thought to join gangs. Members were recruited by family, friends, and neighbors and were recruited in schools, neighborhoods, and in the juvenile detention center" (Decker and Curry 2003, 194). According to the National Youth Gang Survey, instituted by OJJDP, there were 125 active gangs functioning in Detroit in the late 1990s. It was also estimated that the total number of gang members was between 5,000 and 6,000. The OJJDP reported that it is common in cities with a population over 250,000 to average more than 5,000 gang members (Bynum and Varano 2003). In 1996, the Dallas Police Department reported that the city of Dallas had 79 gangs with 6,145 documented gang members (Fritsch, Caeti, and Taylor 2003).

Los Angeles has the dubious distinction as the "street gang capital" of the world. It is estimated that there are well over 100,000 gang members in Southern California. One-half of all homicides are gang-related, and in Southern California homicide is the cause of more deaths than auto accidents. The average life expectancy for a gang member in Southern California is 19. The notorious 18th Street Gang (See Chapter 6) has an estimated 20,000 members alone (Maxson, Hennigan and Sloane 2003).

NON-STREET GANGS

There are many types of gangs. The focus of this book is on street gangs; however, we need to briefly discuss a number of *non-street gangs* as a means of contrasting and comparing them to street gangs. This is important because students generally ask, "Will we be discussing biker gangs? What about skinheads? Is the KKK a gang?" A brief discussion of a few non-street gangs will help to clarify the focus of *American Street Gangs*.

Motorcycle Gangs

Members of motorcycle clubs such as the Hell's Angels and the Pagan Outlaws do not consider themselves *gang members* nor do they believe that they should be subjected to the same behavioral restraints as gangs. The Ventura County (CA) Fair Board voted in July 2003 to ban gang attire in the hope that gang violence would decrease during the annual fair. A Hell's Angels member, wearing a leather vest sporting the group's trademark *winged skull* (or "death head"), was denied admission to the fair and protested that the ban should not apply to him because the Hell's Angels are not a gang. *Motorcycle gangs* first appeared on the American scene in the 1950s. They had a great influence on American pop culture, and some of the more notorious ones were linked to numerous violent crimes.

> Following World War II, lower- and working-class males began forming outlaw motorcycle clubs, groups which refused to register with the respectable American Motorcycle Association (which governs the sport of motorcycle riding). These outlaws, or bikers, became frightening popular culture icons, the focus of movies, such as *The Wild One* (1953), and journalists' accounts, such as Hunter Thompson's (1966) *Hell's Angels*. The biker's frightening appearance, especially his "colors" (the denim or leather vest or jacket bearing the club insignia), and disruptive behavior on club trips ("runs") violated the norms of propriety, and stories of illicit drug use, violence, and theft linked bikers with more serious forms of deviance. Claims that particular gangs control prostitution, drug distribution, and other vice in some areas depict bikers as members of a powerful, highly organized deviant conspiracy (Best and Luckenbill 1994, 55–56).

Despite the "outlaw," nonconformist nature of the biker gang, the more sophisticated ones (e.g., Hell's Angels) have a formal operating structure. Wolf's (1991) participant observation study of the Edmonton (Alberta) Rebels motorcycle club revealed the strong sense of belonging to a brotherhood among the members, but it also revealed its formal structure. The Rebels had a written constitution filled with membership requirements, club officers, and regularly scheduled meetings and required that members pay dues. "This formal structure reflects the difficulty of maintaining organizational stability. Bikers find themselves under perpetual threat of attack. The respectable world, especially law enforcement, seeks to constrain, if not eliminate, outlaw clubs. Moreover, members may have to defend their club's territory from attacks by rival clubs. Finally, there is the danger of violent, uncontrolled internal disputes among the club's members" (Best and Luckenbill 1994, 56). In order to deal with these problems, it was important for the biker club to find a clubhouse to serve as a refuge from external enemies (Wolf 1991). As with street gangs, biker gangs often branch out. Such an affiliation and federation generally involves clubs that are separated by some distance from each other. This is important in order to eliminate conflict and the inevitable competition for resources among the affiliates.

The most famous biker gang is the Hell's Angels. The Hell's Angels were founded by Ralph "Sonny" Barger (called "Sonny" from the Italian tradition of calling the first-born son by that name). According to his autobiography, Sonny had difficulty with authority figures and was continually getting suspended for his mischief in school.

Taking on the role of a gang leader began at an early age. While he was still at Oakland (CA) High School, Sonny organized a small street corner club named the Earth Angels, after the hit song by the Penguins. Barger (2001, 21) explained that the gang "didn't stand for anything, it was just something to belong to. . . . It was all about belonging to a group of people just like you." Sonny's words reflect an important aspect of street gangs, which is the tendency for them to be homogenous in nature, even when they are found in heterogeneous neighborhoods. Sonny's gang spent the majority of their time smoking marijuana and getting into fights at school. Sonny's first experience with a motorcycle club, the Oakland Panthers, was short-lived due to the lack of solidarity (Barger 2001). Some experts on gang behavior believe that individuals seek out gang membership because they are looking for a substitute family that contributes the same kind of support, security, and caring that the "traditional" intact nuclear family is supposed to provide (Siegel et al. 2003). Sonny's search for a substitute family would soon find it in a motorcycle club, the Hell's Angels.

The Hell's Angels are "the world's most respected and feared motorcycle organization" (Jamison 2000, 1). On the surface, the Hell's Angels possess many of the characteristics of a street gang, including the common name, common identifying symbols, and common activities among members. The Hell's Angels are a mix of races and ethnicities, though most of the members are white. Barger (2001) describes the original members of the Hell's Angels as "young high school dropouts in our early twenties who didn't have two nickels to rub together . . . all we owned was the clothes on our back and the bike between our legs" (32). Brotherhood and fraternity are the hallmarks of the Angels. It was an unwritten rule that if you messed with one Hell's Angel, you messed with them all. Furthermore, if a Hell's Angel was locked up in jail, the other members would raise money for bail. The origin of the Hell's Angels name is linked to the U.S. Army's 11th Airborne Division. They were "an elite group of paratroopers trained to rain death on the enemy from above, drifting in behind the lines of battle" (Jamison 2000, 2). Barger (2001) states, "The term 'Hell's Angels' had been bouncing around the military as far back as World War I, when a fighter squadron first took on the name. During the twenties in Detroit, a motorcycle club affiliated with the American Motorcyclist Association named themselves Hell's Angels. . . . WWII had a few groups called Hell's Angels, including an American Air Force bomber company stationed in England" (28–29). A veteran of the Airborne was wearing his "modified Air Force-like patch" while bike riding. Barger and the rest of the club liked the design and made matching patches for everyone in the club. The Hell's Angels motorcycle club was formed.

Beyond the brotherhood that the Hell's Angels provide, recreational opportunities were among the more poignant reasons that an individual chose to join the motorcycle gang. (*Note*: These characteristics—brotherhood and recreational opportunities—are common with gangs as well.) "They swap girls, drugs and motorcycles with equal abandon. In between drug-induced stupors, the Angels go on motorcycle stealing forays" (Thompson 1999, 25). Sonny's own criminal record supports Thompson's claims. From 1957 to 1987, Barger's record includes numerous charges of possession of narcotics and marijuana, oftentimes with the intent to sell. In fact, throughout his autobiography, Sonny describes the continuous cycle of partying (drinking and drugs), bar brawls, and women. Barger believes that women are attracted to outlaw bikers because of their tough-guy image. Law enforcement officers and the townspeople who come in contact with outlaw bikers such as the Hell's Angels describe the chaos and criminal activity that accompany them. The bikers refute such accusations, protesting that their actions are merely innocent fun. Aggravated assaults, theft, and drug and alcohol-related offenses are the most common criminal violations committed by biker gangs. Sonny Barger's own criminal history, however, supports the accusations, as his record shows numerous aggravated assaults, most involving a deadly weapon.

The structure of the Hell's Angels is similar to that of a business or corporation. First, there must be a strong leader if the organization is going to survive and flourish. This leader must demonstrate that he can deal with any problem that may arise. Disputes in the Hell's Angels were handled by Barger, who not only introduced the structure and rules of the biker club but enforced them as well. Sonny insisted on weekly meetings, and if anyone missed a meeting, they paid a monetary fine. Barger also created tactical rules such as a separation of 50 miles between all charters (with one exception—the Oakland and San Francisco charters are less than 10 miles apart). Because of the "pick up and go mentality" of the biker gang, it is hard for members to secure steady employment. Consequently, the majority of the members partake in illegal activities to support themselves. Selling drugs and stolen property (e.g., guns and auto parts) are among the more profitable illegal activities biker gangs participate in. The Hell's Angels also provide illegal services such as protection (e.g., security for the Rolling Stones) and demolition of property.

In their frustration over curtailing the illegal activities of the Hell's Angels and other motorcycle gangs, in the late 1990s the federal government alleged violations of racketeering and organizational corruption against the motorcycle gang (in violation of the Racketeering Influence and Corrupt Organization Act—RICO). "The fifteen million dollar federal prosecution resulted in two mistrials, which prosecutors derived as a miscarriage of justice, while Sonny threw a no-holds-barred bash for the jurors" (Jamison 2000, 5). Despite their exoneration, both local and national law enforcement agencies perceive the Hell's Angels as "a wealthy corporation with a global drug distribution network" (Jamison 2000, 5). In 2004, leaders of the Outlaws motorcycle gang were convicted in Toledo, Ohio of federal charges that included racketeering and conspiracy to distribute drugs (cocaine, marijuana, and LSD) throughout the Midwest. James "Frank" Wheeler, 62, was among the 12 leading members of the Outlaws convicted.

In Canada, outlaw biker gangs, including the Angels, are becoming more powerful and dangerous than ever. In 1997, the Canadian federal government passed legislation (Bill C-95) that gave police more power to fight biker gangs. This legislation made it illegal to participate in criminal organizations such as biker gangs. Since then, tougher legislation (e.g., Bills C-24 and C-36) has been introduced that would give police the right to break the law during some undercover operations. Still, the Canadian legislation does not go so far as the U.S. RICO Act (O'Neill 2002). In recent years, biker gangs have become increasingly violent in Canada, participating in such criminal activities as murder, drug-trafficking, and prostitution. The Hell's Angels are known for trafficking drugs from Toronto into the United States through the Buffalo-Niagara region.

Among the identifying features of the Hell's Angels are the numerous tattoos that they sport and the wearing of leather. A very important characteristic of the Angels is their commitment to their motorcycle—the Harley-Davidson. They generally park their spotlessly clean machines inside their homes at night. Thompson (1999, 85) claimed that the Hell's Angels are pathetic without their motorcycles but further stated that there is nothing pathetic about an Angel on his bike. The relationship between an Angel and his bike is obvious even for those who know nothing about motorcycles. The most identifying feature of the Hell's Angels is the death's-head patch all members have affixed to the back of their jackets. The patch is respected in the same manner as a patriot respects the national flag or a gang-banger protects his colors (e.g., bandanna). The Angels make it clear that only members are to be seen wearing the patch. If a non-member is discovered wearing the patch, severe consequences will occur.

Outlaw motorcycle gangs are often very structured and relatively organized. On the other hand, members come and go, chapters rise and fall, and territories expand and contract. "Ultimately, it is the sense of belonging, of brotherhood—rather than commitment to deviant enterprise—which is at the center of the bikers' world. In this, bikers resemble another deviant formal organization—large street gangs which have adopted formal structure as a way of managing deviant enterprises, compiling resources, and thereby achieving relative stability" (Best and Luckenbill 1994, 58). The Hell's Angels remain one of the most notorious and well known of all biker gangs. The story of the Hell's Angels motorcycle club is the story of a very select brotherhood of men who fight and die for each other, no matter what the cause (Barger 2001). They possess many of the characteristics of a highly organized and influential gang. Their numerous run-ins with law enforcement have seemed only to add to their reputation. Sonny Barger, the founder and leader of the Hell's Angels, is not only well respected by his fellow members but also by those who enjoy the idea of defying the law in search of excitement, thrills, and anarchy.

Organized Crime and Gangsters

Motorcycle gangs such as the Hell's Angels and national super gangs such as the Crips and Bloods have been accused of committing organized crime. Legislation such as the RICO Act was created to fight organized crime but it has been increasingly used to combat the growth of gangs. Civil rights groups, including the American Civil Liberties Union (ACLU), believe that the use of RICO arrests against street gang members is illegal. Consequently, it is important to understand what constitutes "organized crime" and what distinguishes it from crime committed by street gangs. Thus, we must determine what organized crime is.

Simon and Hagan (1999) argued that "organized white-collar crime" has traditionally referred to the infiltration of organized crime groups such as the Mafia into legitimate business, but it may also refer to behavior on the part of legitimate businesses that resemble organized crime operations or alliances between organized crime and legitimate businesses" (114). However, is organized crime limited to the white-collar world? Federal agencies such as the Federal Bureau of Investigation and the U.S. Department of Justice use the Federal Task Force on Organized Crime's operational definition (Simon and Hagan 1999), which is quite broad:

> Organized crime includes any group of individuals whose primary activity involves violating criminal laws to seek illegal profits and power by engaging in

racketeering activities and, when appropriate, engaging in intricate financial manipulations. . . . Accordingly, the perpetrators of organized crime may include corrupt business executives, members of the professions, public officials, or any occupational group, in addition to the conventional, racketeer element (National Advisory Committee 1976, 213–215).

This definition would seem to imply criminal groups that are more sophisticated than the "typical" street gang. However, there are gangs that are highly organized and do participate in financial manipulation. The President's Commission on Organized Crime (1986) focused on the concept of *organized* as the key distinction between groups that may, or may not, qualify as organized crime syndicates (Kenney and Finckenauer 1995, 1). Once again, there are gangs that meet this requirement. It is up to state and federal prosecutors to prove that a street gang is organized enough to justify RICO arrests.

Organized crime (sometimes called *syndicate crime*) involves deviant activity committed by members of formal organizations that exist to operate profitable illicit enterprises (e.g., insurance fraud, counterfeiting, tax evasion, prostitution, and money laundering) (Delaney 2004). Organized crime exists to meet the needs of a public that is denied access to certain goods and services through legitimate means. Wherever there is a demand for prohibited goods and services (e.g., prostitution, drugs, pornography, gambling, or smuggled goods), there is an opportunity for organized crime to become a major supplier (Best and Luckenbill 1994). As McIntosh (1973) states, the provision of illicit goods and services and systematic extortion are the basic operations of organized crime. Highly organized street gangs also provide illicit goods and services to the public that demands it.

After reviewing the work of other researchers (Hagan 1983 and Maltz 1985), Kenney and Finckenauer (1995, 3–6) conclude that organized crime groups have the following dimensions and characteristics:

1. They are nonideological—Meaning that they do not have political agendas of their own. "They are not terrorists dedicated to political change." (p. 3)

2. They have an organized hierarchy—The structure is characterized by persons who possess different levels of authority. There is a boss, a second in command, and so on.

3. They have continuity over time—The group is self-perpetuating; it continues even as members come and go—whether it is permanent because of death, or temporary because of incarceration.

4. They use force or the threat of force—Organized criminal groups use force or threaten to use it in order to accomplish their ends.

5. They restrict membership—This is especially true in terms of limiting their membership to persons of certain ethnic types and backgrounds, kinship, race, religion, or criminal record.

6. They obtain profit through illegal enterprises—Making a profit, through whatever means are considered necessary, is the primary goal of organized criminal groups. This reflects the idea that they are nonideological.

7. They provide illegal goods and services desired by the general populace—Organized crime provides goods and services that are illegal or highly scrutinized (e.g., drugs, gambling, and disposal of toxic wastes).

8. They use corruption to neutralize public officials and politicians—Organized crime neutralizes or nullifies government by avoiding investigation, arrest, prosecution, and conviction through payoffs to the police, prosecutors, and judges. Bribes and kickbacks are common means of inducing corruptible politicians and governmental workers.

9. They seek a monopoly—In order to maximize profits, organized crime groups seek to obtain exclusive control over specific goods and services.

10. They have job specialization within the group—A clearly defined division of labor.

11. They have a code of secrecy—In order to operate efficiently it is imperative that all members keep quiet about all aspects of the organization. Membership, rituals or initiation, rules and regulations, activities, and the leadership of certain organized crime groups are bound by rules of secrecy. Members of the Ku Klux Klan go so far as to cover their faces to hide their identities from others.

12. They plan extensively to achieve long-term goals—In order to keep the organization profitable it is imperative to plan and coordinate activities for the long run, not just the immediate. Most street gangs lack long-term planning and are more concerned with living in the moment.

All of these characteristics could easily apply to highly organized street gangs.

From a structural standpoint, organized crime is generally characterized by violence, corruption, and criminal monopoly. The use, or threat, of *violence* serves two critical functions. First, systematic extortion (the collecting of payments from people), accomplished through the use of threats and intimidation, provides the organization with needed funds (Chambliss 1988; Cressy 1969). Most illicit markets involve a fairly steady demand and extortionists can arrange to collect their payments at regular intervals. Extortionists may also demand that their victims conduct exclusive business relationships with other businesses already under the control of the crime syndicate. For example, organized criminals may demand that a restaurant subscribe to their linen service, garbage removal, liquor sales companies, and so on. This reality underscores the second function of violence, gaining control of the market—a monopoly. A monopoly is accomplished through the threat and use of violence. This market advantage allows the criminal syndicate to maximize its profits (Delaney 2004).

The criminal organization must be sophisticated enough to manage regular supply and collection activities. Large-scale illicit operations are difficult to conceal, especially when they continue over time. One of the most powerful tools used to accomplish freedom from arrest, prosecution, and conviction for crimes is *corruption*. Paying off (e.g., bribery) certain governmental and law enforcement personnel is the cornerstone of corruption. Corruption ensures the cooperation of the authorities and protects the organization's operations. It also facilitates monopoly control by enlisting the authorities in the elimination of rivals (Delaney 2004). "The integrity of the level of the legal and political systems is harmed as law enforcement becomes distorted and the rule of the law is subverted" (Finckenauer 2002, 1427).

Along with violence and corruption, Maltz (1976) argued that theft, economic coercion, deception, and victim participation are means by which organized crimes are executed. *Theft* involves burglary, fencing, cargo theft, chop shops, and distribution of bootleg cigarettes and pirated records and CDs. *Economic coercion* involves such acts as price-fixing and organizing illegal labor strikes. *Deception* often involves creating dummy corporations or businesses that serve as a front for illegal enterprises. *Victim participation* remains a key element in the success of organized crime syndicates. The fact that some people want illegal drugs and others want to have consensual sex with prostitutes guarantees economic opportunities for criminal syndicates. Legalizing drugs and prostitution would quickly eliminate many criminal organizations. Street crime and incarceration rates would also decrease. Because criminals have no legal right to their profits, the members of organized crime syndicates would have to transform their earnings into legitimate investments.

Organized crime syndicates include such groups as the Russian Mafia, the Irish Mob of Boston, and the Italian Mafia/La Cosa Nostra. Other organizations are less organized but as potentially dangerous as organized crime syndicates. These groups include the Ku Klux Klan and skinheads.

Ku Klux Klan

The *Ku Klux Klan* was formed immediately after the Civil War and the resulting freeing of the slaves. The Klan was against the civil rights movement designed to give slaves rights as citizens. The Ku Klux Klan derived its name from the English word *clan*, meaning "extended family," and the Greek word *klyklos*, meaning "circle" or "wheel." Thus, the Klan was designed as a fraternal organization, a close-knit circle of people with similar beliefs and goals. Throughout its history, the Klan has persecuted and targeted Jews, immigrants, Roman Catholics, communists, homosexuals, blacks, and organized labor. The symbolic clothing worn by Klansmen (when conducting activities in the public sphere) makes them easily recognizable: white hoods (or tall pointed hats) and robes—which are supposed to resemble the ghosts of dead Confederate soldiers. When conducting Klan business, the members stand in a circle and carry blazing torches, which are used to burn large wooden crosses to serve as a warning to their intended victims.

The first charter of the Ku Klux Klan was established in Pulaski, Tennessee, in May 1866 by a formal Confederate general and Freemason, Nathan Bedford Forrest, who served as the first Imperial Wizard. The men that founded the first branch were ex-Confederate soldiers. Their mission was to oppose the Reconstructionist policies of Congress as well as to maintain "white supremacy" in America. After the Civil War, a *moral panic* occurred throughout the Southern states: "There were fears of black outrages and even of an insurrection; therefore, informal vigilante organizations, or armed patrols, were formed in almost all communities, allegedly to help better protect the white communities from the blacks" (Schlesinger 1992, 120). These community groups often united and became known as the "Men of Justice," the "Pale Faces," "The Constitutional Union Guards," the "White Brotherhood," the "Order of the White Rose," and the "Ku Klux Klan (KKK)." The KKK became the best known of the groups and it eventually absorbed many of the smaller organizations.

In April 1867, a call went out to all known KKK chapters or "dens" to send representatives to Nashville, Tennessee, for a meeting that would plan the Klan's response to the new federal Reconstruction policy. The Klan grew increasingly violent throughout 1867. Thousands of white citizens from Tennessee, Alabama, Georgia, and Mississippi had joined the Klan by this time. And another phenomenon had occurred as well: Non-Klan-member criminals began wearing the Klan's regalia while committing crimes in order to get away with their acts of deviance. In Nashville, a gang of outlaws that had adopted the Klan disguise came to be known as the Black Ku Klux Klan. Middle Tennessee was witness to a plague of guerilla warfare between real Klansmen and the phonies. The Klan was also coming under attack by Congress and the Reconstruction initiatives.

In 1915, the KKK was reformed by William J. Simmons, a preacher who was heavily influenced by Thomas Dixon's book (1905) *The Ku Klux Klan* (George and Wilcox 1996). The Klan was now expanding its list of enemies to include Asians, immigrants, bootleggers, dope, graft, nightclubs and road houses, violation of the Sabbath, pre- and extramarital escapades, and scandalous behavior (Southern Poverty Center 2002), and the Klan increased its level of hostility against blacks, Jews, Roman Catholics, socialists, and communists. During the 1920s, the Klan played an active role in politics by assisting some politicians in elections (e.g., Klan efforts were credited with helping elect governors in Georgia, Alabama, California, and Oregon) and placing some of their own members in elected offices (especially in Colorado, Arkansas, Oklahoma, Indiana, and Ohio). The KKK, very powerful during this era, is estimated to have had at its highest point 5 million members; today, it is estimated to have about 20,000 members.

By the late 1920s and early 1930s, the Klan began losing its power. The public's general disdain for the Klan's increased level of violence, outspoken political and religious critics of the KKK, and then the Great Depression were all factors contributing to the decline of the KKK. Only in Florida was the Klan still a factor during the 1930s. The Klan had a statewide membership of about 30,000 and were active in Jacksonville, Miami, and the "citrus belt" from Orlando to Tampa (George and Wilcox 1996). In the "citrus belt," the Klansmen still operated under the cloak of the night, hiding behind masks, to intimidate blacks who tried to vote, punish marital infidelity, and clash with union organizers. In the North, Klansmen were beginning to exhibit ties to the American Nazi Party, a move that the Southern Klansmen opposed but were basically powerless to stop. But by the 1950s, the political influence and power of intimidation once held by the Klan had all but disappeared. Klansmen were jailed for the floggings and other criminal acts that they had committed.

Today, the KKK consists of small charters scattered across the country. They are a model of extreme bigotry and violence. They maintain a commitment to white supremacy and work toward transforming American culture to one based on the Bible. In their "ideal" society, homosexuals, nonwhite people, and non-Christians would not be annihilated, but segregated. Posted on the Klan's own website (*www.kukluxklan.org*) are the stated goals of this hate-based organization:

> The Knights of the Ku Klux Klan is a political party of White Christian men and women seeking to preserve the highest attributes of Western Civilization and the people who created them. . . . The highest motivation of our cause is love: love of our people's unique heritage and character, love of freedom, and love of our brothers and sisters who are the vanguard fighters for a new era for our people. . . . We believe that abundant differences between the cultures, nations, and races of man give them the natural right to work toward their own ideals and interests with the least possible interference from others. We believe that all races should have the freedom to associate in their own communities.

The Klan prefers that "undesirables" emigrate from the United States, thus leaving America as a "purified" nation. The United States is, of course, too diversified for such an extreme and distorted vision of society, and the Klan's lack of power today reflects this reality.

Skinheads

Another group with a reputation of being an organization based primarily on hatred is the *skinheads*. Among other things, skinheads vary from street gangs in that they don't necessarily have a neighborhood, or turf, that they call home and find necessary to defend. On the other hand, skinheads are often cited as an example of a white gang. Skinheads are generally identified with shaved heads, swastikas tattooed on their bodies, and certain clothing worn to promote their beliefs (e.g., white-power T-shirts). There is a growing acknowledgement in the academic world that all skinheads are not racists. A "racist skinhead" refers to those who promote "white power" or are neo-Nazis. Racist skinheads dislike Jews, blacks, certain other minorities, and certain religious groups. They dislike these people because they consider them to be inferior in comparison to themselves. Racist skinheads draw directly upon the works of Adolf Hitler, leader of the German Nazis. There also exist nonracist skinheads who may have personal racist beliefs but do not declare them as part of being a skinhead.

The skinheads first emerged in Great Britain, especially in London, in the mid- to late 1960s. The post–World War II era was one of turmoil and social change in Great Britain (England, Scotland, and Wales). After the war, many youths, especially young males, enjoyed a large amount of free time since required military service was eliminated. Young males spent time in arcades, coffee shops, and pubs, where they began to form youth groups. Some of the early recognizable British youth groups were labeled beatniks, hipsters, and Teddy Boys. The Teddy Boys were mainly working-class young people who exuded individualism and sought to rebel against conformist values. The Teddy Boys listened to rock and roll and regarded it as a form of revolt and rebellion against work, school, family, police, and foreigners. With defiance and anger, the Boys adopted a new style of dress and new values and treasured American rock (Moore 1993). Unfortunately, their new values included racism, an element not associated with American rock music. They revolted against foreigners like the Afro-Caribbeans, who took many jobs and moved into white neighborhoods throughout England. As is the common outcome when two diverse cultures come into contact with one another, violent confrontations became commonplace. There were a number of unprovoked attacks on Jamaican and other West Indian men in 1958, which became known as the Notting Hill and Nottingham Race Riots of 1958. The seeds were sown for a growing culture of racial violence among British youth for decades to come.

Along with the Teddy Boys, the Mods were also a strong influence on the formation of the skinheads. *The Mods* were a postwar, working-class subculture based on a sharp new style of fashion that distinguished them from other youth groups. They adopted their own music, which included an interesting blend of Jamaican ska, jazz, and rhythm and blues. Knight (1982) and Marshall (1994) argued that soul was their music of choice. Hamm (1994) contends that the Mods were clean-cut, conservative, and much less confrontational than the Teddy Boys and that the Mods, like the Beatles, were greatly inspired by black soul music. More important than the specific sources of music admired by the Mods is the fact that this subculture identified itself with a particular music. By the late 1960s, the Mods had split into two factions: one faction that included art-college-student types whose style became more trendy (Knight 1982); and the other, the Hard Mods, who kept with the working-class look, acted more like a street gang, and enjoyed violence. The Hard Mods became the British predecessors of the skinheads. (The Hard Mods were the prototype for the gang that Anthony Burgess described in *A Clockwork Orange*.) The Hard Mods distanced themselves from the emerging influence of American rock singers and their style of dress, which consisted of denim, long hair, Harley-Davidson T-shirts, and black leather jackets. The Hard Mods had a cleaner appearance, with heavy boots, work shirts, blue jeans, suspenders, and short hair.

The Hard Mods were influenced by the Rude Boys, a group of working-class youths who listened to Jamaican ska and dressed in the fashion of Jamaican gangsters (thus the early skinheads had both white and black members). The mixture of the Hard Mods and the Rude Boys is what essentially became the skinheads (Hamm 1994). The short hair of skinheads—neither totally shaved off nor a crew cut—is one of the attributes acquired from the Rude Boys. In the late 1960s, the Hard Mods and the Rude Boys often fought against other English youth gangs, including the Teddy Boys, who still identified with the rock-and-roll style. Some of the more violent encounters occurred at soccer (football, or futbol) games. Soccer hooliganism has its roots in these skinhead confrontations. (Today, soccer violence is generally not attributed to skinheads.) According to Knight (1982), at one football match in 1968, 4,000 skinheads were in attendance. By the 1970s, a skinhead reggae subculture had also emerged. Its more Jamaican patriotic theme and antiwhite content distanced whites from the Jamaican style of music. As a result, only the whites remained as skinheads.

At this point, the skinhead groups did not believe in Nazism. Their main ideology was to be rebellious against mainstream culture. They distanced themselves from long-hair hippies, who loved rock music and had conformed to the new trends of British culture. According to Moore (1993), shaving their heads was a way of saying, "Fuck you, I'll do as I please." This fuck-you attitude characterizes the early skinhead groups in England, which began to stray even further away from mainstream society.

During the 1970s, the skinheads became more violent and rebellious. With their strong roots in music and their disenchantment with rock, reggae, and other forms of popular music, punk came to their "rescue." Punk bands and their music were labeled rebellious, just like the skinheads. The punk rockers wrote songs about being fed up and rebellious against the mainstream—an ideology that the skinheads had already developed. Skinheads began to listen to punk music and more bands adapted to their beliefs, especially the fuck-you attitude. The punk scene, with its made-to-shock attitude and new streetwise, aggressive music, brought about the first "Skinhead Revival" (Marshall 1994). Eventually, the punk/skinhead youths began to wear the swastika symbol in order to shock the mainstream public. As punk music became more popular, the London-based skinheads began to recruit other Europeans who could be considered right-wing extremists (Moore 1993).

In 1979, Ian Stuart established a political action group called White Noise in order to promote survival and rebellion (Moore 1993). This group originally started out as a musical band named Screwdriver. White Noise formed an alliance with the British National Front, a racist organization. Eventually, White Noise fell apart and Stuart and his friends adopted a full neo-Nazi ideology. They began to publish pamphlets aimed against Jews, homosexuals, blacks, and immigrants. Stuart's popularity and notoriety increased, especially among those looking to rebel against society, and his crew became the premier white-supremacy group in Britain. Furthermore, they adopted the swastika as their symbol. The skinheads took Stuart's lead and began to vandalize and commit hate crimes against groups they did not like. Their violence included murder. The British skinheads were now identifiable by their swastika armbands, shirts that said "Power," Doc Martens, and the playing of Screwdriver records. Influenced by the long-standing English dislike of Pakistanis, the skinheads soon took to the act of "paki-bashing," the physical assault of Pakistani immigrants. So by the 1980s, the skinheads had become, more or less, foot soldiers for racist organizations.

By the late 1970s and early 1980s, skinheads had begun to form gangs in the United States as well as in European countries outside of Great Britain. The rise of skinhead organizations in the United States can be credited to many individuals who accepted the British skinhead ideology. According to Moore (1993), these individuals suffered from mental and emotional disabilities and had trouble fitting into American society. Obviously, they were not mainstream persons. Among the number of individuals "credited" with introducing the skinhead ideology to Americans is Clark Reid Martell, who established the first official skinhead group in America, Romantic Violence, in 1984. Martell had been sentenced to prison for committing arson—he had burned down a Hispanic family's house in Chicago in 1979. While Martell was in prison, he read *Mein Kampf* by Adolf Hitler. Upon release from prison, he joined the Chicago-based American Nazi Party and drew cartoons for its newsletter; he also formed Romantic Violence. Martell is responsible for distributing the hate music of Ian Stuart and Screwdriver. These efforts caused Romantic Violence to be the first skinhead group noted by private organizations that tracked antiminority activity in the United States (Moore 1993). Martell's group protested Gay and Lesbian Pride Day in Chicago as well as other groups that right-wing extremists were against. Martell met with other hate groups across the country to discuss extreme ideologies, such as the one promoted by the Ku Klux Klan, and he is responsible for widely publicizing the skinhead ideology in Chicago and other parts of the United States.

According to Hamm (1993), Robert Heich is another influential skinhead who helped publicize skinhead ideologies. He started a neo-Nazi gang in San Francisco in 1984 after being influenced by the British skinhead movement in the 1970s. His gang was responsible for publicly protesting against African-Americans, Asian-Americans, homosexuals, and immigrants. Heich's influence on the West Coast arose at the same time as Martell's in the Midwest.

Newsday reporter Jim Mulvaney (1993; reprinted in the *Las Vegas Review Journal*) has argued that Greg Withrow is the founder of the skinhead movement in the United States, dating back to 1978. Withrow has stated that he was raised to be a racist: "Some fathers raise their sons to be doctors, some fathers raise their sons to be lawyers. I was raised to be the next Fuhrer" (Mulvaney 1993). While Withrow was growing up in Sacramento, his father made him study the life of Hitler and read hate literature. At age 14, he joined the Klan. Withrow acknowledged to Mulvaney that " 'it became apparent that I held the youth movement in the palm of my hand. . . . I am sorry for what I have done.' Withrow states that white-supremacist skinheads tend to adopt an anarchistic lifestyle in which race and hate crimes are celebrated. In keeping with this attitude, groups around the country are only loosely confederated. [According to Withrow] . . . 'I called it the "100 Hitlers policy" to set up cells across the country. The police can crush one cell, two cells, but the movement continues.' Leaders of the cells tend to meet each other only through more traditional organizations, such as neo-Nazis, the Ku Klux Klan and White Aryan Resistance, which use skinheads as foot soldiers" (Mulvaney 1993). Withrow quit the skinheads in 1987 after his father died. Ironically, he fell in love with a woman whose family fled Hitler's Germany. Withrow was then attacked by the skinheads, including his former best friend, beaten, had his throat cut in two places, his jaw broken, his hands nailed into a board, like a crucifix, and told that he would die as a Jew. He survived the beating and later became a lecturer for the Anti-Defamation League.

The neo-Nazi element was most successfully introduced into the American skinhead scene by Thom Metzger of the White Aryan Resistance (WAR). Metzger had read Ian Stuart's *Blood and Honour* and joined the KKK under David Duke. Metzger learned of the skinheads during a visit to Great Britain. Members of the National Front explained to him the value of using skinheads for the white-power movement. Metzger returned to the United States and began recruiting skinheads as his "frontline warriors" (Andersen and Jenkins 2001; Marshall 1994).

Today, skinheads can be found all over the country and are generally affiliated with other white-supremacist groups such as the White Aryan Resistance (WAR), the National Alliance, the New Order, and the White Student Union (WSU). As Finnegan (2002, 30) stated, "in the mid-eighties, a host of unholy alliances were formed between racist skinheads and old-line extremist organizations such as the Aryan Nations, White Aryan Resistance, the Church of the Creator, and the Ku Klux Klan." However, it is important to note that skinheads are a very disorganized group of troubled youths. They are similar to gangs in the sense that there is no standardized membership, no dues, no organized meetings, and no formal connection between skinheads in various areas (Moore 1993). Their disorganization is reflected in the fact that they typically are unable to define their own beliefs and often ramble on when challenged to a debate (Korem 1994). Members who are more affluent usually do not remain in the gang into adulthood, because their capacity to rationalize and blend into society has been developed by then. Most skinheads are society's castoffs. Many come from broken homes characterized by drug and/or alcohol abuse. They often do poorly in school or completely drop out. They have always had trouble fitting into society and finding friends.

Their feelings of powerlessness and hopelessness make them vulnerable to a group with like-minded personalities. Most come from the lower socioeconomic strata, but regardless of their social stratification, the majority of skinheads come from a family without a father.

Skinheads are often physically fit and have swastika tattoos covering their bodies (Hamm 1994). They are known for their aggressiveness and often resort to violence to get their message of hate across to others. Vandalism (e.g., defacing synagogues with swastikas) and the use of graffiti are other common crimes committed by skinheads. As with street gangs, skinheads will use hand signs for communication with one another. Music remains as a hallmark of the skinhead subculture. They will listen to hard rock, metal, or punk, anything that is radical and extreme and especially anything that makes proclamations regarding white power. Skinheads often shave their heads and wear T-shirts and black, combat-style boots. Most skinheads proclaim support of Nazism and Hitler's ideals, and it is their racist ideology that keeps them loosely united, for they share a hatred of those who are different from them (e.g., blacks, Asians, Jews, immigrants, and homosexuals).

Some skinheads claim to be nonracist, stating that the true roots of the skinhead movement do not include racism while clinging to the music and the rebellious nature of the skinhead ideology. The nonracist skinhead is likely to come from a family of relative affluence. Blazak (1995) found that nonracist skinheads have a higher need for autonomy. Racist skinheads must give up some of their individual autonomy for an allegiance to a racial ideology. The divide between racist and nonracist skinhead groups may lead to confrontation, with one trying to force the other out of their town. Currently, the best-known example of a nonracist skinhead gang is Straight Edge. The Straight Edge movement was started by Ian MacKaye of the Washington DC hardcore band Minor Threat (Andersen and Jenkins 2001). MacKaye wrote a song called "Straight Edge" in the 1980s as an obituary for a friend who had died of a heroin overdose. Straight Edge skinheads do not take drugs, drink alcohol, or smoke cigarettes and do not have casual sex. Many members choose not to ingest caffeine or aspirin and become vegans. The typical symbol of a Straight Edge member is a bold X (in permanent black marker) etched onto the back of the hand, an idea they got from the X marks that underage youths (at concerts) would have drawn on their hands to indicate that they were not old enough to drink. Thus, by marking their own hands with an X, they are telling society that they shun alcohol. This makes the Straight Edger bipolarly distinct from the typical skinhead, who enjoys consuming large amounts of beer. Straight Edgers enjoy different music than the traditional skinhead, music that could be called "Christian hardcore." Members of Straight Edge insist that their group is not about violence, but brotherhood (Kennedy 1998). Thus, a Straight Edger who beats someone up because they are smoking is not a true Straight Edger; instead, he would be labeled a Hate Edge.

As described, skinheads have many of the characteristics of gang members, although they are clearly not in the same category as street gangs. It is estimated that skinheads number less than 5,000 in the United States, although they can be found in most states. The Anti-Defamation League (ADL), which monitors neo-Nazi skinheads in more than 30 countries, estimated in 1995 that there were only 3,500 active neo-Nazi skinheads in the United States. Finnegan (2002) questions this figure, stating that the ADL must have derived it "from a narrow definition of its subjects, since there were, from everything I could tell, more white-supremacist gang members than that in California alone" (30). Skinhead groups exist in Canada, Australia, New Zealand, South Africa, Scandinavia, and Germany. Presently, there is an escalating problem with skinheads in Germany. There are over 150 neo-Nazi groups active in Germany with over 10,000 members. Many of these groups are skinheads. In September 2001, skinheads marched through the city of Leipzig wearing armbands with swastikas and carrying Nazi flags, demanding that foreigners leave Germany. These skinheads admire, and agree with, all the things that Hitler stood for and think that everybody else should feel the same way. A revitalization of the Nazi movement in Germany should be a frightening thought to anyone who knows twentieth-century history.

PRISON GANGS

A discussion of prison gangs is necessary because many street gang members end up in prison and continue their gang-banging lifestyle behind bars. Violence and angry confrontations directed against rivals on the street continue in prison. *Prison gangs* are known to be in existence in nearly all of the prisons in the United States. According to Fong (1990), prison gangs first formed in 1950 when a group of prisoners at the Washington Penitentiary in Walla Walla organized and took the name of the **Gypsy Jokers**, so for more than 50 years prison gangs have been present in the United States. "Prison gangs are flourishing across the country. Organized, stealthy and deadly, they are reaching out from their cells to organize and control crime in America's streets" (Danitz 1998). The enactment of tougher laws against gang-related crimes, beginning in the late 1980s, has directly led to an increase in the number of gang members in prisons. The judicial system was successful in getting gang members off the streets, but their incarceration has led to increased problems for prison officials. Today, prison gangs are more prevalent than ever before (Martinez 1999). They are also responsible for the majority of problems within correctional facilities. The increasing reality is that today's street gangs are becoming tomorrow's prison gangs; and correctional facilities will have to deal with inmates who are more violent and have better connections to illicit activities outside prison walls (Welling 1994).

Prison gangs are similar to organizational crime syndicates. "The emergence of prison gangs has added to the crisis already being experienced by many correctional systems. Prison gangs pursue more than self-protection; they evolved into organized crime syndicates involved in such activities as gambling, extortion, drug-trafficking, prostitution, and contract murder" (Fong 1991, 66). For example, Larry Hoover, a reputed leader of the Gangster Disciples, was convicted of running a large cocaine enterprise from within a state prison (Tyson 1997). Beyond drug trafficking, organized crime often leads to violence. In Texas, 62% of inmate murders recorded between 1979 and 1985 were committed by prison gangs, and overall, prison gangs account for over 50% of all problems and violence in America's prisons (Fong 1991).

Some prison gangs are very powerful and command respect among inmates and street gangsters alike. Prison gang leaders keep in contact with outside gangbangers in a number of ways, including through individuals who visit gang leaders in prison and receive commands; correctional officers and other staff members who have been bribed, coerced, or extorted; and direct contact with street gangsters via phone calls from prison gang leaders behind bars. As unthinkable as it would seem, some prisoners actually have cell phones and make regular calls to their outside contacts. As Cory Godwin, president of the gang investigators association for the Florida Department of Corrections (DC) stated, "contraband equals power" (Danitz 1998). Judicial intervention in correctional administration has systematically stripped away the legitimate authority of prison officials to discipline and control inmates, experts claim. The existence of this organizational crisis has created an atmosphere conducive to the proliferation of inmate gangs (Fong 1991). Thus, judicial intervention, which has the effect of weakening control over inmates, has created an era in which inmate gangs have begun to dominate the prison setting and that has also led to an escalation of violence in prisons (Fong 1990).

"Prison gangs are flourishing from California to Massachusetts. In 1996, the Federal Bureau of Prisons found that disturbances soared by about 400 percent in the early nineties, which authorities say indicated that gangs were becoming more active. In states such as Illinois, as much as 60 percent of the prison population belongs to gangs" (Danitz 1998). Goodwin has identified 240 street gangs operating in the Florida Department of Corrections (Danitz 1998). Street gangs are viewed as an emerging problem in East Coast prisons; they are already a problem in West Coast and Southwest prisons. Texas officials estimate that of the 143,000 inmates in their prisons, 5,000 have been identified as gang members and another 10,000 are under suspicion. Prison gangs are not great in number in Texas, but they are highly organized and possess a paramilitary-type structure. In other state prison systems, officials have noticed that the gang problem is very serious. "Gangs are so powerful at Stateville maximum-security prison in Joliet, IL, that they control entire cell blocks, run a profitable drug trade, corrupt guards and gain unsupervised interviews with wardens, experts and officials say. The growing influx of gangs—whose members account for 77 percent of inmates at Stateville and more than half of the 36,000 inmates in Illinois—has turned the overcrowded Illinois prison system into what one state gang prosecutor calls 'a powder keg.' Illinois illustrates in the extreme how gangs, already a widespread scourge on U.S. streets, are now emerging across the country as the biggest security threat for U.S. prisons" (Tyson 1997). Through intimidation, Chicago super gangs, such as the Vice Lords and Gangster Disciples, exert great control over gallery and cell assignments in the Illinois prisons. Gangs dominate inmate organizations and some are allowed to paint their cells with gang colors and insignia and enjoy special privileges such as wearing expensive jewelry and personal clothing.

In the following pages, a number of the more powerful prison gangs are briefly discussed. We begin with the three most familiar ones—the Mexican Mafia, the Texas Syndicate, and the Aryan Brotherhood—and continue with a description of Neta, the Black Guerilla Family, and La Nuestra Familia.

La Eme (Mexican Mafia)

The largest of all prison gangs is the Mexican Mafia, which has a highly organized and paramilitary-type of structure. The **Mexican Mafia**, or **La Eme** (*eme* is Spanish for the letter "m"), was started around 1957 at Duel Vocational Institute, a center for youthful offenders in Tracy, California. The original leaders, believed to be Joe "Peg Leg" Morgan and Rudy "Cheyenne" Cadena, formed a gang of about 20 Mexican-Americans, mostly gang members from the Maravilla area in Los Angeles. The original reason for the formation of La Eme was for protection against African-American inmates. As more Los Angeles Hispanics came into prison, they were recruited into La Eme. As La Eme grew in members, it was soon the hunter and not the hunted. The early years of La Eme were portrayed in the movie *American Me* with Edward James Olmos. Current members of La Eme vehemently deny that the film is factual. They were especially upset about a scene that suggested the rape of one of their leaders, as they are dead set against homosexuality in any form, declaring it violates their creed of *machismo*. Allegedly, advisors to the film were murdered on the orders of La Eme.

By the late 1960s, La Eme began to exert its power over the outside community. La Eme has a dual purpose: ethnic solidarity and the control of drug trafficking. Violence, extortion, vandalism, and pressure rackets are the tools La Eme uses to control drug trafficking. Commands given from inside the prison are carried out by street gangs. Street gangs must pay the Mexican Mafia a "commission fee" to sell drugs in what La Eme considers its outside territory. The gang frequently resorts to murder as a means of intimidation and gaining respect. Why would outside gang members obey the commands of a prison gang? A simple answer: Most gang members either end up dead or in prison. Going against the Mexican Mafia outside the prison means dealing with the repercussions on the inside. Additionally, members of other gangs who cooperate with La Eme while on the outside will be protected in prison for their loyalty.

The organizational structure of the Mexican Mafia consists of a specific, military-style chain of command. Instructions from generals are carried out by captains, lieutenants, and foot soldiers. Membership is based primarily on race and is open to Hispanics; members are identified by a large "M" tattooed on their chest, back, or arms. It is believed that in order to become a member of La Eme one has to kill another prisoner. The members of La Eme are considered members for life, and it is very difficult and dangerous for a member to try to leave the gang. Among the rivals of La Eme are the La Nuestra Familia, Arizona's New Mexican Mafia, and Northern Structure. Some of the allies of La Eme are the Aryan Brotherhood and Arizona's Old Mexican Mafia.

Since its formation, it is estimated that the Mexican Mafia is responsible for more than 700 murders, both inside and outside prison walls. In 1997, this crime syndicate was weakened by a racketeering and conspiracy trial in Los Angeles Federal Court (Ramos 1997). Using the federal RICO Act, prosecutors were able to get convictions of 13 members of La Eme on 26 counts of murder, conspiracy to commit murder, drug dealing, and extortion. They were also found guilty of "shaking down" actor Edward James Olmos. In San Diego, La Eme members commit crimes on both sides of the border, making it more difficult to apprehend them. In November 1997, Mexican Mafia hitmen were arrested for the slaying of a Tijuana journalist who was a vocal advocate for stronger sanctions on La Eme members (O'Connor 1997).

Despite the legal setbacks of the late 1990s, La Eme continues to grow. There are hundreds of Mexican Mafia members in prison systems throughout the Southwest region of the United States. In Texas, La Eme is also known as *Mexikanemi*, which means "soldiers of Aztlan." The confirmed membership of the Mexican Mafia in Texas is 340, which makes it the largest inmate gang in Texas (Fong 1990).

Texas Syndicate

The **Texas Syndicate (TS)** originated in California's notorious Folsom prison in the early 1970s. It was established in direct response to the other California prison gangs—especially the Aryan Brotherhood and the Mexican Mafia—that were attempting to prey on native Texas inmates. Membership is rising today due to expanded recruitment efforts. As expected, the TS is very strong in Texas, and the Florida Department of Corrections indicates that there are efforts to recruit inmates from its prisons.

TS has a solid organizational structure. A TS member is called a "carnal," a group of members is called a "carnales," and a TS recruit is called a "cardinal." The institutional leader, called the "Chairman," oversees the vice chairman, captains, lieutenants, sergeants, and soldiers. Just as with La Eme, the TS attempts to avoid intragang conflict by having a ranking member automatically revert to the status of soldier when prison officials reassign him to a different facility. Texas Syndicate members generally have TS tattoos located on the back or the right forearm, but they also have been found on the outside calf area, neck, and chest. As with nearly all organized gang syndicates, the TS has precise rules of conduct, which are outlined in its constitution (Fong 1990):

1. Members must be a Texan.
2. Once a member, always a member.
3. The Texas Syndicate comes before anyone, and anything.
4. Right or wrong, the Texas Syndicate is right at all times.
5. All members will wear the Texas Syndicate tattoo.
6. Never let a member down.
7. All members will respect each other.
8. Keep all gang information within the group.

As mentioned earlier, the TS was originally designed as a means to protect fellow Texans from other gang members. It is violent and resorts to extreme methods of violence, including murder, to deal with its enemies. As with the Mexican Mafia, the TS attempts to expand its crime base beyond prison walls by participating in drug trafficking. TS members who are released from prison and secure an income are expected to contribute 10% of their earnings to the syndicate.

Aryan Brotherhood

Prison gangs break down along racial lines: white, black, and Hispanic. Whites make up a small percentage of the prison population and become automatic targets inside prison walls. If their criminal offense was nonviolent, other prisoners are especially tough on them. White inmates are often beaten, raped, and sold from gang to gang (Selcraig 1999). If they are to survive their prison terms, white inmates need protection. This was especially true in the turbulent 1960s as the nation's racial unrest spilled into the nation's prisons. Gangs formed by white inmates in the California prison system were among the early gangs whose roots were entrenched in state penitentiaries. The **Aryan Brotherhood** gang originated in the mid-1960s in San Quentin State Prison, Marin

County, California. The early members were mostly motorcycle bikers and a few neo-Nazis. United together, the Aryan Brotherhood decided to strike against the blacks, who were forming their own militant group called the **Black Guerrilla Family (BGF)**. "Initially, the whites called themselves the **Diamond Tooth Gang**, and as they roamed the yard they were unmistakable: pieces of glass embedded in their teeth glinted in the sunlight" (Grann 2004, 158). The Aryan Brotherhood continued to grow throughout the 1970s. "By 1975, the gang had expanded into most of California's state prisons and was engaged in what authorities describe as a full-fledged race war" (Grann 2004, 159).

Today, the Aryan Nation has unaffiliated splinter groups who use the name of their state with the name "Aryan Brotherhood," for example, the Aryan Brotherhood of Texas (ABT). In the Texas prisons alone, there are over 300 identified full-fledged members of the Aryan Brotherhood. Members express white-supremacist, neo-Nazi characteristics and ideology and identify themselves in such ways as wearing racist tattoos. The primary reason the Aryan Brotherhood exists within the prison is for protection from non-white gangs (especially African-American gangs) and to get "high." As with other prison gangs, they attempt to secure contraband. They are especially concerned with attaining drugs and therefore work in cooperation with a few other prison gangs (e.g., La Eme). They are involved in violence and are known for committing murder against their enemies. Law enforcement officials have uncovered evidence that the Aryan Brotherhood, sometimes called the Brand (Grann 2004), is involved in an increasing level of violence behind prison walls. In California, for example, authorities report that the Aryan Brotherhood, all convicted felons, have "gradually taken control of large parts of the nation's maximum-security prisons, ruling over thousands of inmates and transforming themselves into a powerful criminal organization" (Grann 2004, 158). Upon their release from prison, Aryan Brothers are expected to continue to assist or score drugs for the members remaining in prison. They abide by the creed "blood in, blood out," which means you spill someone's blood to get into the Brotherhood, and your own blood will be spilled if you try and leave the Brotherhood.

The Aryan Brotherhood is not the only white-supremacist prison gang. In 2005, prosecutors filed murder, assault, and racketeering charges against the **211 Crew**, a 300-member gang found in the Colorado prison system (*Syracuse Post-Standard* 2005).

Neta

The **Neta Association** was established in 1970, in the El Oso Blanco Prison (Rio Piedras, Puerto Rico) by an inmate named Carlos Torres-Irriarte (a.k.a. *La Sombra*— "the Shadow"). Torres-Irriarte vocally advocated against the injustices experienced by fellow inmates at the hands of prison officials and other prison gangs. Among the more significant prison gangs in Puerto Rico was **Grupo (Group) 27**. As Torres-Irriarte became more popular among prison inmates, the gang leader of Group 27 (G27) ordered his execution. On March 30, 1981, the hit was made. Seven months later, members of Neta executed G27 gang leader *El Manoto*. During the 1980s, the Neta Association would continue to grow in strength and numbers.

Members of Neta view themselves as victims of American oppression. They are strongly patriotic and have associated themselves with revolutionary groups in Puerto

Rico. It is their hope that Puerto Rico will some day become an independent nation, free from American involvement and citizen status. They have aligned themselves with numerous street gangs in order to bring anarchy to the streets. All Neta members are required to procure 20 prospective recruits for the gang in order to guarantee its growth.

A classic Neta technique of survival in prison is to keep a "low profile" while other Hispanic gangs draw attention to themselves. In this manner, members of Neta are often underestimated by prison officials and work "beneath" the watchful eye of correctional officers. The Neta have quietly entrenched themselves in the drug trade and use the common tactics of extortion, violence, and threat of violence against their enemies. The Neta have become so violent that they perform "hits" for other gangs. They attack and kill without regard to the consequences. Neta members wear the colors of red, white, and blue, although black may be substituted for blue. Displaying colors is a typical trademark of all gangsters. Common clothing of Neta street gangsters includes wearing beads, bandannas, white tops, and black shorts. Neta is actively recruiting new members in correctional facilities and rapidly climbing up the ranks of the most feared prison gangs. It is primarily found in Northeastern prison such as New York and Connecticut.

Black Guerrilla Family

The **Black Guerrilla Family (BGF)** is among the dominant African-American prison gangs. It was created by former Black Panther member George L. Jackson in 1966 at San Quentin State Prison. The most politically oriented of the major prison gangs, BGF was formed as a Marxist/Maoist/Leninist revolutionary organization with three sociopolitical goals: to eliminate racism, to maintain dignity in prison, and to overthrow the United States government. Life-long allegiance is a requirement of BGF membership, who are identified by tattoos with the initials BGF, crossed sabers and shotgun, and, more elaborately, by a dragon overtaking a prison or prison tower. They are allies of La Nuestra Familia, the Black Liberation Army, the Symbionese Liberation Army, the Weather Underground, and black street gangs (including both the Bloods and the Crips). Membership in the BGF traditionally comes from black inmates.

The BGF has members nationwide in both state and federal prisons and is strongly represented on both the East and West coasts. Its membership grew rapidly throughout the 1990s due to its alignment with black street gangs. Recently, a rift has developed between the older members, who see the BGF as a political group, and the newer members, who see the BGF as the "New Man/New Woman" association. The BGF is believed to have created a paramilitary subgroup known as the New Afrikan Revolutionary Nation (*Black Guerrilla Family* 2003).

Another powerful Black prison gang is the **Five Percenters**. The Five Percenters are a loose-knit religious organization that split from the Nation of Islam (NOI) in 1964. Founded by Clarence 13X Smith (also known as "Father Allah"), the Five Percenters believe that 5% of the population is righteous and teach and know about "truth," 10% try to hide the truth, and 85% have not yet received knowledge of the truth. Smith was expelled from the NOI for disagreeing with some of the group's teachings. Five Percenters believe that blacks are the original people of Earth, that they founded all civilization, and that black men are gods (women are known as "earths" and children as "seeds"). They also believe that whites have deceived the whole world, causing it to honor and worship false gods and idols.

The Five Percenters, also known as the Universal Flag of Islam (Anti-Defamation League 2005), have become a presence in the form of prison gangs throughout the East, especially in New York, New Jersey, Massachusetts, Ohio, North Carolina, and South Carolina. In New Jersey, there are an estimated 400 prison inmates who belong to the Five Percenters; 60 are identified as gang members. To many prison officials, the Five Percenters are simply a violence-prone black-supremacist prison gang. The Five Percenters teach that white people are devils, a teaching that corrections officials find dangerous behind prison walls. Despite prison officials' efforts to suppress the teachings of the Five Percenters, the U.S. Supreme Court (in 1987) held that prison walls "do not form a barrier separating prison inmates from protections of the Constitution" (*Turner v. Safley*, 482 U.S. 78, 84). On September 22, 2000, President Clinton signed the Religious Land Use and Institutional Persons Act (RLUIPA), which enhanced the religious rights of prisoners. Although the RLUIPA protects religion, it leaves it to the courts to define what beliefs actually constitute a religion. New Jersey, for example, has been able to levy restrictions on the Five Percenters on the basis of their designation as a "security threat group" rather than as a religion (*Fraise v. Terhune*, 283 F.3d 506, 3d Cir. 2002). In South Carolina, prison officials also prevailed against Five Percenter inmates in a pre-RLUIPA suit (*Inmates Designated as Five Percenters, 14 F.3d 464, 4th Cir. 1999*) (Levin 2005).

La Nuestra Familia (Norte)

La Nuestra Familia (NF) originated in Soledad Prison in California in the mid-1960s. It was established to protect younger, rural, Mexican-American inmates from other inmates. La Nuestra Familia is the primary rival of La Eme. The cultural and social differences between urban and rural Mexican-Americans are the main reason for the split between these two Hispanic prison gangs. The L.A. gangsters disrespected the Northern members by calling them "Farmers" and "Busters"—terms used in a derogatory manner. When one gang member sees a rural gang member, he is to kill him right away. Thus prisons have had to separate gang members from La Eme and La Nuestra. La Nuestra Familia represents northern California Chicano inmates. The Nuestra, or Norte, gang members brand themselves with the letter "N" as a symbol of their allegiance and also to separate themselves from La Eme, which uses the letter "M" for tattoos. Additionally, since the letter "N" is the 14th letter of the alphabet, La Nuestra incorporates the number in its graffiti and symbolism. La Eme members will often wear the color blue; consequently, La Nuestra members wear red. The color red is also symbolic of the United Farm Workers and Cesar Chavez, a champion of civil rights for migrant workers.

Norteno members are much fewer in number than their counterparts the Surenos, but they are much more organized. Battles between the two prison gangs are common in California institutions. The struggle to gain power has led NF to increase its participation in criminal activities. La Nuestra is attempting to control the introduction of contraband into facilities. Membership in NF extends beyond the prison setting.

The prison gang problem is of such concern in California that in 2004 state policy dictated the racial segregation of inmates for the first 60 days of imprisonment. California Assistant Attorney General Frances Grunder argued that the policy is strictly a matter of safety, because mixing white and black inmates in their early prison time could lead to riots and other disturbances. Many white inmates join the Aryan Brotherhood because of their minority status within the prison system. Blacks often join black gangs. The California policy is being challenged by a California inmate who deems the initiative a violation of the Constitution. The case has reached the Supreme Court (the decision is currently pending).

SUMMARY

Street gangs are a growing social problem in the United States. Their exact numbers are hard to determine, but most likely, the total number is still below 1 million. The latest U.S. census data indicate that there are approximately 290 million Americans. Consequently, gang members make up less than a half percent of the total population. But although their numbers are relatively small, their impact on society, especially in particular neighborhoods, is immense. As described in this chapter, there is no single definition of a gang. However, there are many general characteristics that help to identify certain groups as gangs. This chapter also revealed that there are a wide variety of gangs and that they can be found in very diverse environments.

CHAPTER TWO

A History of Gangs

As stated in Chapter 1, people have formed groups since the beginning of human history. This is also true of youths. As we also explained in Chapter 1, the designation of young people as a special group—children—is recent. Children were expected to obey their parents unconditionally and they worked to earn their keep. Many children were treated very poorly and in some cases orphaned or abandoned by their parents. They learned that there was safety in numbers and that group formation increased their odds of survival. Much has changed in the modern era. Most children have a great deal of free time and few are expected to work 8–10 hours a day—a typical occurrence in the past, especially in agricultural families. Today, children still form groups primarily for play, games, organized sports, and a wide variety of activities. Sometimes they organize as youth gangs.

Street gangs are not, however, a recent phenomenon. Documentation of gangsters and street thugs dates back many centuries. Savelli (2000) stated that the word *thug (thugz)* originated in India (A.D. 1200) and referred to a gang of criminals that roamed the country, pillaging towns along their path. They were famous for strangling people. These thugs used their own symbols, hand signs, rituals, and slang. Savelli (2000) also suggested that pirates should be considered gangs because they engaged in similar types of brutal behavior. Evidence supports the existence of youth street gangs committing criminal acts in Europe throughout the Middle Ages. Hay and associates (1975) stated that gangs in England committed such crimes as theft and robbery, extortion, and rape. Pearson (1983) described fourteenth- and fifteenth-century London as a place where citizens were terrorized by such gangs as the Mims, Hectors, Bugles, and Dead Boys, who enjoyed violent acts such as breaking windows, demolishing taverns, and assaulting the watch (a sort of law enforcement). These gang members distinguished themselves, especially while in battle, by wearing different colored ribbons (colors). Other research has shown that street gangs fought one another in France during the Middle Ages and in Germany during the seventeenth and eighteenth centuries (Covey, Menard, and Franzese 1992).

There are references (Sanders 1970) to gangs in colonial America, but these "gangs" were mostly orphans who banded together, forming a substitute or surrogate family, with the simple idea that there is greater protection in numbers. Gurr (1989) documented at least 500 vigilante groups (gangs) between 1760 and 1900. Taylor (1990, 1–2) stated that "gangs have existed in the United States since the Revolutionary War. The infamous Jean Laffite led his band of buccaneers against the British in Louisiana in support of General Andrew Jackson. Countless gangs rode during the early days of the Wild West." During the early 1790s, gang members in Philadelphia participated in the activity of flying candle kites, a harmless behavior until the candle kites crashed down into buildings and caused fires.

"By the early 1800s teenage gangs were a fixture, albeit unwanted, of most large cities" (Grennan, Britz, Rush, and Barker 2000, 3). Most gang researchers agree that the first "real" street gang in the United States was the Forty Thieves, founded in New York City around 1826. This Irish-American immigrant gang consisted of youths and adults, a common characteristic of the early Irish gangs in New York City during the early-to-mid-1800s.

THE EARLY 1800s: THE BIRTH OF STREET GANGS

In 1820, there were approximately 123,000 inhabitants of New York City, most of whom were concentrated in lower Manhattan, below Fourteenth Street. These city residents were native-born Americans and Protestants. The once major ethnic division between citizens of English and Dutch ancestry had subsided by this point (Lardner and Reppetto 2000). New York was a relatively peaceful city, lacking in gangs, drug dealers, and the threat of street gun violence. There were no police forces as well. Local newspapers were more interested in reporting information like ship departures and arrivals, treaty negotiations, and legislative debates than they were in writing about crime. "Little if anything was said about the unsolved case, the unapprehended suspect, or the uncontrolled disturbance—about any of the incidents with the potential to embarrass the guardians of law and order. New Yorkers, by all reports, were reasonably satisfied with the level of public safety" (Lardner and Reppetto 2000, 4).

The fate of New York City would change with the opening of the Erie Canal in 1825. "It was Mayor-turned-Governor Clinton's 'Big Ditch,' connecting the Great Lakes to the Hudson River, that turned the city into something more than a provincial port. With the opening of the Erie Canal, in 1825, transportation to, from, and within the new nation evolved into a hub-and-spoke system with just about everything and everybody passing through New York" (Lardner and Reppetto 2000, 7). Dramatic changes in all phases of transportation coincided with the rapid rise of industrialization. Cheap labor was necessary in order to build the Erie Canal and the railroads. Many labor-intensive jobs would be filled by the numerous immigrants entering the United States through New York. The city grew quickly, and its growth was accompanied by a lack of any logical planning. Apartment tracts sprung up on streets lacking sewers and safe drinking water. Drastically overcrowded living conditions and the lack of proper sanitation gave birth to medical (e.g., cholera) and criminal epidemics. Newly arrived immigrants, lacking education and English proficiency, continued to pour into densely populated ethnic ghettos. The number of immigrants was so great in the early 1800s that, by 1850, "immigrants comprised more than two-thirds of the population of the largest cities in the northeast, more than three quarters of those in New York, Boston, and Chicago" (McCorkle and Miethe 2002, 32).

Among the immigrants entering New York in the 1820s, the largest number were the Irish. The Irish immigrants, poor and Catholic, were America's first urban ethnic group. Attempting to maintain their ethnic heritage, the Irish opened their own "cheap green-grocery speakeasies" throughout their ghetto neighborhood, known as the Five Points. The first street gangs of the United States arose in the Five Points and neighboring Bowery. The Five Points was an area, in the Paradise Square district, where five streets (Cross, Anthony, Little Water, Orange, and Mulberry) once converged (today there are just three streets that converge in this area). The green-grocery speakeasies were little more than "fronts" for illegal activity that was conducted in back rooms.

> The first of these speakeasies was established about 1825 by Rosanna Peers in Center Street just south of Anthony, now Worth Street. Piles of decaying vegetables were displayed on racks outside the store, but Rosanna provided a back room in which she sold the fiery liquor of the period at lower prices than it could be obtained in the recognized saloons. This room soon became the haunt of thugs, pickpockets, murderers, and thieves. The gang known as Forty Thieves, which appears to have been the first in New York with a definite, acknowledged leadership, is said to have been founded in Rosanna Peers' grocery store, and her back room was used as its meeting place and as headquarters by Edward Coleman and other eminent chieftains (Asbury 2002, 56).

Lardner and Reppetto (2000) refer to this grocery as belonging to Rosetta Peers; regardless, this is the place that the Forty Thieves called home. Edward Coleman, the founder of the Forty Thieves, was obviously literate, as he named his gang in honor of "Ali Baba and the Forty Thieves" from *Arabian Nights*. The Forty Thieves dominated the Five Points for 10 years, until 1836, when Coleman was arrested for murdering his wife, for which he was hanged in 1838. The rising gang activity in this urban ghetto led to all Irish being labeled "no good." The Kerryonians, composed of natives from County Kerry, Ireland, were also a result of Peers's enterprise. This gang "seldom roamed beyond Center Street and did little fighting; its members devoted themselves almost exclusively to hating the English" (Asbury 2002, 57).

A number of other gangs were organized and met in different grocery stores, including the Chichesters, Roach Guards, Plug Uglies, Shirt Tails, and the Dead Rabbits. The Roach Guards took their name from a local grocery owner, Ted Roach. "One night, a dissident faction of the Roach Guards was holding a meeting when somebody threw a dead rabbit in their midst; because a rabbit meant a rowdy and *dead* was an adjective connoting sharp or best, they took the name for their own. Another gang wore oversize plug hats, stuffing them with wool and leather to provide protection from brickbats and bludgeons. Soon other gangs adopted the practice, and the term *plug ugly* became a synonym for street hoodlums in general" (Lardner and Reppetto 2000, 8). The Tail Shirts earned their name because of their habit of wearing their shirts outside of their trousers—an uncommon practice at the time. The Dead Rabbits, when going to battle, carried with them a dead rabbit impaled on a stick. Asbury (2002, 1927) described the Plug Uglies as "gigantic" Irishmen and as the most notorious of all the street thugs found in the Five Points. The Roach Guards and the Dead Rabbits wore colors to distinguish themselves, the Guards with a blue stripe on their pants, while the Rabbits wore red (McCorkle and Miethe 2002, 33). The Roach Guards and Dead Rabbits were sworn enemies of one another, but they, along with all the other Irish gangs of the Five Points, would unite against the "Yankee" gangs from the Bowery.

The Bowery was a slum area to the north of the Five Points. Here, many young men worked as butcher boys (a term that became associated with a rowdy) in the numerous slaughterhouses located throughout the Bowery. There were native-born "Yankee" gangs and Irish-American gangs. Among the most distinguished Bowery gangs were the Bowery Boys, the True Blue Americans, the American Guards, and the

Atlantic Guards. Asbury (2002, 1927, 62) described the often epic battles between the Bowery Boys and the Dead Rabbits:

> For many years the Bowery Boys and the Dead Rabbits waged a bitter feud, and a week seldom passed in which they did not come to blows, either along the Bowery, in the Five Points section, or on the ancient battleground of Bunker Hill, north of Grand Street. The greatest gang conflicts of the early nineteenth century were fought by these groups, and they continued their feud until the Draft Riots of 1863, when they combined with other gangs and criminals in an effort to sack and burn the city. In these early struggles the Bowery Boys were supported by the other gangs of the Bowery, while the Plug Uglies, the Shirt Tails, and the Chichesters rallied under the fragrant emblem of the Dead Rabbits. Sometimes the battles raged for two or three days without cessation, while the streets of the gang area were barricaded with carts and paving stones, and the gangsters blazed away at each other with musket and pistol, or engaged in close work with knives, brickbats, bludgeons, teeth, and fists. On the outskirts of the struggling mob of thugs ranged the women, their arms filled with reserve ammunition, their keen eyes watching for a break in the enemy's defense, and always ready to lend a hand or a tooth in the fray.

Although most of the gang members were males, females did participate in the early Irish gang clashes. "From the sidelines, female companions supplied emotional support, ammunition, and medical aid. Sometimes they actually participated in the battles. One legendary female gangster was Hell-Cat Maggie, a fierce moll who fought alongside the Dead Rabbits, armed with teeth filed to sharp points and long artificial fingernails made of brass" (McCorkle and Miethe 2002, 33). Often, troops had to be sent in to break up the battles between these rival gangs. A great deal of attention would be directed toward the growing gang problem in the following decades. Newspapers had already begun to change their focus to issues related to crime and the rise of street thug gangs.

MID-1800s: THE ESCALATION OF NEW YORK CITY STREET GANGS

The population of New York had risen to 300,000 by 1840. It was a city besieged by street thugs and rampant criminal activities (e.g., pickpockets, street robbers, violent attacks on merchants and tourists). New York was not the only city claiming a gang problem. In Philadelphia, a study covering the years 1836 to 1878 identified 52 different gangs that plagued the city (Shelden et al. 2001). However, New York City would remain the gang capital of the nineteenth century. According to Spergel (1995), there were an estimated 30,000 men who owned allegiance to gang leaders in New York City in 1855. The media took notice. The rise of the "penny press" allowed more citizens access to news events covered by local newspapers. Noteworthy is the fact that the penny press often covered stories about the city's elites and their misdoings. However, the focus of most newspaper reports rested with street crime. The citizens needed someone to blame, a scapegoat, for all the ills of society. Longtime inhabitants of New York and the other Northeastern cities had their target—the Irish.

Old World/New World Rivals

The Irish had been a visible presence in New York since the early 1820s. However, due to dramatic events in Ireland in the mid-1840s, the presence of the Irish would greatly increase in the United States, especially New York. This dramatic event was the Irish potato famine. "The Irish potato famine set off the greatest migration the world had ever seen: 2.5 million people left Ireland in a single decade. Most of them went to America, and more than a million settled in New York, where the gentry railed against their drinking and carousing and their foreign religion, with its lax attitude toward the Sabbath. For the native-born working class, the biggest problem with the Irish was their readiness to take almost any job at any pay. Framing the threat in apocalyptic terms, the Know-Nothing Party proposed a twenty-one-year naturalization period for immigrants, a ban on Catholics in government, and the deportation of foreign-born criminals and paupers. Of the various foreign elements capable of getting the city riled up in those years, however, nobody topped the British. Worshipped by many upper-crust New Yorkers, they were loathed by the working class, regardless of ethnicity." (Lardner and Reppetto 2000, 26). The Irish and anti-Irish gangs would suspend fights against one another to fight the English. English snobbery and the Protestant religion were in direct conflict with the Irish, Catholics, and other ethnic poor groups that were migrating in great numbers to New York.

To better understand this New World conflict, it is beneficial to understand the long history of resentment between the Irish and English in the Old World. For centuries, the English dominated the Irish, militarily, culturally, and economically. The English treated the Irish like barbarians and less than human. During eighteenth- and nineteenth-century occupation, the English army stored their horses in Irish churches. More relevant was the Irish "potato famine," referred to in Irish as *Gorta Mor*, or the Great Hunger, because, while there was a failure of the potato crop in Ireland in the 1840s, it was not the cause of the Irish famine. In fact, there was enough food grown in Ireland to feed its own people, but the Irish were forced to pay food as "rent" to England. Most of the more than 1 million Irish who starved to death could have been spared if not for the yearly demand of 15 million pounds worth of wheat, oats, barley, beef, mutton, pork, poultry, eggs, butter, milk, fruit, and vegetables grown by the Irish that was collected by England. The Irish who refused to pay this "rent" were evicted from their land, and their homes were destroyed. The potato "famine," as perpetrated by England, that occurred in Ireland from 1845 to 1850 is an equal rights violation similar to genocide and slavery. Because of England, 1 million Irish died and more than 2 million were forced to flee.

Needless to say, the Irish brought with them a great deal of cultural "baggage" and resentment toward the English. In America, the English were still trying to tell the Irish how to behave. The young Irish-Americans fought back via gang participation. Condemned to the ghettos of New York's Five Points district, many of the newly arrived Irish were willing to take any job offered as a means of improving their lives in the New World. Others joined the existing street gangs. Battles between the Irish Dead Rabbits and the native Bowery Boys waged on throughout the 1850s. A famed riot occurred in 1857, leaving more than a dozen combatants dead. Shortly afterward, Charles Dickens visited the Five Points and declared that it was much worse than the slums of London, which he made famous in *Oliver Twist*.

The Rise of Law Enforcement

Demands among the citizenry for more law and order and control over the gangs led to the formation of local police forces. Professional law enforcement agencies are a relatively new phenomena. Throughout most of human history, law and order was maintained by community elders, tribal leaders, armies loyal to a monarch, or some other variation of "might makes right." Most citizens were powerless against existing social hierarchies, and the concept of innate human rights was something left to philosophers to debate. With industrialization, modernity, a longer life span, and democratic societies came the idea that citizens should have certain basic rights. Primary among these rights was granting citizens certain protections under governmental supervision (e.g., the right to own property free from threat that others may take or destroy it). Professional (governmental) law enforcement rose to serve this function.

"The first professional police force was London's Metropolitan Police Force, established in 1829 by Sir Robert Peel. . . . The English were ahead of us in their organization of a formal police department. Early nineteenth-century Manhattan (until the consolidation of the five boroughs in 1898, Manhattan *was* New York City) was still dependent on the volunteer patrolmen and night watchman who walked informal beats. These early New York cops—called roundsmen—were armed with nightsticks, rattles, or whistles" (Safir 2003, 23). London's policemen were called "Bobbies" in honor of Robert "Bobbie" Peel. The Metropolitan Police, established in 1845, was New York's first structured police force. Marilynn Johnson (2003, 13–14) explains the origins of the NYPD:

> Founded under a state act in 1845, the New York Police Department was established as a bulwark against urban crime and disorder. A growing metropolitan economy had attracted new immigrants, spurred the development of poor tenement districts, and fueled class and ethnic tensions that produced a wave of urban disorder in the 1830s and 1840s. Poor neighborhoods such as the predominantly Irish Five Points were plagued by high rates of property crime, violence, vice, and a series of street riots that convinced city officials to create a full-time professional police force along the lines of London's Metropolitan Police.

In comparison to London's metropolitan police, the early New York police force was a bit disorganized and not always professional (e.g., citizens often had to make payoffs to the police to get stolen property returned—they sometimes still do). During the 1840s, the police seldom used firearms because of the simple fact that they did not work very reliably—often backfiring or exploding in one's hand during use. Companies such as Colt, Derringer, and Smith & Wesson were already working on guns that would kill more efficiently and that would ultimately become integrated as a common component of the policeman's arsenal. Even so, the reality of a police force was met with a great deal of reluctance by the majority of New Yorkers. Many New Yorkers were worried about the growing crime rate, but the idea of a "standing army" in the city was something that most Americans were against.

> New Yorkers had gotten a department that reflected their conflicted feelings about police protection. A more disciplined and centralized force might have

come across as a "standing army"—something that many early Americans, not just New Yorkers, had hoped to do without. Uniforms, besides the military connotations, were servant's "livery"—a symbol of the Old World class distinctions that Americans had fought a revolution against (though the immigrants who already predominated among the servant class did not object so strongly; they couldn't afford to). And yet the department was moving slowly and haltingly down the path of what we would consider professionalism. The term of appointment, originally two years (the same as an alderman's term), was increased to four in 1849 (Lardner and Reppetto 2000, 31).

The concern among Americans about the need for a standing army is firmly entrenched in Amendment II of the U.S. Constitution, ratified in 1791. The "founding fathers" of the United States hoped that it would be unnecessary to have a standing army, but just in case, they wrote that "a well regulated Militia, being necessary to the security of a free State, the right of the people to keep and bear Arms, shall not be infringed." Clearly, the Constitution was granting the right for a future army (a well-regulated militia) to bear arms. New York citizens of the mid-1800s, not exposed to the evils of guns on the streets, were greatly dismayed to see police (or anyone else) armed.

The gangs were not impressed by the early New York police forces and often attacked them with great intensity. For the Irish gangs, the disdain shown toward the police was more personal and reflected their "cultural baggage" from the Old World. The early New York police dressed in uniforms that attempted to imitate the English bobbies, something that further fueled the Irish-English rivalry. "So much ill-feeling arose because of this . . . that the uniforms were called in, and for several years the police appeared on the streets with no other insignia than a star-shaped copper shield, whence came the names coppers and cops" (Asbury 2002, 59). The Irish eventually infiltrated the ranks of the police and would come to dominate their numbers.

Politics, Fire Brigades, and Gangs

In 1850, the population of New York City had soared to well over one-half million residents. There were an estimated 30,000 gang members at this time. During the mid- and late 1800s, street gangs directly shaped the outcome of New York's political elections. Political institutions such as Tammany Hall used gangs to control elections. The gangs received favors from elected officials; in return, they would scare people away from the voting polls.

> The political geniuses of Tammany Hall were quick to see the practical value of the gangsters, and to realize the advisability of providing them with meeting and hiding places, that their favor might be curried and their peculiar talents employed on election day to assure government of, by, and for Tammany. Many ward and district leaders acquired title to the green-grocery speakeasies in which the first of the Five Points gangs had been organized, while others operated saloons and dance houses along the Bowery, or took gambling houses and places of prostitution under their protection. The underworld thus became an important factor in politics, and under the manipulation of the worthy statesmen the gangs of the Bowery and Five Points participated in the great series of riots (Asbury 2002, 68–69).

The police force was equally corruptible. Politicians such as Fernando Wood learned how to use both the gangs and the police to their political advantage. Born in Philadelphia in 1812, Wood came to New York with his family and went into the liquor and cigar business as a young man. Through the backing of Tammany Hall, Wood was elected to Congress in 1840. After losing his 1850 bid for New York mayor, Wood learned how to use the new emerging "political games" to his advantage. "His more serious innovations had to do with getting votes and collecting graft. . . . In the 1852 primary, gangs had seized ballot boxes and barred entrance to the polls while the cops did nothing. Control of the police was estimated to be worth 10,000 votes in a mayoral election; at a time when fewer than 100,000 votes were cast . . . Wood was not subtle. While his predecessors had tried to maintain a certain veneer of respectability, he openly ran city government to benefit himself and his Tammany Hall cohorts" (Lardner and Reppetto 2000, 37). Wood was one of the first politicians to pursue the Irish vote. The Irish, large in numbers, represented a huge political block of votes. Newly arrived immigrants were sent to Tammany Hall, naturalized, and given the right to vote— something that the Irish did proudly, as they were not allowed to vote in Ireland because of English domination. The corruption of Wood's administration led to the creation of rival police forces and the governor's (John King) attempt to serve Wood a summons. Street gangs were amused by the whole ordeal.

Another interesting development during the mid-1800s in New York was the creation of fire brigades. Before the Civil War, fire brigades generally consisted of gang members, most of them Irish and loyal to Tammany Hall. Fire companies did not work cooperatively with one another; instead, they were in competition. As a result, a number of rival fire companies were formed. Prominent politicians (even George Washington was once the head of a New York department) aligned themselves with various fire brigades. The bitter rivalry between the fire departments often led to disastrous results. Insurance companies paid compensation to only one fire department that fought a fire. When members from rival companies met at the scene of a fire they would fight one another over the right to fight the fire. Sometimes entire buildings burned to the ground while the firemen did battle. Another dysfunctional fire-fighting tactic involved the practice of early arrivals at a fire of covering the fire plug with a barrel, disguising it from the rival company until one's own members arrived. If the fire plug was discovered, the battle ensued until the rest of the brigade arrived. The fight for fire plugs frequently resulted in the building burning down before anyone even attempted to put it out.

THE CIVIL WAR PERIOD–1900

The outbreak of the Civil War had a profound effect on the residents of New York City. "There was considerable antiwar sentiment in New York. To the Irish, the abolition of slavery raised the specter of more low-wage workers competing for scarce jobs. (In 1853, Black workers armed with revolvers had been hired as scabs after Irish laborers struck against the Erie Railroad, seeking a salary of $1.25 a day and a limit of ten hours)" (Lardner and Reppetto 2000, 43). Other outspoken opponents of Lincoln and going to war were Fernando Wood (who had become mayor again in 1859), New York Governor Horatio Seymour, and Tammany leader William "Boss" Tweed. Speaking in front of a predominantly Irish crowd in 1863 and flaming the feelings of resentment against the impending draft, Seymour stated that "the bloody, treasonable and revolutionary doctrine of public necessity can be proclaimed by a mob as well as by government" (Lardner and Reppetto 2000, 43).

The country's first draft was enacted in July 1863. The draft was initiated to fill the ranks of the Union Army. Any time a draft is in existence it risks a negative backlash; this is especially true if citizens are not completely behind the war in question (e.g., the Civil War, the Vietnam War). As unpopular as this draft was, it also included a highly discriminatory "buy-out" clause for those draftees who were willing to pay $300 in order to avoid serving their country. No working-class persons could afford such an amount, but clearly the wealthy could buy their drafted sons' freedom from the military. Immigrants (mostly the Irish) who had the misfortune of arriving in New York at this time were welcomed, made American citizens, and told that they were drafted into war. During the draft registration process, signs of trouble emerged.

The Draft Riots

On the third day of the draft, Monday, July 13, 1863, an unruly crowd began to disturb the draft procedures at Forty-Sixth and Third streets. The state militia, which had been assigned to maintain law and order during draft announcements, had been summoned to Gettysburg to help stem Lee's invasion of the North. This left the local police to defend the draft office. They were unsuccessful. Rioters burned the office to the ground and fought the police. Mobs destroyed telegraph lines and broke into a gun factory. They attempted to overtake the *Tribune* office, primarily because of its support for the war. For days, rioters fought with the police, who were eventually supported by a company of soldiers with orders to kill every man with a club. The rioters were originally expressing their opposition to the draft, but they soon found other targets, including the wealthy and blacks.

"The riots had started out as a protest against the draft. As they continued blacks were more and more often the main targets. They were attacked everywhere mobs found them. . . . The police and troops showed no mercy, nor did the rioters. An army colonel, himself a local Irishman, fired artillery at a mob and then unwisely went home, where he was caught and tortured to death" (Lardner and Reppetto 2000, 48). In all, a hundred buildings were burned to the ground and the city was nearly taken over by the rioters. Authorities speculated that the draft riots were stirred up by Southern agents attempting to cause havoc. They used the gangs to fight the police while they sought out blacks.

Interestingly, Asbury (2002, 63) noted that during the draft riots it was the women who inflicted the most fiendish tortures upon blacks, soldiers, and policemen captured by the mob, "slicing their flesh with butcher knives, ripping out eyes and tongues, and applying the torch after the victims had been sprayed with oil and hanged to trees." The most famous of the female battlers was Hell-Cat Maggie, who ran with the Dead Rabbits during the 1840s. (The gangs of New York during the mid-1800s and the draft riots serve as the primary subject of the film *Gangs of New York*, 2002.)

Drug use among gang members became predominant in the post–Civil-War period and is directly linked to technological innovations and discoveries, such as morphine (1803), the hypodermic syringe, cocaine, chloral hydrate (1868), and heroin (1898), by the medical profession. At this time, medicine was crude at best and its inability to cure disease led physicians to turn to narcotics for their anesthetic properties. "Proprietary medicines containing morphine, cocaine, and laudanum could be bought at any store or ordered through the mail. In addition, many soldiers from both the North and South had become addicted during the war and returned to their communities heavily addicted to morphine, and spreading addiction even further by recruiting new users" (McCorkle and Miethe 2002, 41). Gang members increasingly turned to cocaine, and as many "as 90 percent of members may have been cocaine addicts" by the late nineteenth century (McCorkle and Miethe 2002, 41).

Post–Civil-War gang activity extended to the South in the form of the Ku Klux Klan. The Klan was started by former Civil War veterans (see Chapter 1).

The Late 1800s

In the world of gangs, the Irish dominated the streets for decades and made "claim" to a number of notorious characters, beginning with the Forty Thieves founded in 1826 and ending with Edward Delaney, alias Monk Eastman. At the end of the nineteenth century, Eastman was the boss of 1,200 men (Borges 2002, 89–90). Tammany politicians hired Eastman (Delaney) to stir up trouble. Eastman had set prices for "jobs" (e.g., $19 to break and arm or leg, $25 to stab someone, and $100 to kill someone). However, by the late 1800s, the Irish, for the most part, had assimilated into American culture. They were now the "natives" and "flag-wavers" of the country. They dominated the police force. Their immigrant status had all but disappeared, and their reign as street gangsters vanished along with their old status.

Replacing the Irish as a "menace" to society were the new immigrants arriving in the United States via New York. By 1910, New York City's population reached a staggering 2 million. These people faced the same obstacles as the Irish—living in ghetto conditions, difficulty speaking the language, lack of job skills, and so on. As with the Irish, these immigrants formed ethnic street gangs, eager to cut out a piece of territory and respect for themselves and their people. As in New York City in the late 1800s, youth gangs emerged in the slums of Philadelphia, Boston, Chicago, St. Louis, Detroit, and Pittsburgh.

THE EARLY 1900s: THE SPREAD OF STREET GANGS

The early 1900s witnessed the spread of street gangs to many urban cities in the Northeast and Midwest. The use of guns increased the level of violence. Many would-be gangsters were taken off the streets and placed in the military during World War I. The postwar period initially brought about economic opportunities for adult males, lowering the average gang member's age. During Prohibition and the Depression years, two distinct types of gang activity occurred: Street gangs were committing petty crimes, and organized crime syndicates were making huge amounts of money selling liquor. During Prohibition, law enforcement efforts were concentrated on such characters as Al Capone, the Bonnie and Clyde gang, the Ma Barker gang, and so on. For some reason, the public seemed to glamorize and support these criminals (the "Robin Hood" scenario), and decades later the mass media immortalized these thugs in film. With the end of Prohibition in 1933, organized criminals lost control of the streets, and street gangs flourished once again until World War II.

New York City

At the turn of the century, the Irish still had a presence in the New York gang world and were led by politician/theatrical impresario "Big" Tim Sullivan, who was successful not only in legitimate business and politics but also as an overlord of crime. "From his headquarters inside the Occidental Hotel . . . Sullivan oversaw gang activities, delivering votes, jobs and graft opportunities—doing more for the downtown poor than other politicians of his day" (Vergano 2002, 8D). His position with Tammany Hall provided Sullivan with opportunities to champion the voices of the common person, even in such matters as the fight against police brutality and their use of excessive force. In 1909, Sullivan "sponsored a state legislative bill banning police use of blackjacks, brass knuckles, and other unorthodox weapons. Although opponents claimed the bill was designed to protect gangsters allied with Tammany Hall, Sullivan insisted that the law was necessary to prevent police from establishing a 'rule of armed terrorism' in his district" (Johnson 2003, 96). As Sullivan demonstrated, the perception of what constitutes acceptable forms of violence is in the eye of the beholder. The power and influence of Tammany Hall was still quite strong in the 1910s. The only time in New York State history that a governor was removed from office occurred in 1913. According to historians, then-governor William Sulzer wasn't removed because of a citizen's revolt (as in the recall of former California Governor Gray Davis in 2003); it was because he turned his back on the Democrats of Tammany Hall who got him into office (Case 2003).

Following the lead of the Irish, young males from the emerging immigrant ethnic groups began to form street gangs. In fact, from this point on in U.S. history, a noticeable trend emerges: The most recent immigrants, and those most marginalized from society, tend to dominate the gang world. By 1910, the Irish gangs were all but replaced by Jewish and Italian gangs. The Eastmans, who were mostly Jewish and resided east of the Bowery, formed one gang confederation; the Five Pointers, who were mostly Italian and resided to the west, represented the other major gang confederation of New York. The Eastmans and Five Pointers often waged battle with one another using handguns. The Five Points Gang was led by Italian immigrant Paolo Antonini Vaccarelli, also known as Paul Kelly, and his second-in-command, Johnny Torrio. Torrio later became a significant member of the Sicilian Mafia (La Cosa Nostra) and recruited street hoodlums from the Five Points Gang. The Five Points Gang gained a reputation as a type of "farm club" for the Mafia. The most notorious recruit was Alphonse Capone, who later gained a notorious reputation and became known by his nickname, "Scarface." In 1919, Capone was summoned by Torrio to move to Chicago, where his assistance was needed in maintaining control of the Chicago mob territories (Savelli 2000).

The post–Civil-War period saw an increased use of guns among criminals and gang members. In 1911, the Sullivan law made the possession of guns without a permit a crime—a move that greatly aided the fight against gang-related crimes. Two years later, Mitchell was elected mayor of New York City, and he became instrumental in prioritizing the NYPD's commitment to containing the street gang problem. The beginning of the twentieth century was a period when reform efforts were instituted in an attempt to control the power of gangs, especially in relation to political elections. "In the early 1900s, reform efforts targeted widespread police corruption, just as election laws eliminated the uselessness of gangs. The cops took after the gangs, driving their most entrepreneurial members underground" (Vergano 2002, 8D). These reform efforts certainly did not eliminate gangs. To eliminate gangs completely (a seemingly impossible goal), numerous socioeconomic issues would have to be addressed; and with the huge numbers of immigrants arriving in the United States, it became obvious that gangs would become a permanent fixture of society. The early 1900s witnessed such events as the Tong Wars, which involved gangs from Chinatown; the emergence of Italian gangs, which would eventually evolve into organized crime syndicates; and Jewish street gangs.

The Gorilla Boys

At the beginning of the twentieth century, there were a number of Jewish street thugs who engaged in a variety of criminal acts. Richard Cohen (2002) chronicled the life of Louis "Lepke" Buchalter, born in Williamsburg, Brooklyn, in 1897 to Russian-born Jews, in his book *Tough Jews* (1998). His mother called him *Lepkeleh*, a Yiddish variation of "Little Louis." His friends would simply call him Lepke. The Buchalters were a large, middle-class family with 14 children, and Louis, the youngest brother, sought attention that his parents could not provide. Whenever he had the chance, Louis would sneak away and roam the immigrant streets looking for adventure and excitement. Lepke's father died when he was 13, and his mother, feeling distraught, moved to Colorado, leaving Louis under the guidance of an older sister. Lepke paid little attention to his sister, skipped school often, and fell into a group of older gangsters (for example, Joseph "Doc" Stacher, Louis "Shadows" Kravits, Hyman "Curly" Holtz, and Phil "Little Farvel" Kovolick). These men taught him various criminal acts: how to be a pickpocket, roll a drunk, spy on cops, and so on (Cohen 2002). As Albert Fried (1980, 130) described Lepke at this age, "he was, to put it candidly, a delinquent—an audacious and ruthless one, according to the sparse accounts we have—who spent most of his time across the river on the Lower East Side where he committed petty thefts and extortions and other random acts of violence."

Louis Buchalter's criminal career officially began in 1915, "the year of his first arrest and conviction on a felony charge (for stealing luggage in Bridgeport, Connecticut, where he had gone to work for an uncle). From then on he was true to his calling. One arrest followed another, and he shuttled back and forth between the various punitive, retributive, and rehabilitative agencies" (Fried 1980, 131). When he returned to the Lower East Side, Lepke began stealing pushcarts. During one robbery, he met Jacob "Gurrah" Shapiro, a notorious downtown figure. Shapiro's very presence and mannerisms identified him as a street gangster. Shapiro "had come to New York as a boy from Odessa, Russia, home of the brutal, farcical Jewish gangsters immortalized in *Odessa Stories* by Isaac Babel, whose descriptions could apply as well to the Jewish hoods of New York as to those of Russia" (Cohen 2002, 351). In 1918, Lepke was convicted of robbery and sent to the Tombs (a jail that his gangster friends called "City College"), and then sent to Sing Sing prison. Upon his release, Lepke was reunited with Gurrah.

They formed a gang of street criminals that came to be known as the Gorilla Boys. These Jewish gangsters had now gone into the extortion business, threatening merchants unless they paid "protection" fees from such "accidents" as failed deliveries and fires. Lepke and Gurrah especially targeted bakeries. "Over the years they extorted money from the biggest bakeries in New York: Gottfried's, Levy's, Fink's, California Pies, Rockwell's, and Dugans. By the mid-thirties Lepke and Gurrah were receiving about a million a year in tribute from the industry" (Cohen 2002, 352).

New York Jews had a strong presence in the garment industry in the early 1900s. When workers began organizing into unions (one of the first unions in New York was the United Hebrew Trade Union) and went on strike to demand higher pay and safer working conditions, the garment bosses hired Jewish street gangsters to bust them up. "One employer hired Monk Eastman to drive the strikers back to work. Monk and his boys attacked the strike leaders on Allen Street. While breaking strikes, gangsters often beat workers with a length of metal pipe wrapped in newspaper. They called this schlamming. In the coming years, as the nation was rocked by strikes, even the most down-on-his-luck hood could get work as a schlammer" (Cohen 2002, 353). Thus, Jewish gang members were being used to bust up strikes by Jewish garment workers and were hired by Jewish garment bosses. By the 1920s, labor unions began to hire gangsters like Lepke and Gurrah to defend the strikers against the strike busters. And just as the schlammers had taken it directly to the strikers, Lepke's crew took it to the bosses by setting fires and throwing bombs. It was only natural for this tide to turn. The gangsters had far more in common with the workers than they did with the bosses and most of the workers were Jews from Eastern Europe, whereas the bosses were German Jews who looked down on the Eastern Europeans. Street gangsters enjoyed labor racketeering. It offered them economic opportunities that were lacking during the 1920s and it kept them from having to do factory work. As the power behind the unions, these racketeers had access to union dues and kickbacks from workers—cash in exchange for jobs or promotions. Years later, the federal government would intervene and stop this practice.

Lepke and Gurrah, the Gorilla Boys, would lead an interesting and colorful life as successful gangsters. Their crimes, along with those already described, included murder. Lepke was not one of those glamorous gangsters who lead a high-profile, playboy lifestyle; instead, he was in it for the money and power. Gurrah himself lived in Brooklyn, moving to Flatbush. By the early thirties, Lepke was more of a businessman than gangster, with young gangsters seeking his help and advice on how to survive in the underworld. Although there would be other Jewish gangs, given the overall success that Jews have experienced in the socioeconomic strata of the United States, their presence in contemporary street gangland is extremely limited.

Detroit Street Gangs

Among the many American cities experiencing a rapid population growth fueled by industrial and economic development at the beginning of the twentieth century was Detroit. As Taylor (1990, 2) explained, "the origin of serious youth gang development is rooted in the shift from agrarian to industrial society. Gangs of young toughs were plentiful in early urban American. From the early 1900s to the mid-1930s, industrial cities experienced drastic population increases. . . . Detroit is a microcosm of urban America. . . . As immigrants entered America, Detroit attracted foreign and domestic job seekers to fill the demand for well-paying jobs. Detroit experienced rapid growth during the 1920s, 1930s and, with the industrial needs of World War II, even more. . . ." By the early 1940s, Detroit was a city faced with numerous racial troubles. "No city expected racial trouble more than Detroit, and none did less to prevent it" (Sitkoff 1971, 673). More than 50,000 Southern blacks moved to Detroit in the early 1900s, and they found a city with severe shortages of housing, recreation, and transportation and an overabundance of agitators and extremists of every color and persuasion (Sitkoff 1971). African-Americans had not formed significant gangs during this era in Detroit, but the Jews had.

The Jewish population was another group with minority status that experienced discrimination. "During the industrial boom of the early 1900s to the mid-1930s, many immigrants moved into the city in greater numbers, neighborhoods were established along ethnic lines. The earliest gangs in Detroit can be traced to the dynamics of these ethnic neighborhoods where loose groups of youth banded together to 'protect' local merchants and neighborhood residents from outsiders. One of the best examples of a protective youth group was the Jewish gang known as the Sugar House Gang, formed to protect Jewish merchants in the 1920s by Harry and Louis Fleisher and Irving Milberg" (Taylor 1990, 3). Greed would eventually lead them to join forces with Norman Purple and his group. This new gang would be known simply as the Purple Gang. "The Purple gang reaped the financial rewards associated with distilling operations and other organized crime activities. Starting in the 1920s, the Purple Gang represented one of Detroit's first true organized gang syndicates" (Byrum and Varano 2003, 215).

The **Purple Gang** was one of the most ruthless organized crime groups in United States history. Whenever Purple Gang members were brought to trial, witnesses were afraid to testify against them, and jurors were afraid to convict them. Witnesses and jurors were often bribed or threatened with death. Detroit prosecutors were unable to gain any convictions against Purple Gang members until the early 1930s. With their predisposition to violence and acts of intimidation, the Purple Gang flourished during Prohibition.

The Purple Gang had its genesis with the Bernstein family. In 1902, a young shoemaker, Harry Bernstein, arrived in Detroit with his wife and their six children. Harry opened a small shoe store located on Gratiot Avenue, in the lower east side of Detroit, not far from the Jewish ghetto district (Kavieff 2000). The east side of Detroit was a typical urban, industrial ghetto, marked by uncontrolled diseases, dense living conditions, poverty, and a high crime rate. Observing how difficult a life their parents had in supporting their family, the Bernstein children took to the streets in an effort to help out the family financially. Abe Bernstein, the eldest of the children, became a skilled card dealer and stick man. Gambling, which was illegal at the time, allowed Abe to meet many corrupt politicians, police officials, and other members of the underworld (Kavieff 2000). Abe's brothers, Joe, Raymond, and Isadore (Izzy), took to the streets, claiming "turf." Their territory consisted of the Jewish ghetto that stretched from Jefferson Avenue to East Grand Boulevard. The outer boundaries of their territory stretched for about two blocks east and west of Hastings Avenue. Many of the Purple Gang members would come from this area (Kavieff 2000).

The Purple reign in Detroit began in 1918, when on May 1 the state of Michigan's Prohibition Referendum, which had been approved 2 years earlier, became law. Detroit was the first major American city to go completely "dry" (no alcohol) as an experiment to test the new "dry law" for the rest of the country. The Prohibition Act (18th Amendment) was a huge failure. People want alcohol, and wherever there is a need and desire for a good or commodity that is not provided by the government or legitimate business enterprises, a black market will rise to satisfy this need. Prohibition, in effect, gave criminal syndicates financial leverage for legitimate business ownerships, spawned rackets to provide people with alcohol, and corrupted every level of government (Albanese 2002).

The Purple Gang's rise to power during the mid-1920s was the result of a merger between the newly formed Purples and the older, established **Oakland Sugar House Gang**. The Oakland Sugar House Gang was a fiercely violent gang designed to protect Jewish merchants from rival gangs. The newly emergent Purple Gang sought out the services of Abe Bernstein to run the rackets that the new liquor laws inspired. Bernstein and his crew were referred to as the Original Purple Gang (Kavieff 2000). The designations of Original Purple Gang and the new Purple Gang revealed that there was a lack of complete harmony between the gangs' members and that there was still a gang within a gang allied by friendships and birth.

Among the Original Purple Gang members was Jack Selbin, one of the first illegal liquor merchants of Detroit. Charles Auerbach, the elder statesman of the Detroit Jewish mob, was known as "The Professor," because of his appearance and refinement and the fact that he was a self-taught educated man who had a collection of rare books. Mike Gelfeld (a.k.a. One-Armed Mike), a noted racketeer, was one of the leaders of the "Little Jewish Navy"—a faction within the Original Purple Gang. Sam Solomon, a bookmaker, was known as the brains behind the Little Jewish Navy. Raymond Bernstein, known as a "ladies" man, who ran rackets, was a noted card dealer, hijacker, and gunman, who was not opposed to violence. Joe Bernstein, who was considered the toughest of the four Bernstein brothers, managed to make a great deal of money. Joe eventually left the Purples to become a legitimate businessman in the oil industry (*The Crime Encyclopedia* 1998). Internal turmoil and power struggles between Purple Gang members eventually led to the downfall of the gang. By 1935, the rule of the Purples was over. At least 18 members of the gang had met violent deaths at the hands of one another.

In 1935, Abe Bernstein, along with several other Purple Gang members, saw the "handwriting on the wall" and had begun to meet with the Italian Mafia to turn over the Detroit rackets peacefully. Bernstein and his cohorts thought that this was the best way to go about things because the Italian Mafia was growing stronger and would eventually take over the rackets anyway. In addition, the Purple Gang was much weaker as a result of the internal killings and long prison sentences of other members. In return for the rackets, the Italians gave Abe Bernstein enough money to take care of himself for the rest of his life (Kavieff 2000). Abe Bernstein removed himself from Detroit's underworld and attempted to get his brother Raymond out of the prison system, a losing battle that he continued until his death in 1968. Joe Bernstein became a legitimate businessman and eventually moved to California with his brother Izzy. Most of the other Purple Gang members met the same fate as Raymond Bernstein—life sentences in prison for such crimes as murder, conspiracy to commit murder, and racketeering. The Purple Gang had its roots in street crime and flourished under the misguided laws of Prohibition. Its success was due to "street smarts" and strong-arm tactics. Its failure was a result of high-profile methods, lack of organization, greed, and mistrust of fellow gang members.

THE MID-1900s: AN EXPANSION AND SHIFT IN GEOGRAPHIC GANG DOMINANCE

During World War II, the public was obviously distracted from such issues as street gangs. Most of the young, able-bodied males were off fighting wars on two fronts. As Decker and Curry (2002, 756) explained, "during the Depression and World War II, gang activity declined. When gangs reemerged in the 1950s, they included large numbers of African-American, Puerto Rican, and Mexican-American youths. In addition, levels of violence were higher than in previous periods of gang activity. This can be attributed to the presence of guns and automobiles."

The change in immigration laws and internal geographic relocation during the mid-century led to a focus on the emergence of gangs in the West. The legal migration of nearly 2 million Mexicans to the United States in the twentieth century (beginning during the 1920s) would have a major impact on the growing numbers of gangs throughout America's Southwest region. Additionally, and following the pattern established by the Irish more than a century earlier, these Mexican immigrants were low-skilled workers—poorly educated, lacking basic English-speaking and writing skills, and from agricultural, rural areas—who were suddenly thrust into densely populated urban ghettos. These people were met with the same indifference and discriminatory actions as were all the other immigrants prior to their arrival. The big difference was their skin color. They were not black, but not quite white either. Consequently, they suffered from a marginalized status that others (white European immigrants) did not. Derogatory terms such as *greasers* and *wetbacks* (because they had to cross the Rio Grande River in Texas and the All-American Canal in California to gain entry to the United States) were applied to these Mexican immigrants, most of whom resided in Southern California, especially Los Angeles.

Internal migration patterns were also important in the expansion of street gangs. Large numbers of African-Americans were moving from the rural South to the North and West. With a history that already included slavery, blacks have historically been discriminated against in the United States. Thus, their marginal status in society had already been well established by the mid-1900s. Seeking a better life and hoping for more opportunities than could be found in the South, blacks moved to the industrial cities of the North and the West.

Northern Cities: 1940s–1960s

New York City was still experiencing a gang problem—the continuing influx of immigrants guaranteed it. European ethnic groups still fought against one another, but when Puerto Ricans starting arriving in large numbers, they would become the common enemy of white street gangs. Interestingly, during the 1950s the Hollywood movie industry began to romanticize street gangs with movies like *The Wild Boys, Rebel*

Without a Cause, and especially *West Side Story*. *West Side Story* depicted a Puerto Rican gang fighting a white gang and was filled with dancing and singing and a love story—a far cry from reality.

An increasing number of African-Americans in the cities would also lead to more turf battles between rival gangs. In Detroit, the Purple Gang was long gone, and the emerging power on the streets was not organized crime syndicates, but street gangs. Bynum and Varano (2003, 215) explained:

> Many African-Americans migrated from the rural South to Detroit during the 1940s and 1950s. Like many European ethnic groups, African-Americans were attracted to the promise of well-paying factory jobs. There were almost immediately tensions between the growing black population and whites. African-Americans were generally restricted to living in a few neighborhoods in the eastern side of the city, and many found it difficult to gain quality employment. Growing tensions and distrust eventually resulted in two riots that would change Detroit forever.

The Detroit riot of 1943 was caused mostly by segregation and racism and did little to change the economic plight of African-Americans (Farley, Danziger, and Holzer 2000). The years following World War II was a boom time for Detroit, especially because of the growing automobile industry. Unfortunately, African-Americans did not prosper like their white counterparts. The riot of 1967 had a dramatic and lasting effect on Detroit, as many businesses that were instrumental in Detroit's economy withdrew from the city.

The existence of street gangs in Boston throughout the 1940s and 1950s is documented in Walter Miller's (1958, 1959, 1973) studies of delinquent street-corner groups. Miller's evaluative research was based on social workers' intervention programs with gang members. The gang members committed such delinquent acts as fighting, theft, truancy, and vandalism. Their primary concern was protecting turf. The gangs generally consisted of 50 to 70 youths, ranging in age from 12 to 20 (Miller 1957). "This early research documented the territorial nature of Boston gangs, which for the most part continues today. These groups had clearly defined enemies and allies, and the issue of honor or respect was then, as now, a common cause of conflict" (McDevitt, Braga, Nurge, and Buerger 2003, 55).

One more thing that Miller's research revealed was the fact that gang members were becoming younger in age. In this brief review of the history of gangs, the ebb and flow of the age of gang members has become apparent. When gangs first appeared, they were often comprised of children abandoned or orphaned by their parents. During the mid-1800s, many of the Irish gang members were as likely to be adults as children; and during Prohibition and the Depression, the gangsters were almost always adults. The 1940s and 1950s would be a period in gang history dominated by young gangsters. This was especially true in Los Angeles.

Los Angeles Gangs: 1940s–1960s

Gangs are a relatively recent phenomena in Los Angeles. In fact, "prior to World War II, gangs, as we understand them today, did not exist in Southern California" (Shelden et al. 2001, 9). Unfortunately for the residents of Southern California, the late arrival of gangs to their streets would not mean that the gang problem would be less severe than that found in eastern cities. In fact, within a few decades, beautiful Los Angeles would hold the dubious distinction of "gang capital of the world." The proliferation of gangs in Southern California would be the result of the two-pronged migration of millions of Mexicans from rural Mexico and large numbers of African-Americans from rural America. Given the sheer number of Mexicans, especially compared to the relatively small percentage of blacks in Los Angeles during this period, causes us to turn our attention first to Mexican-American gangs during the mid-1940s rather than African-American gangs in the same period. In the later decades of the twentieth century, however, African-American gangs will be the focus.

Mexican-Americans and Cholo Gangs

Southern California experienced an economic boom in the 1920s that had two distinctive results. On the one hand, the aggressive marketing of California real estate created large enclaves of white, middle-class, conservative Midwesterners in Los Angeles and Orange Counties. These transplants brought with them a strong sense of patriotism, nativism, and the presence of the Ku Klux Klan (*PBS: American Experience* 2002). In turn, the economic prosperity enjoyed by some created the need for workers to perform a large number of low-skilled jobs (e.g., agricultural laborers, housekeepers, etc.). Mexicans moved north to fill this void and to find their own economic windfall. Predominantly poor and undereducated, Mexican-American have often been victims of prejudice and discrimination by mainstream society. Their reception in Los Angeles was less than friendly, and they were often treated as poorly as African-Americans. Because of their poverty, they ended up in neighborhoods near downtown and to the east of downtown. Lacking political power, they often saw their homes destroyed for civic expansion projects such as the Civic Center in the 1920s and Dodger Stadium in Chavez Ravine in 1951. Many of the poverty-stricken barrios of the mid-1900s have not faded into the past, but still exist today throughout the Southwest.

Immigrants from Asia and Mexico had been working as agricultural workers in California since the time of the Gold Rush of 1848. The 1882 Chinese Exclusion Act and the 1902 Gentlemen's Agreement, which expelled Asian agricultural workers, aided the Mexican immigrants and their search for employment. Mexicans arrived in the United States in large numbers in the period between 1900 and 1929 in a search for economic opportunity especially after the Mexican Revolution and the Depression of 1929. During the 20 years from 1930 to 1950, 5 million more workers arrived under the Bracero Program to assist in agricultural work during World War II. However, beginning in 1954, the political tide turned against Mexican immigrants. "Operation Wetback" was a governmental program designed to expel any Mexicans illegally overstaying their visas. Many legal Mexican-American citizens were forced to deal with unannounced "sweeps" in their homes, workplaces, recreational centers, and churches well through the 1960s.

The Mexicans who moved to Southern California brought with them a tradition known as *palomilla*, which refers to a number of young men in a village who group together in a coming-of-age cohort (Vigil 1990). Within the palomilla tradition there is a general "boys-will-be-boys" attitude about their juvenile behavior. In other words, it was expected within the Mexican culture that boys will bond together for "mischief and adventure." In Southern California, these cohorts identified with a specific parish or neighborhood known as *barrios*. Boys grow up thinking that it is necessary to protect their barrio. These groups of boys would become the forerunners of modern Chicano (Mexican-American) gangs, also known as *cholos* (a Mexican-American, or Chicano, gang member).

Vigil (1990) identified a process of *choloization* (or marginalization) within the Mexican-American community, which suggests that various cultural ingredients make Chicano youths more susceptible to becoming gang members. The marginal status that Mexican-Americans have experienced in Southern California can be traced back to the nineteenth-century American conquest of the indigenous Californian people (Mexicans). In addition, many Mexican-Americans were sent back to Mexico during the Depression era. The more than 1 million who were deported to Mexico became known as *repatriadas*. Since most of these Mexican-Americans were born in the United States, they lived as stigmatized strangers and outcasts in Mexico, where they had to learn the Spanish language because it had been prohibited in the schools of Los Angeles (Hayden 2004). All of this further fueled the negative feelings that Mexican-Americans held toward whites.

The Zoot-Suit riots mark the starting point in the growth of Chicano gangs throughout Los Angeles. Joan Moore (1991) has stated the cholo gangs that originated in the 1940s were a product of a climate of hysteria. She uses Cohen's (1980) term *moral panic* to describe the general feelings toward Mexican-Americans in Southern California. "American cities are swept by periodic waves of fear and outrage about poor and racially distinctive young men. These outbreaks of fear usually begin with reports from law enforcement people, and are greatly helped along by newspapers and other media and especially by television in recent years. . . . These moral panics occur periodically, almost by generations" (Moore 1991, 1). Moore identified the Zoot-Suit riots and a gang-related incident, now famous as the "Sleepy Lagoon" case, as a hugely significant moral panic that led to the formation of Chicano gangs in Southern California.

The "moral panic" concerning the growing level of delinquency among Mexican-American youths started on June 12, 1942 when nineteen-year-old Frank Torres was ambushed and shot to death outside a track meet at the Los Angeles Memorial Coliseum. The chaos that ensued nearly led to a riot. Newspapers begin writing articles suggesting that wartime juvenile delinquency among Mexican boy gangs was out of control. The Los Angeles Police Department, drastically reduced by the wartime draft, tried its best to control the growing concern and problems with crime in the Mexican-American neighborhoods. On July 27, 1942, a crowd fought back against a police attempt to break up a craps game at the corner of Pomeroy and Mark streets in Boyle Heights. On August 1, 1942, a fight broke out between kids from the 38th Street and Downey neighborhoods near a reservoir on the Williams ranch nicknamed the "**Sleepy Lagoon**," after a popular song of the times. The Sleepy Lagoon was the larger of two reservoirs used to irrigate crops in what is now Bell, California. For many of the young people in the area, the lagoon was a swimming hole by day and a lover's lane by night, and it was frequented mostly by Mexican-American youths, who were routinely denied access to city-owned recreation facilities.

On the night of August 1, several young couples from the 38th Street neighborhood were parked at the reservoir when they were suddenly and violently attacked by members of the Downey Street neighborhood. After the beating, one of the boys successfully rounded up the 38th Street crew to seek revenge against the Downey boys. However, instead of finding the Downey boys, members from the 38th Street crew found a birthday party on the Williams ranch, where Jose Diaz and other immigrant families worked and lived. Diaz was just a few days short of reporting for induction into the Army. The 38th Street gang was convinced that the party on the Williams ranch involved Downey boys—it did not—and they attacked the partygoers. Jose Diaz died during the battle, prompting front-page coverage of the "Sleepy Lagoon" murder. A police dragnet resulted in over 600 people being brought in for questioning. Eventually, the police narrowed the murder suspects to 22 gang members from the 38th Street crew. On October 13, 1942, the criminal case *People v. Zammora* went to trial: including 17 of the 22 defendants (five of the boys' families were able to afford separate trials), it was the largest mass trial in California history. On January 12, 1943, 5 of the 17 defendants were found guilty of assault; 9 were found guilty of second-degree murder and sentenced to 5 years to life; and 3 were found guilty of first-degree murder and sentenced to life. The 5 suspects who had secured separate trials were acquitted. The harsh penalties and perceived lack of evidence left Mexican-Americans very upset. They questioned the legitimacy of the court decision and made claims of discrimination. (*Note*: On October 2, 1944, the Second District Court of Appeals overturned the Sleepy Lagoon verdicts, dismissed the case, and cleared the records of all the defendants. Authorities declined to retry the case, meaning that whoever killed Diaz got away with murder.)

Animosity between Mexican-Americans and whites was escalated by the Sleepy Lagoon case. The impending war further complicated the city's social dynamics. White men went off to fight in a segregated military, and women and minorities filled the jobs in the defense industry that were previously reserved for white males. (It is important to note that Japanese-Americans were also highly discriminated against in Southern California, as their homes were taken from them and they were sent to live in internment camps set up in the rural West.) Newspaper and radio reports warned the public about Mexican zoot-suit gangs. The *zoot suit* was initially an African-American youth fashion closely connected to the jazz culture. Mexican-Americans began wearing them in the 1940s. "The zoot suit was associated with black urban youth when it appeared on the scene around 1940. Malcolm X's autobiography recounted the importance of his first zoot suit and suggested the style had racial connotations as the preferred choice of hip black men and entertainers. Youth of Mexican and Filipino descent were the prototypical wearers of the garb in Southern California, however" (Daniels 1997, 201).

In an era of segregation and discrimination and unwritten rules which demanded that people of color remain unseen and unheard in public places, the zoot suit, with its broad shoulders, narrow waist, ballooned pants, and long coats, seemed to defy conventional expectations of proper behavior. Those who wore zoot suits were often called *pachucos*. Blacks and Mexican-Americans who wore zoot suits generally referred to them as "drapes" and "chukes," probably from the word *pachuco* (Daniels 1997, 202). The zoot-suit ensemble included a felt hat with a long feather in it, called a *tapa* or *tanda.* The baggy pants were referred to as *tramas* and the shirt as a *lisa.* A *carlango,* a long, loose-fitting coat, was worn over the shirt and pants. The shoes, called *calcos,* were always well shined. To complete the style, the zoot-suiter had to have a long chain attached to the belt loop and hanging past the knee and into the side pocket of the pants. Zoot-suiters walked with a confident swagger that seemed to derive from the fabric itself. The amount of material and tailoring required for the suit made them a luxury item that even upset older, conservative Mexican-Americans.

Resentment toward Mexican-Americans who wore zoot suits was not simply because they were presumed to be gang members, it was also grounded on the fact that during the war there was a garment shortage and a limit was placed on how much fabric could be allocated for civilian clothing. Since an excessive amount of fabric was used to make zoot suits, wearing such outfits was considered unpatriotic. Police routinely conducted raids on neighborhoods inhabited by zoot-suiters. On December 31, 1942, reports that a policeman was shot and killed by "a drunken Pachuco" led to weekly clashes between young Mexican-Americans and police and military personnel.

In light of the Pearl Harbor bombing, Los Angeles considered itself vulnerable to attack. Civilian patrols were established throughout the city and Los Angeles beaches were fortified with antiaircraft guns. Southern California also was a key military location and consequently on any given weekend up to 50,000 servicemen could be found in Los Angeles. Many of the single servicemen on leave would attempt to "hook up" with Mexican-American girls. Those who were married or involved in a relationship accused Mexican-American males of taunting their wives and girlfriends. This atmosphere of "normal" jealousy and an anti-zoot-suiter attitude could only lead to a violent conclusion. What was not so predictable was the extent of the violence. Anglo servicemen on leave in the city engaged in a series of bloody clashes with Mexican-American youths. By spring, the clashes occurred up to two or three times per day. The servicemen did not take the time to distinguish between gang-member zoot-suiters and bystanders who happened to wear zoot suits. As Hickey (2003, 540) explained, "The riot was partly rooted in xenophobia fueled by World War II hysteria. Some thought the Zoot suiters' darker skin resembled the enemy. . . . Servicemen were frustrated and anxious about the war and needed to vent. When the media began focusing on the Zoot suits, tensions soon became explosive."

By May 1943, the rioting boiled over into the Venice Riot. Local high school boys had complained that "Zoots" had taken over the beachfront. A crowd of 500 sailors, soldiers, and civilians appeared at the Aragon Ballroom in Venice on May 1 and attacked Mexican-American young people as they desperately tried to exit the dance. On May 31, approximately 50 sailors clashed violently with Mexican-American boys near downtown. Seaman Second Class Joe Dacy Coleman, U.S.N., was badly wounded. On June 3, sailors on leave from the Naval Reserve Armory revenged the attack on Coleman. They attacked anyone wearing a zoot suit, thus giving the name to the Zoot-Suit Riots. On the second night of fighting, Mexican-American young men drove back and forth in front of the armory, hurling obscenities and epithets at the guards. Later in the night, when sailors could not find zoot-suiters, they took the fight into the Mexican-American neighborhoods of East Los Angeles and Boyle Heights. Los Angeles police seemed unwilling to do anything about the fighting. They stood by and even encouraged the servicemen. Police officers had their own problems—they were under-paid and under strength (there were fewer police in 1943 than in 1925 and the wages had not increased during that period). Many were World War I veterans and certainly not likely to arrest servicemen.

Intense fighting between servicemen and Mexican-American gangs (as well as civilians) continued for over a week. The fighting on June 7 was the worst, with ser-vicemen from San Diego traveling to Los Angeles to join in the fracas. Approximately 5,000 civilians and servicemen gathered downtown to fight Mexican-Americans. Young males throughout the barrios organized counterattacks and often lured the sailors into ambushes. When the rioting finally ended, the governor of California or-dered the creation of a citizens' committee to determine the cause of the riots. The committee concluded that racism was the key element, but Mayor Fletcher Brown stated that the riots were caused by juvenile delinquents and that racial prejudice was not a factor. Turner and Surace (1956, 16–17) explained:

> It is, of course, impossible to isolate a single incident or event and hold it re-sponsible for the riots. Local, state, and federal authorities and numerous civic and national groups eventually tried to assess blame and prevent further violence. The most prominent charge from each side was that the other had molested its girls. It was reported that sailors became enraged by the rumor that zoot-suiters were guilty of "assaults on female relatives of servicemen." Simi-larly, the claim against sailors was that they persisted in molesting and insulting Mexican girls. While many other charges were reported in the newspapers, including unsubstantiated suggestions of sabotage of the war effort, the sex charges dominated the precipitating context.

"Zoot-suit" riots were not restricted to Los Angeles in 1943. Daniels (1997) indi-cated that similar riots took place in such cities as Detroit and New York, where whites not only attacked and beat Mexican-Americans and blacks but stripped them from their zoot suits as well. Before long, the zoot-suit style disappeared. The reservoir known as the Sleepy Lagoon was later filled in as a result of urban sprawl. The primary impor-tance of the Zoot-Suit Riots to the gang world was the reaction by Mexican-Americans to the attack by sailors on their neighborhoods. Many of the young Chicano males began to idolize the gang members who fought the sailors and police and treated these Mexican-Americans as heroes. "In fact, one particular boy gang known as *Purisima* (the name comes from a local parish) began to call itself *White Fence* (named after the surrounding barrio). Currently, this gang is one of the oldest, most well-established gangs in Los Angeles, having offshoots in other cities, such as Las Vegas" (Shelden et al. 2001, 9). Among the most prominent of the Mexican-American gangs of the mid-1900s was White Fence and its rival, El Hoyo Maravilla.

WHITE FENCE Most of the Mexican-American gangs of Los Angeles reside in an area known generically as East Los Angeles, which has the highest concentration of Mexican-Americans in the United States. The **White Fence** gang lived in a city neighborhood called Boyle Heights and was called "White Fence" because of a white picket fence that ran along much of its territory near the Los Angeles River. Boyle Heights was developed before World War I as an exclusive suburb on the heights east of downtown and across the Los Angeles River. Cheaper housing became available during the 1920s, attracting a great diversity of people, among them Armenians, Jews, Russians, and Japanese. The poor Mexicans who migrated to LA during the 1920s began building shacks in the ravines and hollows of Boyle Heights, and by the 1940s, Mexicans dominated the region. The Japanese population had been forced out of the community and into internment camps during World War II. Most of the Mexican-Americans in East LA stayed poor, living in shacks without services (e.g., running water, sewers, etc.). They were generally reluctant to accept American culture and usually refused to become citizens (Moore 1991, 12). The Mexican-American residents of East LA during the 1930s and 1940s did not consider their boys to be gang members, but simply "boys from the barrio." Youths hanging out together was a part of Mexican tradition (palomillas), but the original White Fence gang members had a reputation for being very violent.

EL HOYO MARAVILLA To the east of Boyle Heights lies a cluster of neighborhoods known as Maravilla, an unincorporated part of Los Angeles county that Angelenos refer to as East LA. There are several gangs in Maravilla; one of the more prominent call itself El Hoyo Maravilla (*el hoyo* means "the hole" in Spanish). Mexicans had began settling in Maravilla prior to the 1920s, but the migration process increased dramatically with the construction of the Belvedere Gardens development. Although postwar Los Angeles experienced an economic boom, it bypassed Maravilla and Boyle Heights, primarily because the Mexican-Americans lacked adequate education and had poor English-language skills. The new industry was mostly in the aerospace field, an industry that demands technological know-how.

The Maravilla neighborhood had a number of gangs, which were named for specific streets, with each territory being quite small. As one of the neighborhoods invaded by servicemen during the Zoot Suit Riots, Maravilla's gang boys fought back and earned the respect of Mexican-Americans in the barrio. The young boys especially admired the gang members who fought back to protect their neighborhood. With the advent of World War II, many of the older gang boys had been drafted, creating an abrupt void of young males to protect local neighborhoods. But in the case of White Fence and El Hoyo Maravilla, the boys (and girls) managed to carry on the traditions and generally surpass the level of violence and staunch determination necessary to defend their neighborhoods. They remain powerful gangs today, with White Fence a highly visible presence in East Los Angeles.

The area of East Los Angeles still suffers from low levels of education and economic success. Its lack of political power has been apparent since the 1940s as the neighborhoods have often been ripped apart in the name of civic improvement—especially the development of freeways in the 1950s. "A tract in one of the barrios actually lost 60 percent of its population in the 1950s. Community myth held that the freeway was deliberately designed to cut through the neighborhood and thereby break up the gang. . . . East Los Angeles is now crisscrossed by no less than four freeways" (Moore 1991, 15–16). It is worth noting that sensationalized newspaper articles continued to condemn Mexican-American gangs throughout the 1950s.

African-American Street Gangs

African-Americans have longed suffered from oppression in the United States. After being granted freedom from slavery, their access to legitimate opportunities in the higher socio-economic strata of society was severely limited. Seeking a better life than the one offered in the rural South, blacks moved to such places as Southern California. "The origin of African-American gangs in Southern California are similar to those of the Chicano gangs. . . . Like their Mexican counterparts, African-Americans came from rural areas (mostly the rural South) to Southern California, a sprawling urban and industrial society. Their traditional way of life in the South was mostly church based with close family ties. However, the second-generation children (again like the cholo youths) faced many pressures in the new culture in Los Angeles" (Shelden et al. 2001, 10). By the late 1920s and early 1930s, African-American street gangs had formed on the east side of Los Angeles near Central and Vernon avenues. They formed clubs in the downtown area of Los Angeles as well. During the late 1930s and 1940s, the black population of Los Angeles moved south from downtown Los Angeles down Central Avenue toward Slauson Avenue. The area between Slauson Avenue and Firestone (Manchester) had been occupied by white residents during the 1920s and 1930s. The African-American population had already been growing in Watts between 92nd Street and Imperial. Thus was created an area known as South Central, the primary residence of the African-American population of Los Angeles.

Among the early black gangs in Los Angeles during the 1920s and 1930s were the Goodlows, Magnificents, and the Boozies. The Boozies were a family of many brothers and friends who ran a prostitution ring and committed robbery. Their turf was the Jefferson Park area. The Magnificents were a group of youths from Central Avenue. These juvenile gangs disappeared by the late 1930s, but during the 1940s, blacks were forming social clubs throughout the African-American community and these clubs eventually evolved into gangs. Among the notable gangs of this era were the Purple Hearts and the 31st and 28th Street gangs. Some of the clubs had been attempts at forming political organizations, but most of them served as a protective mechanism against white gangs. Some of these black crews were involved in petty theft, robbery, and assaults, but murder was quite rare. Weapons of choice were usually limited to bats, chains, and knives, with disputes settled by hand-to-hand combat.

During the 1950s, car clubs modeled after the white car clubs that were popular throughout Southern California were formed by African-Americans. Among them were the Low Riders, Coasters, Highwaymen, and Road Devils. Other clubs such as the Slausons, Rebel Rousers, Businessmen, Watts, and so forth were tied to area high schools. These clubs were not labeled as gangs by the LAPD. In fact, it was not until the Watts Riots of 1965 that African-American youth groups were considered a serious problem. Before the riots, black people were not on the minds of whites. Johnson and Sears (1971, 698–699) referred to this as "Black invisibility" meaning "a condition describing the perceptual world of the white American. He is physically isolated from blacks, hence they are physically invisible to him, and his few physical contacts with them are structured so that blacks are psychologically invisible to him as well. Thus, Blacks essentially do not exist in the subjective world of the white American." In 1964, blacks had reason to believe that their invisible status would change with the passing of the federal Civil Rights Act. However, California responded with Proposition 14, which was designed to block the fair housing components of the act. This development added to all the other feelings of injustice and despair among inner-city blacks helped to fuel the 1965 Watts Riots.

Watts was a rundown district of Los Angeles, 98% black and characterized by numerous social problems (poverty, overcrowding, high unemployment, a high crime rate, etc.). The police force in Watts was nearly all white. The Watts residents viewed the police as an occupying army. On August 11, in the middle of a heat wave, police pulled over a black youth on suspicion of drunk driving. A crowd gathered and yelled angry chants at the police. Eventually, bottles and other items were thrown at the police. When police reinforcements arrived, they were greeted by a hail of stones and bottles. As day turned into night the level of violence escalated. Angry black youths began throwing missiles and Molotov cocktails at white motorists. Stores were looted and buildings torched. Thousands of National Guardsmen were sent in and were met with machine gun fire. News coverage of this six-day riot made Los Angeles look like war-torn Vietnam. When the riots finally ended, 34 were dead, over a thousand people injured, and nearly 4,000 had been arrested. The Watts Riots sparked other urban uprisings in cities across the United States for the next 2 years. The importance of the Watts Riots cannot be understated:

> The Watts riots of 1965 did for African-American gangs roughly what the Zoot Suit riots did for Chicano gangs. One result of the Watts riots was that young African-Americans were seen in a more negative light by the media and by the rest of society. Also, African-American youths began to see themselves differently. It is important to note that although African-American youths did not have the palomilla tradition of their Mexican counterparts, they did have already-developed Chicano gangs to imitate (Shelden et al. 2001, 11).

During the 1950s, some African-American youths (along with some whites) had already begun to copy the cholo style of Mexican-American youths. After the Watts Riots, blacks began to borrow many of the Chicano gang traditions, including flashing colors, defending turf, using graffiti, hanging out, and jumping in new members. By the 1960s, black gang members began forming alliances with one another, forming "super gangs." The most notorious gang of all, the Crips, have their roots in the mid-1960s. (For a full description of the Crips, see Chapter 6.)

CONTEMPORARY GANGS (1970s TO THE PRESENT): AN EPIDEMIC

Throughout the history of street gangs, it has become apparent that youths formed protective-type groups in order to increase their odds of survival. This is true whether we are talking about youth gangs from the Middle Ages or colonial America who united for basic survival reasons or ethnic-based gangs beginning with the Irish-Americans in the 1800s. The largest percentage of gang members came from disadvantaged ethnic and racial groups. They were primarily concerned with protecting their turf and protecting "their own." However, around the mid-1960s and early 1970s this philosophy began to change to the reality that is today's gangs; namely, they are now far more *offensive*. They seek larger territories, they have become mobile and conduct such behaviors as drive-by shootings, and they have seemingly taken claim to the economically profitable illegal drug industry. "The spread of crack cocaine in the late 1980s had produced an epidemic of gang-related violence and corruption" (Johnson 2003, 287). Indeed, the culture of gangs has changed a great deal in the contemporary era.

An examination of contemporary gangs is limited in this chapter for a couple of reasons. First, estimates of the total number of gangs and gang members today were provided in Chapter 1. Second, a large number of contemporary gangs (especially those found in Los Angeles, Chicago, and New York City) and their criminal activities will be discussed in greater detail throughout the book, but especially in Chapters 6 and 8. The following pages help to provide a glimpse into the reality of the changing nature of gangs over the years.

During the 1960s, local neighborhood gangs began to merge, forming "nations." The Crips were the first to make alliances. Rival gangs of Crips formed an alliance under the Blood banner. In Chicago, the **Vice Lords**, having started with just eight original members in 1957, had reached the 8,000 mark by the mid-1960s. An offshoot of the Vice Lords, the **Conservative Vice Lords**, had incorporated into a legitimate business in 1967. Chicago Mayor Daly and rival gangs questioned the legitimacy of the "new" Vice Lords and their attempted peace movement, and by 1969, the Conservative Vice Lords had fallen apart. But in response to the formation of the Vice Lords, a number of other super gangs would rise in Chicago (e.g., Latin Kings, Latin Disciples, Black Gangster Disciples), who in turn formed greater alliances of "Folks" and "People." While all of this was going on, the general public did not seem to take notice. Shelden and associates (2001, 2–3) explain this rather odd occurrence:

> By the end of the 1960s Americans were tuned into nightly exhibitions of civil disorder (related to the civil rights movement and the Vietnam War), the Vietnam War, and a new type of gang—the hippies. Strangely, with high levels of crime and violence occurring throughout most of the 1970s, very little attention was paid to gang activities. America's loss in Vietnam, inflation, fuel shortages, existentialism, and disco captivated the public's attention.

The public's attention to gangs would resurface in the 1980s. The primary reason for the earlier lack of a public outcry, or moral panic, was the fact that gangs were still restricted to certain cities. "Gang activity increased in the 1980s. At the beginning of that decade, gang problems were recognized in only a few large cities, particularly Chicago, Detroit, and Los Angeles. But, by the end of the decade, gangs appeared in large and medium-sized cities as well as in many rural areas. The levels of violence were much higher than in any previous wave of gang problems, corresponding with even more widespread availability of automobiles and firearms" (Decker and Curry 2002, 756). The seriousness of the gang problem has persisted into the twenty-first century.

Boston

Boston is a city with approximately 575,000 residents and is marked by small, ethnically/racially identified neighborhoods (e.g., the North End, South Boston). Currently, the city's population is 59% white, 24% black, and 11% Hispanic (with 6% other). The segregated nature of Boston led to the development of housing projects for minorities. As a result, a large number of project gangs emerged in Boston during the 1980s (McDevitt et al. 2003). Like many jurisdictions, Boston's governmental authorities were reluctant to admit that there was a gang problem in their city. "Boston officials did not use the term 'gang' or publicly admit to having a 'gang problem' during the 1980s, despite the increasingly lethal consequences of gang conflicts. The mayor and police commissioner at the time decided against acknowledging the existence of gangs, fearing it would hurt the city's image and create publicity that might inadvertently stimulate additional gang development. It became an informal but explicit policy of the police and city officials to deny that gangs were involved in any criminal incidents" (McDevitt et al. 2003, 56). What city officials denied, researchers, residents, and gang members already knew—that there were in fact many gangs in Boston during the 1980s. Boston's "going into denial" approach is common in many police departments, but nonetheless, gangs exist whether they are labeled as such or not.

One researcher, Jankowski (1991), found that Irish-American gangs in Boston followed the traditional link from childhood friendship groups to adult Irish-American social clubs. (Thrasher would label this formation of groups into gangs as spontaneous—see Chapter 3. This is also similar to the Mexican tradition of palomilla.) These gangs came from families in working-class neighborhoods. Gang participation reflected pride in and loyalty to their ethnic heritage. Jenkins's (1995) research revealed that marginalization was the primary reason for gang formation among Boston's minorities. The gangs he studied were loosely organized, neighborhood-based, and involved in typical gang behaviors: drug sales, delinquency, and violence. By 1990, Boston officials, faced with growing homicide and violent youth crime rates, admitted that there was a gang problem and implemented programs designed to combat the growing street-gang problem. "The year 1990 was a turning point in the city's efforts to combat youth violence. As the homicides mounted to record numbers, the community was transfixed by the violence: many residents viewed Boston as a city out of control" (McDevitt et al. 2003, 58). The increased use of firearms was the primary reason for the rising numbers of homicides.

St. Louis

Census data reveals that St. Louis had a population of roughly 335,000 in 2000. St. Louis is a city with considerable violent crime, and throughout the 1990s it has ranked among the top five cities in the United States in its rate of homicide, robbery, and aggravated assault. "Mirroring national patterns, young black males, especially those aged 15–24, were the most likely victims of homicide in St. Louis . . . firearms accounted for virtually all deaths" (Decker and Curry 2003, 194). In the mid-1990s, St. Louis had nearly 300 different gangs, with a total membership of 3,500. The desire to make money and perceived "gaining of respect" are the two most common reasons gang members stated for joining a gang. Members were recruited in the typical fashion: by friends, family, schoolmates, and in the juvenile detention center. St. Louis gangs are generally bound together by neighborhood ties or associational characteristics (Decker and Van Winkle 1996). As in many large cities, the gang problem in St. Louis is generally limited to a small number of neighborhoods (i.e., College Hill and Fairground Park, located in the Fifth Police District—which contains many of the most dangerous neighborhoods in the city).

Little Rock

Steve Nawojczyk, a noted gang researcher, has chronicled gang activity in Little Rock and traces it to the 1980s. Prior to that time there were neighborhood gangs of various groups, but these were mainly social in nature. The current gang structure has become increasingly visible since the introduction of crack cocaine on the streets. Nawojczyk (1997) believes that the Highland Court Crew has been in existence since 1984, and they are among 40 gangs that he and his associates have identified in Little Rock. Most of these gangs are directly associated with four major national coalitions of gangs: Crips, Bloods, Folks, and the People. Due to the fluid nature of gangs, Nawojczyk (1997) noted that gangs sometimes change affiliation. Contemporary Little Rock street gangs are similar to those found in larger urban areas: They are often violent and involved in drug sales and distribution. According to Nawojczyk (1997, 4), "feelings of fear, hatred, bigotry, poverty, disenfranchisement, and the general breakdown of social values are considered motivations for joining a street gang."

Detroit

Contemporary street gangs generally form for three reasons: racial/ethnic pride and loyalty, protection of turf, and economic gain. The increasing number of gangs and gang members is almost always directly attributed to marginalized status and the lack of economic opportunities (including the lack of desire to pursue economic gain by legitimate means). In the early 1970s, the economy of Detroit and several other Michigan cities such as Flint and Saginaw suffered from tremendous cutbacks in the auto industry (due to increased competition from foreign imports and an oil embargo). During this same time, a number of delinquent groups began to take on gang characteristics and identify themselves with street names. By 1975, the loosely organized street gangs were being replaced by structured, confederated street gangs. Mieczkowski's (1986) research linked the increased gang activity to the heroin epidemic that hit Detroit during the late 1970s and early 1980s. The drug trade continues to be an integral aspect of Detroit's gangs today.

It is difficult to determine the number of gangs in contemporary Detroit. Data provided by the National Youth Gang Survey (NYGS) have been very inconsistent: It reported the total number of gang members in 1996 as 2,000; as 3,500 in 1997; and then as 800 in 1998. It is more likely that the 1996 and 1997 statistics are more accurate. Ascertaining the exact number of gang-related crimes in Detroit is also nearly impossible. "The Detroit Police Department's crime information system does not contain fields that denote 'gang-related' crimes" (Bynum and Varano 2003, 220). Logic would dictate, and anyone who has been to Detroit for any significant amount of time can tell you, that there are a large number of gangs and they *do* commit crimes. In their own research, Bynum and Varano (2003, 222) concluded that "gangs pose a significant problem in the city of Detroit."

Chicago

Chicago has the distinction of being the "Third City" of the United States in total population at nearly 3 million people, and is a metropolitan hub of more than 9 million people (U.S. Census Bureau 2001). Chicago is very ethnically and racially diverse, having populations of white non-Hispanics (30.4%), African-Americans (39.3%), Hispanics (24.4%), and Asian-Americans (5.6%). It is a city still experiencing a large influx of immigrants, with nearly 175,000 arriving between 1990 and 1995. These new immigrants came from such places as Mexico, Poland, India, and former USSR countries. Traditionally, Chicago has been a highly segregated city, with whites living in the north, northwest, southwest, and far south sides, and African-Americans on the west and south sides (Coldren and Higgins 2003).

Chicago has a huge gang problem, second only to that of Los Angeles, and since the mid-1980s, the number of gangs has increased dramatically. The violence and homicide rates are also staggering. The city serves as a home base to many super gangs, with the People and Folks the most significant (see Chapter 6 for a full description). The Folks and People both are a collection of other, highly identified gangs. For example, Chicago's largest gang (at 35,000 members) is the **Black Gangster Disciples**, who along with the **Latin Disciples** are under the Folks nation. The People's major Chicago affiliates are the Latin Kings (18,000 members) and the Vice Lords (20,000 members). These numbers are estimates from law enforcement and media sources, but it should be made clear that no one knows for sure how many gang members make up these nation gangs.

The Black Gangster Disciples are descendants of the Woodlawn Disciples and are predominant in Chicago's South Side (Block and Block 1993). The Latin Disciples are a racially and ethnically mixed gang (a rarity among gangs, as they tend to be homogeneous) allied with the Black Gangster Disciples, forming the Folks nation. The Latin Disciples are generally found in the northwest part of the city in and around Humboldt Park and Logan Square. The enemies of the Folks nation are the gangs that comprise the People nation: the Latin Kings and the Vice Lords. The Latin Kings are the oldest and largest of the Hispanic gangs and are found in a variety of diverse neighborhoods, but especially on the southwest side. The Vice Lords are the oldest of the four super gangs, dating back to the 1950s, and are generally found in the poor West Side neighborhoods (Shelden et al. 2001, 15). The Latin Kings and Vice Lords formed an alliance (the People) primarily in response to the formation of the Folks (Block and Block 1993).

The gangs of Chicago are heavily involved in illegal drug distribution and drug sales. Drugs are viewed by many disadvantaged youths as a means of gaining quick and easy money. This has been true since the 1970s and is excellently chronicled in Padilla's *The Gang as an American Enterprise* (1992). As in most of the cities of the North and Northeast, the departure of industry left the poorly skilled and undereducated youths of Chicago with little hope of economic security. Padilla (1992, 39) describes Chicago's public schools as the "worst education system of the nation." The gang members he interviewed described horrible teachers who had prejudged them as "no good" even before giving them a chance. Consequently, many gang members dropped out of school, never earning a high school diploma. Chicago's public schools had a 40% dropout rate (Padilla 1992). When hopelessness is added to marginalization, delinquency cannot be far behind. Throw in a neighborhood in a state of despair and with drastic economic shortcomings, and the ingredients for gang formation and participation become fairly evident. (Further discussion of contemporary Chicago gangs will be found in Chapters 5 and 8.)

Los Angeles

The city of Los Angeles and Los Angeles County are home to the most street gangs in the United States (and most likely the world). This reality began to reveal itself in the 1970s. East Los Angeles remained a poor area during the economic boom years of the 1970s and disenchantment grew among the youth. The African-American Crips super gang was in full bloom, and the rise of the Bloods super gang would become an inevitable response to the newly found power of the Crips. Mexican-American gangs continued to develop, led by White Fence, and a number of Asian American gangs (e.g., the Triads and Tongs) emerged, with roots dating back centuries. While African-American gangs were forming alliances with various neighborhood gangs, the Mexican-American gangs, and Hispanic gangs in general, were not. The number of gangs and gang members continued to increase, however, and White Fence remains a highly visible gang among LA's Hispanic gangs.

For the most part, public concern over gangs in Southern California did not reemerge until the 1980s. Gangs were hard to ignore—1980 estimates had more than 30,000 gang members in Los Angeles County, and by 1982, gang members started dealing heavily in narcotics. Crack cocaine sales were huge during the 1980s, and the gang members controlled a large percentage of the market. Gang-related violent crime and murder has become a constant topic of discussion in Southern California. The Southern California region (consisting of the seven counties of Ventura, Los Angeles, Orange, Riverside, San Bernardino, San Diego, and Imperial) is the second-largest metropolitan area in the nation, with roughly 15 million residents. "It has become known nationally as an incubator for gangs" (Maxson et al. 2003, 240). According to the National Youth Gang Survey (2000), there are nearly 2,000 gangs and over 165,000 gang members in Southern California. Los Angeles, the nation's second-largest city, has been labeled the gang capital for some time now, a title this city appears destined to keep into an indefinite future. Los Angeles now serves as a home base for the Crips and Bloods, who have set up affiliations in nearly every large city in the nation, including Seattle, Denver, and Buffalo.

New York City

As this chapter has revealed, New York City has played a significant role in the development of street gangs. The European, white, ethnic-based gangs of the 1800s have long been replaced by such contemporary gangs as the Bloods, Latin Kings, Netas, Crips, and Mara Salvatrucha (MS-13). Other new immigrant groups (especially from Central American countries) have also formed street gangs. There were an estimated 15,000 gang members in New York City in 2001. The Bloods claim about 5,000 members, but only about half are "blooded in" (the initiation process—discussed in Chapter 5—that makes them "real" Bloods). The Bloods in New York now outnumber the Latin Kings, once the largest and most violent gang in the city. But the gang scene in New York is anything but monolithic. Prison officials at Rikers Island reported that in 2001, 1,775 of the 15,000 inmates were members of as many as 47 gangs, the major ones being Bloods (600), Latin Kings (300), Netas (151), Five Percenters (80), and Crips (50) (NYPD and Department of Correction 2001). Nation gang members, such as the Bloods, are far different in New York than in Los Angeles. In LA, most Bloods who live near each other know each other; this is not true in New York (O'Shaughnessy 2001). Thus, Los Angeles street gangs are generally far more organized than New York gangs.

In 2004, Long Island, New York, witnessed a huge, growing gang problem spearheaded by MS-13 (discussed in further detail in Chapter 6). MS-13, a Salvadorian street gang, has challenged all existing street gangs on Long Island and is also rivaled by its fellow Salvadorian street gang Salvadorans with Pride (O'Shaughnessy 2001). In October 2004, six MS-13 members were charged in Nassau County with the murders of two fellow gang members who they believed were informants for law enforcement. MS-13 policy is to "get rid of all the people that are rats" federal officials said (Kessler and Smith 2004). Nassau police reported that 6 of the 22 homicides in 2003 were gang-related and that 5 of the 18 homicides from January to October 2004 were also gang-related. Law enforcement officials estimated that 3,000 to 5,000 gang members lived in Nassau alone (Dowdy 2004). Another Long Island jurisdiction, Suffolk County, estimated that it had nearly 2,000 active gang members (Dowdy 2004). Federal officials and local officials both agree that MS-13 is responsible for the large increase in gang activity on Long Island. Mexican gangs have also made their presence known on Long Island. Law enforcement officials in Newburgh accused the Benkard Barrio Kings (BBK) gang of operating a street-corner cocaine market and of at least one homicide. An 18-month investigation of the BBK led to the deportation of 23 Mexican nationals and the arrest of 27 others (*Syracuse Post-Standard* 2004, C).

SUMMARY

Gangs are so prevalent today that they have reached institutional status. Beginning in the 1820s, with the Irish, America's first ethnic urban minority group, youth street gangs have become permanent fixtures of the urban landscape. By the end of the twentieth century, gangs had proliferated in nearly all geographical areas of the United States. Gangs can be found in the suburbs, in small cities, and on Native-American reservations. Today, their numbers continue to grow, and street gangs will remain as a major social problem in American society for some time to come.

CHAPTER THREE

Theoretical Explanations of Gangs

Perhaps the most fundamental question involving street gangs is why they exist in the first place. Many people—social researchers, gang experts, law enforcement personnel, school administrators, citizens, and gang members themselves—have given various explanations. In this chapter, a number of theories on juvenile delinquency will be presented and analyzed. Since there are very few theories that specifically address gangs, general theories are applied to gang formation and gangster behavior.

It is very important to examine theoretical explanations of gang formation primarily because the way a particular agency or governing body views a gang directly impacts the programs and types of law enforcement used in relation to them. "All delinquency programs used now and in the past are based on one or more theories to explain why adolescents are delinquent. Theories identify the causes of delinquency, and programs are designed to eliminate or counteract these causes" (Trojanowicz et al. 2004, 7). Champion (2004) believed that the way in which one explains and accounts for juvenile behavior directly affects the way individuals are processed in the juvenile justice system. "Theories are integrated explanatory schemes that predict relationships between two or more phenomena. They provide rational foundations to account for or explain things and help us to understand why juveniles are processed different ways by the juvenile justice system" (Champion 2004, 83). The theoretical approaches employed reflect contemporary social currents and knowledge available at the time. As Thornton and Voigt (1992, 107) explained, "each generation of social scientists has sought explanations for the causes of delinquent and criminal behavior. These explanations have been tied to the knowledge and techniques available at the time of their origins. Some explanations of delinquent and criminal behavior are called theories. Although there are many definitions of **theory**, we generally call it a speculation, usually stated in some logical framework, about why and how certain behaviors or events occur."

Researchers committed to the scientific tradition view theory as much more than speculation, for speculation seems to imply uncertainty; and uncertainty is contrasted with established truths (Delaney 2005). Goode (1997, 65–66) explained that "to a scientist, a 'theory' is not mere speculation. In fact, theories may already be established as true. To a scientist, theories possess three characteristics: First, they are *empirically verifiable*, second, they provide an *explanation* or *account for*, third *a general class of phenomena*." "Empirically verifiable" refers to science's commitment to support theory with systematic observation and data collection, known as research. It is a commitment to scientific research that allows researchers to go beyond "common-sense" explanations of gang behavior. Furthermore, a commitment to sound scientific principles greatly assists in the creation and implementation of programs designed to help mainstream gang members. Research offers a cause-and-effect account of phenomena; it provides the "explanation or account" for why something occurs. When the explanation is general enough, it can be applied to "a general class of phenomena," and not just a few cases (e.g., Newton's theory of gravitation).

Theories are used as an attempt to explain and put order to the world that surrounds us. They provide the road map for our daily activities. We anticipate (theorize) how certain people are going to behave in given situations based on past experience and knowledge (research). For example, it is safe to assume (theorize) that if a student falls asleep in class, or an employee falls asleep on the job, that there will be negative consequences such as a lower grade in class and possible dismissal from work. Research will indicate that this theory is generally accurate. It may be "speculative," but it is also subject to the laws of probability, especially in cases where the student/employee has been warned against engaging in this deviant behavior. Theories that can be tested and are supported by empirical research are the "best" theories. "Good theory offers new explanations for patterns that have been observed through research, or predicts findings that might be expected based upon the theory's argument. Good research may test a relationship proposed in a theory, or it may identify new patterns or relationships in need of explanation by a theory" (Farley 1998, 3–4).

"Good" theory is always expressed in general terms, with specific tenets supported by social research. Theories of juvenile delinquency and gangs need to be abstract enough to generalize to other gangs but specific enough to concretely address specific issues critical in the scientific analysis of gang formation and gang behaviors.

BIOLOGICAL AND PSYCHOLOGICAL THEORIES

Before the last half of the nineteenth century, little scientific research had been conducted to explain why delinquency and crime occurred. Most explanations reflected moral beliefs and religious ideals. Biologists developed many of the earliest theories on crime and delinquency. They believed that genetic inheritance or other physical attributes were the cause of crime. Although these theories have been shown to be "useless" (Trojanowicz et al. 2004, 7) in explaining criminal behavior, discussion of theoretical explanations of juvenile delinquency and gangs begins with biological theories.

Biological Theories

Many biological theories attempt to link crime and delinquency to genetics, raising controversial issues such as the concept of a "born criminal" and the suggestion that crime is hereditary. Other biological theories have examined body types as a means of determining an individual's character, suggesting that the person "looks like a criminal." A layperson may think that a person looks "shifty" and must therefore be a criminal. "The notion that an individual's character could be read from a physical examination dates to the ancient Greeks and Romans. Known as *physiognomy*, practitioners of this 'science' studied faces, skulls, and other physical features that they believed revealed a person's natural disposition. . . . In the medieval period there was even a law that specified that if two people were suspected of having committed the same crime, the uglier one should be regarded as more likely the guilty party" (Curran and Renzetti 1994, 39). The essential aspect of biological theories of crime and delinquency rests with the premise that such behaviors are caused by some mechanism internal to the individual or an outwardly visible physical trait possessed by the individual. As a rule, biological theories can be divided into two classification schemes: the **classical** and the **positive**.

THE CLASSICAL SCHOOL   The classical school of criminology emerged in the eighteenth century, and its name is derived from that entire period, known as the "Classical Period." The classical school was not interested in studying criminals; rather, it focused on law-making and legal processing (Williams and McShane 1994). The eighteenth century was an era of great social change, faith and tradition were being challenged, and the rise of industrialization and ideals of democracy dominated in the Western world. The classical school of thought was developed by Cesare Beccaria, an Italian nobleman (1738–1794), in his book *On Crimes and Punishment* (1764). He believed that humans were free to choose courses of action and that they are capable of making rational decisions. People can choose whether to follow the rules or be deviant. Thus, an individual is free to choose whether to become a gang member or not. Another important contributor to this school of thought was Jeremy Bentham (1748–1832), an English philosopher, in his book *An Introduction to the Principles of Morals*. Bentham was known for promoting the idea of **hedonism**—humans seek pleasure and avoid pain in their activities. He also believed in utilitarianism—the greatest good for the greatest number.

According to Williams and McShane (1994, 21) the basic tenets of the classical school are

1. an emphasis on free will choices and the human rational
2. a view of behavior as hedonistic
3. a focus on morality and responsibility
4. a concern with political structure and the way in which government deals with its citizens
5. a concern for the basic rights of all people

These generic ideas and concerns when applied to criminal justice produced the concepts of deterrence, civil rights, and due process of law. Within this framework, individuals are expected to conform to the expectations of society, as Bentham held, for the greater good of society. As Champion (2004, 85) explained:

> Societal progress and perpetuation are paramount, and individuals must each sacrifice a degree of their freedoms in order that all persons can pursue happiness and attain their respective goals. Evil actions operate adversely for societal progress and merit punishment. Because evil acts vary in their seriousness, the severity of punishments for those actions should be adjusted accordingly. Becaria believed that punishments should be swift, certain, and just, where the penalties are appropriately adjusted to fit particular offenses. The primary purpose of punishments should be deterrence and just deserts. In an ideal world, people will refrain from wrongdoing in order to avoid the pain of punishment.

Punishments were to fit the crime, with those found guilty of serious offenses the most harshly punished.

From the classical school perspective, since all behaviors are freely engaged upon, the judicial system merely needs to find a way to make crime so unappealing that individuals dare not violate society's rules. Free will allowed people to choose behavior; the judicial system needed to make sure that that offenders would "unwill" to commit future crimes.

> The offenders' mental makeup, background, and extenuating circumstances were irrelevant. Because offenders were viewed as being very rational, the pleasure-pain principle was invoked as the major method of dealing with them. The pleasure-pain principle proposed that if the punishment for the particular act produced negative consequences that were more severe than the pleasures derived from committing the act, potential offenders would be discouraged from being so deviant. Offenders were presumed to be rational enough and to have enough "good sense" to choose right from wrong (Trojanowicz et al. 2004, 40–41).

The classical approach to crime and delinquency served a useful function in the transition from the old days of rule by monarchy and religion, where punishment varied based on who committed the crime. The idea of creating a rationally based criminal justice system in an effort to fight delinquency and crime represented a good start in establishing a fairer and just social system of justice. However, the ideas that all people act rationally all the time and that legitimate extenuating circumstances do not exist are just a few of the flaws in this approach.

THE POSITIVE SCHOOL The classical school consisted mostly of writers and philosophers. The proponents of the positive school were generally scientists, mathematicians, doctors, and astronomers. Where the classicalists believed that humans possess a rational mind and were therefore capable of making rational choices, "the Positivists saw behavior as determined by its biological, psychological, and social traits. The primary characteristics of positivist criminological thought are a deterministic view of the world, a focus on criminal behavior instead of on legal issues such as rights, and the prevention of crime through the treatment and rehabilitation of offenders" (Williams and McShane 1994, 29). The positivists' rejection of the idea that people were free to make their own decisions in life led them, in effect, to view offenders of the law as being "sick." The belief that such offenders were "sick" implied that researchers needed to find the "cause," or determinants, of such social pathology among individuals. "The determinants would be the offender's biological, psychological, sociological, cultural, and physical environment. Treatment would include altering one or more of the determinant factors that contributed to the unlawful behavior" (Trojanowicz et al. 2004, 41). Once these determinants were identified, treatment would involve altering one or more of the determinant factors that contributed to unlawful behavior.

Although the true roots of the positive school are hard to ascertain, given the fact that the attribution of criminality and delinquency to biological causes dates to prebiblical times, it is the work of Italian physician and criminologist Cesare Lombroso (1835–1909) that generally receives credit for influencing the beginnings of the positive school (Champion 2004). Lombroso, known as the "father of modern criminology," is best known for his early views on the "born criminal." The born criminal, in Lombroso's conception, possessed physical inferiorities. "Trained as a psychiatrist, Lombroso came upon the idea of the 'atavistic man' as a special type of criminal while dissecting cadavers in the prisons and asylums of Pavia, Italy. . . . Lombroso (1911) thought that most deviant individuals were biologically inferior types resembling earlier and more primitive human beings. Possessing unrefined instincts, the atavistic man—the most extreme of the biological misfits—was, Lombroso believed, predestined to engage in criminal activities" (Thornton and Voigt 1992, 111). Furthermore, Lombroso "also reported that criminals manifest traits of sensory impairment; a lack of moral sense, particularly the absence of remorse, and the use of slang and tattoos" (Williams and McShane 1994, 33). Enrico Ferri, one of Lombroso's students, later added other types of criminals to the "born criminal" category: the habitual criminal and those who committed crimes of passion. Using scientific research, common to those who studied criminals from the positivist perspective, Lombroso attempted to categorize anatomically atavistic types. In the first edition of *The Criminal Man*, Lombroso labeled criminals on the basis of physical characteristics (e.g., thickness of the bones in the skull, pigmentation of the skin, hair type). Lombroso believed that criminals were products of heredity.

> Successive generations of human beings inherited not only physical features genetically from ancestors, but they also inherited behavioral predispositions such as propensities toward criminal conduct or antisocial proclivities. Since heredity is more or less binding on future generations, it made sense to Lombroso and many of his disciples that certain physical characteristics would also be inexorably related to criminal behavior. Therefore, physical appearance would be a telling factor whether certain persons would be predisposed to criminality or other types of deviant behavior (Champion 2004, 87–88).

Trojanowicz, Morash, and Schram (2004, 41) summarize Lombroso's work as follows:

1. Criminals were a distinctive type at birth.
2. They could be recognized by certain stigmata, that is, such as distinguishing characteristics as "a long lower jaw," and "a low sensitivity to pain."
3. These stigmata or physical characteristics did not cause crime but enabled identification of criminal types.
4. Only through severe social intervention could born criminals be restrained from criminal behavior. The Lombrosian school of thought relied heavily on *biological determinism*.

The logical flaws of biological determinism alone should had been enough to stop this school of thought from becoming as influential as it did. Furthermore, with our knowledge of white-collar crime and the criminals that commit such offenses, the idea of some sort of biological or physical characteristics as indicators of criminals can easily be dismissed. However, the positive school did, and continues to, contribute to the field of knowledge in crime and delinquency.

Among the more bizarre attempts to link body types to delinquency is the use of somatotype. "A *somatotype* is the overall shape of the body, in consideration of the relative development of the various parts of the body in comparison with each other. An important feature of the somatotype explanations of delinquency is that one's character and behavior can be correlated with the shape and structure of the body" (Shoemaker 2000, 22). William H. Sheldon was one the proponents of this perspective. Sheldon (1949) provided three categories of body types: the **mesomorphs** (strong, athletic, aggressive, extroverted individuals), **ectomorphs** (thin, frail, and introverted individuals), and **endomorphs** (fat, jovial, and extroverted persons). Sheldon believed that the mesomorphs were the most likely to commit crime. Although it is true that some criminals fall into the mesomorph's category, research, of course, has never been able to substantiate a correlation between these body types and criminality. As hard as it is today to believe that anyone took Sheldon's work seriously, the positive school did enjoy relatively high esteem. Sheldon also attempted to link body shape and intelligence. Beginning in the early 1900s, it was common for frontal and profile nude photos to be taken of generations of elite college students. All freshmen at some colleges—including Ivy League schools—were required to pose in the buff (Among them former President George Bush, Hillary Rodham Clinton, Diane Sawyer, and George Pataki). For some time, the photos were available at the Smithsonian Institution, where the public had access to them—they have since been destroyed or made unavailable. Most scientists today consider Sheldon's work as "quackery" (*Billings Gazette* 1995, 1A).

In the late twentieth century, biological explanations of the connection between crime and delinquency have attempted to link specific characteristics (e.g., chromosome analysis and gene identification, brain activity) to behavior. At one time, students who did poorly in school might have been labeled slow, feebleminded, dumb, or uninterested in schoolwork and preferring to cause trouble. In the early 1960s came the "discovery" of "learning disabilities" and the realization that individuals learn differently from one another. There are several forms of learning disabilities, with the most common being dyslexia, aphasia, and hyperkinesis. Thus, descriptions of many of the students once labeled "impulsive" and "unwilling to learn" were inaccurate. "In short, children with learning disabilities are thought to have a breakdown in the usual sensory-thought processes that enable other children to understand societal punishment-reward systems attached to behavior. Thus, the general effectiveness of sanctions on behavior is lessened" (Shoemaker 2000, 35). Many of today's delinquents in the schools may in fact suffer from some learning disability. If the disability can be properly identified and dealt with, then many of these delinquents will do better in school and may not end up in a gang.

The only way biological theories will serve any use and purpose in the field of criminality (and the social sciences, for that matter) is if they can clearly link genes and chromosomes to crime and delinquency. Studies involving the **XYY syndrome** have attempted to show that the presence of a Y chromosome signals the secretion of the male hormone testosterone. Testosterone has been linked to aggressiveness. Consequently, it is theorized that the presence of an extra Y chromosome will lead to increased aggressiveness and, by implication, increased levels of criminality. Studies have shown that XYY males are disproportionately found among the institutionalized. "Nevertheless, it must be kept in mind that most studies of XYY males to date have utilized small, selective samples which may have seriously compromised findings. More importantly, even if criminality is associated with this abnormality, XYY syndrome can account for only a tiny proportion of crime. The vast majority of crimes are still committed by chromosomally normal XY males" (Curran and Renzetti 1994, 66). As Shoemaker (2000, 41) summarized:

> The biological approach to delinquency has undergone several changes in this century. First, modern biological theories seldom display the evolutionary themes so common in the eighteenth and nineteenth centuries. Delinquents are no longer seen as evolutionary throwbacks or degenerates. . . . Second, modern theories are much more interdisciplinary than in the past. Personality factors and environmental conditions are often considered, if not formally included, in the propositions of the theories and in research designed to test them. Seldom are claims made that solely profess biological explanations of delinquency. Third, research on the biological contributions to delinquency is more sophisticated than in the past. Control groups are more often used, longitudinal designs are beginning to emerge, and definitions of key variables are being revised and refined.

Biological theories seemingly have little value in explaining human social behavior in general, and that is especially true in the study of gang behavior. There are two primary reasons for this. First, making a claim that certain persons are destined to be gang members based on physical or biological characteristics would most likely lead to charges of racism in contemporary society. It is true that the vast majority of present-day gang members are either African-American or Hispanic. But they do not possess a predisposition, or genetic trait, for this behavior—there is no such thing as a "gang gene." Second, history (see Chapter 2) has already shown us that in the nineteenth century the vast majority of gang members were white. Did whites lose their gang gene? Of course not. Socioeconomic conditions changed for the ethnic white gangs. Furthermore, as Chapter 5 will demonstrate, gangs today come from all socioeconomic classes and all races.

Psychological Theories of Delinquency

Psychological theories, although not as fundamentally sound as sociological theories on gang behavior, represent an improvement over biological explanations. Psychological theories of delinquency start with the premise that there are individual differences in intelligence, personality, and learning.

INTELLIGENCE-BASED THEORIES At their most basic level, intelligence-based theories on crime and delinquency center around the idea that certain individuals are mentally deficient, possess some hereditary degeneration, are feebleminded, or just too plain dumb to understand the consequences or meanings of their delinquent behaviors. The development of the concept of insanity, particularly moral insanity, represents the earliest attempt to link psychological or mental aspects of the individual to criminal behavior (Fink 1938). "It was typically suggested that criminals and delinquents were deficient in basic moral sentiments and that, furthermore, this condition was an inherited trait and contributed to the fusion of biological and psychological properties in the explanation of criminality" (Shoemaker 2000, 47). With the introduction of intelligence tests in the early twentieth century, attempts were made to attribute criminality to those who were unable to comprehend their actions. However, these early intelligence tests worked with the assumption that intelligence was somehow an inherited trait, and thus these theories were as much biological as they were psychological.

Hereditary studies attempted to explain criminality as some form of mental deficiency. "At the heart of the early hereditary studies was the belief that intellectual inferiority or low intelligence was a basic cause of crime. With the development of Alfred Binet and Theodore Simon's *Scale of Intelligence* in 1905, numerous studies conducted on prison inmates tested the hypothesized relationship between low intelligence, especially feeblemindedness, and crime" (Thornton and Voigt 1992, 143). Goddard (1914) reported in *Feeblemindedness: Its Causes and Consequences* that 89 percent of one inmate population under study was feebleminded, but only 29 percent in another study (Vold 1979). During this same period, Charles Goring published his study *The English Convict* (1913), in which he found no evidence to support Lombroso's theory of atavism. "However, he found that criminals were abnormally low in intelligence and he took this as an indication of hereditary inferiority" (Curran and Renzetti 1994, 91). This represents quite a jump, for even if convicts are, as a whole, less intelligent than the general population, how does that prove heredity had anything to do with it? The general feeling of the early twentieth century among researchers who studied criminality was that criminals were lacking in intelligence and morality.

In 1912, a German psychologist named W. Stern revised Binet's method for calculating general intelligence by introducing the idea of dividing mental age by chronological age, arguing that this gives a better estimate of degree of deficiency. Through division, the resulting score ended up being a fraction, so Stern multiplied the quotient by 100 to get rid of the decimal point and thus gave birth to the concept of the intelligence quotient, or IQ (Curran and Renzetti 1994). There have been numerous adaptations of intelligence tests over the years. Psychological theories of delinquency no longer assume that criminality is a result of mental deficiency and have instead come to the conclusion that socialization and school experiences are important factors in criminality. Psychological theories in the modern era believe that personality and learning techniques are correlated to delinquency.

PERSONALITY TRAIT THEORIES In order to develop a personality-based theory of delinquency, the concept of personality must be defined. Curran and Renzetti (1994, 99) define personality as "the organization of characteristics that define an individual and determine that person's pattern of interaction with the environment." This definition, which has not been adopted by all psychologists, still does not solve the problem of how personality develops and how it changes. Among the more famous psychologically based theories of personality is Freud's psychoanalytical theory. Freud did not study delinquency, because he did not feel delinquents and criminals were worthy of his attention (Ewen 1988). Instead, his theory has been applied by others to crime and delinquency. Freud felt that the personality consisted of three parts: the id, ego, and superego. The theory is based on the belief that the *id* component of the personality is concerned with satisfying primal needs, such as sexual gratification and aggressive tendencies. The *superego*, which is the personality trait that symbolizes society's expectations of proper behavior, comes in conflict with the id. Consequently, the *ego* attempts to find the balance between individual needs and society's rules and expectations on how to best attain them. The theory suggests that if the child was not properly taught how to incorporate the superego into the personality, then the child's id would become overly active, ultimately leading to delinquent behavior. Later in life, "the youth may demand immediate gratification, lack compassion and sensitivity for the needs of others, disassociate feelings, act aggressively and impulsively, and demonstrate other psychotic symptoms. Antisocial behavior then may be the result of conflict or trauma occurring early in a child's development, and delinquent activity may become an outlet for violent and antisocial feelings" (Siegel et al. 2003, 84). Thus, the *underdeveloped superego* syndrome leads to a personality that is more conducive to crime and delinquency. An *overdeveloped superego* may also lead to deviancy—feelings of guilt leave the child with a need for punishment. Among the many criticisms of this theory is the realization that there are those who did not suffer from childhood trauma and yet still end up committing delinquent and/or criminal acts. Additionally, there is no way of empirically testing such a theory as Freud's.

Personality-based theories on deviant behavior have led to the development of such concepts as *neurosis* and *psychosis* being applied to criminality. People who are dominated by their primitive id are known as *psychotics*. Their behavior may be marked by bizarre and inappropriate behaviors. *Schizophrenia* is the most common form of psychosis and is characterized by an illogical thought process (e.g., hearing voices that are not really there). The field of psychology has convinced nearly everyone of the validity of the phenomenon of individuals with multiple personalities. Erik Erickson speculated that delinquents suffer from an *identity crisis*. Multiple personality disorder is believed to be caused by severe childhood trauma, in particular sadistic child abuse. "In order to deal with the abuse, the individual disassociates from it by separating into different selves, each of which has its own way of thinking, feeling, and acting" (Curran and Renzetti 1994, 115).

Many of these disorders are used successfully in courtrooms to excuse improper social behavior. Terms such as *psychopath* and *sociopath* often arise when discussing delinquency, even though attempts by the American Psychiatric Association to standardize the meaning of these concepts have not been successful (Thornton and Voigt 1992). The sociopath represents a personality type that has surfaced in biopsychology research. The sociopath possesses an "antisocial personality." "The *sociopath* is thought to be a dangerous, aggressive person who shows little remorse for his or her action, who is not deterred by punishments, and who does not learn from past mistakes. Sociopaths often appear as someone with a pleasant personality and with an above-average level of intelligence. They are, however, marked by an inability to form enduring relationships" (Lyman and Potter 2000, 70). Gang members would not appear to be sociopaths. They do, in fact, generally display little remorse for their actions and are not deterred by punishments; however, they do form loyal, life-long relationships with their fellow gang members.

SOCIAL LEARNING THEORIES Like sociological theories, psychological social learning theories are based on the idea that delinquency, as with nearly all behaviors, is socially learned. "Traumatic early childhood experiences may be important determinants of subsequent adult personality characteristics, but the primary factors influencing whether one conforms to or deviates from societal rules are those experiences youths have while learning from others such as their parents. Adults in any institutional context (e.g., schools, churches, homes) provide role models for children to follow" (Champion 2004, 94). In simplest terms, children learn to become delinquents based on interaction with significant others. Children model the behavior of the adults that they are in close contact with, especially parents, and also the behaviors they see on television and at the movies. "By implication, social learning suggests that children who grow up in a home where violence is a way of life may learn to believe that such behavior is acceptable and rewarding. Even if parents tell children not to be violent and punish them if they are, the children will still model their behavior on the observed parental violence. Thus, children are more likely to heed what their parents *do* than what they *say*" (Siegel et al. 2003, 87).

Social learning generally takes place through two primary methods: reinforcement of behavior and modeling of behavior. The relationship between **reinforcement** and delinquency is both predictable and, perhaps, surprising to some readers. First, when aggression is rewarded instead of punished, the odds of aggressive delinquency increase (Bandura and Walters 1963). Second, "parents of aggressive youths are more inclined to encourage and condone aggression in the home than the parents of nonaggressive youths. The reinforcement of aggression toward siblings or other children at home can cause the child to be aggressive outside the home, at school, and in the community" (Thornton and Voigt 1992, 146). Reinforcement is the result of contact between a great number of people in society, and although parents and the immediate family are the most important agents of socialization, when the child reaches a certain age (around the third grade) the reinforcement of peers becomes very important. If the child associates with a number of other delinquents, the reinforcement of deviant activity becomes stronger and may take hold as a significant modifier of behavior. When a child becomes identified with a particular subculture, the reinforcement becomes stronger.

Along with reinforcement, the child learns behavior through **modeling**. Direct contact between the child and the person who serves as a model is not needed in order for the child's behavior to be influenced. Simply observing how others behave represents a learning opportunity. Thus, a child may learn how to play ball by observing the older kids or by watching professional athletes on television. Thus, one may serve as a model without knowing it, or without wanting to serve as a role model. This happens to athletes a lot—they may not see themselves as role models, but children regard them as such anyway. Delinquents in the neighborhood have a direct influence on younger children. This is especially true in the gang world. Many youngsters grow up as "wannabes"—meaning that they want to be a gang member when they grow older. In fact, the psychological theory involving the impact of modeling on gang participation seems to have a high degree of validity—certainly not as a cause of gang participation, but as a partial explanation as to why youngsters grow up wanting to be gang members. When young children growing up in poverty see gangsters with new clothes, shiny jewelry, and cash, they see a "role model."

SOCIOLOGICAL THEORIES

Sociological theories of crime and delinquency are often applied to the study of gangs. They generally incorporate a diverse, multicausal framework in their explanation of criminality. Sociological theories are grounded by the belief that delinquency is caused by environmental factors. They are supported by empirical data and represent, by far, the most scientific approach in explaining crime and delinquency. Let us begin with the social disorganization theory, which emphasizes that certain neighborhoods are more likely to produce crime and delinquency.

Social Disorganization Theory (the Chicago School)

Social disorganization theory developed from the early ecological research on urban development conducted by sociologists at the University of Chicago during the 1920s and 1930s. Established in 1892, the University of Chicago is home to the first academic department of sociology in the United States. Until the mid-twentieth century it was one of the most dominant forces of sociological thought. The city of Chicago was experiencing dramatic change due to rapid industrial growth and a high migration rate at the turn of the twentieth century. The social problems of high-density urban life presented a golden opportunity for researchers to use the city as a sort of living social laboratory. Many of the new residents of Chicago were from rural areas and were not able to cope with the social problems that urban life presented. The researchers at Chicago attempted to provide some sort of explanation for why certain neighborhoods produced high rates of crime and delinquency, including gangs, while others did not.

Robert Park, Ernst Burgess, Louis Wirth, and others from Chicago, identified several areas of the city that expanded outward in a pattern of **concentric circles**. The outlining areas (Zones 4 and 5) were populated predominantly by white, middle- and upper-class homeowners who had lived in their communities for many years and were well integrated into the dominant culture of society. In an area between the center of the city and the outlying districts (Zone 3) were working-class neighborhoods occupied mostly by second- and third-generation immigrants. In the area closest to the center (Zone 2) were found the poor, the recent immigrants, and transients that faced poor housing conditions. This is the area where the ghettos were found. The core of the city (Zone 1) contained the downtown area where businesses and government buildings were located. "The Chicago sociologists observed that not all urban zones were plagued equally by alcoholism, high rates of mental illness, and other similar problems. Indeed, the further one moved away from the city center, the lower the incidence of social problems. According to the Chicago School, this was the result of the social disorganization that characterized city areas" (Curran and Renzetti 1994, 136). Social disorganization most directly affects those people experiencing poor living conditions. Feelings of hopelessness foster deviant manifestations. No zone was found to be free from delinquency, but the highest rates were found in Zone 2. However, the farther one moved away from the center of the concentric zone, the fewer social problems were confronted. Because all cities do not grow in the same manner, other models were created to explain delinquency in different cities (the other two popular models are the sector and multinuclei). The importance of the concentric zone model is that it stimulated subsequent research to analyze delinquency rates by incorporating fundamental environmental factors such as neighborhood location.

Social disorganization was believed to be caused by "rapid social change that disrupts the normally smooth operation of a social system. In a socially disorganized area, dominant values and norms compete with other, sometimes illegitimate, values and norms. Various cultures, conflict, and members of younger generations clash with one another as well as with members of older groups. Social cohesion breaks down, and social deviance is one common result" (Curran and Renzetti 1994, 137). Thus, high rates of crime and delinquency will be found in areas with a high degree of social problems (e.g., unemployment, single-parent families, and low levels of education). During the early 1900s, social disorganization became the primary explanation for the emergence of crime. In neighborhoods where the family and friendship groups were solidly grounded, neighborhoods were stable and cohesive, and where people had a loyalty to the neighborhood, social organization existed. Without these elements, a neighborhood becomes socially disorganized, and normal social control, which prevents delinquency, becomes ineffective (Williams and McShane 1994). Sampson and Groves (1989) outlined four elements that constitute social disorganization:

1. Low economic status

2. A mixture of different ethnic groups

3. Highly mobile residents moving in and out of the area

4. Disrupted families and broken homes

The high degree of mobility, and implied lack of stability, is a major factor in the disorganization of an economically poor neighborhood.

Social disorganization stimulates the creation of subcultures that are in opposition to the dominant cultural values and norms. Delinquent and criminal subcultures tend to flourish in poor areas (Zone 2) that, over time, lead to a subculture of deviance that has values in contrast to conventional ones. "One of the classic works about gangs coming from a social disorganization perspective was that by Frederic Thrasher. His book *The Gang*, published in 1927, seems to be as relevant today as it was when originally published" (Shelden et al. 2001, 162–163). Thrasher is considered the pioneer of gang-formation research. He believed that gangs grew naturally from spontaneous play groups. Thrasher (1927, 32) stated that gangs originate from "the spontaneous effort of boys to create a society for themselves where none adequate to their needs exists. What boys get out of such associations that they do not get otherwise under the conditions that adult society imposes is the thrill and zest of participation in common interests, more especially in corporate action, in hunting, capture, conflict, flight, and escape." Threats from youths outside the neighborhood provided delinquents with the rally call of coming to arms to protect the neighborhood. Protecting the neighborhood would work only with the involvement of other cohorts. "Thrasher maintained that those play groups that eventually become gangs go through an evolutionary process, in which a loosely organized group develops into a closely knit gang with strong group loyalty, ready to present a united front against enemies. He characterized gangs as being either *diffuse* or *solidified*. Diffuse gangs are loosely organized; those that are solidified have developed a strong internal structure and *esprit de corps*" (Kratcoski and Kratcoski 1996, 95–96).

Thrasher was firmly entrenched within the Chicago School/social disorganization tradition. He systematically documented gang activity and rigorously attempted to analyze all facets of gang activity—an accomplishment probably never equaled. He identified at least 1,313 gangs with a total membership of nearly 25,000. His studies allowed him to distinguish between what activities are normal for adolescents and what activities are unique to gangsters (Trojanowicz et al. 2004). Furthermore, "Thrasher's view of gang causation was consistent with the social disorganization perspective. Specifically, gangs develop within the most impoverished areas of a city. More specifically, Thrasher noted that gangs tend to flourish in areas he called *interstitial*. These areas lie within the 'poverty belt' within a city" (Shelden et al. 2001, 163). For Thrasher (1927), the poverty belt was an area of the city characterized by deteriorating neighborhoods and mobile residents. He believed that gang membership provided many youths a sense of self, an identity, and status and maybe even increased their self-esteem. The gang often becomes a substitute family for its members. Their loyalty to the gang supercedes the one to the greater community or society as a whole.

The social disorganization theory, or Chicago-school approach, is known as an ecological theory. Social ecological theory concerns itself with the organization and structure of society and its impact on localized environments, or communities. "Even at the height of its popularity, the ecological school recognized that American crime patterns might be different from those found elsewhere in the world and that crime zones might exist in city areas other than those surrounding the core" (Schmalleger 2004, 209). According to Schmalleger (2004) the most significant contribution from ecological theorists of the Chicago School was its "formalized use of two sources of information: (1) official crime and population statistics and (2) ethnographic data. Population statistics, or demographic data, when combined with crime information, provided empirical material that gave scientific weight to ecological investigations" (p. 209).

Anomie/Strain Theory

Anomie theory, sometimes called *strain theory*, was articulated by Robert Merton, who borrowed Emile Durkheim's term *anomie*. Durkheim was very concerned with what he perceived as the decline of common morality in French society. "Industrialization in particular, according to Durkheim, tends to dissolve restraints on the passions of humans. Where simple societies—primarily through religion—successfully taught people to control their desires and goals, modern industrial societies separate people and weaken their social bonds as a result of increased complexity and the division of labor. Durkheim believed that members of Western society are exposed to the risk of *anomie*" (Delaney 2004, 101). The term *anomie* comes from the Greek *anomia*, meaning "without law." In his 1893 book *The Division of Labor in Society*, Durkheim used the word *anomie* to refer to a condition of "deregulation" occurring in society. "By this he meant that the general procedural rules of a society (the rules that say how people ought to behave toward each other) have broken down and that people do not know what to expect from each other. This deregulation, or normlessness, easily leads to deviant behavior" (Williams and McShane 1994, 87). Feelings of normlessness lead members to deviant behavior because a common morality of society no longer exists. It was in *Suicide* (1897) where Durkheim used *anomie* to describe a general state of moral deregulation, which had left people inadequate moral controls over their behavior.

> Individuals are confronted with *anomie* when they are not faced with sufficient moral constraint, or do not have a clear concept of what is and what is not acceptable behavior. . . . Durkheim viewed *anomie* as a pathology. By thinking

of *anomie* as a pathology, Durkheim was saying that deviant behaviors and the problems of the world could be "cured." Thus, the proper level of regulation, both in terms of issues of morality and civility, would guarantee a cohesive and smoothly operating society (Delaney 2004, 101–102).

In short, *anomie* refers to the breakdown of social norms and rules and a condition in which existing norms no longer control the activity of individuals.

Robert Merton was intrigued by Durkheim's notion of anomie and how persons adapt to the *strain* of chaotic social conditions. In 1938, Merton borrowed Durkheim's concept of anomie and used it in an attempt to explain deviant behavior in the United States: "Whereas Durkheim conceived of anomie as a problematic social condition resulting from sudden and rapid social change, Merton saw it as an endemic feature of the everyday operation of certain types of societies" (Curran and Renzetti 1994, 149). Merton conceived of society as consisting of two primary components: the cultural structure and the social structure. The *cultural structure* consists of society's goals— what all members are supposed to strive to attain; whereas the *social structure* refers to the institutional means of attaining these goals. Merton believed that functional societies have an integrated blend of these two aspects. Dysfunctional societies, however, place an undue emphasis on one of the societal components. Merton viewed the United States as a dysfunctional society because it places great emphasis on cultural goals— primarily economic and material success—but is characterized by a social structure that does not provide everyone with an equal opportunity to reach these goals.

Merton's "goals-means" scheme of describing different societies shines a light on how good a job a particular society does in providing its members with opportunities to reach desired ends. "Merton contended that society generally prescribes approved cultural goals for its members to seek (e.g., new homes, jobs, automobiles). Furthermore, appropriate, legitimate, or institutionalized means are prescribed for the purpose of attaining these goals. But not everyone is equally endowed with the desire to achieve societal goals nor are they necessarily committed to using the prescribed means to achieve these goals" (Champion 2004, 102). Social systems found throughout the world differ a great deal. Some societies do not value capitalism and materialism; they also vary a great deal in the manner of which they distribute their accumulated wealth. In repressive regimes, the wealth is kept in the hand of a few (e.g., Iraq, Saudi Arabia), whereas in democracies, it is theoretically possible for anyone to attain a certain measure of wealth. "Merton saw our society as being extremely productive, but at the same time creating frustration and strain because all groups do not have equal access to the institutional norms, and when there is a disjunction between goals, means, and institutionalized norms, and when there is an overemphasis on goals or means" (Trojanowicz et al. 2001, 62). Thus, Merton believed that deviance was a result of the social strain that anomie created. "Deviance, then, is explained as a symptom of a social structure in which 'culturally defined aspirations and socially structured means' are separated from each other. Or, in other worlds, deviance is a product of anomie" (Williams and McShane 1994, 88).

Approved means of reaching the success goal of American society are not readily available to all members of society. Certain people, especially those found in the lower social classes and minority members, often find barriers to their path of success that the wealthy and privileged persons of society do not. "The individuals caught in these anomic conditions (largely from the lower classes) are then faced with the strain of being unable to reconcile their aspirations with their limited opportunities" (Williams and McShane 1994, 91). Because many individuals find conventional or legitimate means unavailable to them in their pursuit of culturally defined goals, they often resort to illegitimate and illegal methods of reaching society's goals. (In fact, it should be noted that legitimate means of attaining society's goals are not always the most efficient.) The strain of finding oneself in a disadvantageous position leads many individuals down the path of deviancy.

According to Merton (1968), when individuals are faced with the strain caused by anomic conditions they have a choice between five **modes of adaptation**. Three of these behavioral adaptations are considered deviant (innovation, retreatism, and rebellion) while the other two (conformity and ritualism) are generally not. (Note that many social scientists consider ritualism as a deviant adaptation.)

MERTON'S MODES OF ADAPTATION

1. **Conformity**—Involves accepting things as they are. Conformists have accepted the goals of society and the prescribed ways of attaining them. According to Merton, this is the most common mode of behavior. Furthermore, this reality helps to explain why, no matter how high the crime rate is in some neighborhoods, most citizens are not criminals.

2. **Innovation**—Involves an emphasis on striving for the approved goals of society but legitimate means have been replaced by illegitimate ones. Innovation represents the most common deviant adaptation of behavior. For many members of society, deviant adaptation (e.g., bank robbery) may actually represent a more efficient means of reaching a goal than the approved means to do so (e.g., working hard at a menial job making minimum wage). It is this reasoning that has a direct effect on why a disproportionate number of street criminals are from the lower socioeconomic classes (e.g., a successful businessperson has little need to rob a convenience store for 50 dollars).

3. **Ritualism**—Ritualists reject goals but work toward less lofty goals by institutionally approved means. "In this mode the means can become the aspirations of an individual, as when one may attempt to treat a job (means) as a form of security instead of using the job as a means of achieving success. In this example, keeping the job has become a goal by itself, resolving the frustration of unsuccessfully chasing the original goal" (Williams and McShane 1994, 92). Clerks and petty bureaucrats are examples of ritualists. Ritualists simply go through the motions day after day, are never really happy with life, but have found salvation through scaled-down ambition. Deviant behavior occurs when clerks exercise a sense of power by breaking the rules. For example, a clerk may give out private and confidential information to reporters or to people who offer bribes.

4. **Retreatism**—Occurs when people reject both society's goals and the means of attaining them. Rather than innovate, or simply accept society (conformity), these people choose to cut themselves off from the world (e.g., hermits, drug

addicts, street people, and "bag ladies"). This mode of adaptation seems to be more common today than in Merton's era.

5. **Rebellion**—This mode of adaptation interests those persons who are so strained by society that they wish to replace both the goals and the means of attaining them (e.g., anarchists, militant groups).

One other variation of strain theory worth mentioning comes from the work of Cloward and Ohlin in *Delinquency and Opportunity* (1960). These authors believed that blocked opportunities in the pursuit of culturally determined goals leads to feelings of frustration and poor self-concepts. These frustrations lead to delinquency, especially within a gang context (Shelden et al. 2001, 170). Culturally frustrated youths are disproportionately found in the lower economic social classes. Within these environments exist greater opportunity and reinforcement to commit acts of delinquency and crime. Thus, there is a difference in opportunity to commit crime based on one's social class. Cloward and Ohlin used the concept of *differential opportunity structure*, meaning that there is an uneven distribution of legitimate and illegitimate means of achieving society's success goal. This "opportunity theory" stressed the importance of the social environment in determining which opportunities individuals choose. Youths from wealthy families have more legitimate opportunities afforded to them, whereas youths from poorer neighborhoods have far fewer legitimate and realistic means of attaining desired goals.

The fact that the largest percentage of gangs can be found in lower-class neighborhoods would seem to give validity to anomie/strain theory. Kratcoski and Kratcoski (1996, 56), however, believed that "today, anomic behavior is not restricted to youths living in poverty areas or those lacking educational or social advantages. Changes in American life, notably in the stability of family life, have caused young people of all social classes to experience a lack of structure, continuity, and goal orientation in their day-to-day existence. . . . The emphasis on personal gratification and immediate pleasure, which can be sought without concern for the needs, wishes, and rights of others, promotes normlessness as a way of life."

Subculture/Cultural Deviance Theory

By the 1950s and early 1960s, sociologists were studying juvenile delinquency in the context of the new sociological term *subcultures*, which represented an evolutionary step in the study of gang behavior. "Combining these two topics, criminologists began studying gang delinquency and theorizing about delinquent subcultures" (Williams and Voigt 1994, 105). Subcultural theories offer great insight into gang behavior, as the gang is most definitely a subculture of the greater society. "Subcultural theorists perceive delinquency to be simultaneously a reaction to the larger cultural value system and an adherence to group norms. Subculturalists maintain that delinquency is an expression of standards espoused by one's reference group—in this case, other members of the subculture. For subculturalists, delinquency constitutes behavior consistent with a set of norms" (Thornton and Voigt 1992, 171). In brief, a subculture is a group of people found within the greater society. They generally share many of the same ideas and values of the greater society, but go about things differently. If the subculture group participates in deviant behavior, new members will feel the pressure to conform to deviant norms. Subcultural theory concentrates on this group dynamic. As Goldstein explained (1991, 12), "Subcultural deviance theory holds that delinquent behavior grows from conformity to the prevailing social norms experienced by youths in their particular subculture groups."

Subculture and cultural deviance theories were influenced by the Chicago School tradition (looking for the relationship between community and delinquency), Merton's anomie theory, and even social disorganization theory. As Shelden and associates explained, "cultural deviance theory proposes that delinquency is a result of a desire to conform to cultural values that are to some extent in conflict with those of conventional society. In part, this perspective is a direct offshoot of social disorganization theory because part of that theory . . . suggests that criminal values and traditions emerge within communities most affected by social disorganization" (2001, 172). It is safe to conclude that subcultural theories were influenced by the previous sociological theories on crime and delinquency.

During the 1950s, along with the term *subcultures* came the concept of **reference groups**. In many ways, reference groups are similar to subcultures; in fact, it is this "reference point" idea that leads to the formation of subculture. Subcultures are formed when reference group members share a number of common goals and traits. The reference group serves as the point of reference in making comparisons or contrasts, especially in forming judgments about one's self. Reference groups provide points of comparison in evaluating one's own status. The reference group concept is particularly useful in accounting for the choices made among apparent alternatives, particularly where the selections seem to be contrary to the "best interests" of the actor. "The concept of reference group can . . . greatly facilitate research on the manner in which each actor's orientation toward his world is structured" (Shibutani 1955, 562). Within the framework of the reference group, members feel a great sense of loyalty to each other, they aspire to gain or maintain acceptance, and consequently, group norms take on a higher value than society's. When these events occur, a subculture has been formed.

Among the more significant theorists of the subcultural format of explaining crime and delinquency is Albert Cohen. "Delinquent subcultures exist, according to Cohen, within the greater societal culture. But these subcultures contain value systems and modes of achievement and gaining status and recognition apart from the mainstream culture" (Champion 2004, 100). Cohen's *Delinquent Boys: The Culture of the Gang* (1955) is one of the first versions of cultural deviance theory that explains how delinquent subcultures form. Cohen began his analysis with a simple premise, that everyone seeks social status. Unfortunately, not all youths can compete equally for status. "By virtue of their position in the social structure, lower-class children tend to lack both material and symbolic advantages. As long as they compete among themselves, the footing is relatively equal; it is in competition with middle-class children that lower-class children fall short" (Williams and McShane 1994, 108). Cohen did not imply that delinquency is a product of lower socioeconomic status (SES) per se: "Rather, children from lower SES are at greater risk than others of being susceptible to the rewards and opportunities a subculture of delinquency might offer in contrast with the system's middle-class structure" (Champion 2004, 100). It is this "middle-class measuring rod" against which many youths of lower SES fall short.

Cohen's (1955) subcultural deviance theory works with the following assumptions:

1. A high proportion of lower-class youths (especially males) do poorly in school.

2. Poor school performance relates to delinquency.

3. Poor school performance stems from a conflict between dominant middle-class values of the school system and values of lower-class youths.

4. Most lower-class male delinquency is committed in a gang context, partly as a means of meeting some basic human needs, such as self-esteem and belonging (Shelden et al. 2001, 173).

Working with these assumptions, Cohen (1955) identified five central characteristics of lower-class delinquent gangs, which, when combined, comprise the **delinquent subculture**:

1. **Nonutilitarianism**—The acts of delinquency committed by delinquents are not always done for a specific purpose (utilitarianism). Instead, profound satisfaction from committing crimes, such as theft, may come from the act itself—being delinquent.

2. **Maliciousness**—A great deal of delinquency is committed simply for the purpose of being mean and the corresponding rush and thrill of committing deviant acts. Vandalism is a primary example of malicious behavior.

3. **Negativism**—The delinquent subculture is not only at odds with the greater society, it attempts to take its norms and turn them upside down.

4. **Short-term hedonism**—There is little planning in regard to long-term goals, instead, gang members live for the moment and immediate gratification.

5. **Group autonomy**—Delinquents, and especially gang members, do not recognize any authority figure (e.g., parents, teachers, agents of social control) other than those in charge of the gang (Curran and Renzetti 1994, 153–154).

Cohen concluded that gang members are at complete odds with the middle-class goal structure (e.g., delayed gratification, good manners, self-control, being a productive member of society). When the schools try to impose such goals, they rebel. The strain caused by middle-class expectations placed on lower SES youths causes **status frustration** (Cohen 1955). The fact that some neighborhoods produce more delinquents than others can be explained (at least partially) by Cloward and Ohlin's use of the concept of **degree of integration**. As this term implies, the degree to which delinquents are, or are not, tied to the community will impact their degree of delinquency. Where individuals are at great odds with the prevailing value system, a high degree of delinquency and gang activity will most likely be found. The greater the degree of integration, the lower the rate of delinquency and crime.

Richard Cloward (1959), noting Merton's anomie theory, developed a "differential opportunity theory." Cloward believed that there exist both a legitimate opportunity structure toward desired societal goals and also an **illegitimate opportunity structure**. This illegitimate opportunity structure served as the backdrop for a theory Cloward proposed with Lloyd Ohlin in *Delinquency and Opportunity: A Theory of Delinquent Gangs* (1960). Their theory is known as *differential opportunity theory*. Cloward and Ohlin argued that "whereas legitimate opportunities are generally available to individuals born into middle-class culture, participants in lower-class subcultures are often denied access to them. As a consequence, illegitimate opportunities for success are often seen as quite acceptable by participants in so-called illegitimate subcultures" (Schmalleger 2004, 218). The inference is that delinquent (and gang) behavior may result from the availability of illegitimate opportunities and their acknowledgment, within the subculture, as acceptable. Cloward and Ohlin described three types of delinquent subcultures:

1. criminal subcultures—criminal roles are readily available for adoption
2. conflict subcultures—participants seek status through violence
3. retreatist subcultures—groups that participate in drug use and/or withdrawal from the predominant society

The works of Walter B. Miller represent a significant influence on subcultural theory. Miller argued that Cohen's analysis of gangs from the perspective of the middle class resulted in his missing important aspects of gang life. Miller believed that gang members did not see their activities as nonutilitarian, malicious, and negativistic. Instead, Miller believed that gang behavior supports and maintains the basic features of lower-class values and a way of life. Miller (1958) identified six basic features that characterized the lower-class value system. He referred to them as **focal concerns**. Focal concerns are features or aspects of a subculture that require constant monitoring, attention, and care. Miller's (1958) focal concerns are

1. **Trouble**—Getting into trouble is in direct contrast to the middle-class value system. Delinquents, especially gang members, thrive on getting into trouble and having confrontations with law enforcement officers, rival gang members, and others not a part of their subculture. As Miller explained (1958, 8), "the dominant concern over 'trouble' involves a distinction of critical importance for the lower class community—that between 'law-abiding' and 'non-law-abiding' behavior." Middle-class people value "achievements" of the conventional nature; while lower class youths value getting into trouble and general non-law-abiding behavior. "From the lower class male perspective, trouble often entails getting into fights, drinking, and the sexual conquest of women" (Thornton and Voigt 1992, 172).

2. **Toughness**—The most important aspect of toughness is physical strength, prowess, being masculine, and bravery in the face of physical threat. It involves a general macho attitude (or machismo). Miller explained (1958, 9) "the genesis of the intense concern over 'toughness' in lower class culture is probably related to the fact that a significant proportion of lower class males

are reared in a predominantly female household, and lack a consistently present male figure with whom to identify and from whom to learn essential components of a 'male' role." The lower-class male raised in a female-headed family becomes overly concerned with issues of what it means to be a man. Being tough is viewed as a critical element. Toughness "also includes a lack of sentimentality, a disdain for art and literature, and a view of women as sex objects. Concern over toughness may derive from being reared in a female-headed household and lack of male role models. The concern with toughness precludes males from assuming roles that might be seen as feminine, such as caring for one's children and acting responsibly toward fathering children out of wedlock" (Shelden et al. 2001, 174).

3. **Smartness**—This quality has nothing to do with academic smarts, but rather with "street smarts." Being street smart can often be more important for basic survival than being tough. "Smartness, as conceptualized in lower class culture, involves the capacity to outsmart, outfox, dupe, 'take,' 'con' another or others, and the concomitant capacity to avoid being outwitted, 'taken,' or duped oneself" (Miller 1958, 9). Street smartness is highly valued because it allows individuals an opportunity to attain desired material goods.

4. **Excitement**—This focal concern refers to the constant search among lower-class persons for "thrills" and "taking risks." Drinking, taking drugs, having lots of sex, and fighting are all forms of excitement. Miller also pointed out that gang members need a counterbalance from all this excitement and that's why they spend a great deal of time just "hanging out" doing nothing.

5. **Fate**—Many lower-class persons are raised in an atmosphere of hopelessness, resulting in a belief that fate has worked against them, and that no matter how hard they try, they will never succeed outside the lower-class world. They believe that their lives are controlled by forces (socioeconomic) that they cannot control.

6. **Autonomy**—Involves attempts by lower-class persons to take charge of their lives, to regain some sense of control. Autonomy actually becomes a contradiction of sorts in that the gang member does not want to be told what to do (by outside cultural social control agents), but seems to want the structure provided by the gang (the subculture). As Miller (1958, 12) explained, "many lower class people appear to seek out highly restrictive social environments wherein stringent external controls are maintained over their behavior." Besides the armed forces and disciplinary schools, the gang becomes a great source of desired structure for lower-class males.

Often many, or all, of these focal concerns come into play on a regular basis. Miller believed that the gang subculture reflected the lower-class value system and that gang participation provided a means to an end.

Subcultural theories had substantial impact on American policy because they offered hope to a new generation of liberal-thinking people in the early 1960s. The Kennedy and Johnson presidential administrations attempted to implement the major concepts of opportunity theory by spending millions of dollars on the Great Society and War on Poverty efforts, especially the Peace Corps.

Control/Social Bond Theory

There are many variations of control theory; its roots date back to the late nineteenth century but its greatest impact on the field of delinquency developed in the 1950s and 1960s.

> Control theories of delinquency cover a wide range of topics. Lamar Empey (1982) characterizes nineteenth-century and early-twentieth-century individualistic theories of delinquency as "control" theories, especially psychoanalytic explanations. Travis Hirschi (1969) traces the ideas of control theory as far back as Durkheim in the nineteenth century. Most often, however, control theories of delinquency are equated with self-concept research and social control mechanisms, such as family and school experiences. In this context, control theories may be historically placed in the 1950s and early 1960s, with the development of Walter Reckless' self-concept or containment explanation of delinquency. In the late 1960s Travis Hirschi extended Reckless' ideas to broader social contexts, thus leading to the social or psychological perspective, which became synonymous with control theory (Shoemaker 2000, 159).

Social control theories of crime and delinquency examine the standard variables studied by sociologists: family, education, peer groups, socioeconomic status, etc.).

The common link among social control theories is their rather unusual way of examining delinquent behavior. Whereas most theories of delinquency ask why people commit acts of crime and delinquency, social control theorists ask why doesn't everyone commit acts of crime and delinquency?

> Control theorists adopt a Hobbesian view of human nature; to them, everyone is basically criminal at heart. Everyone is equally motivated to commit crimes because fulfilling one's desires usually can be done most effectively, efficiently, and pleasurably by violating the law. . . . To the control theorist, then, the question criminologists must answer is *"Why do people obey the rules of their society?"* In answering this question, control theorists argue that it is a person's ties—or, depending on the individual theorist, a person's links, attachments, binds, or bonds—to conventional social institutions, such as family and school, that inhibit him or her from acting on criminal motivations (Curran and Renzetti 1994, 199).

Thus, social control theorists emphasize that individuals must form a bond with society, and in that manner they are less likely to deviate from cultural expectations. The key to forming bonds and attachments to society rests with proper socialization. "Proper socialization leads to conformity, while improper socialization leads to non-conformity. Delinquency is one consequence of improper socialization" (Shelden et al. 2001, 175). Delinquency, then, is the result of the weakening, the breakdown, or absence of effective social controls.

Juvenile delinquents are youths who have not developed bonds to the society that spawned them. Juveniles that remain unattached to society's norms are free to engage in a variety of deviant activities, including delinquency. In other words, control theorists say, delinquency occurs because it is not prevented (Nye 1958). In order to prevent delinquency, adequate controls must be placed on youths. According to Thornton and Voigt (1992), there are two general categories of controls: personal, or inward, and societal, or external. For example, a youth who refrains from stealing an item from a store because his/her conscience forbids the breaking of laws has expressed personal or inward control. On the other hand, a child who has developed a healthy respect for the authority of the police and refuses to steal, fearing arrest, has displayed external control.

There are a number of variations of control theory, but they all assume one basic point: "Human beings, young or old, must be held in check, or somehow controlled, if criminal or delinquent tendencies are to be repressed" (Shoemaker 2000, 160). In the following pages a brief review of some of the major variants of social control theory will be presented.

As mentioned earlier, the roots of control theory can be traced back to the works of Durkheim. It should first be noted that Durkheim believed that society will always have a certain number of deviants. His idea that even in a "society of saints" there would still be sinners is a perfect example of this belief. In this type of society, there would be no crime as we know it, but even saints may be guilty of committing crimes like failing to say a blessing before a meal or using the Lord's name in vain. "If crime represents harm to society, such behavior for the saints could threaten their social order. Controls, then, are necessary for order to exist and for people to understand the boundaries of accepted behavior" (Williams and McShane 1994, 184). Durkheim's analysis of anomie was related to the existence of controls. According to Durkheim, a normal (nonanomic) society is one in which social relationships are working well and society's norms and expectations (regulations) are clearly defined. "When relationships and norms begin to break down, the controls they create begin to deteriorate. Durkheim noted that a breakdown of those controls leads to crime and suicide. He was particularly concerned with situations in which uncontrolled rising aspirations lead to suicide. Whenever anomie exists in society, controls begin to disappear" (Williams and McShane 1994, 184). Durkheim argued that the extent to which society is integrated (bound to one another morally) and committed to common goals—thus forming a *collective conscience*—the more deviant behavior is controlled. In Durkheim's view, society exerts social control over individuals through custom, tradition, laws, and religious codes. "When members of a society accept and internalize these guidelines for behavior, conformity exists. Durkheim thus explained suicide through the bonding of the individual to the norms of society. Some criminologists have developed theories of juvenile delinquency from this model. The basic premise of social control theories of delinquency is that juveniles who accept societal goals and feel a moral tie to others will engage in less delinquency that those who are not committed to social goals and are not attached to important others" (Thornton and Voigt 1992, 179).

Personality-oriented social control theories, such as the one developed by Albert Reiss, Jr. (1951), are based on the idea that social control efforts have gone through dramatic changes since the time of Durkheim. Reiss combined concepts of **personality** and **socialization** with the work of the Chicago School and created a version of social control theory that suggested there are three components of social control that explained delinquency:

1. a lack of proper internal controls developed during childhood

2. a breakdown of those internal controls

3. an absence of, or conflict in, social rules provided by important social groups (the family, close others, the school) (Reiss 1951, 196).

These three elements have appeared in almost every version of social control theory from the time Reiss first presented them. Reiss believed that delinquency was behavior that represents a failure of personal and social controls to produce behavior in conformity with the norms of the social system. Since individuals learn core values during early childhood (via the family and school), delinquency is the result of a failure of primary socialization. Reiss (1951, 197–200) found that delinquents on probation who were most likely to fail to live up to the terms of their probation usually came from the following types of circumstances:

1. They came from a home supported by welfare.
2. The parents were divorced, or one parent was deceased.
3. There was an open breach or gross incompatibility with the natural parents.
4. Unfavorable moral ideas had been institutionalized.

Reiss concluded that the parents and family play a critical role as to whether or not a youth becomes a delinquent. But the family is not the only agent of socialization, and therefore, the peer group also has a great impact on whether a youth becomes delinquent.

Another variation of social control theory comes from Walter Reckless and his **containment theory**. Reckless (1961) described delinquency as a character disorder on the one hand and as a social pursuit on the other. "Reckless's approach represents a socio-psychological synthesis. According to Reckless, not everyone is susceptible to the 'pull' of certain delinquent and criminal activities because some individuals are contained or restrained from these behaviors through various **outer** and **inner containments**" (Thornton and Voigt 1992, 180). Delinquency is explained as the interplay between these two forms of control (containment). Reckless believed that inner containments are self-controls that develop during the socialization process. Although he never clearly articulated the term *inner containment*, Reckless (1961) provided a number of its characteristics: self-control, self-concept, ego strength, tolerance of frustration, identification with lawfulness, goal-directed, and realistic objectives. Outer containment was equated to society and the agents of socialization. Reckless believed that in order to avoid delinquency a child must avoid the external pressures from deviant subcultures. A child with a positive self-image and a sense of direction in life will more easily be able to avoid the deviant temptations confronting him or her, whereas a child who does not possess a positive self-concept, or who is "drifting" aimlessly, becomes more susceptible to a deviant way of behavior.

Gresham Sykes and David Matza (1957) proposed that one becomes "free" to commit deviant acts when one has found a way to justify one's behavior. Their famous description of the **techniques of neutralization** (a concept that all sociology and criminology students are taught) illustrates how delinquents and norm violators attempt to rationalize their deviant behaviors. "These techniques allow individuals to neutralize and temporarily suspend their commitment to societal values, thus providing the freedom to commit delinquent acts" (Williams and McShane 1994, 186). In an article (1957) and in Matza's book *Delinquency and Drift* (1964), Sykes and Matza argue that delinquency cannot be explained simply as an absence of social controls, instead it must also involve a "will to delinquency." Sykes and Matza believed that lower-class males are especially prone to delinquency because of their feelings of desperation. They supplement their role as passive societal victims through perceived positive acts of delinquency. Not feeling tied to society, these individuals manage to justify their deviant behaviors through neutralizing techniques.

The five techniques of neutralization that individuals use to justify their delinquent behavior described by Sykes and Matza are as follows:

1. **Denial of Responsibility**—The first of any deviant defense is simply denying that involvement in the act of delinquency under question. It can also refer to cases when an individual attempts to escape responsibility by means of insanity (temporarily, or otherwise). Thus, gang members might claim that they did not commit certain delinquent or criminal acts, even though a witness and/or the police saw them do it.

2. **Denial of Injury**—Occurs when individuals can neutralize any guilty feelings they might have for committing deviant acts as long as no one was hurt. Gang members will justify many behaviors when people are not harmed (e.g., theft, selling drugs, painting graffiti on buildings).

3. **Denial of the Victim**—When offenders retaliate for previous acts of the victim, they justify their behavior by denying the "victim status" of their enemy (victim). Gang members use this technique often by saying things like "they had it coming" or "we were just getting even."

4. **Condemnation of the Condemners**—Another tactic used by deviants is to "attack" those who disapprove of their behavior. Delinquents, gang members included, will accuse the police of being corrupt and teachers as playing favorites. "The effect is an attempt to shift attention away from the delinquent's own actions and to neutralize the normative sanctioning system these authority figures represent" (Thornton and Voigt 1992, 182).

5. **Appeal to Higher Loyalties**—Many deviants (as well as extremists) use this technique of neutralization. They disobey society's rules and values in favor of some other "higher" authority. Gang members claim a higher sense of loyalty to their gang than to society's laws. Religious extremists claim a loyalty to God, or Allah, or some other deity in order to justify their criminal behavior (e.g., a person who kills a doctor who performs abortions because they believe God commanded them to do so). Terrorists justify their behavior using the same illogic. Inadequate socialization leads many people to believe that they can pick and choose which laws, if any, to obey.

In his later work, Matza (1964) used the term *bond to the moral order* to mean the tie that exists between individuals and the dominant values of society. Once individuals use the techniques of neutralization to justify their delinquent behavior, they are in a state of limbo or **drift** that makes deviant acts permissible. The key to rehabilitating deviants is to find some component of society that they can "attach" themselves to through reinforcement and the rewarding of proper behavior.

The most popular version of social control theory is the one presented by Travis Hirschi. In his book *Causes of Delinquency* (1969), Hirschi gave his analysis of empirical data he had collected on delinquency. (Hirschi conducted a survey of 4,000 high school students in California.) He believed that deviant acts are the result of an individual's weakened or broken bond to society. Especially important is the youth's relationship with the family. "Regardless of their social class, the most delinquent youths were least attached to their parents, as reflected by low levels of parent-child intimacy and communication. Beliefs reflected by such things as lack of respect for the police and the law, and lack of involvement with homework were other predictors of delinquency" (Trojanowicz et al. 2001, 72). Like Durkheim, Hirschi believed that behavior reflects varying degrees of morality. "He argued that the power of internalized norms, conscience, and the desire for approval encourage conventional behavior. As did Sykes and Matza, Hirschi saw that a person becomes 'free' to engage in delinquency. Instead of using neutralizing techniques, however, he blamed broken or weakened bonds to society" (Williams and McShane 1994, 188).

Consequently, Hirschi promoted the idea that individuals must form a solid bond with society. Hirschi (1969) specified four elements of the social bond:

1. **Attachment**—A tight connection to significant others (especially parents and peers) and to the school provides the best mechanism on constraining delinquent behavior by youths. Affection to parents and family is a positive sign of attachment. The importance of attachment to significant others rests with the realization that primary socialization takes place while youths interact with parents and peers. "Thus, attachment to others facilitates the internalization of society's norms and the development of a conscience" (Curran and Renzetti 1994, 199).

2. **Commitment**—Involves the amount of time that individuals spend with conventional behavior and their dedication to long-term goals (delayed satisfaction). The reasoning here is simple: The more time that individuals spend with conventional activities, the less time is available for delinquency. Engaging in conventional activities (e.g., sports, spelling bees, dance and music lessons, planning for college) teaches people that there are rules, that they must be followed, and that there are negative consequences for violating these rules. In short, individuals who possess a commitment to conventional activities are less likely to engage in delinquent activities.

3. **Involvement**—Participation in conventional activities, such as doing homework, working at a job, or doing chores, generally means less time for delinquency. In other words, if a youth has too much free time, he or she is more likely to eventually commit deviant acts.

4. **Belief**—The final element of Hirschi's social bond refers to the simple belief in the law, especially the morality of the law. Successful socialization can only take place if the individual has a willingness and belief in the ideals of law and order. Thus, individuals come to realize that stealing, littering, and similar acts are just wrong and know better than to engage in them. Obviously, from Hirschi's perspective, those who do not believe in law and morality are more likely to commit deviant acts.

Hirschi believed that these bonds are interrelated. From the perspective of control theory, the most critical element of proper parenting is creating a social bond between their children and society. When this bond is strong, delinquency is less likely to occur; conversely, when the bond is weak, delinquency is more likely to occur.

Social Learning/Differential Learning Theory

As the name social learning theory implies, individuals *learn* how to become delinquent. "One of the first theorists to associate the origins of crime with a learning process was Gabriel Tarde. In his book *The Law of Imitation*, Tarde argued that crime results from one person's imitating the actions of another. Although he also took into account biological and psychological factors, he believed that crime is essentially a social product" (Kratcoski and Kratcoski 1996, 56). An individual learns behavior through interaction with others. For example, the reason children speak their "native" tongue is that they were taught that language. In fact, without socialization, people would not even be "human," nor would they develop language. Consequently, social learning theory has a great deal of credibility for the simple reason that all behaviors are learned. Through interaction with others, individuals learn of the norms, beliefs, attitudes, and values treasured by the interactants. According to this perspective, individuals become delinquent not only through direct contact with delinquents but also through exposure to various values, beliefs, and attitudes that are supportive of criminal and delinquent acts (e.g., through the media and music). However, direct association with deviant others, especially over a period of time, is the most likely way to elicit delinquent behavior according to social theorists.

From the social learning theory perspective, youths learn to become delinquent through three related processes: acquisition, instigation, and maintenance. *Acquisition* refers to the initial introduction to a deviant form of behavior. This opportunity allows for reinforcement through modeling. Thus, if a youth is introduced to violence at home or at school, and finds this behavior positively rewarded (or negative sanctions lacking), he or she is more likely to imitate it. *Instigation* occurs when the individual actually participates in some form of delinquent behavior (e.g., beating someone up at school as an initiation requirement to join a gang). *Maintenance* refers to participating in the delinquent behavior consistently over a period of time. This is the only way that criminal or delinquent behavior will persist. "In order for delinquent or criminal behavior to persist, there needs to be consistent reinforcement or *maintenance*. Social learning theory suggests four specific kinds of reinforcement: (1) direct reinforcement, (2) vicarious reinforcement, (3) self-reinforcement, and (4) neutralization of self-punishment" (Shelden et al. 2001, 178).

Edwin Sutherland is considered the most prominent of all the social theorists. He developed a theory of **differential association**, which he first introduced in the third edition of his textbook *Principles of Criminology* (1939). The final version appeared in 1947, after he had made revisions based on criticisms and comments on his first version. Sutherland was highly critical of biological and psychiatric theories of crime. "Sutherland expressly incorporated the notion that all behavior is learned and, unlike other theorists of the time, moved away from referring to the varied cultural perspectives as 'social disorganization' and used the term 'differential social disorganization' or 'differential group organization.' This allowed him more clearly to apply the learning process to a broader range of American society" (Williams and McShane 1994, 75–76). Sutherland recognized that many youths are introduced to, and associate with, a diversity of people, some of whom will encourage and participate in conventional behaviors and others who engage in delinquent and criminal behavior. Individuals exposed to such diverse groups of people may experience internal conflict in trying to decide which set of values, attitudes, and codes of behavior to accept and internalize. Many young people who attempt to embrace society's conventional norms, but who grow up in gang-infested neighborhoods and experience the pressures to join a gang, deal with this internal conflict on a daily basis.

Sutherland put together nine basic and formal theoretical propositions that, when taken together, constitute differential association theory, which is reminiscent of Tarde's imitation theory (Thornton and Voigt 1992). The final version of Sutherland's differential association theory is as follows (Thornton and Voigt 1992, 165–166):

1. Criminal behavior is learned.

2. Criminal behavior is learned in interaction with other persons in a process of communication.

3. The principal part of the learning of criminal behavior occurs within intimate personal groups.

4. When criminal behavior is learned, the learning includes (a) techniques of committing the crime; (b) the specific direction of motives, drives, rationalizations, and attitudes.

5. The specific direction of motives and drives is learned from definitions of the legal codes as favorable or unfavorable.

6. A person becomes delinquent because of an excess of definitions favorable to violation of law over definitions unfavorable to violation of law.

7. Differential associations may vary in frequency, duration, priority, and intensity.

8. The process of learning criminal behavior by association with criminal and anticriminal patterns involves all the mechanisms that are involved in any other learning.

9. While criminal behavior is an expression of general needs and values, it is not explained by those general needs and values, since noncriminal behavior is an expression of the same needs and values (from Sutherland and Cressey 1978, 80–82). [*Note*: Donald R. Cressey was a former student of Sutherland's and worked on the final modifications of differential association theory.]

The point that Sutherland makes repeatedly is that criminal behavior is learned and not an inherited trait. It is learned through socialization. In short, if the greatest number of associations that youths have are the positive, conventional ones of society, the more likely they are to embrace those values. Conversely, if the primary associations that youths have are with delinquents, the greater the likelihood they will become delinquent.

The primary criticism of this theory is related to the vagueness of the term *association*. Sutherland and Cressey (1978) admitted that their differential association theory was not precise enough to undergo rigorous empirical testing; thus, the theory is difficult to prove or disprove. But differential association theory remains one of the most popular theories of delinquent and criminal behavior. It has worked its way into everyday thinking, as reflected by the familiar instruction of parents to their children. "We don't want you hanging out with that person, or group of people, because they are a bad influence on you."

Labeling Theory

The labeling perspective does not examine how or why people become delinquents and criminals, rather it concentrates on the effect of being labeled a delinquent or criminal. Labeling theorists attempt to uncover the processes that lead to who gets to decide what is deviant and criminal (the labelers) and how it is that certain behaviors come to be labeled criminal while others are legal. For example, why is tobacco legal when it kills over 400,000 Americans a year, and marijuana illegal when no deaths have ever been attributed to it? Somehow the tobacco smoker is not generally considered a deviant but the marijuana smoker is. The answer, of course, lies with economic-political factors. Thus, individuals are subjected to the demands of conventional behavior, and if they fail to embrace these cultural ideals, they risk being negatively labeled and stigmatized.

No one wants to acquire a label that they themselves consider to be an inaccurate assessment of their character. Everyone attempts to *negotiate* their *role-identity*. Generally, individuals have a stake, and want a say in, the outcome of the role-identity allocation process (Spencer 1987, 131). However, the allocation of labels is often determined by "outside" social control agents, and there are times when these attached, unwanted labels come to consume the identity of individuals. For example, a child who is truly interested in learning at school and repeatedly pesters the teacher might then be labeled by the teacher, and ultimately by the school, as a "troublemaker." In an attempt to restore and maintain cherished identities, individuals often engage in the use of *disclaimers* as a means of fighting unwanted identities and labels (Hewitt and Stokes 1975, 1). Similar to disclaimers are *accounts*. "An account is a linguistic device employed whenever an action is subjected to valuative inquiry. . . . By an account, then, we mean a statement made by a social actor to explain unanticipated or untoward behavior—whether that behavior is his own or that of others, and whether the proximate cause for the statement arises from the actor himself or from someone else" (Scott and Lyman 1968, 46). Accounts, then, like other techniques of neutralization, represent the efforts of labeled individuals to modify their image to the outside world. Scott and Lyman (1968, 47) identified two general types of accounts: *excuses* and *justifications*. Excuses are used when mitigating circumstances are involved with the behavior in question. Justifications are accounts in which an individual admits to some undesired behavior but denies the pejorative quality associated with the act in question.

A label having been attached to a person means that the person must now find a way to neutralize it. Individuals can no longer go about their daily business in the same manner prior to being labeled. As Fontana (1973, 179) explained, "labeling places the actor in circumstances which make it harder for him to continue the normal routines of everyday life and thus provoke him to 'abnormal' actions." Once labeled, the individual's self-identity may not change immediately, but the way that others see that individual may. "The degree to which youngsters are perceived as deviants may affect their treatment at home and at school. Parents may consider them a detrimental influence on younger brothers or sisters. Neighbors may tell their children to avoid the 'troublemaker.' Teachers may place them in classes reserved for students with behavior problems, minimizing their chances of obtaining higher education" (Siegel et al. 2003, 124).

One of the first to reveal the consequences of official labels of delinquency as potentially negative was Frederick Thrasher in his work on juvenile gangs. "A few years later, Frank Tannenbaum (1938) introduced the term 'dramatization of evil,' in which he argued that officially labeling someone as a delinquent can result in the person *becoming* the very thing he is described as *being*" (Shoemaker 2000, 196). Tannenbaum suggested that delinquents were not the result of a lack of adjustment to conventional society, but the fact that they had adjusted to a special group. "Tannenbaum (1938) wrote that a 'tag' becomes attached when a child is caught in delinquent activity. The tag identifies the child as a delinquent, may change the child's self-image, and causes people to react to the tag, not the child. Thus, his argument was that the process of tagging criminals or delinquents actually helps create delinquency and criminality" (Williams and McShane 1994, 133). From the labeling perspective, when an individual continually receives negative feedback from significant others and then begins to accept the negative label, a **self-fulfilling prophecy** has been created. When people take to heart the labels bestowed upon them and then act according to those labels, they have come to see themselves as others have labeled them. In his book *The Gang as an American Enterprise* (1993), Padilla described in great detail how negative school experiences negatively influenced the gang members he studied (the fictitiously named "Diamonds"). These negative experiences and labels contributed to their transformation into delinquency. Retelling the story of a gang member named Lobo, Padilla (1993, 73) described the effects of labeling:

> In Lobo's earliest school memories one of his teachers' name-calling routines led to his subsequent stigmatization and treatment as a troublemaker. He described how, after being labeled a troublemaker for arriving late to class on several occasions, every mischievous act that happened in school was blamed on him. "One time," he says, "we were in the hallway, walking to the bathroom, and someone threw a rock through a window, and all the kids said, 'Lobo did it'. . . I became the explanation for everything that went wrong in that school. So, I retaliated by fighting. And there were lots of fights."

Labeling is an important factor in the creation of a deviant identity. When conventional society shuns delinquents, the deviant group will accept them and teach them to reject their rejectors (similar to the neutralization technique of condemning the condemners). The deviant subculture teaches the newly arrived delinquents to show contempt toward those who labeled them. "These actions help solidify both the grip of deviant peers and the impact of the labels" (Siegel et al. 2003, 125). Edwin Lemert

(1951) developed the concepts of *primary* and *secondary* deviance to illustrate the transitional status of labeled delinquents. *Primary deviance* refers to individuals who are guilty of committing acts of deviance but whose actions are undetected, or unrecognized by others. With *secondary deviance*, the actor has been identified and labeled as a deviant. The process of moving from primary to secondary deviance is often complex, but the critical determinant is societal reaction and identification.

Howard Becker is a significant contributor to the labeling perspective. In his book *Outsiders: Studies in the Sociology of Deviance* (1963), Becker explained that "social groups create deviance by making rules whose infraction constitutes deviance, and by applying those rules to particular people and labeling them as outsiders" (p. 9). Becker adds that we should "view deviance as the product of a transaction that takes place between some social group and one who is viewed by the group as a rule-breaker" (1963, 10). Individuals are subjected to the rules created by social control agents, and if they fail to meet the demands of others, they risk being negatively labeled. "Once a rule has come into existence, it must be applied to particular people before the abstract class of outsiders is created. . . . This job ordinarily falls to the lot of professional enforcers who, by enforcing already existing rules, create the particular deviants society views as outsiders" (Becker 1963, 162–163). Individuals who accept, or believe in, the labels that are attached to them will begin to see themselves differently. They *are* different in the eyes of "mainstream" society. As these labeled people think of themselves more as deviant, they may view themselves as more "outside" than other outsiders. They may also view themselves as more outside than do those who labeled them in the first place (Becker 1963).

Becker was concerned with who the people are that are capable of affixing a label onto others and who and why certain people are singled out as "outsiders." Not surprisingly, he found that those who control power, control the labeling process. The rule makers can be thought of as "moral entrepreneurs" (Becker 1963). Moral entrepreneurs are people who try to correct the wrongs—as they see them—of a society. Becker believed that power people create rules for one simple reason: personal gain.

Increasingly in society it is law enforcement that is responsible for labeling criminals and delinquents. This is especially true for gangs. The decision whether or not to label a particular group of juveniles as a gang, or just a group of delinquents, directly impacts the manner in which the police and judicial system will deal with them. Labeling theorists examine the criminal justice system, especially the legislation that describes behaviors that will ultimately be labeled criminal or delinquent. Quinney's (1970) theory of the *social reality of crime* presents a clear look at crime and criminal behavior from a labeling perspective. He based his theory around six interrelated principles:

1. Crime is a definition of human conduct that is created by authorized agents in a politically organized society. This is the starting point of any theory on criminal behavior. Defining a particular behavior as criminal reveals the fact that crime is not inherent in behavior.

2. Criminal definitions describe behaviors that conflict with the interests of the segments of society that have the power to shape public policy. The people in a

position to define certain behaviors as criminal have the *power* to translate their interests into *public policy*. "In other words, those who have the ability to have their interests represented in public policy regulate the formulation of criminal definitions. . . . The interests of the power segments of society are reflected not only in the content of criminal definitions and the kinds of penal sanctions attached to them, but also in the *legal policies* stipulating how those who come to be defined as 'criminal' are to be handled (Quinney 1970, 17).

3. Criminal definitions are applied by the segments of society that have the power to shape the enforcement and administration of criminal law. As Quinney (1970, 18) explained, "the probability that criminal definitions will be applied varies according to the extent to which the behaviors of the powerless conflict with the interests of the power segments."

4. Behavior patterns are structured in segmentally organized society in relation to criminal definitions, and within this context persons engage in actions that have relative probabilities of being defined as criminal. "Once behavior patterns are established with some regularity within the respective segments of society, individuals are provided with a framework for developing *personal action patterns*" (Quinney 1970, 21).

5. Conceptions of crime are constructed and diffused in the segments of society by various means of communication. The most critical conceptions are those held by the power segments of society because these are the conceptions that are certain of becoming incorporated into the social reality of crime.

6. The social reality of crime is constructed by the formulation and application of criminal definitions, the developments of behavior patterns related to criminal definitions, and the construction of criminal conceptions. The first five propositions are collected into a composite. "The theory, accordingly, describes and explains phenomena that increase the probability of crime in society, resulting in the social reality of crime" (Quinney 1970, 23).

In his theory, Quinney attempted to show how a theory of crime can be consistent with some revisionist assumptions about man and society. His theory serves as the foundation of the labeling perspective, a theory with great validity and relevance today—especially in the study of gang behavior.

Marxist/Conflict/Radical Theory

Marxist, conflict, and radical theories are each unique but are linked by a general belief that the capitalistic economic structure is responsible for the formation of gangs. Social conflict theory, according to Siegel et al. (2003, 127), "finds that society is in a constant state of internal conflict, and different groups strive to impose their will on others. Those with money and power succeed in shaping the law to meet their needs and maintain their interests. Those adolescents whose behavior cannot conform to the needs of the power elite are defined as delinquents and criminals." Similarly, Shoemaker (2000, 214) wrote "the radical theory of criminality argues that criminal behavior is a result of the repressive efforts of the ruling class to control the subject class. The effects of this repression are not only higher instances of crime and delinquency among the subjugated class (the lower class, generally), but also greater tendencies among the middle and upper classes to label the actions of the lower class as criminal in order to facilitate their control." The works of Karl Marx had the greatest impact on the formation of conflict theory. Quinney and Wildeman (1991) used a Marxist perspective to explain delinquency, an expansion on Quinney's earlier work in *Class, State and Crime* (1977), where Quinney "linked crime and the reaction to crime to the modern capitalist political and economic system" (Shelden et al. 2001, 185).

It is interesting that the general **Marxist paradigm** used to explain crime and delinquency comes from the works of a man who never made law or crime primary topics in his theories. Like the theorists who developed the conflict perspective of social theory, Marxist criminologists must piece together Marx's ideas about conflict in society to formulate a theory on delinquency. Marx paid close attention to forces that gave rise to the capitalistic system; he was especially interested in the role of production and theorized that power was related to one's position in the economic structure. Marx believed that those who controlled the means of production (the bourgeoisie) could exercise their will and power over those who did not control the means of production (the workers, or proletariat). Marx viewed society as basically a two-class system consisting of the workers and of the owners of the means of production. One's relation to production dictated one's relative position in life. "Social classes, understood as conflicting groups arising out of the authority structure of imperatively coordinated associations, are in conflict with one another" (Delaney 2004, 75). Those in a position of authority will want to maintain their advantageous position—this is a matter of common sense. They maintain their power position through the creation of a rationally based political system. Marx believed that the economically powerful are in a position to dominate the political system and therefore are in a position to create laws to maintain their power position over the masses (the economically poor).

In contemporary societies of the West, the masses, of course, are found in the middle class. Nonetheless, the most powerless are still found at the lowest end of the economic strata, and not coincidentally this is where the greatest number of delinquents and gang members are found. Marx, as a humanist, truly hoped that all individuals could reach their full *human potential*, but because of *alienation* (caused by the unequal distribution of power in society) he believed all citizens of a capitalist society would never reach their full human potential. Marx viewed the capitalist society as unnatural and as the primary source of alienation. In this system, the wealthy stood to make great fortunes while the poor were likely to remain poor and powerless. Marx encouraged a workers' revolution that would overthrow the existing capitalist system, hoping to replace it with communism—a political and economic structure in which all people would somehow be treated equally and share equally in society's resources. This naive and utopian ideal, classless system of Marx, in which all people would be treated equally, has never been successfully achieved as he envisioned it, and yet, other utopian idealists have hoped to create such a system.

Contemporary Marxists might be tempted to label street gangs as revolutionary groups attempting to overthrow the existing social structure. Some see gangs as an example of a classless system where all members are created equal. However, even gangs have a structured hierarchy, and, just as in capitalist systems, members are not all treated equally. It should be pointed out that gang leaders do come from the same economic class as members and therefore there is little difference between the leader and the members of the rank and file. Gang leaders, who come from the rank and file, have achieved their position through merit and not some other form of power (e.g., inherited power found in monarchies) and are subject to immediate removal from their leadership position if they prove to be ineffective leaders. Additionally, the gang is a communist society in the sense that all the activities of the gang are done for the overall benefit of everyone in the gang. Their rebellion against the conventional rules of society can be likened to the proletariat revolution against capitalistic society. Joining a gang generally reduces the alienation that members feel in relation to the greater society through the familial association of the gang and also because gang members benefit directly from what they do. Thus, from a Marxist perspective, it could be argued that the gang is communistic, in the sense that everyone in the gang exists for the good of the gang and its members.

Conflict and radical theories are based on the idea that conflict and contradictions are constant forces in society. Conflict theorists "see consensus as a temporary state of affairs that will either return to conflict or will have to be maintained at great expense. It is the use of power to create and maintain an image of consensus, then, that represents the problems to be studied" (Williams and McShane 1994, 155). For conflict theorists, the most important variable to study is **power**—who has it, and how do they maintain it? Those in power will exercise both legitimate and illegitimate means of maintaining their advantageous position—they have a **vested interest** in doing so. On the other hand, the conflict perspective teaches that those without power will want some, and they will find some way of demonstrating what little power they have. This often entails participating in illegal and delinquent activities. Conflict theorists believe that laws are created and enforced because some people have a virtual monopoly on power while others are basically powerless (Quinney 1970).

> Because power can be equated with resources, then it seems evident that those who are higher up in the social class structure will be the more powerful members of society. Their influence in the making of social decisions, and their ability to impose values, will also be greater than those of the lower social classes. For conflict theorists, this explains the presence of a dominant middle-class value system in society. Similarly, the important statements of a society, its laws for example, are bound up in middle-class values. This is because, historically, the merchant class helped create the form of society we have today. We may now begin to ask whether the middle class has reached its peak of influence and some higher class is beginning to exert more control in society (Williams and McShane 1994, 158).

The **law** represents one of the most valuable resources that the powerful manipulate to maintain the **status quo**. The poor, on the other hand, have a vested interest in changing the law to better meet their needs and demands. According to social conflict theorists, those in power use the justice system to maintain their high status in society while keeping others subservient.

> Social conflict theorists view the law and the justice system as vehicles for controlling the have-not members of society; legal institutions help the powerful and rich to impose their standards of good behavior on the entire society. The law protects the property and physical safety of the haves from attack by the have-nots, and helps control the behavior of those who might otherwise threaten the status quo. The ruling elite draws the lower-middle class into this pattern of control, leading it to believe it has a stake in maintaining the status quo (Siegel et al. 2003, 127).

Conflict theorists believe the very fact that a disproportionate number of the poor are arrested for criminal activities and the minority poor claim to be victimized by the police is proof of the imbalance of power found in society. In short, conflict theory views delinquency as a normal consequence of the conditions created by the capitalist system's inherent inequality. From this perspective, the best way to eliminate delinquency is to find quality jobs for the disadvantaged.

Radical theories of delinquency propose that capitalism is the root cause of much criminal behavior, especially of crimes committed by the economically poor. Among the great variety of radical theorists are those who promote such extreme ideas as political anarchy (Tifft 1979). Two of the more prominent radical theorists are William Chambliss and Robert Seidman. Chambliss (1964) focused on the importance of labor, resources, and social control methods as the key ingredients used by capitalists to maintain their position of power. In their 1971 publication, *Law, Order and Power*, Chambliss and Seidman argued that the ruling class maintains its power by exercising control in two ways: through the creation of laws that are focused on controlling the behaviors of the poor, and by creating a "myth" that the law serves the interests of everyone.

Donald Shoemaker (2003, 215–216) described the basic assumptions of the radical approach to delinquency as follows:

1. Most behavior is the product of a struggle among the classes within a society, particularly between those who own the tools of production (the bourgeoisie) and those who do not (the proletariat).

2. The economic system of capitalism is primarily responsible for the class divisions within society.

3. The bourgeoisie, either directly or through its agents, such as the State, controls the proletariat, economically, institutionally, or legally.

4. Most official crime and delinquency is committed by the lower and the working classes as a form of accommodation to the restraints placed on them by the bourgeoisie.

For Marxist, conflict, and radical theorists, crime and delinquency are not the result of some individual pathology, or immediate environmental factors, but are instead the result of an economic system that, by its very design, will leave some people behind in a disadvantaged situation in the pursuit of the American dream.

SUMMARY

In this chapter, a number of major theories of crime and delinquency were discussed and applied to gangs in an attempt to understand why they exist. The theories included biological and psychological explanations and the traditional sociological theories: social disorganization (Chicago School), anomie/strain, subculture/social bond, social learning/differential learning, labeling, and Marxist. Each of these approaches offers great insights in the study of gang behavior. Researchers, professors, and students all have their personal preferences among the various theories, but the fact remains that there are a lot of reasons why certain adolescents join a gang; consequently, every theory is eventually applicable.

CHAPTER **FOUR**

Socioeconomic Explanations of Gangs

The theoretical analyses presented in Chapter 3 provided a variety of explanations as to why someone might join a gang. Many times, however, the reasons someone chooses to join a gang come down to simple socioeconomic factors. Furthermore, many juveniles are attracted to street gangs because they find the gangbanger lifestyle so exciting that they experience a "rush." An analysis of socioeconomic explanations of why there are gangs can be quite beneficial to this study.

TRADITIONAL SOCIOECONOMIC FACTORS

Gang researchers and social policymakers have identified and discussed a number of traditional socioeconomic factors that impact on an individual's decision to join a gang. These factors are the shifting labor market, the development of an underclass (a nontraditional explanation, as the term *underclass* is a relatively new concept, but the conditions that led to the development of an underclass have traditional roots), poverty and the feminization of poverty, the breakdown of the nuclear family, lack of a quality education, and the gang's offering of acceptance, protection, and survival.

The Shifting Labor Market

The prime motivator for nearly all actions is security, and, despite those who argue otherwise, security is best accomplished through economic means—money. Although this statement may seem cynical, it is money that allows someone to live in a neighborhood that is relatively free from the daily onslaughts of violence, murder, and mayhem. Money may not "be everything," but it is a very important "something." Having a good job is the best way of making money. A good job provides workers with the money needed to take care of themselves and their families. When Bill Clinton ran for the presidency in his first term, he popularized the expression "It's the economy stupid"—meaning what the voters cared about the most was the economy. The economy is all about jobs. Political and social extremist Karl Marx, an economic determinist, believed that all of social life revolved around matters related to economics. For gangs, economics is also a critical element. A team of university-affiliated medical researchers found that "of all the factors contributing to gangs and their epidemic of violence in Los Angeles, none is more significant than the staggering rates of unemployment in their communities. . . . The researchers found that employment and per capital income were more closely associated with the city's gang homicide rate than a variety of other social, economic or other demographic factors including age, race, education or the proportion of single-family households" (Krikorian 1997, B1). The researchers suggested that the best hope of curbing gang carnage rested in community-based economic programs that would reduce the conditions that give rise to gangs and their violence.

Clearly, there are other important aspects of life, including love, family, personal security, and happiness, but most of these pursuits come at a cost. As the psychologist Abraham Maslow (1951) explained, there exists a *hierarchy of needs*, which consists of the five basic needs that all humans have and try to fulfill:

1. **Physiological/biological**—The basic survival needs, such as food and shelter, which should be met by the child's parents and family from birth until adulthood.

2. **Safety and security**—Refers to stability, protection, freedom from fear, found in a structured family environment.

3. **Love and belongingness**—Everyone wants to feel as though they belong to a group or family, and especially to have someone special to share in a loving relationship.

4. **Self-esteem**—Feeling good about oneself, self-respect, confidence, a positive reputation.

5. **Self-actualization**—The stage where one has found peace within oneself, of reaching one's full human potential. One accepts oneself and is relatively independent.

According to Maslow, if the first three needs are met by the family, the adolescent has a good chance of attaining the next two levels. When these needs are not fulfilled by the family, the youth will seek out other groups to provide them. In many cases, youths seek out gangs for these economically driven needs. For gang members, having **respect** is perhaps the most critical need they possess. Any perceived violation of this is often met with extreme prejudice. Being disrespected is one thing that gang members will not tolerate. When a gang member is "dissed," he will fight back to maintain his reputation. (*Note*: The importance of respect will be discussed in greater detail in Chapter 5.) Self-actualization can only be reached when the first four needs have been satisfied. Few people reach this level, and for gang members, the likelihood of ever reaching their full human potential is very slim. The constant struggle for economic survival generally means that any chance of self-actualization, according to Maslow's description of the hierarchy of needs, is slim to none.

In simplest terms, economics is about jobs. Traditionally, immigrants, minorities, and poorly educated persons could find jobs in factories. Unfortunately, U.S. manufacturing has shifted to foreign countries, eliminating job opportunities for millions of people. Capitalists, seeking to maximize their profits, often move their industries to foreign countries to get cheap labor, which allows for a higher profit margin. According to a 2002 Census Bureau report, the number of people employed in the manufacturing industry dropped by almost 5%, or 830,000, to under 17.1 million in the year 2002 (*Syracuse Post-Standard*, 2003). There were also slight decreases in the retail and warehousing industries. These are jobs that potentially could have employed youths, who, instead, turned to gangs rather than seek conventional employment. Furthermore, most Western societies have reached the last stage of the Industrial Revolution, resulting in the elimination of many factory jobs. Despite the claims made by President Bush (2004) during the annual State of the Union Address that the "economy is strong, and growing stronger," statistics tell another story. According to the Annenberg Political Fact Check, a nonpartisan, nonprofit "consumer advocate" for voters, total employment in January 2004 was 2.3 million below where it stood in January 2001 when Bush first took office.

The shifting labor market now provides more opportunities in the service economy, but many of these jobs often require relatively high levels of education. This economic reality has caused many lower-class persons to lose out on opportunities for financial success, especially the poorly educated. From this viewpoint, the capitalist system disadvantages the lower classes, creating inequality, and results in the development of an **underclass**.

The Underclass

The changing nature of America's occupational opportunity structure has dramatically changed many urban areas. The loss of significant numbers of manufacturing jobs has left many inner-city persons without gainful employment opportunities. When people are unemployed, their financial stability is greatly compromised. Anyone who remains unemployed for an extended period of time generally ends up poor. Many of the nation's poor live in the core of America's cities. The term *underclass* (popularized by William Wilson in his 1987 book *The Truly Disadvantaged*) generally refers to the extremely poor, who live in neighborhoods, or census tracts, where the poverty rate exceeds 40%. Underclass members are generally poorly educated, "unskilled" in terms of the economic market, are likely to have been in the poverty category for generations, are dependent on the welfare system, and appear to have little chance to break out of the cycle of poverty (Wilson 1987, 1996). *Underclass* is not meant to refer to a racial or ethnic group, but because the vast majority of the underclass are racial minorities, some oppose the use of the term. "This term is used to, in effect, stigmatize those who fall within the general category of the 'underclass'—the homeless, those who live in 'the projects,' addicts, young poor women with babies, and of course gang members. Needless to say, the term is often used interchangeably with racial minorities" (Shelden et al. 2001, 193).

It was during the 1970s that the shift in the labor market began to have a significant negative effect on American blacks. Blacks were heavily represented in manufacturing, and the decline in production in such sectors as automobile, rubber, and steel hurt urban African-Americans profoundly. Blacks were also adversely affected by the mechanization of Southern agriculture and the large number of baby-boomers and white women who entered the labor market in the 1970s. These socioeconomic factors contributed greatly to adding large number of blacks to the underclass. Thus, Wilson argued, public policies, such as race-based programs and policies, were doomed to fail because they ignored the core economic explanation of poverty, delinquency, and gang membership—the elimination of industry-based jobs. Wilson's use of the term *underclass* was not racist; instead, it was a condemnation of government policies that disadvantaged blacks more than any other group of people. African-Americans are overrepresented in the underclass, but generally, they are so because of social and economic forces that they cannot control. Criticism of the term might be a little more appropriate if it were aimed at the person who first coined the term in 1982: Ken Auletta, a writer for *The New Yorker*. Auletta used the word broadly to include individuals with "behavioral and income deficiencies" (Papadimitriou 1998).

The inner cities have suffered the most from the shifting labor market. When industries move (capital flight), they take with them job opportunities and tax revenue necessary to maintain the areas in which they had resided. When economic opportunities disappear, those who can afford to move will also abandon the deprived area ("white" flight—the exodus of middle- and upper-class people, generally white). The consequences of these developments are lower tax revenue and, eventually, impoverished neighborhoods that lack basic civil services, political power, and the representation needed to help the community. The lack of political power is exemplified in a number of ways, including the inability of poorer communities to stop civic projects that rip them apart. The location and building of freeways clearly demonstrate whether or not a community has political power. In *Going Down to the Barrio*, Moore (1991) explained how freeways ripped apart Mexican-American neighborhoods in Los Angeles. Robert Powell, in *We Own This Game* (2003), described how expressways dissected Overtown, a poor section in Miami and a vibrant neighborhood once considered the Harlem of the South.

Capital flight and white flight are the two most critical forces leading to the formation of an underclass. "The emergence of this underclass, particularly in the Eastern and Midwestern cities of the United States referred to as the 'rust belt,' is related to a drastic decline in employment opportunities in the large cities, primarily through the loss of the types of factory jobs that provided employment for the unskilled, poorly educated children of the immigrants who came to these cities at the height of the industrial revolution" (Kratcoski and Kratcoski 1996, 106). Inner-city youths recognize the fact that there are few legitimate job opportunities. They are aware of the poverty that surrounds them, and the lure of gangs that calls out to them is often tough to resist. Joining a gang is often viewed as the *only* opportunity to get ahead, especially for those from the underclass. As Kratcoski and Kratcoski (1996, 106) argued, "those from the underclass, having few options or opportunities, are more likely to remain with the gang structure. In these families, younger brothers follow older ones into the gang, and remain with the gang after they have reached adulthood." The hopelessness associated with the underclass not only implies that these people will never reach self-actualization; they may also never find economic stability. The gang appears as an attractive alternative.

The underclass does not consist of just blacks. Puerto Ricans, especially those in the South Bronx, also face the challenge of the lack of quality job opportunities. Among the larger Hispanic groups, statistics show that Puerto Ricans are far more disadvantaged than Mexican-Americans or Cuban-Americans. Puerto Ricans are more likely to be afflicted by the secondary effects of poverty, such as family breakups and not trying to find employment, which work to ensure that poverty will continue beyond one generation (Lemann 1991). In New York City, the black median family income is substantially higher than the Puerto Rican rate, the black homeownership rate is more than double the Puerto Rican rate, Puerto Rican families are more than twice as likely as black families to be on welfare and are about 50% more likely to be poor (Lemann 1991). "The question of why poverty is so widespread, and so persistent, among Puerto Ricans is an urgent one, not only for its own sake but also because the answer to it might prove to be a key to understanding the broader problem of the urban underclass" (Lemann 1991, 3). Lemann suggested that the reason Puerto Ricans in New York were so disproportionately poor was the result of two economic factors (unemployment and welfare) and cultural factors (e.g., neighborhood ambience and ethnic history). On the mainland, Puerto Ricans still face a great deal of prejudice, which partially contributes to their being shut out from quality job opportunities, which ensures that they live in poor neighborhoods and instills a defeatist attitude among many Puerto Ricans. In short, persistent poverty is more common among Puerto Ricans than among blacks. Disenchanted Puerto Rican youths are increasingly turning to gangs as a means of gaining economic salvation.

It is interesting to note that the United States is not the only country to apply the term *underclass* to a group of statistically poor people. In Australia, social researchers have used the term *rural underclass* to describe rural Victoria. Bureau of Statistics data revealed that not a single full-time job had been created in rural Victoria in 13 years (1990–2003), leaving it a land of part-time work despite a decade of solid economic growth in Australia as a whole. The lack of full-time jobs has led to the formation of a rural underclass with countless people in country towns stuck in low-income jobs or unemployed altogether, leaving them caught in a poverty trap—they can't afford to move and they can't afford to stay. The problem is not unique to rural Victoria, as throughout Australia almost two-thirds of all jobs created since 1990 have been part-time (*The Age* 2003). Industrial leaders argue that it is not viable to set up businesses in country towns. It is up to the government to provide legitimate economic opportunities for these citizens to meet their survival needs. Otherwise, Australia may some day have their own gang problem.

Poverty and the Feminization of Poverty

Some people are tempted to blame the capitalistic system for **poverty**. They claim that the capitalistic system guarantees that there will always be some people at the top and some people at the bottom of the economic hierarchy. Although it is true that there are poor people in countries with capitalism, the reality is capitalism did not create poverty; poverty was inherited from past social systems that created the class distinctions of the "haves" and the "have-nots." Even today, the poorest nations in the world are those without capitalism. According to the World Bank, there are over 1 billion people in the world who live in constant poverty. People who live in poverty are personally affected by almost every problem having to do with basic human needs—striving for self-actualization is the furthest thing from the minds of people who suffer in poverty. Worldwide, people living in poverty are generally malnourished; they are refugees, homeless, or have inadequate shelter; they have no health care; their homes and neighborhoods have little or no sanitation or clean water supplies; they are usually illiterate and have no access to education or educational opportunities; they have no energy supplies; they are often unemployed or underemployed; and because they are generally powerless, they have the least amount of human rights. Additionally, many of the poor people around the world face severe environmental problems such as deforestation, desertification, soil erosion, and inadequate drinking water.

In the United States, the prosperous middle class, whose members are economically secure, is the result of capitalism. Coupled with democracy, capitalism guarantees the rights of all individuals so that they may pursue their own economic freedom. In fact, there are very few people (e.g., the mentally retarded, crippled, and orphans) in capitalistic societies who are truly unable to help themselves find economic salvation. Capitalism, then, provides plenty of opportunities for people who are properly motivated to get ahead. Convincing testimony to this is the fact that many of the really "poor" immigrants (most of whom could not speak a word of English) who arrived in the late nineteenth century and early twentieth century in America are now among America's elites. Many recent immigrants have had the same positive experience. The "rags to riches" story usually takes a few generations; but for those who are willing to work hard, gain an education, and embrace cultural norms, the future is indeed very bright for those lucky enough to have all the advantages that capitalism offers. Unfortunately, there are large numbers of Americans who have not attained economic security for a variety of reasons. Many of these people end up poor, and poverty is often correlated with gang involvement.

Historically, gangs have developed in economically depressed neighborhoods. Poorer neighborhoods are characterized by high rates of unemployment, high population density, and transients. Growing up in poverty leads many youths (and adults) to seek unconventional means of making money. Schools in economically depressed areas generally experience higher crime and drug problems.

> Poverty in a school's surrounding area influences the social characteristics of students. They may lack the readiness and interest to learn when compared with students from more affluent neighborhoods. Poor areas may find it difficult to hire and retain the most qualified faculty and/or provide students with the most up-to-date equipment and books. Because poor communities have lower tax bases, they are handcuffed when they want to provide remedial programs for students with learning issues, or conversely, enrichment programs for the gifted. Finally, parents and other students have neither the time nor resources to become involved in school activities or participate in governance. These factors may eventually undermine school climate and destabilize the educational environment, which leads to school crime and disorder (Siegel et al. 2003, 283).

The lack of job opportunities not only contributes to the formation of an underclass, it helps to create conditions of poverty. Conditions of poverty, in turn, cause increasing harm to youths who find themselves caught in a continuous downward spiral. Poverty causes human suffering and stunts human potential. It is a major cause of social unrest, crime, and even revolution. A recent study at the University of Virginia has shown that poverty can lower a child's IQ score a number of points. Impoverished children struggle to reach their full intellectual potential; inadequate nutrition during early life can also stunt a child's potential for learning. The findings of the IQ and nutrition studies reveal the importance of environment over genes for mental development (Kotulak 2003).

According to the U.S. Census Bureau, the official poverty rate in 2002 was 12.1%, up from 11.7% in 2001. In 2002, people below the official poverty thresholds numbered 34.6 million, a figure 1.7 million higher than the 32.9 million in poverty in 2001. At 16.7%, the poverty rate for children did not change between 2001 and 2002, but the number of children in poverty increased to 12.1 million in 2002, up from 11.7 million in 2001 (U.S. Census Bureau 2003). In 2002, 7.2 million families (9.6%) were in poverty, up from 6.8 million (9.2%) in 2001. Because racial and ethnic categories were redefined in 2002 (and more and more people are refusing to identify their race on census forms), the Census Bureau does not have a single comparison of poverty rates by race between 2001 and 2002 that meets all the definition requirements. However, it remains statistically clear that non-Hispanic whites and Asians have lower rates of poverty than do blacks and Hispanics. Interestingly, the poverty rate remained the same in the years 2001 and 2002 in the central cities and nearby metropolitan areas, whereas the number in poverty and the poverty rate for people living in the suburbs rose from 12.1 million and 8.2% in 2001 to 13.3 million and 8.9% in 2002 (U.S. Census Bureau 2003).

Further analysis of poverty statistics is quite enlightening. The federal poverty level for a family of four is currently $18,400. However, it takes double the income considered "poverty" level for most families to provide their children with adequate and basic necessities, such as food, stable housing, and health care. The families that live in the "gray" area, between poverty and the realistic minimum income necessary to function, face material hardships and financial pressures. Families with income in this gray area make "too much" money to qualify for public benefits but "too little" to provide all the "necessities" of family life. Thus, in addition to the 12.1 million children living in poverty in the United States, it is estimated that there are another 27 million children living in low-income families. This figure represents nearly 40% of all American children. So, as the statistics reveal, there are millions of poor children in the United States. However, it is also obvious that the greatest percentage of poor people are not gang members; consequently, poverty alone does not lead an individual to gangs.

A large number of economically poor youths, especially gang members, come from single-parent families, usually headed by a female. The dramatic increase in female-headed, single-parent families is often cited as a major reason why young malcs seek out gangs. These boys are looking for the male presence that is lacking in their lives. African-American families are far more likely to be headed by a female than are white families, and in extreme poverty areas, only around 15% of African-Americans are married. As a result, the majority of black children in inner-city urban areas are raised by a single female, who is generally poor. Of all the poor families in the nation, almost half are headed by a female (Shelden et al. 2001, 204). According to the U.S. Census Bureau (2003), the number of female householder families with no husband present in poverty increased to 3.6 million in 2002 from 3.5 million in 2001. The poverty rate for these families remained the same as in 2001, at 26.5%.

Women disproportionately are found to have lower-paying jobs than men. This fact is underscored by the reality that, worldwide, women earn on average slightly more than 50 cents for every dollar that men earn. The United Nations Development

Fund for Women reports that women are the poorest of the world's poor, representing 70% of the 1.3 billion people who live in absolute poverty. They also estimate that nearly 900 million women in the world earn less than 1 dollar a day. Not surprisingly, females are much better off socially and economically in societies of the West. In the United States, women earn 76 cents for every dollar that a man earns. As more and more women enter the workforce, especially in full-time jobs, this average pay differential will continue to shrink—at least in capitalistic societies such as the United States. Globalization and capitalism have greatly impacted women throughout the world; where these two socioeconomic forces are present, the rights and privileges of women have increased dramatically. However, in many nations today women still do not have property and inheritance rights, which all but guarantees their lower economic-class standing. In many of these nations, political and religious ideas of what constitutes a woman's "place in society" overpower economic forces. Thus, any effort to improve the lives of women throughout the world will have to move beyond economic considerations and concentrate on cultural ones instead. In other words, it is culture that needs to be changed, as even capitalism is not powerful enough to overcome thousands of years of repressive ideology. The United States, however, is a different story. Democratic ideals are overpowering the sexist ideologies of the past; even so, American women are disproportionately more likely to be poor than American men.

Many single-parent poor women who are conscientiously trying to put food on the table for their children will work two or more jobs (most likely, low-paying and part-time jobs). This is highly commendable behavior. Unfortunately, the result of single-parent women spending many hours away from home working is that their children have many unsupervised hours of time at their disposal. Furthermore, because the jobs these women are working at are low paying, they still end up "poor." Since women are more likely to be poor than men, sociologists generally use the term *the feminization of poverty* to describe the huge number of women living in poverty, most of whom are single mothers or heads of families. "Unlike men, who often can escape poverty by getting a job, women tend to remain poor even when they are employed. Why? Because in the gender-segregated labor market, women are much more likely to work in low-paid, low-status jobs" (Thio 2003, 185–186). The term *feminization of poverty* was popularized by Diana Pearce in her 1978 article "The Feminization of Poverty: Women, Work, and Welfare." In this article, Pearce cited data to support her claim that almost two-thirds of the poor over the age of 16 were women entering the labor force between 1950 and the mid-1970s. She argued that the blame for this feminization of poverty belonged to the government because it did not find a way to support divorced and single women.

Women are about 50% more likely to be poor than men. Single parenthood has affected women's poverty rates far more dramatically than it has men's. Among the problems facing single-parent women living in poverty are they often have bad credit, or no credit of their own established, their own health care and nutritional needs become secondary to their children's, and they lack sufficient access to education and support services. There are many possible explanations as to why women are more likely to be poor than men. Pearce (1978) argued that one of the consequences of women's fight for independence from men has led to their pauperization and dependence on welfare. Clearly, a major contributor to the rise of single-parent families is the dramatic increase in the number of divorces. Thus, the various changes in family structure (especially the large number of children born out of wedlock) have contributed to the feminization of poverty. The poorest of the poor females come from generations of poverty, and when these single women have children they almost guarantee themselves a life of poverty—especially if they fail to receive a quality education or job training. Many of these poor women do not have families to support them and are left with one primary option, government support. Putting off having children until they have a quality job would solve this problem, but since unplanned pregnancies are fairly common, abortion is often used as a method of birth control. However, the increased feminization of poverty coincides closely to the period when abortion became increasingly legalized. Some have argued that the availability of abortion should help reverse this trend, because job loss due to childbirth would be avoided, as would the burdens of child care which so clearly contribute to the impoverishment of women. "Abortion advocates claim that the right to abort unplanned pregnancies empowers women. They view unplanned children as the cause of lost education and career opportunities. Abortion, they claim, enables women to control their lives, pursue their dreams, and ultimately improve their socioeconomic status" (Reardon 1993). Studies have shown that aborting unplanned children has not increased the socioeconomic status of women (Strahan 1991). According to research conducted by Thomas Strahan (1991), women who have abortions are more likely to subsequently require welfare assistance, and the odds of going on welfare increase with each subsequent abortion. When first abortions are followed by adequate family planning counseling and services, the woman is more likely to practice effective contraception in the future. Those who do not receive adequate counseling and assistance risk repeat abortions. Furthermore, women who have repeat abortions tend to have an increasing number of health problems and greater personality disintegration, which increase the likelihood of their needing public assistance. Multiple abortions are particularly problematic. Various studies have shown a weakening of social bonds (especially with male partners) with multiple abortions, and communications with others tend to break down (Bracken and Kasl 1975). This controversial subject matter is one that demands further research.

The effects on children being raised in a single-parent, inner-city environment are often devastating, with abuse and neglect often the end result. Consequently, many youths seek out the "comfort" of a gang.

Breakdown of the Nuclear Family

As the family structure changes (same-sex partners raising children, commuter marriages, childless families, etc.) and growing acceptance for varied families is becoming commonplace, it may seem politically incorrect to point out that the *breakdown of the nuclear family* is still a prime factor related to delinquency. "There is a long-standing belief among many juvenile justice practitioners and criminologists that broken homes are conducive to the development of a pattern of delinquent behavior. . . . It is logical to conclude that broken homes can contribute to delinquency for they can result in economic hardships, the loss of some affection, the loss of proper role models necessary for socialization, and fewer barriers to the development of friendships with delinquents"

(Trojanowicz et al. 2001, 141). Despite empirical evidence that links broken families to delinquency, there are those who still fail to admit this correlation exists. Based on a research review of this area, the safest conclusion is that single-parent families do not cause delinquency, but they are a risk factor.

Perhaps a further analysis of the family function and its relationship to delinquency is more fruitful. Other family problems are just as likely to be risk factors for youths becoming delinquent. "Research efforts have consistently supported the relationship between family conflict, hostility, and delinquency. Adolescents who are incarcerated report growing up in dysfunctional homes. Parents of beyond-control youngsters have been found to display high levels of hostile detachment" (Siegel et al. 2001, 198). Emotional deprivation as the result of a lack of parental love is also a cause of delinquency. "Rejected or neglected children who do not find love and affection, as well as support and supervision, at home, often resort to groups outside the family; frequently these groups are of a deviant nature. The hostile or rejecting parent is usually not concerned about the youngster's emotional welfare or about providing the necessary support and guidance" (Trojanowicz et al. 2001, 143). Research has shown that a relationship exists between parental rejection and aggressive delinquent behavior. The lack of consistent and adequate discipline is another indicator of delinquent behavior.

Youths who come from "broken" homes or dysfunctional homes are more likely to become delinquents, whereas children who are raised in healthy, intact homes are less likely to become delinquent. "Some studies have found female delinquency to be more deeply influenced by broken homes than males. Psychological disruption of the family through alcoholism, mental illness, emotional disturbance of parents, or home atmospheres characterized by internal conflict and constant tension has been identified as factors in delinquency production. Conversely, a number of studies have shown that a happy and well-adjusted family life is related to lack of delinquency and successful adjustment to society" (Kratcoski and Kratcoski 1996, 136). In short, the family, as the primary agent of socialization, continues to have a significant influence on whether the youth will, or will not, become a delinquent. There is not a direct cause-and-effect relationship between the breakdown of the nuclear family and delinquency, but it is an important indicator.

The Role of Education

Youths who do not perform well in school, or do not like school, are more likely to be involved in delinquent behavior. Youths who are seriously delinquent report that their school experiences were negative ones. Who is to blame for this? Ideally, schools are institutions where youths learn about society's rules and earn an education. Education is commonly viewed as the most effective way of achieving economic and social advancement in the United States. There is a strong correlation between the level of education one attains and the amount of money one earns. As a result, the best way to get out of poverty is through proper education (Althaus 1995). European immigrants, beginning with the Irish, Italians, and Poles, all learned this valuable lesson. But today many minority members have failed to embrace education as a means of getting ahead. This is especially true with Hispanics, who traditionally have not valued higher education.

Changing the cultural habits of people and getting them to accept the value of education is an important goal of sociologists and criminologists who conduct research on delinquency and gangs and their relationship to the school experience.

Unfortunately, some school environments are not very conducive to learning. In some cases, the teachers and/or administrators are incompetent and guilty of labeling certain children as no good (or other negative labels). In many more cases, the students who come to school do not come properly prepared to learn. Parents are responsible for the child's readiness and preparation to perform and behave properly in the classroom. Especially important is language skills. Immigrant children often perform poorly in the schools because of their lack of adequate English language skills. When English is not spoken in the home, immigrant schoolchildren will have an even more difficult time mastering the materials necessary to earn good grades in school. If children have not been properly socialized to accept education as a vital aspect of their future, even the best teachers will not be able to motivate them. If the youth is struggling in the classroom, it is hard to persuade him or her to continue education in the face of continuing poverty. Parents, especially single parents and agricultural parents, may encourage their child to skip school in order to work and help support the family. This negative cultural ideology has been associated with Hispanics in particular. Yablonsky's research on Los Angeles high school students revealed that approximately 39% of Chicanos drop out of high school, and that number significantly increases for youths who belong to Chicano gangs (Yablonsky 1997). The inference is that the gang has a greater attraction for certain youths than the school environment. Many gang members report that the schools were like a form of "incarceration."

Disenchanted with school, youths may become truants, the first step on the path to delinquency. When youths are out of school during scheduled hours, they find and associate with other deviants. For many, the gang is now just one step away. Parents, teachers, school administrators, and community organizations all need to come together with some effective plan for keeping children in school and fostering an environment conducive to learning for all youths.

Acceptance, Protection, and Survival

In simple terms, many youths turn to the gang for **acceptance**. Youths who experience alienation and a sense of powerlessness from their environment find acceptance in the gang. Mexican-Americans develop, in the words of Diego Vigil, a "cholo style," composed of ways of "walking, talking, dressing, overall demeanor . . . nicknames, graffiti, tattoos, dancing, car culture, and music styles" (Vigil 1997, 5). Gangs present an outlet for youths whose culture has been suppressed in the school and discriminated against by society. Gang members form their own subculture, including a style of dress, mannerisms, and communication, sometimes called *slanging*. The simple activity of "hanging out"—something that gang members do more than anything else—provides physical evidence of their existence and establishes turf. As gang expert Irving Spergel summarizes, "gangs often form out of need for acceptance in a culture that tends to shun poor, first-generation Americans" (Duffy 1996, A16). Spergel's own research on Chicago gangs and his analysis of the growing presence of the Latin Kings in Syracuse led him to believe that Latino gangs in particular form out of a need for acceptance, but that this is no different from what Irish youth did a century-and-a-half ago.

In many high-density urban areas throughout the United States, a youth's motive for joining a gang can be described in one word: **survival**. Existing rival gangs attempt to recruit new members on a regular basis. Consequently, even when a youth tries to remain neutral and stay out of the gang life, he (or she) may be perceived as a member of a rival gang because he is not a member of "your" gang. In other words, if he's not one of ours, he must be one of theirs. To survive on the streets, one generally needs **protection**. Within the gang, youths believe they are safe from attacks by other gang members or conventional youths who are bullying them. Therefore, the threat of being beaten or shot by rival gangs is often an important reason youths join gangs. The gang becomes a substitute family that offers not only acceptance but also protection and the opportunity to survive in a neighborhood filled with dangerous obstacles.

KICKS AND THRILLS

Delinquency is not without its appeal. Youths often feel as though everyone is telling them what to do and how to do it. A desire to violate norms crosses the minds of most people, at least from time to time. The allure of the deviant culture comes from many sources. Some youths are tempted by the drug and alcohol subculture. Media-induced glamorization of delinquency and gang behavior attracts other youths. Firearms in the hands of those once abused or beaten are a source of comfort. And at the simplest level of all, some people simply find delinquency and gang behavior exciting, fun, and thrilling.

Drug and Alcohol Use

Drugs and alcohol have a fascinating appeal to most adolescents. Sneaking a drink while underaged is far more exciting than having a drink when you are in your forties. Consuming the forbidden drink gives youths a thrill and a sense of excitement because they feel that they are getting away with something. If the first-time experience of drinking is pleasurable, youths are likely to continue the behavior. According to research, many youths are experimenting with drugs and alcohol.

> The use of drugs and alcohol by high school students has been documented by a number of self-reported-use research studies. On the basis of their findings, it appears that the vast majority of adolescents experiment with various kinds of illegal substances (alcohol, marijuana, and other drugs) at some time during their growing-up years. Self-reports by high school seniors showed that 87 percent of the students in a nationwide survey had used alcohol at least once, and more than 50 percent had used it within the last 30 days (Kratcoski and Kratcoski 1996, 171).

Most teenagers will try alcohol and a slightly smaller percentage will try some sort of illegal drug. However, it should be clear that the number of adolescents who go on to become serious delinquents, or gang members, is small. Those youths who find drinking and taking drugs exciting and continue their use are at the greatest risk of becoming delinquents. The problem lies with the fact that "the consumption of alcohol and drugs may encourage or facilitate criminal behavior, especially violence and aggression, because these substances are known to lower inhibitions, impair judgment, and increase recklessness and risk-taking behavior" (Curran and Renzetti 1994, 122). Heavy drug users with no source of income to support their habits often resort to crime (e.g., theft, robbery). The type of drug used will dictate behavior which, at times, may be violent (e.g., especially under the influence of PCP). In the past, gang members' association with drugs was generally restricted to consumption. But in the past couple of decades, street gangs have begun to take control of drug sales on the street. It is estimated that "approximately 42 percent of youth gangs were involved in the street sale of drugs for the purpose of financial gain. The extent of their involvement was associated with population size: Large cities had the greatest percentage of youth gangs involved in drug sales (49 percent)" (Trojanowicz et al. 2001, 198). The most common drugs sold by gangs are crack cocaine, marijuana, powder cocaine, methamphetamine, and heroin. (*Note*: In this chapter, the focus is on drug consumption; see Chapter 8 for an analysis of the criminality of gangs and drugs.)

Getting high and being drunk are ways that delinquents cope with their unhappiness in conventional society. They find drinking and taking drugs enjoyable alternatives to their unpleasant realities.

Firearms

Possessing a **firearm** and aiming it at someone represents power. This is true not only for military personnel, law enforcement officers, and hunters; it is true for gangbangers as well. For gangsters, having a gun is fun. It gives them automatic respect because they know people will do almost anything that is asked of them when there is a gun pointed at their head. Gangbangers find this form of intimidation very exhilarating. Gang members have been known to laugh at their victims while watching them shake in terror. Firearms are often used during the commission of a crime and are regularly used in disputes with rivals. Relaxed regulations of gun sales in this country make it very easy for gang members to find guns. "The easy availability of guns has contributed to a stunning upsurge in killings by teenagers and young adults. Since 1985, the homicide rate has declined among older adults but has soared among young people. . . . Most of these killings take place in large cities' poor neighborhoods, where many teenagers carry guns, a relatively new phenomenon" (Thio 2003, 144). Although the number of juvenile murder victims decreased from the peak year of 1993, when there were 2,900 juvenile deaths, to 1,300 in 2000, about half of these deaths were from firearms.

There is a great debate in the United States over the availability of firearms and whether harsher restrictions should be placed on the purchase and possession of firearms. Organizations such as the National Rifle Association (NRA) cite the U.S. Constitution and its justification of citizens' right to bear arms. Amendment II (ratified December 15, 1791) states, "A well regulated Militia, being necessary to the security of a free State, the right of the people to keep and bear Arms, shall not be infringed." (Readers can decide for themselves whether to emphasize "a well-regulated militia" or "the right of the people to bear arms.") Other people (e.g., social workers, law enforcement groups) believe that there should be stricter gun laws. In some states, it is relatively difficult to obtain a gun legally; in other states, people can legally carry guns with them in their automobiles or on their persons. There should be little wonder why there is a gun problem in the United States. On the one hand, various policies and laws have been passed to intervene in gun-related violence, sources of illegal guns have been increasingly interrupted, penalties have been increased for illegal possession and carrying of guns, and people who supply guns to youths at risk for violence (e.g., probationers, gang members, and drug traffickers) are being prosecuted more aggressively (Champion 2004, 71). The hypocrisy of all this is the fact that the United States is the world's largest supplier of weapons, selling more than $7 billion worth in 1999 (Raum 1999). Despite this huge figure, it is actually far below the $21.5 billion in U.S. arms sales in 1993. The highest number of juvenile deaths in the United States also occurred in 1993.

A popular saying during the early 1990s was that "guns don't kill people, people do." I suggest an alternative: "people with guns kill." Firearms themselves do not kill or cause violence; instead, they are the result of the poor judgment of people with guns. "While firearm availability is not per se a cause of violence, it is certainly a facilitating factor: a petty argument can escalate into a fatal encounter if one party or the other has a handgun. It may not be a coincidence that the United States, which has a huge surplus of guns and in which most firearms (80 percent) used in crimes are stolen or obtained through illegal or unregulated transactions, also has one of the world's highest violence rates" (Siegel 1995, 297).

Firearms are a source of power that both provides the possessor a great sense of being in control and often leads to someone being hurt, or killed. (*Note*: Chapter 9 includes a discussion on weapons-related homicide; the discussion here is limited to the idea of the "thrill" people get from owning a gun and using it as a means of intimidation.)

The Mass Media

Another influence on the behaviors of juveniles is the **mass media**, by which is generally meant television, radio, motion pictures, newspapers, books, magazines, and sound recordings. The mass media are forms of a one-way flow of information (Ryan and Wentworth 1999, 10). (The Internet, a form of two-way communication, is generally considered a form of the media as well.) People's attitudes and beliefs about crime and criminals are often shaped and influenced by media representations of crime. These opinions carry over to other aspects of the social world. "What people believe about crime and criminals influences Supreme Court decisions, criminal justice policies, the election of public leaders, and routine activities of the public" (Thompson, Young, and Burns 2003, 206). The increased level of gang violence has become "one of the most prevalent crime news topics of the past two decades. . . . News stories that focus on gangs have influenced attitudes and opinions by providing vivid public images of gang crime and criminals. Gang news not only presents information, it also articulates ideological messages concerning the meaning and definition of gangs" (Thompson et al. 2003, 206). As Nawojczyk (1997, 3) explained, gang culture is "highly glamorized by the media including television, big screen releases, and powerful, idolized hard-core rap artists who rap about revolutions and killing. This music is in great demand by both white and black kids and provides the role models for many of the dress habits and slang of today's street culture."

The media glorify gang violence in all of its mass outlets, but especially in music. The music most often associated with gangs is known as "hip-hop" or "gangsta rap." "Rap" music is the forerunner of hip-hop and gangsta rap. Cheryl Keyes (2002, 17) defined rap as "a confluence of African American and Caribbean cultural expressions, such as sermons, blues, game songs and toasts and toasting—all of which are recited in chanted rhyme or poetic fashions." Keyes traced the rap style in music to the "jive-talk" popularized by jazz musicians and Harlem Renaissance writers in the first half of the twentieth century. Radio disc jockeys, such as Daddy-O Daylie (Holmes Bailey), Doc Hep Cat (Lavada Hurst), and Rufus Thomas, would rhyme over the music while it played on the air (Keyes 2002).

The "rap style" was embraced by two diverse groups in the 1960s. Hippies used the term *rap* to mean a form of communication. A common expression would be "Let's rap about it, man." Their idealistic outlook on life incorporated a belief that people should rap (talk) about problems and differences rather than go to war and use violence on one another. Counselors employed the technique of "rap sessions" with their clients as a treatment method. By the late 1960s, African-Americans began expressing a new racial consciousness that promoted Afrocentrism in all spheres of social life, including the arts. African-American writing workshops began to spring up throughout the nation. Poetry and rhymes were performed live and were generally accompanied by African music or drum beats. Performers like *The Last Poets of Harlem* gained national prominence. By the early 1970s, soul and funk artists like Barry White and Isaac Hayes began to incorporate raps into their songs (Keyes 2002). In the mid-1970s, another, now common aspect of hip-hop began to emerge: the DJ (disc jockey). The DJ spun records at clubs and private parties. Over time, DJs developed such techniques as "phasing," "back spinning," and "scratching" (Keyes 2002). By the mid-1980s, rap had become popular in urban neighborhoods throughout the country. These relatively mild lyrics and themes gave way in the 1990s to rappers whose angry messages were laced with profanity. The new lyrics glorified violence and often disrespected women (women are often referred to as "bitches" and "ho's"). It was in the 1990s that gangsta rap gained popularity. Many rappers, such as the late Easy-E and Tupac Shakur, along with current rappers Dr. Dre and Snoop Dogg have used their actual gang and street credentials to give their lyrics legitimacy—"keeping it real." Rap music had now been transformed into gangsta rap and gangsta rap is all about street credibility.

The story of Tupac Amaru Shakur sheds light on the relationship between gangsta rap and street credibility. Shakur is the son of Afeni Shakur, a former Black Panther and prison inmate who was once charged with conspiracy to blow up several Manhattan buildings. Born on June 16, 1971, by 1991 Tupac was a gangsta rapper and part-time poet and thug who sold millions of albums and starred in Hollywood movies. His troubles with the law included six arrests, convictions for assault and sexual abuse, and an eight-month prison term. In 1994, he was shot five times but lived. In 1996, he was shot four times and died (Carlson 2003). Tupac's lyrics included references to police officers he may have shot in Atlanta, the child he might have shot in 1992, the woman he sexually assaulted in New York, and the rival rappers he assaulted with bats and fists and guns (Solotaroff 2002, 256). On the night of September 7, 1996, Tupac was in Las Vegas to watch the Tyson-Seldon fight. He arrived with Marion "Suge" Knight, the head of Death Row Records. Suge worked with Dr. Dre, the creator of the Death Row gangsta sound, basically inventing a genre, which brought in a South-Central (Los Angeles) kid named Snoop Dogg to get the label off the ground (Solotaroff 2002, 262). Suge was a Blood from LA and he hung out with a crew called MOB (Members of Bloods). Tupac had his own road entourage and bodyguards, the Outlaw Immortalz. Flanked by their crews, Suge and Tupac headed toward their fourth row VIP seats inside the MGM hotel. Members of the rival Crips gang were already sitting in Tupac and Suge's seats; a minor confrontation took place but ended quickly. Early in the first round Tyson knocked out Seldon. As the spectators left the arena, Tupac and his crew met up with members of the Crips outside the hotel and a fight between these rivals started in earnest. The MOB crew beat up a Crip, and when MGM security arrived, they let Tupac and his crew leave and detained the beaten Crip.

Las Vegas is a city with at least 5,000 gang members, most of whom came from Los Angeles. "The cops even have a joke about it: They migrate here for the dry heat to spell the rheumatism that comes from having bullets lodged in your spine or skull. But their sense of territory is dead serious and testy—what with other guys always coming over from LA" (Solotaroff 2002, 260). Feeling good about themselves, Suge and Tupac drove around the Vegas strip and were eventually confronted by assailants in a white Cadillac that opened fire on Suge's BMW 750. Tupac died shortly after. Tupac's death started a chain reaction, beginning with the murder of Notorious B.I.G., or Biggie Smalls, Tupac's East Coast rival, in Los Angeles. A number of incidents between East Coast affiliates and West Coast affiliates took place in such diverse cities as Los Angeles, New York City, Salt Lake City, and Omaha, to name a few. The deaths of rappers Shakur and Notorious B.I.G. represented a turning point and the coming of age of a hip-hop generation (Kitwana 2002).

Gangsta rap is about street credibility, and the claims of contemporary artists such as 50 Cent—who says he has been shot nine times—add to the allure for youths who see delinquency and gang behavior as something to emulate. Interestingly, rap music itself has become more conventional, with suburban white kids listening to it and creating it. Rapper Eminem is one of the few white performers who has credibility in this genre. White former rapper Vanilla Ice was long ago revealed as a poseur. The absence of white women in rap speaks volumes about their lack of credibility on the streets. This review is not meant as a condemnation of rap music—after all, most people who listen to rap do so simply because they enjoy it. In the 1970s, white kids were condemned for listening to Led Zeppelin—the "Devil's music"—and some of those juveniles turned out to be college professors!

The mass media are not consistent in their portrayal of gangs. As with some police agencies, certain media outlets are in denial about the reality of gangs in their communities. For example, some newspapers (e.g., *The Los Angeles Times*) will report incidences of violence that are gang related *as* gang related, whereas other newspapers (e.g., the *Buffalo News*) seldom describe particular acts of juvenile violence as gang related. In my own studies of Buffalo street gangs, I was often aware of events that were gang related, and yet the *Buffalo News* did not report it (editorial policy) as such (it would describe the events but seldom used the term *gang-related*). It appeared that the newspaper did not want to alarm the public as to the true level of gang activity in Buffalo. The media has often been criticized for its glamorization of violence in the movies, television, and video games. The great debate regarding the impact of the media's portrayal and glamorization of violence on the behavior of youths has not reached a conclusion. But it seems logical to believe that it does have an impact, greater for some than for others. As Thio (2003, 144) explained, "Media violence may not *cause* violence among the majority of young men, but it is likely to turn the few susceptible, violence-prone youngsters to violence." The media do exercise a great influence on the American public and it shapes our perception of events. The media have great control over the manner in which they describe events to the public. "Contemporary society can be characterized by a *mass-mediated culture*, that is, a culture in which the mass media play a role in both shaping and creating cultural perceptions. The media do not simply mirror society, they help shape it" (Delaney and Wilcox 2002, 201).

Nearly everyone enjoys at least one aspect of the media. This might include waking up in the morning to an alarm clock-radio set on a news or music station, then turning the television on to watch sports, followed by reading the newspaper and maybe some magazines, reading a book, listening to music in one's car, and later in the day going to a movie. In short, most people find some form of the mass media exciting and enjoyable, so it should come as no surprise that this is true for juvenile delinquents. The effects of the media on juveniles are usually much different than on adults, because juveniles are much more susceptible to the influence of the media. Wannabe gangsters are heavily influenced by gangsta rap and movies that glorify gangs. The content of material that youths are exposed to is important and should be monitored by responsible adults.

The Rush

By this point, a number of socioeconomic explanations have been presented to explain why youths turn to gangs. Chapter 3 provided many theoretical explanations. Perhaps one of the simplest, and most overlooked, reasons why people commit acts of deviance, criminality, and join delinquent groups is that they find it fun and exciting. Deviant behavior has its appeal, to young and old alike. The oldest bank robber in U.S. history, "Red" Rountree, was asked why he robbed banks. As retold in newspapers, Rountree replied, "You want to know why I rob banks? It's fun. I feel good, awful good. I feel good for sometimes days, for sometimes hours" (Carter 2004, A13). Rountree committed his first bank robbery a week before his 87th birthday, on December 9, 1998, in Biloxi, Mississippi. He was arrested within minutes and eventually given three years' probation. Less than a year later, Rountree robbed his second bank, in Pensacola, Florida. He was quickly caught and sentenced to three years. At age 87, he became the oldest inmate in the Florida prison system. Two months after his Florida release, Rountree was arrested for his third bank robbery, in Abilene, Texas. His twelve-year Texas sentence nearly guarantees that he will die in prison. Rountree stated, "I know I'm going to die in here. That's OK. I've led a good life and I have no regrets" (Carter 2004, A13). Clearly, criminal behavior does not have an age limit. However, behavioral indiscretion is usually reserved for the young.

Preteens and teenagers enjoy testing the bounds of acceptable behavior. Sometimes lacking a mature sense of morality, young people, far more often than the elderly, are attracted to deviant forms of behavior. For some, the gang becomes symbolic of taboo behavior that is viewed as exciting, thrilling, and fun. Thus, it is this writer's contention that many individuals join gangs, at least in part, simply because of the lure of the "rush" of excitement that the gang provides. This idea should seem fairly logical—after all, nearly everyone seeks excitement and thrills and this is especially true for youths. Jankowski (1991) suggested that gangs provide individuals with entertainment opportunities much as a fraternity does for college students. Many youths join gangs because they represent the primary social institution of their neighborhood capable of delivering such a desirable want and need. Many gangs throw huge parties just as college fraternities do. They may have a clubhouse or meeting place where they all hang out and party. Such a meeting place might come equipped with a bar, pool tables, video games, dart boards, and even slot machines.

However, what distinguishes most gangs from most fraternities is the commitment to violent behavior among gangsters. They get off on the "rush" of often flirting with death. Although most people understand what is meant by a **rush**, fewer know how to explain its occurrence. A neuropsychological explanation of the rush is that an individual experiences an increase of adrenaline, cortisone, and testosterone, which are released into the bloodstream. This explains how military personnel are able to push on despite fatigue or how athletes are able to play through extreme pain immediately after experiencing an injury. The individual is loaded with adrenaline. Adrenaline is also known as epinephrine, the substance that medics inject into the heart of an individual who has experienced heart failure. It is meant to be a short-term response to a threatening situation. **Epinephrine** is a hormone important to the body's metabolism. It is a *catecholamine* (any of several compounds occurring naturally in the body that serve as hormones or as neurotransmitters in the sympathetic nervous system), and together with *norepinephrine* (a neurotransmitter that mediates chemical communication in the sympathetic nervous system, a branch of the autonomic nervous system) is secreted by the medulla of the adrenal gland. The body's sympathetic nervous system activates arousal by directing the adrenal gland atop the kidneys to release the stress hormones (Myers 1998). The physical body endures a number of changes during this arousal period. The pupils dilate, widening to allow in more light; the heart beat is faster; breathing speeds up; and blood sugar rises, providing the body with more energy to act. Digestion will also slow down so that blood flow can be diverted from the stomach and intestines to muscles, all with the purpose of preparing the body to respond quickly to danger, threat, and excitement (Wade and Travis 2002). The heightened secretions, caused by such reactions as fear and anger, result in an increased heart rate and the hydrolysis of glycogen to glucose. This chemical reaction, often called the "fight or flight" response, prepares the body for strenuous activity.

The fight or flight response is critical for survival, as many times people who are victimized freeze and fail to react to signs of danger. The "flight" response is the reaction to run from danger. Individuals not trained for combat are best advised to use this tactic when confronted with a hostile situation. Thus, if one "senses" trouble or notices visible signs of impending danger (e.g., gang members emerging from a dark alley), a basic survival strategy is to run for safety. Even gang members, police, and military personnel recognize the wisdom of surviving to fight another day when the odds are better. The "fight" response is the more typical response among gang members. For many gangbangers, fighting and combat are the very elements that enticed the individual to join the gang in the first place. Gang members will fight rivals even when greatly outnumbered rather than risk being labeled a punk for running. In Chinese gangs there exists the "Red Pole Member," whose sole duty in the gang is to fight and protect the other members (Booth 1999). An abundance of adrenaline rushes has a direct correlation to violence (Klinteberg 1989). In addition, higher levels of testosterone are found in both men and women with aggressive tendencies, something that is necessary to the "fight" in the "flight or fight" response (Harris, Rushton, Hampson and Jackson 1996). Aggression, linked to testosterone, can range from simple irritation to full-blown rage.

Testosterone levels have also been linked to levels of anger in adolescence (Archer 1991). High testosterone and cortisol levels, contributors to increased aggression and violence, have been linked to prefrontal cortex dysfunction. The prefrontal cortex is essential in executive cognitive functioning. It controls working memory, planning and organization, and most importantly self-regulation and inhibition. A prefrontal dysfunction may cause a breakdown of regulatory control and cause permanent antisocial behavior. Adolescents who do not learn to channel their emotions properly risk involvement in deviant and criminal behavior. Furthermore, it is during adolescence that males experience an increase in testosterone. The hormone testosterone is released at high levels during puberty, and it does not begin to decline until around 23 years of age (Martin 2000). The adolescent years are also the high-risk years for males to join a gang. The gang provides an outlet for the feelings of rage and anger experienced during adolescence.

Norepinephrine, like other neurotransmitters, is released at synaptic nerve endings to transmit the signal from a nerve cell to other cells. Norepinephrine is almost identical in structure to epinephrine, which is released into the bloodstream from the adrenal medulla under sympathetic activation, usually in response to short-term stress. The activation of epinephrine and norepinephrine causes an increased heart rate as well as blood pressure. Other actions caused by the release of norepinephrine include increased glycogenolysis (the conversion of glycogen to glucose) in the liver, increased lipolysis (the conversion of fats to fatty acids) in adipose (fat) tissue, and relaxation of bronchial smooth muscle to open up the air passages to the lungs. All of these actions represent a mobilization of the body's resources in order to meet a stressful challenge (*The Columbia Encyclopedia* 2001). Thus, the "rush" that one experiences is actually a release of hormones that the body creates naturally in response to stressful situations (Stamford 1987).

It is important to note the potential harmful effects of catecholamines on individuals:

> Chronic release of catecholamines due to psychological stress may cause a wear-and-tear effect on the body that increases the risk of coronary heart disease, hypertension, and ulcers. A bout of mild exercise can produce an acute tranquilizing effect because mild exercise increases metabolism to use up the excess catecholamines produced by stress. If exercise is intense, however, more catecholamines are released, which can lead to a state of arousal. This is why taking a walk is a successfully calming solution to a stressful situation, whereas running an intense mile is not (Stamford 1987, 184).

Chemical reactions in the body affect individuals differently. Furthermore, the "rush" experience is different from one person to the next. Consequently, all gang members do not share the same "rush" experience, but this theory (that youths join a gang in part because gang life provides a rush) does help to explain why wealthy kids join a gang—they are looking for thrills and excitement. It would be interesting to conduct research experiments to determine whether chemical reactions among gang members vary compared to those with more "conventional" lifestyles. It might also be interesting to test for gender differences. For example, are males more likely to experience the "rush" than females, considering that a larger percentage of "conventional" males than "conventional" females engage in dangerous activities? According to Walker-Barnes and Mason (2001) a higher percentage of males report that they joined a gang because they found it fun and exciting. But this does not indicate whether males experience the "rush" more than females. Gang members certainly feed off of the energy created by catecholamines and generally thrive in violent crisis situations. Conversely, conventional citizens prefer to avoid volatile and violent situations.

There appears to be a decreasing level of civility in society today, although historians and sociologists will state there have always been great levels of incivility throughout history. Perhaps what has really manifested itself lately is an increasing number of outward displays of rage that so many people feel today. As Bonnie Berry (1998, 1) stated, "It seems that there is more rage and less tolerance in the United States lately. We see intense rage leveled at, for example, crime and criminals; we see less tolerance for diversity. Actually, there may or may not have been a change in the number of rage-filled people or in the level of rage experienced by people, but rage certainly has a greater voice in the last several decades." A prime example of the outward display of rage today is "road rage." Road rage takes many forms, from such behaviors as aggressive driving so that another driver cannot pass or turn off and waving the middle finger in hostility to cutting someone off, getting in fist fights, and drive-by shootings. A great number of people exhibit car rage—old and young, male and female—who are otherwise mellow individuals. So why do drivers become so irritated by the slightest perceived form of disrespect? Is it the anonymity of the situation by which the individuals involved feel the incident is so isolated that it does not impact their personalities? Is it related to the fact that when driving a car, especially one made of steel, drivers feel power—power that they might not possess in any other social sphere? The answers are complex and multiple. But the implication is almost scary. Only gang members seem to take being "disrespected" so seriously that it warrants a physical retaliation. Perhaps conventional citizens are becoming more like gang members than gang members are becoming like regular citizens.

Rage is an emotional response to stimuli. It is an "expression of a primitive explosive affective state" (Cartright 2002, 22). The emotion of rage may be the result of a number of factors: the trauma associated with growing up in a bad neighborhood, being a victim of abuse, the lack of a trusted family member to turn to when in trouble, and victimization outside the home. "The emotion of rage is like hatred but it is bigger, more colorful, and more intense. Rage is usually thought of as personal. Rage can also be social, as when a number of people focus their rage on a social event (like Waco), a social phenomenon (like affirmative action), or a social category of people (like the poor, immigrants, and prisoners)" (Berry 1998, 1). Some people find rage to be an irrational behavior, whereas others view it as a final, desperate, but calculated undertaking perpetrated by individuals to reach a desired end. Intolerance toward others is generally involved with rage. The person displaying the rage is deeply upset with the actions of someone else or simply the very presence of the other. "Intolerance is a catalyst for rage. Rage is an emotional overreaction to intolerance; the words 'backlash' and 'violence' come to mind. People who are into rage and intolerance today seem willing to preach violence, listen to and agree with violence, and either engage in it themselves or support the conduct of violence as committed by others" (Berry 1998, 2). Gang members are very intolerant of rivals and they almost always display violent rage toward rivals. The very presence of rival gang members is enough to "set off" gang members. Violence is the only way they know to deal with confrontation: it is taught, accepted, and carried out on a regular basis. Rage is the very life blood of many gangsters.

Certain people, sometimes called **rage junkies**, seem to feel much better when their system is operating on increased levels of adrenaline. Rage junkies have become addicted to the "druglike high" that the adrenaline rush provides. It intoxicates the rage junkie. Highly violent people experience this "rush" of adrenaline; in fact, they feel far more comfortable with this high stress level. The adrenaline high combined with hate is deadly. Hard-core gang members are especially high-strung and will act violently at the slightest provocation. There are many **rage junkies** in American society, as there are in all societies. Most are violence-prone and angry. They are angry over personal and socially defined failures and they need a target at which to direct their anger. Usually these targets are **scapegoats**—readily available, often "weaker" persons blamed for society's wrongs (e.g., immigrants).

Rage is a form of retribution, but it is not therapeutic. For example, murder victims' families generally do not feel better or even satisfied when the condemned are executed (Verhovek 1997). Rage is a type of "expressive justice" that generally does not satisfy the people who vented the rage and intolerance although they expected that it would (Anderson 1995). Thus, rage seldom provides the relief anticipated by conventional people. Conventional people, those who have developed a strong bond to society, will find positive ways to deal with their rage by taking out their aggressions on a punching bag or participating in some other rigorous activity as a means of "blowing off steam." However, gang members appear to receive great satisfaction from rage aimed at rival gang members as well as toward law enforcement.

Jack Katz, in his book *Seductions of Crime* (1988) described how individuals experienced "sneaky thrills" through various property crimes. "A common thread running through vandalism, joyriding, and shoplifting is that all are sneaky crimes that frequently thrill their practitioners" (Katz 1988, 53). Katz explained that the sneaky thrill is created by a series of three events:

1. **Being seduced to deviance**—The person flirts with the idea of committing a crime. "In most accounts of shoplifting, the shoplifters enter with the idea of stealing but usually do not have a particular object in mind" (Katz 1988, 53). When a situation arises where it appears to be "easy" to steal, the seduction becomes stronger.

2. **The ability to create an aura of "normal appearances"**—Amateur thieves often draw attention to themselves because they become so self-centered that they believe everyone is looking at them. "At some point on the way toward all sneaky thrills, the person realizes that she must work to maintain a conventional, calm appearance up to and through the point of exit" (Katz 1988, 59).

Remaining "cool" under pressure is a trait desired by criminals as well as by conventional persons.

3. **Appreciation of success**—When the criminal has successfully accomplished the crime, a feeling of elation is derived. This is when the thrill is completely experienced. "Usually after the scene of risk is successfully exited, the third stage of the sneaky thrill is realized. This is the euphoria of being thrilled" (Katz 1988, 64).

Katz (1988, 73) concluded that deviant persons appreciate the act of doing evil because "it is literally wonderful." In order words, the thrill of committing acts of delinquency may be enough of a stimulus to entice certain individuals to engage in criminal pursuits.

Committing property crimes is not nearly exciting enough for some people; they seek more extreme forms of thrills. For these people, "thrill killing" is the ultimate expression of criminality. If the reader has a hard time understanding how someone could kill for the "thrill of it," consider that research conducted by McDevitt, Levin, and Bennett (2002) led to the conclusion that some hate crimes are committed simply because the individual reported having nothing better to do. Two-thirds of hate crimes committed were done merely for the thrill and immature desire to display power and to experience the rush at the expense of someone else (McDevitt et al. 2002). If simply being bored and having nothing better to do can lead to hate crimes, then taking the next step of actually killing another living being becomes a little more understandable. There are many types of **thrill killers**. Poachers represent one category of thrill killers. Poaching is the illegal taking or possession of any game, fish, or nongame wildlife. Hunting out of season or out of the district for which one has a valid license, hunting at night with a spotlight, taking more than the legal limit, and a nonresident buying a resident license all fall into the poaching category (*Colorado Department of Natural Resources* 2002). Poaching is a big problem in places like Colorado. Poaching and thrill-killing of game animals leaves more dead and wounded animals than those killed by licensed hunters. Poachers kill for a trophy. According to John Bredehoft, chief of law enforcement for the Colorado Division of Wildlife (DOW), most poachers are not poor people trying to feed their families. They kill for the thrill of killing, for trophies, and for profit—since trophy heads, antlers and bear gall bladders are worth thousands of dollars (*Colorado Department of Natural Resources* 2002). Colorado authorities have found poachers to range from sophisticated and well-organized crime rings to groups of teenagers who wantonly kill elk, deer, and antelope for the sheer fun of it.

Another category of thrill killers are also involved in the taking of animal life. These people kill animals as a form of religious sacrifice or black magick (magic). Animal sacrifice was once a common feature of many of the world's major religions—it is a common theme in the Old Testament. Today, religious animal sacrifice is usually attributed to Satanists and cultists who mutilate and kill an animal as part of a "religious" ceremony, much like Christians and Jews of the past. Killing an animal for magick is a "thrill kill." A thrill kill occurs when adolescents believe that killing a neighborhood dog or cat in the name of Satan will gain them "points." Many Satanists and cultists believe that if an animal is sacrificed, it must be eaten as well. Satanists describe how in medieval times animal sacrifice was a part of the black magick ritual; however, in modern times, most Satanists believe that the taking of an "innocent life" to attain one's own selfish needs is wrong. Whether or not they are Satanists or cultists, the fact remains that there are many individuals who kill animals simply because they find it thrilling. They may enjoy watching the animal suffer, or they may enjoy the perceived power associated with the ability to take a life. Whereas conventional people see dogs and cats as pets (or "companions"), animal thrill killers see them as expendable objects.

Serial killers represent another category of thrill killers. A serial killer is someone who murders many victims with some common trait in a designated time frame. American serial killers are almost always white males in their early 20s to 40s who lack a strong family environment. A mass murderer is not the same thing as a serial killer, as mass murderers kill a large number of people during a state of rage, often in quick succession, but then do not kill again (e.g., Michael McDermott, the 42-year-old employee of Edgewater Technology in Wakefield, Massachusetts who opened fire on his coworkers, killing seven of them; and Eric Harris and Dylan Klebold, Columbine High School). Serial killers find a far greater thrill in killing by instilling fear into the general public. "Serial killer Andrew Cunanan terrified the nation during the summer of 1997 by staying on the loose after he killed people in Minnesota, Illinois, and New Jersey. More than two months later, Cunanan committed suicide in Miami Beach, but not before he shot to death his final victim, fashion designer Gianni Versace (Fox and Levin 2002, 1037). There are four types of serial killers: the *visionary*, who kills because he feels internally compelled to do so; the *missionary*, who kills to rid his world of perceived evil; the *thrill-motivated* killer, who does so simply because he enjoys it; and the *lust-motivated* killer, who has sexual motivations for killing. Thrill killers represent perhaps the most dangerous of the serial killers, as the motivation to kill comes from the enjoyment it brings to the killer—it makes them feel good. Thrill-motivated serial killers are also the most likely ones to commit gory murders, often after they have tortured their victims in some heinous fashion. Thrill killers enjoy the rush of the hunt as much as the thrill of the kill. They love running from the police, and if they receive media attention, their thrill level increases all the more. They are truly addicted to adrenalin and need more and more of it because their bodies have become conditioned to adrenalin rushes. Murder represents the ultimate rush for thrill killers.

Although a large number of street gangsters will not commit murder, there are many gang members who will. Consequently, gang members may also represent another category of thrill killers. These gangsters are the hard-core members whose very existence and sense of self are dependent on their gang identity. They will engage in whatever behavior is necessary for the maintenance of the gang. Not all gang members are thrill killers, but nearly all of them will indicate that they get a thrill from gang life, a high that is often incomparable to anything else they have ever experienced. Gang members involved in drive-by shootings state that the desire for excitement provided the necessary momentum to carry out their cowardly deed. When taunts from rivals precede the drive-by shooting, gang members are especially aroused and motivated to action (Davis 1995). Hard-core gang members enjoy life in the "fast lane," as there is a rush of power and excitement from living on "the edge."

Activities that qualify as **living on the edge** vary from one group to another. For adults in the conventional world just finding a way to pay the bills each month on a salary constitutes life on the edge. For children, self-mutilation and self-injury constitutes living on the edge. Self-mutilation includes such activities as burning the skin, taking multiple punches to the arm or body, smoking, multiple piercings, and tattoos. Young people are especially susceptible to thinking that these behaviors are somehow "cool." They are activities utilized by adolescents as a means of showing their independence from parental and societal rules and expectations. Gangs recognize that these behaviors draw impressionable youths to the gangs and take full advantage of self-injury by requiring gang recruits to go through a physical initiation and brand themselves with gang tattoos. Individuals who can justify self-mutilation have a much easier time justifying injuring others, especially rival gang members.

One need not be a delinquent to understand the lure of excitement from living on the edge, or enjoying life in the fast lane; many conventional people embrace this ideology and consider themselves to be "adrenaline-rush junkies." They seek the rush in such "legitimate" ways as rock and mountain climbing, skydiving, parachuting, swimming with sharks, surfing huge waves, riding on roller coasters, auto racing, playing chicken with on-coming traffic, hopping trains, watching scary movies, playing video games like *Grand Theft Auto: Vice City*, and so on. When someone climbs Mt. Everest they are commended, even though there is the constant risk of death. Large ocean swells can be very dangerous, but for surfers, the lure of waves caused by ocean storms or surfing the Pipeline in Hawaii are the ultimate rush. Many people wish that they could fly. Skydiving and parachuting are forms of human flight. Trapeze performers are able to temporarily fly in the air. The artists who perform their daring feats high above the crowd and without a net are both excited and scared at the same time. Their hearts beat fast as they swing on the trapeze. For a moment in time, when they let go of the trapeze and wait for their partner to reach out and grab them, they are experiencing human flight. They have achieved "air and speed," a rush that is difficult to match. Stunt fliers who perform such feats as cutting the power to their engines while tumbling toward the ground and restarting just in time to swoop safely upward speak of the rush of adrenaline and fun they receive from performing their tricks. Driving a car fast on an open expressway is a rush that many "common" (non-adrenaline-rush junkies) people enjoy. People who enjoy riding on roller coasters do so because they find it both fun and semiterrifying—it gives them an adrenaline rush.

Endorphins also provide individuals with an adrenaline rush. Endorphins are morphine-like substances in the brain that block pain, heighten pleasure, and have been associated with some addictions. "Narcotics are thought to mimic or enhance the activity of endorphins, which are proteins produced by the brain that control pain and influence other subjective experiences" (Schmalleger 2004, 416). Endorphins may be stimulated into action by a variety of seemingly harmless behaviors. For example, friends of mine who belong to a hot chili club state that eating hot chilies provides them with a rush. In other words, people who enjoy eating hot chilis seek to "ride the endorphin rush." Recent research published by Steven Feldman and associates (2004) reveals that tanning is addictive because it appears that the exposure to UV rays triggers the release of endorphins. In their research on tanners who utilize tanning beds, participants reported that they could not go more than a few days without another tanning session or they would feel depressed (Feldman et al. 2004). Tanning may be viewed as addictive (defined as any behavior that makes you feel good but is unhealthful and is a habit that is hard to break without significant effort) because tanners *need* the endorphin rush provided by UV rays. Thus, the reason that people tan extends beyond the perception of improved appearance (the belief that people look better tanned than pale) to the possibility of a physiological effect of UV rays that drives tanning behavior (Feldman et al. 2004). Another example of a mundane trigger of endorphin release may be found in the workplace. Workaholics experience a "rush" from taking on tasks and challenges with a high stress level. They "get off" on doing large amounts of work. A great number of law enforcement officers and military personnel report that they receive a rush from performing their jobs because of the realization that they face potential death on a regular basis. In short, many people seek the rush; it should not be surprising that this same idea can be applied to gang behavior as well. In my own interviews with gang members, it is clear to me that many gangsters enjoy the violence of gang activity because they get a "rush" from it.

Clearly, many people have incorporated legitimate ways of satisfying their need for thrills and the rush. Conventional people fantasize about ways of filling their otherwise boring lifestyles with excitement. An extreme form of "fantasy rush" (as I call it) was detailed in a 2002 *Newswire* report. Controversial Detroit rapper Mr. Scrillion, a.k.a. Adam Thick, offered "extreme kidnapping adventures" to hard-core thrill seekers. The rapper began kidnapping people for his profit and their fun. Extreme kidnapping takes thrill seeking to new heights. The rapper stated, "This service caters to the extreme sports adventurer who is bored with what's currently available; this takes it to a whole new other level. . . . The kidnappings are very realistic, and not for the faint of heart, as every nuance and detail of an actual kidnapping are replicated to provide the most intense experience possible" (*Newswire* 2002, 1). Three different kidnap scenarios are available and each kidnapping comes with a videotape copy of the adventure so that the client can relive the experience. Extreme kidnapping hardly seems like the type of activity society would like to promote as a means of alleviating boredom.

Clients of extreme kidnapping share something in common with criminals and gang members—they do not go about fulfilling their cravings for the adrenaline rush in ways that mainstream society would prefer. With this idea in mind, it should be understandable why criminals and delinquents have a high disregard for their own safety and the safety of others. In *The Unknown Darkness* (2003, xv), former FBI agent Gregg McCrary described a case where two fugitives, driving from Ohio to Buffalo, had a fully functioning but unstable bomb in their car. "What made it really dangerous was that the shunt of the blasting cap was unprotected. This meant that any extraneous radio transmission or static electricity could have detonated the bomb. They could easily have blown themselves up and some of the bomb techs who dismantled the device were surprised that they hadn't." The fugitives found the ordeal very exciting and reported getting a rush from it all. And that is the way many gangbangers feel about their lives in the gang. They feel as though no one cares about them, so why should they care about themselves. They turn cold and are capable of watching people bleed and die without feeling any remorse. Their disregard for life coupled with the rush that they receive from gangbanging is far more rewarding to them than the alternative, conventional, poverty lifestyle. Furthermore, the fact that people from all socioeconomic classes, races, and ethnicities enjoy experiencing the rush helps to explain why youths from "good" neighborhoods turn to crime and delinquency. In an attempt to experience the rush, both legitimate and delinquent opportunities are available.

SUMMARY

There are a number of socioeconomic reasons that entice gang members to join a gang. The shifting labor market has left many unskilled workers without work, which in turn has led to the development of an underclass in many urban inner-city neighborhoods. Economics remains a guiding force that lures youths into the gang. Growing up in a life of poverty will stimulate many to take the path that leads directly to a gang lifestyle. The lack of a male role model remains a contributing factor that influences a young male to join a gang. Beyond the traditional socioeconomic explanations of gang formation is the reality that many gang members simply enjoy gang life and would lead no other. In short, gang members report getting a "rush" from gangbanging activity. The gang lifestyle is fun, exciting, and dangerous. The adrenaline rush experienced by gang members would be difficult to duplicate by legitimate means. Thus, the "rush factor" becomes a potentially major contributing explanation of why an individual chooses to join a gang. This is an area of study in need of further research.

CHAPTER FIVE

Gang Structure and Process

B ased on the information provided so far in this book, it should be clear that there is no such thing as a "typical" gang. However, when focusing solely on street gangs, it is possible to describe the basic structure and the processes that are common to most of them. This chapter analyzes the organizational structure of gangs, gang typologies, and the processes involved in "turning" to a gang. Beyond all, gang members demand respect—it is the "code of the street."

GANG STRUCTURE

Typically, gangs develop spontaneously, or, as Thrasher (1927) explained, they emerge from playgroups. Children in playgroups hang out with one another for a large portion of their free time and maintain their friendships as they grow up together. "Age seems to be one of the most important characteristics of gangs because the clique is one of the basic building blocks of gangs" (Shelden et al. 2001, 36). Cliques and friendship cohorts sometimes organize into street gangs. This is more apt to be true in urban environments. Cohort gang groupings are called *klikas* (the term *clique* is more common) in cholo gangs and *sets* in African-American gangs (Reiner 1992). The degree to which they organize into gangs is dependent on many factors.

The Organizational Structure

"The organizational structures of gangs have varied widely over time, from city to city, and even within cities" (Regoli and Hewitt 2003, 309). The Vice Lords, based out of Chicago, are an example of a highly organized gang, having created an administrative body called the "board" designed to deal with matters affecting the entire Vice Lord Nation. Keiser (1969) found that the Vice Lords held regular meetings with representatives from all the subgroups present. The gangsters were given printed membership cards with the Vice Lords insignia (a top hat, cane, and white gloves). But the highly organized structure of the Vice Lords is more the exception than the rule, as most gangs are not nearly so established. At the opposite extreme of the Vice Lords' structural arrangement are gangs that Yablonsky (1959) described as "near groups." "Such near-groups fit the needs of their members, whose social abilities are so rudimentary that they cannot meet the criminal demands of a more organized or stable group" (Regoli and Hewitt 2003, 309). Other researchers, such as Short (1974) argue that gangs fall somewhere in the middle. In my research I found that most Buffalo gangs are loosely confederated, with the exception of the local Crips gangs, which possessed many structured qualities.

Most gangs are centered on a core group of about 10 to 12 members, who form the nucleus of the gang. Their primary function is to oversee the total unit. The core clique generally consists of the most violent members, and it is from this group that a leader emerges.

> Most gangs have leaders. This should not be surprising, as few organizations can survive without some form of leadership. However, gang leaders in most cases are less likely to resemble corporate executives than they are to be like captains of sports teams, a role that can change from one circumstance or one day to another. Not surprisingly, leadership roles are better defined in those gangs and gang cities where gangs have operated the longest. Thus, in Chicago and Los Angeles, we find gang leaders who are older, more specialized in their activities, and more powerful. In other cities, those we have called emerging gang cities, leadership roles have a far more informal character. In these gangs, the leader of a gang can change from one day or one function to another (Curry and Decker 2003, 81).

The **gang leader** is generally a long-time member who has climbed the ranks and is generally looked up to by the other members. The gang leader is expected to remain calm under pressure and lead by example. In most cases, the leader gains his or her position based on reputation, as opposed to any "voting-in" procedures by the members. (*Note*: This "might makes right" mentality exists in the animal kingdom, for example, an alpha male in dog and gorilla packs.) As might be expected, the leadership role is a fleeting one.

> The stereotype of the gang leader is someone who is tough, with a long criminal history, and who has strong influence over the members. To the contrary, the typical leader does not maintain influence over a long period of time. Leadership tends to be very situational, and contrary to the belief that to eliminate the gang all you need to do is "cut off the head" and the rest will die off, someone else will generally take his place. This is because gang leadership is, as with most groups, a function of the group rather than individuals (Klein 1995, 63).

Nonetheless, gangs have clear leaders, and when a gang leader loses the leadership position, another gang member will step in to take over. As with many organizations, there are different types of leaders. Some leaders are charismatic, ruling by the dynamics of personality. A gang led by a **charismatic leader** has certain differences from a gang led by a militaristic leader. The charismatic leader "is usually older and stronger than, and is revered by, the gang's members. In the violent gangs studied by Lewis Yablonsky, leaders would occasionally manipulate other gang members into aggressive or violent actions just to satisfy their own emotional needs. By a combination of charisma and intimidation, the leaders of violent gangs tended to be more permanent in their positions, while turnover among the general membership was high" (Regoli and Hewitt 2003, 310). In gangs that are more highly structured, the leader is more militaristic, or Mafia-styled. The **militaristic leader** gives orders to the next in command, who in turn transmits them throughout the ranks by a chain-of-command system (Regoli and Hewitt 2003). According to Krisberg (1975), the most important feature of gang leaders is their superior verbal ability. In his research of black gangs, Krisberg found that leaders had the "gift of the gab," which allowed them to draw approving attention from the other gang members.

Turf protection appears to be the most common reason that gangs organize in particular neighborhoods. This has been evident since the formation of Irish gangs in New York City in the early and mid-1800s. Traditional street gangs (those who have been in existence the longest) have the highest regard for the notion of protecting turf, or the neighborhood (Shelden et al. 2001). Moore (1991) explained that the importance of turf for the two traditional gangs (White Fence and El Hoyo Maravilla) that she studied was due to the direct connection that members had to each other and to the barrio. "The gangs started out as friendship groups of adolescents who shared common interests, with a more or less clearly defined territory in which most of the members lived. They were committed to defending one another, the barrio, the families, and the gang name in the status-setting fights that occurred in school and on the streets. They were bound by a norm of loyalty" (Moore 1991, 31).

Recently, turf protection has not been as important for many of the newer gangs. Spergel (1990) explained that "many urban gangs identify with particular neighborhoods, parks, housing projects, or schools. At one time, crossing turf boundaries and entering another gang's territory, often clearly marked by graffiti, involved taking serious risks. However, automobiles have increased the mobility of teenagers, and slum districts have been sliced up by highways and urban renewal, blurring the old dividing lines. In addition, identification with specific turf has been drastically altered for many gang members, largely because of frequent relocation of gang members' family residence" (Regoli and Hewitt 2003, 311). The growth of prison gangs has also impacted the structure of street gangs, as over the past several years the two have become more closely intertwined. Prison gangs such as the Aryan Brotherhood, the Mexican Mafia, Nuestra Familia, the Black Guerilla Family, and the Texas Syndicate have begun to recruit and train street gang members into their more established and structured organizations (Welling 1994). The influence of organized prison gangs added to the increased mobility of gangs and their growing control of the illicit drug market has made it clear that street gangs have evolved from their early, simple goal of protecting turf. According to Welling (1994, 148), "it is difficult to find a community or correctional system whose local gangs have not been influenced by outside groups. As a result, local street gangs are evolving into multi-jurisdictional drug organizations throughout the nation."

As stated earlier, some gangs have a militaristic style of leadership. These gangs tend to be similar in organizational structure to the military in other ways besides leadership. A closer examination of the military reveals some of the similarities to gangs.

ORGANIZATIONAL PARALLELS BETWEEN STREET GANGS AND THE MILITARY Among the similarities between street gangs and the military are the reasons members join, ceremonies of induction and violation ceremonies for disobeying rules, specific clothing and style of dress, a ranking structure, the use of symbols and acronyms, and protection of turf.

The United States Army was established on July 14, 1775. Gangs have existed in the United States in one form or another since the colonial era. In some cases, people have been drafted into the armed services, just as some youths find themselves "drafted" (or recruited) into the local gang (youths as young as age 8 are considered "at risk" in certain large urban neighborhoods). In most cases, however, people have volunteered their service to the military, just as most youths voluntarily join the gang. Sociologists have identified a number of specific reasons why youths join a street gang: identity, discipline, recognition, love, belonging, and money (Nawojczyk 1997). Young people join the army for these same reasons.

Induction into the military and the street gang involves **initiation ceremonies**. Gang members are typically "jumped"—beaten severely to find out how tough they are and to determine if they can take a beating—as a form of initiation. Other ceremonies of initiation may involve acts that range from robbery to shooting someone. Once youths have satisfactorily met the demands of initiation, they become a member of the gang. The military puts its recruits through nine weeks of basic training (boot camp). (*Note*: A Syracuse gang that calls itself "Boot Camp" will be discussed in Chapter 6.) When recruits have successfully met the physical requirements, they graduate into the military. Graduation is accompanied by a ceremony held to recognize the accomplishments of the recruits. Gang members likewise hold celebrations. When gang members violate a group rule, they risk a "violation" ceremony (a form of punishment) that may involve a physical beating or some form of compensation. Military personnel who violate rules are subject to the loss of privileges and risk possible military imprisonment.

Clothing and **style of dress** are important elements and a means of identification for both the military and the gang. There are different uniforms for each branch of the military and specific uniforms that are to be worn for certain occasions and ceremonies, along with guidelines as to how they are to be worn, and camouflaged-colored uniforms to be worn in specific environments in order to blend into the background. Among the restrictive rules governing military dress (as dictated by the *Officer's Guide*) are these: "There is authorized material as to weave, color, weight, design, and manner. The uniforms will be worn when on duty as to represent the United States military" (*Officer's Guide*, 115). In wearing the cotton uniform or BDU (Battle Dress Uniform) there are certain ways to wear the uniform. Socks must be knee length, sufficient to provide for a turnover of $2\frac{1}{2}$ to 3 inches at top, to reach a point about 1 inch below the bottom of the knee cap. The shirt worn must be cotton, with 8.2 ounces brown in color, Army shade No. 1; and appropriate dress wear is expected at social functions" (*Officer's Guide*, 130). Clearly, military personnel dress in a manner that distinguishes them from the civilian population. Gang members also dress in a manner that distinguishes them from the general population. Military clothing is worn just loose enough to break up the silhouette of the body, it is not so loose that it nearly falls off the service person or presents an unprofessional look. Gang members, however, wear their clothing loose to help conceal weapons. Although gang members are often stereotyped as wearing baseball caps backwards, big necklaces with crosses and stars, and gold jewelry, this look can be deceiving for many "wannabes" also dress in this manner. Gang colors and clothing are a trademark of street gangs. In Schneider's (1999) research on gangs, he found that "most gang members employed some insignia or wore some item of clothing that, like colors on a ship, declared the wearer's allegiance" (p. 145). The African-American super gangs of the Bloods and Crips are known for their colors of red and blue, respectively. The flashing of colors is most notable in the wearing of bandannas. The bandanna is often treated with the same level of respect as the military pays to the American flag. In time of battle, the flag, or bandanna, is never to be left behind for enemy capture. Tattoo branding is another notable method of displaying one's loyalty to a specific gang, or branch of the military. Nearly all gang members, male and female, have had extensive ink done as a way of displaying their gang affiliation.

The military shares another characteristic typically found in street gangs, **rank** and **structure**. The military's very foundation is built on a strict hierarchical structure with a clear-cut ranking system. Orders are to be followed without question and individuality is completely lost. At the bottom of the ranking system is the private, and at the other extreme is the general. Promotion through the ranks is possible after years of service and distinguished performance. As in any organizational structure, the higher the rank, the greater the responsibility. Gangs are also built around a hierarchical structure, although this ranking system varies greatly. As mentioned, the Vice Lords are known to be a highly organized gang with a clear-cut stratification system. Examples of the many different typologies of gangs will be presented later in this chapter.

Symbols and **acronyms** are common to both street gangs and the military. The primary function of symbols and acronyms is in communication between personnel. Effective communication is essential in the military. One example of an attempt to avoid confusion includes associating words with letters of the alphabet during radio and phone transmission (e.g., *Alpha* equals A, *Bravo* is used for B, etc.). Symbols and acronyms allow the military to code messages so that enemy personnel cannot steal important information. Gangs rely heavily on symbolism, especially when communicating through the use of graffiti. "Graffiti serves three main purposes for gangs: it defines turf; it provides the opportunity to issue a challenge or a warning; and it reports the neighborhood news" (Schneider 1999, 151). A great deal of information can be learned about gangs through their use of graffiti (see Chapter 9 for further analysis).

Protecting **turf** remains important for many gangs, but as mentioned earlier that concept has changed for some street gangs. However, as gangs continue to take control of the drug market, it remains important to be able to protect their expanded turf. As for the military, its primary function and reason for existence is the protection of turf—American territories—to protect U.S. citizens from their enemies and outside threats to basic democratic freedoms.

All these characteristics reveal that street gangs and the military share many similarities. In addition, by their very design, both the military and street gangs are violent entities, value camaraderie and group goals and values, seek goals, insist on respect for internal authority, demand respect and honor, and appear to be permanent fixtures of society. But despite the many similarities between street gangs and the military, there is at least one glaring difference: The military is a legitimate social institution, whereas street gangs are illegitimate in purpose and design.

COMPARING STREET GANGS TO A VIOLENT TRIBE In their 1998 book *Waorani: The Contexts of Violence and War*, Clayton and Carole Robarchek compare street gangs to the Waorani tribe, found near the Amazon River in Ecuador. Anthropologists have described the Waorani as the most murderous people on Earth. "Virtually no one lived to old age. Entire families were routinely wiped out with 9-foot spears. And the notion of killing a child was no more abhorrent than the notion of killing a snake. A staggering six out of 10 Waorani deaths came at the hands of another Waorani" (Fiore 1997, A1). As the Robarcheks (1998, 1) explained, "The Waorani resisted outside contact and 'pacification' longer and more successfully than any other indigenous group in Amazonian Ecuador. They were engaged in warfare with all surrounding groups and in lethal vendettas among themselves well into the last half of the twentieth century." In the past century, more than 60% of Waorani deaths have been the result of homicide; consequently, anthropologists consider the Waorani as the most violent society known to exist (Yost 1981). A few clans of Waorani still remain hidden in the vast expanse of the rainforest that spans the disputed frontier between Ecuador and Peru and are still at war with each other and with outsiders (Robarchek and Robarchek 1998, 1).

The Robarcheks (1998, 3) used their research on the Waorani to defend their central theoretical premise that human behavior "is not the determined result of ecological or biological or socioeconomic forces acting on them, but, rather, is motivated by what they want to achieve in their world as they perceive and understand it. Within their experienced reality, people make choices based on the information available to them—information about themselves, about the world around them, and about possible goals and objectives in that world." The Robarcheks contend that gang members, like the Waorani, choose to behave violently not because of a biological predisposition or because of socioeconomic reasons. As for the Waorani, their western Amazon habitat has been a violent place for many centuries. "The ultimate roots of this widespread culture of war are lost in antiquity, but the devastating destabilizing impacts of Spanish and later internal colonialism must certainly have contributed to its continuation and intensification. Still, the earliest accounts, even prior to the colonial period, describe the bellicosity of the region's inhabitants. The Incas attempted to colonize the eastern foothills, but their armies were repelled by the Indigenous peoples. Early incursions by the Spanish were similarly repulsed, and resistance continued even after the establishment of Spanish control" (Robarchek and Robarchek 1998, 85). From this perspective, gang members are viewed as a part of a violent culture that has accepted their role in defending turf against all rivals and invaders. The use of extreme violence and homicide are considered the expected norm. "We want to make it clear that we are *not* arguing that human behavior is independent of or unconstrained by the environment or by human biology. We are simply insisting that human beings do not respond, either automatically or otherwise, to some 'objective' environment, to 'nature in the raw' whose 'reality' is imprinted on passive minds. The worlds that people inhabit and interact with are worlds whose characteristics, meanings, and implications are attributed to them *by* human minds" (Robarchek and Robarchek 1998, 137). The Robarcheks compared modern-day street gangs to the Waorani in this way (177):

> Urban gang warfare, like Waorani warfare, is premised on loyalty to a very small group, territoriality, bravado, blood vengeance, and the use of violence, both instrumentally to achieve specific goals and for self-validation. Human identity, here as in Amazonia, is extended only to those in a small face-to-face group, and the human emotions of empathy, sympathy, and compassion are simply not relevant in relations with those outside it. Killing a nongang member for a pair of sneakers or a leather jacket is as easy and inconsequential for a gang member as it was for a Waorani to kill a *kowudi* for an ace or machete. . . . Here, as among the Waorani, there is a self-perpetuating culture of violence.

Regardless of whether or not it has its ultimate origins in the socioeconomic "roots of violence" that obsess social reformers, it is clear that, here as in Amazonia, it is maintained and perpetuated by a psychocultural dynamic. For those caught up in it, gang violence is a way of life that gives identity, meaning, and purpose.

The Robarcheks also described how the Waorani, were transformed, virtually overnight, from a murderous tribe to a relatively peaceful people after being convinced by missionaries that less violent behaviors possessed worthwhile benefits. The murder rate fell by more than 90%. The Robarcheks believe that the behavior of gang members can also be altered. Critics of their theory have difficulty getting past the comparison of urban gangs to a jungle tribe, finding it racially insensitive. The Robarcheks insist that the two "jungles" are similar in what they lack—a community acting as a moral force that is more powerful than personal impulse. In urban areas, the community is viewed as merely an amorphous and amoral aggregation with no psychological saliency, nor a consistent model with which to identify or build upon (Robarchek and Robarchek 1998). "Young people, lacking any other psychologically meaningful communities, create their own, and these most certainly *do* provide a reference group and a sense of identity. They also often present a realm of new opportunities and goals—excitement, money, drugs, sex—and they provide the means for achieving them. Some of the behaviors they promote reflect values, such as loyalty, courage, individualism, and materialism, that are shared with the wider society. Many other behaviors—intimidation, vengeance, and murder—do not" (Robarchek and Robarchek 1998, 179). The "solution" promoted by the Robarcheks is that gang members must learn to embrace society's rules and sense of morality, rather than the subcultural values of their immediate group (as the Waorani had done when they were a murderous tribe). The Robarcheks' theory is similar to that of social bond theorists, who assert that everyone is capable of crime and delinquency and so the key to the solution is to establish social bonds between the gang member and the greater society in order to eliminate delinquent and criminal behavior.

Gang Typologies

The structure of gangs can be differentiated in many ways other than their organizational component. Distinctions can be made based on such variables as age (e.g., a baby posse or veteranos), race and ethnicity (Hispanic, African-American, Asian, White, Native-American, or, in rare cases, mixed), gender composition (all males, all females, or mixed), setting (e.g., streets, prison, or motorcycle), type of activity (e.g., drug sales, protection, violence, turf defense, etc.), degree of criminality (e.g., minor or serious), and so on. These distinctions, along with others, provide a number of typologies with which to classify gangs.

AGE-GRADED GANGS The hierarchical structure of street gangs is often determined by the simple variable of age. Hagedorn's studies of street gangs in Milwaukee revealed that they emerged from ordinary street-corner peer groups (in the same sense that Thrasher described). Some of the gangs evolved from local dance groups. Conflicts with other groups and the police accelerated the transition from a cohort group to a gang. Hagedorn concluded that Milwaukee street gangs could be classified as **age-graded**. Furthermore, the age of the youth would determine the level of commitment to the gang. Hagedorn (1988) found that there were four main age groupings:

1. the Ancients—20 years and older
2. the Seniors—ages 16–19
3. the Juniors—ages 12–15
4. the Pee Wees—ages 8–11

In Moore's (1991) study of Mexican-American street gangs in East Los Angeles, she found that the gangs started out as friendship groups of adolescents who shared common interests and then rapidly developed into "an age-graded structured" gang (p. 31). The original members of White Fence and El Hoyo Maravilla, having aged, would eventually leave the gang to pursue legitimate concerns. "As the boys of the founding clique matured, some of them got married and settled down, generally tending to drop their ties with the gang. Girls left even earlier—usually when they got pregnant. Others, usually the least stable, remained involved in the street life-style. . . . Clearly, the original members—now in their late teens and early 20s—didn't have much in common with the 13- and 14-year-old boys who clamored for admission" (Moore 1991, 31). The differences in ages imply differences in life experiences. The younger boys would often create their own clique in an attempt to make a name for themselves. The original members would be known as *veteranos*.

In my own studies of Buffalo street gangs, I found that neighborhood street gangs generally evolved from neighborhood playgroups and schoolmates. Among the more famous Buffalo street gangs is the **Fruit Belt Posse** (named after an area of Buffalo where the streets are named after fruit trees). The Fruit Belt Posse (FBT), which developed in the early 1980s, mostly as an offspring of the **Mad Dogs**, can be divided into an age-graded typology:

1. Senior Posse—ages 16–20
2. Junior Posse—ages 11–15
3. Baby Posse—10 and younger

Buffalo street gangs will be discussed in greater detail in Chapter 6.

DEGREE OF CRIMINALITY Gangs exist for different reasons. In some cases, the primary function is "defense," as in defending turf. Other gangs exist to make money, so they sell drugs. And still others find extreme pleasure being on "offense"; that is, they are criminal and predatory in design. Huff (1989), who studied gangs in Cleveland and Columbus, found that most of them emerged from break-dancing or rappin' groups (informal groups of peers). Other gangs evolved from regular street-corner groups as a result of conflict with rival groups. Some of these Ohio gangs were influenced by gangsters from Chicago and Los Angeles, who brought with them leadership skills learned from larger urban environments. Huff's (1989) typology of Cleveland and Columbus gangs reflects the level of commitment that gang members had to criminal activities:

1. **Hedonistic**—These types of gangs are mainly into drug use and commit little crime, especially violent crime.

2. **Instrumental**—Gangs that commit property crime, use drugs and alcohol, but seldom sell drugs.

3. **Predatory**—Gangs that are heavily involved in serious crime (e.g., robbery, murder), seriously abuse addictive drugs (e.g., crack), and may sell drugs, but not in an organized fashion.

DEGREE OF ATTACHMENT TO AND INVOLVEMENT WITH THE GANG Vigil (1988) and Vigil and Long (1990) distinguished four basic types of gang members based on their degree of attachment to and involvement with the gang:

1. **Regulars (hard cores)**—Those who are strongly attached to the gang, have few interests outside of the gang, and started in the gang at an early age. These gang members usually had tough childhoods and tend to be very violent as gang members. They usually lacked a consistent male adult authority figure in their lives. They are often called "hard core" members because their very identity is directly tied to their gang affiliation. They are very influential within the gang structure, and have the highest level of attachment and commitment to the gang.

2. **Peripheral (or associates)**—These gang members have a strong attachment, but participate less often in gang activities than the regulars, or hard cores. They have some interests outside of the gang and hope to eventually get out. Their commitment and attachment level is strong but not lasting.

3. **Temporary**—These gang members are marginally committed, and joined the gang later in life than the regulars or associates. Their attachment and commitment to the gang is not nearly as intense as the others. They remain in the gang for a short time.

4. **Situational**—These members are very marginally attached, have limited involvement, and try to avoid violent situations (Shelden et al. 1997).

In other degree-of-attachment typologies, classifications could include:

1. **O.G.s**—The original gangsters of a gang. They are members for life.

2. **Hard cores**—The die-hards of the gang, usually comprising only about 10% of the gang.

3. **Regular members**—Like the associates described by Vigil and Long. They usually range from 14 to 17 years old and have the primary job of robbing and stealing. If they stay in the gang long enough, they will become hard core.

4. **Wannabes**—Usually 11 to 13 years old, these youths have yet to be initiated into the gang, but they are waiting to be invited.

5. **Could bes**—Usually kids 10 and younger who are raised in an environment conducive to gang behavior.

Reiner (1992) studied street gangs in Los Angeles and established his own typology, also based on an individual's level of commitment to the gang:

1. **At risk**—These are youths that are not in a gang presently, but run a high risk of joining a gang in the near future. They can be described as *pregang* youths. They have shown some interest in the gang, either by fantasizing or experimenting by wearing gang attire and talking the talk of gang members.

2. **Wannabe**—As the term implies, these are youths who know and admire gang members and want to be just like them. They are viewed as future "recruits" of the gang. They are usually of preteen age and are already dressing and acting like a gang member. Mentally they are ready to join, they are just waiting for an invitation.

3. **Associate**—Generally these members are at the lowest level of the gang and are sometimes referred to as "fringe" or "little homies."

4. **Hard core**—Regular members that spend most of their time with gang-related activities. They have some friends and interests outside of the gang. They are small in number, usually representing no more than 10–15% of the total membership of the gang.

5. **Veteranos/O.G.s**—Usually men (or women) in their 20s, maybe their 30s, who still actively participate in gang activities. The term *veteranos* is usually used in correspondence to Hispanic gangs; whereas the term O.G. is applied to elder statesmen of African-American street gangs. They may be old, in gang terms, but generally command a great deal of respect. Moore (1991, 27) stated that the term *veteranos* is far more specific and refers to the original clique in any barrio and to men in any gang who have been through prison.

TYPE OF ACTIVITY   Some researchers (Taylor 1990 and Shelden et al. 2001) categorize gangs by the type of criminal activities involved. Four major types of gangs can be identified in this way. (*Note*: Taylor used the first three of these categories and defined gangs in terms of their motivation.)

1. **Scavenger gangs**—Gangs that are loosely organized and prey on the weak. "Members of these gangs often have no common bond beyond their impulsive behavior and their need to belong. . . . They have no particular goals, no purpose, no substantial camaraderies" (Taylor 1990, 4). They sometimes participate in violence for fun and impulsive reasons. They are low academic achievers, found the challenge of school too difficult to handle, and dropped out for a life on the streets where survival of the fittest still implies physical superiority.

2. **Territorial gangs**—These gangs are associated with a specific area or turf. Protecting turf often leads to conflict with rival gangs. Their specific goal is to protect their turf from perceived outside threats. The turf sometimes serves as a business market for illicit activities such as drug sales, which further highlights the importance of protecting it from external threats. Taylor (1990, 6)

stated that "when scavenger gangs become serious about organizing for a specific purpose, they enter the territorial stage."

3. **Organized/corporate gangs**—These are the most cohesive of gangs and are heavily involved in regular and well-organized criminal activities. They often represent a corporate type of division of labor and are specifically motivated by generating a profit. "These well-organized groups have a very strong leader or manager. The main focus of their organization is participation in illegal money-making ventures" (Taylor 1990, 7). Gang members are expected to follow strict orders and promotion is based on merit—as is generally found in the corporate world.

4. **Drug gangs**—These gangs are focused on making a profit, and selling drugs is the business they employ. Padilla's (1992) *The Gang as an American Enterprise* provides an excellent description of a drug gang and the methods employed to maintain its market. The strict division of labor is designed to benefit the group, but the leaders and members found at the top are the ones who generally enjoy the greatest profits—again, similar to most corporations and businesses.

RACIAL AND ETHNIC DISTINCTIONS OF GANGS   One of the most common ways to identify and categorize gangs is by race and ethnicity. Generally speaking, gangs are homogeneous, even in heterogeneous communities; in other words, gangs almost always consist of members from one race (e.g., African-American) or specific ethnic group (e.g., the Irish, Mexicans, or Chinese).

Hispanic/Latino/Chicano Gangs   Hispanics are the largest minority group in the United States. The largest ethnic groups found within this racial classification are Mexican-Americans, Cuban-Americans, and Puerto Ricans. Which term is more acceptable—Hispanic, Latino, or Chicano—is a matter of great debate. The U.S. Bureau of the Census has been struggling over the distinction for some time now. Shelden and associates (2001) prefer to use the term *Chicano*, stating that "Chicano gangs in Southern California have perhaps the longest history of any gang in America; they have been in existence for over 50 years. Family and community ties are most apparent among these gangs, which may often be traced back several generations" (p. 42). Regoli and Hewitt use the term *Latino*. "Most Latino gangs are organized around age cohorts or *klikas*, separated in age by two or three years, and are territorially based" (Regoli and Hewitt 2003, 315). Regardless of the terminology used, Hispanic gangs are very territorial; the gang is linked to a specific barrio, and loyalty to one's barrio is often the basis of much intergang violence. Chicano gangs do not identify with colors in the way that African-American gangs do, but most of them favor colors such as black, white, brown, and tan (Dickie pants are a favorite). Many of their rituals are similar to those of gangs of any racial background.

Membership in Latino gangs is achieved through initiation rituals designed to establish a member's loyalty to the gang. The ritual typically consists of a beating at the hands of three or four members of the gang. Serious beatings in the initiation are rare, since the intent is to see if and how the would-be member stands up and defends himself. The ritual is also intended to solidify the new member's integration into the gang. Much time is spent partying and drinking in casual settings or in structured settings celebrating a baptism, birthday, or wedding. The automobile is also very important to Latino gang members. For many members, cruising in their "low-riders" (cars with lowered front and rear ends) projects a "cool" image to others while at the same time distinguishing themselves from white cruisers (Regoli and Hewitt 2003, 315).

Today, Hispanic gangs are a permanent fixture, especially in such places as Southern California and parts of Texas and Arizona.

African-American Gangs According to Perkins (1987), African-American gangs formed in reaction to institutional racism. He also suggested that blacks join gangs for the typical reasons of developing a sense of belonging, identity, power, security, and discipline. The most noted, and widespread, contemporary black gangs are the Los Angeles-based Bloods and Crips. "These gangs have become essentially confederations of smaller sets or subsets. Sets are generally organized around neighborhoods and typically have between 20 and 30 members, although a few of the larger sets may have more than 100 members" (Regoli and Hewitt 2003, 314). It is believed that the Crips outnumber the Bloods by about three to one (Lavigne 1993). (African-American super gangs will be discussed in detail in Chapter 6.)

Asian-American Gangs Asian gangs are a relatively new development in the United States and their activities vary by ethnicity. There are Chinese, Japanese, Korean, Vietnamese, Cambodian, Samoan, and many other ethnic Asian gangs. They tend to be very secretive and are difficult for law enforcement agents to penetrate. Asian gang members are generally clean-cut and act with respect toward the police; they generally victimize people from their own culture. According to Reiner (1992), Asian gangs are highly entrepreneurial in nature. (Asian gangs will be discussed in further detail in Chapter 6.)

White Gangs White ethnic youths once dominated the gang world. As described in Chapter 2, the Irish formed the first real street gangs in the United States. Nearly all of the white ethnic immigrant groups that followed the Irish formed gangs as a mechanism for coping with their marginal status in society. Presently, white gangs represent only about 10–12% of the nation's total gang population (they make up only 2% of all gang members in Los Angeles). Furthermore, as described in Chapter 1, most of the contemporary white gang members do not belong to street gangs; instead, they belong to such groups as the skinheads, KKK, the Aryan Brotherhood, and so on. Oddly, Shelden, Tracy, and Brown (2001) described white **stoner** groups as a type of gang. These white youths are generally from higher socioeconomic backgrounds than typical street gangs. They are from suburban areas and are generally labeled underachievers by their parents and schools. They typically engage in heavy drug use (e.g., speed, LSD, marijuana, cocaine, and PCP) and are almost always into heavy metal music. Shelden and associates, referencing Jackson and McBride (1992), describe stoners in the following manner: "Stoners typically dress in red or black clothing, with athletic jersey tops portraying heavy music stars; metal-spiked wrist cuffs, collars, and belts; earrings; long hair; and tattoos. They often wear satanic relics or sacrilegious effigies. Stoners use graffiti to mark territory, not necessarily geographic, but musical—to claim music groups or types of music" (p. 52). Stoners may share a couple of characteristics of gangs, but most gang researchers would not classify stoners as gang members.

A group of white immigrants that more clearly reflects the traditions of street gangs would be **Armenian Power (AP)**, a violent youth group formed in the early 1990s. These youths wear the classic uniform of a barrio street gang: baggy khaki pants, pressed white T-shirts, hair nets, and navy blue ski caps. They are tattooed and armed with Berettas and Glocks and Kalashnikovs and speak in Spanish street jargon. But this is not a Latino gang; they are a new street gang in the heavily Armenian areas of East Hollywood and Glendale. "With only 120 members, the gang is now blamed by authorities for a dozen murders—almost exclusively of rival gang members—and more than 100 shootings. To thousands of Armenian Americans whose parents and grandparents came here after escaping the horrors of World War I and genocide, the existence of an Armenian gang is a stain on the tight ethnic community that has achieved success beyond its small numbers in politics, art, business and farming" (Krikorian 1997, B1). For the recent Armenian immigrants who fled the war-ravaged streets of Beirut, the political upheavals of Iran, and the Armenian homeland itself, the gang is a painful reminder of the lawlessness they sought to leave behind. The members of AP see themselves as the guardians of young Armenian-Americans who have come under attack from older, larger gangs (Krikorian 1997).

Native-American Gangs Perhaps the surest sign that gangs exist nearly everywhere in the United States is the fact that gangs exist on Native-American reservations. "In recent years, much attention has been given to the proliferation and emergence of street gangs among ethnic groups in locations formerly gang-free. Navajo tribal members and officials have expressed strong concerns over both the presence of male youth gangs and what has been perceived as growing levels of violence" (Henderson, Kunitz, and Levy 2004, 122). The Navajo Nation reservation in Window Rock, Arizona, the largest reservation in the United States, is now home to numerous gangs. "On this 25,000-square-mile reservation, which has seen about 75 gangs emerge during the past five years, the murder rate has skyrocketed to four times the national average—and nearly double the rate in Los Angeles" (Sahagun 1997, A18). The crime rate on reservations has soared in the past decade. Homicides, assaults, robberies, kidnappings, and weapons and drug trafficking are among the crimes being reported in record numbers. This increased crime rate is attributed to the growing gang presence on reservations.

Gangs have existed on Native-American reservations for at least three decades. "The earliest references to self-identified gangs come from about 1970 in an agency town located near the eastern boundary of the reservation. In that year, one interviewee claims to have formed a gang, the Cruisers, with about a dozen other schoolmates between the ages of thirteen and fifteen. The primary activity consisted of drinking together at the town's drive-in theater on weekends. They shoplifted items 'a bunch of times' to pay for liquor, which they got someone older to buy for them" (Henderson et al. 2004, 129). Gangs at varying stages of development and organization exist on nearly all reservations. However, structured gang activity is still rare. One of the reasons cited for the increased presence of gangs on the Navajo reservation is the fact that the Native-American population is growing increasingly youthful, largely because of high fertility rates—the median age is 24.2 years, compared with 32.9 years for all Americans, according to the Bureau of the Census (Sahagun 1997). Navajo gangs have adopted many of the same behaviors as urban street gangs. They find status through the use of violence and they have been known to possess a range of weapons, from .22-caliber handguns to AK-47s. Drug trafficking provides the capital to help sustain their existence.

On the Pine Ridge Reservation of South Dakota, home to about 20,000 Lakota Sioux, authorities have acknowledged 3,500 known gang members. The village of Pine Ridge is home to 12 gangs alone. Potato Creek, a small town with just 40 residents, has 15 gang members. The gangs have brought a life of terror to this reservation. They exist primarily to deal in drugs, especially cocaine, marijuana, and methamphetamines. Some of the gangs, such as the **Nomads**, have a command structure with a ruling council and a set of laws. The gangs on this reservation are responsible for 70% of the crimes—assaults, sexual assaults, intimidation, harassment, burglaries, vandalism, graffiti, and murder. There are 10 to 12 homicides each year on the Pine Ridge Reservation, which includes Wounded Knee in its territory. Gangs are so prevalent at the local schools that most youth simply drop out; in fact, the graduation rate is a dismal 1% (Elsner 2003).

Native-American youths experience many of the same problems as juveniles off the reservation. But the oppression and discrimination experienced by nearly every other group of Americans pale in comparison to that experienced by Native-Americans. They are victims of attempted genocide and today face high levels of unemployment and poverty. As with urban gangs, economics is a significant factor in the increased level of gang activity on Native American reservations. The Navajo Nation is now faced with important decisions regarding a gang-prevention policy that will effectively meet the growing problem of youth gangs.

A Typology of Ex-Gang Members It is generally understood that once a youth decides to become a gang member, four outcomes are possible: death, imprisonment, life-long membership in the gang, and life outside of the gang. It is interesting to discover what happens to the gang members who have left the gang. Many will find success, but most continue to struggle due to the fact that they wasted their early lives in a gang. Joan Moore (1991) created a typology of ex-gang members from her studies of Mexican-American gang members in East Los Angeles.

1. **Tecatos**—Heroin use is a big part of the Mexican-American gang subculture. A **tecato** is a heroin user. According to Moore, tecatos represent slightly more than a quarter of the male gang members and a much smaller proportion of the female gang members that she studied. Breaking the gang habit is much easier than breaking a heroin habit; consequently, these ex-gang members will continue to struggle in mainstream society.

2. **Cholos**—A **cholo** generally is a Mexican-American gang member. Cholos are not addicted to heroin, but they do use drugs (e.g., PCP, marijuana). In Moore's study, cholos represented about one-third of the men and women who have left the gang. They still use drugs, although not to the extent of tecatos, associate with active gang members, and have usually served prison time. Because of their cholo lifestyle, they have difficulty finding conventional jobs.

They also experience family problems and unstable marriages, especially if their first marriage was to another gang member.

3. **Squares**—These ex-gang members are the ones who are successfully leading a conventional lifestyle. Approximately 40% of the men and around the same number of women fell into this category of ex-gang members that Moore studied. Becoming a part of this category of ex-gang member is generally directly associated with the level of involvement that the gang member had with the gang originally. Hard-core members almost always find it impossible to lead a conventional lifestyle, whereas the peripheral members were the most likely to enjoy a successful transition to a conventional lifestyle.

As this review of gangs and their organizational components has revealed, there are great differences among gangs and their structure and purpose for existence. On the other hand, gangs do share a number of common characteristics. First, they are generally upset by their marginalized status in society and view joining a gang as a viable alternative. Second, their marginalized status helps to develop highly competitive behaviors motivated by self-reliance and a survival-of-the-fittest attitude. Third, they have a general distrust of society's criminal justice system, especially the police and the courts. Fourth, because of their self-inflicted social isolation from the rest of society, they have learned to become self-reliant. This self-reliance often directs them toward delinquent and criminal activities. Fifth, their aura of defiance guarantees that their marginal status will continue.

TURNING: THE SOCIALIZATION OF A GANG MEMBER

Interacting with people one feels comfortable with is a behavioral characteristic shared by nearly all humans. Forming, or joining, a group one feels comfortable in is another vital aspect of human behavior. "Social interaction plays an important role in an individual's life. The individual wants to feel that he or she fits into a group or a society. Individuals want to experience a sense of unity with their fellows. Hence, by joining together in groups, the individual becomes a part of a whole" (Delaney 2001, 126). **Socialization** is the process whereby individuals learn to get along with others in order to form groups. The socialization process is also the mechanism that society utilizes to teach its youths how to conform to cultural expectations.

Socialization

To properly understand human behavior, one must comprehend the critical aspect of socialization. "What makes socialization both necessary and possible for human beings is their lack of *instincts*, biologically inherited capacities for performing relatively complex tasks. Whatever temperament and potential abilities human infants may be born with, they are also born helpless, depending on adults for survival. What may be more surprising is the extent to which traits that seem very basic and essential to human nature also appear to depend on socialization" (Thio 2003, 67). The importance placed on socialization dates back to the Puritan era in the United States.

The earliest Puritan communities in the United States used informal methods of controlling juveniles. Probably the most effective of these informal methods was *socialization*, by which youths were taught the rules of society from the time they were born until the rules became internalized. If a youth violated a law, the family, church, and community stepped in to bring the youth back into line. The family was expected to punish the youth, and, if the family failed, church and community elders turned to other punishments (Bartollas and Miller 2001, 65).

Socialization is a learning process by which individuals learn the expectations of society and are taught the proper guidelines of expected behavior. It is a process by which people learn, through interaction with others, what they must know in order to survive and function as a productive member of society. Successful socialization has occurred when the individual internalizes the norms, values, and beliefs of a society. "Socialization is the process of guiding people into acceptable behavior patterns through interaction, approval, rewards, and punishments. It involves learning the techniques needed to function in society. Socialization is a developmental process that is influenced by family and peers, neighbors, teachers, and other authority figures" (Siegel et al. 2003, 119). Proper socialization ensures that the norms and values of a society are instilled within a child. Each of us becomes a part of society because of the socialization process. From a functionalist perspective, "socialized individuals keep society going after the older generation dies. Without socialization, anarchy would likely reign, threatening the survival of society" (Thio 2003, 74). Conversely, improper socialization contributes to deviancy, criminality, and, sometimes, gang behavior.

Juvenile delinquency and criminal behavior, therefore, is the result of poor socialization and/or the individual's unwillingness to accept the rules of society. The child is exposed to cultural expectations by the **agents of socialization**: parents and family, the schools, peers, the media, religion, employers, and the government. The primary influence on children is the parents and the immediate family. Early socialization is referred to as **primary socialization**. Early childhood socialization is especially critical for instilling the proper guidelines for acceptable behavior. This fact is underscored by the reality that most youths, even those found in high-crime areas, do not become criminals and gang members.

> Early socialization experiences have a lifelong influence on self-image, values, and behavior. Even children living in the most deteriorated inner-city environments will not get involved in delinquency if their socialization experiences are positive. After all, most inner-city youths do not commit serious crimes, and relatively few of those who do become career criminals. More than 14 million youths live in poverty, but the majority do not become chronic offenders. Only those who experience improper socialization are at risk for crime. Research consistently shows a relationship between the elements of socialization and delinquency (Siegel 2003, 119).

Primary socialization is not always successful, as many families fail to properly socialize their children.

> When parenting is inadequate, a child's maturational process will be interrupted and damaged. Although much debate still occurs over which elements of the parent-child relationship are most critical, there is little question that family

relationships have a significant influence on behavior. One view is that youths socialized in families wracked by conflict and abuse are at risk for delinquency. For example, there is now evidence that children, who grow up in homes where parents use severe discipline, yet lack warmth and are less involved in their children's lives, are prone to antisocial behavior. In contrast, parents who are supportive and effectively control their children in noncoercive fashion— parental efficacy—are more likely to raise children who refrain from delinquency (Siegel et al. 2003, 119).

Thus, socialization should be a process where love and affection are also demonstrated. Parents who nurture their children by first holding and cuddling them as infants and then sharing in their growing experiences will have children that love and respect them. Ideally, the "socialization of children further teaches parents to be patient, understanding, and self-sacrificing, qualities useful for enhancing human relations in society" (Thio 2003, 74). On the other hand, poor parenting can contribute significantly to delinquency. For example, research has demonstrated a relationship between parental rejection and aggressive delinquent behavior. Research has also shown that deviant or unacceptable behavior by youths is closely related to emotional stress and high levels of tension in the family environment (Kratcoski and Kratcoski 1996, 130–131). In short, "the mechanisms used within families for controlling youthful behavior can have a significant bearing on the activities of children" (Kratcoski and Kratcoski 1996, 132).

The family is also a **primary group**. Charles Cooley (1909) viewed primary groups as intimate, face-to-face groups that play a key role in linking the individual to the larger society. The primary group is relatively small and informal, involves close personal relationships, and has an important role in shaping the self. Primary groups become the most important sources of the individual's ideals, which derive from the moral and ethical unity of the group itself (Delaney 2004, 157–158). Primary groups include individuals with whom we form our closest relationships, which eventually evolve into a sense of "we" or belonging. "Members of a primary group share a sense of 'we-ness,' involving the sort of sympathy and mutual identification for which 'we' is a natural expression. Individuals share a sense of feeling toward the whole (the group)" (Delaney 2001, 126).

Children generally start school at age 4 or 5. This begins the **secondary socialization** process. The child is now exposed to the influences of both the institutional demands of the school and the interpersonal pressures associated with having peers and attempting to blend into bonding groups. At home, the child was used to being treated as unique, whereas at school, the child is treated in the same manner as all other children. This can be a dramatic experience for some children. Getting along with their teachers will be a critical component to proper continued socialization. "Whereas socialization by families often contributes to the diversity of society, schools are more likely to contribute to uniformity. Society, in effect, officially designates schools as its socializing agents. They are expected both to help children develop their potential as creative, independent individuals and to mold them into social conformity—two goals that seem contradictory" (Thio 2003, 82).

Delinquents and gang members almost always report having difficulty with school, either because of the way teachers treated them or the manner in which their peers treated them. In Padilla's gang research on the Diamonds, he reported that

> a wide range of school-related experiences contributed immensely to the
> youngsters' positive outlook toward the gang, which in turn, led to their subse-
> quent affiliation with it. Their affirmative judgment of the gang and decision to
> join were developed over time as contact and interaction with teachers and
> some schoolmates already familiar with or actually belonging to gangs resulted
> in their being labeled "deviants" and troublemakers and treated accordingly.
> Members of the Diamonds responded to these conditions by joining with others
> so labeled and engaging in corresponding behavior. In response to teachers' la-
> beling them negatively, which in most cases occurred during their elementary
> school years, youngsters adopted different forms of "oppositional behavioral"
> (for example, misbehaving in the classroom, refusing to do work in the class-
> room and at home, fighting with classmates, and cutting school) (1992, 68–69).

Negative labels by teachers, coupled with the poor English skills of the Diamonds, led
to unsatisfactory academic performances in school. These negative feelings would
have dire consequences on their future lives. The negative labels assigned to the
members of the Diamonds led them to feel stigmatized, which in turn fueled a poor
self-image. By the time these youths reached high school, many of them had already
joined the gang and participated in gang activity. However, for most of them, turning to
the gang occurred when they entered high school.

Critics of the educational system wonder why the schools are not doing a better
job controlling the level of delinquency and violence found on many school campuses.
They believe that the school is actually fostering delinquent behavior. As Kratcoski and
Kratcoski (1996, 160) explained:

> The indictment of many schools as delinquency-producing institutions seems to
> center on two types of accusations: (1) that the schools have failed as socializa-
> tion institutions—that is, delinquency is produced because young people have
> not been taught the social skills that enable them to interact appropriately with
> peers and adults; or (2) the failure in academic subjects leads to situations in
> which youths are shamed or down-graded by peers and teachers, or in which
> they develop such negative self-images that they undertake delinquent behavior
> as a defense mechanism or a method of gaining attention or status.

It is important to note that often the children who do poorly is school are not receiving
proper parental help with their schoolwork at home. It is critical that parents work with
their children on homework projects or, at the least, check over the homework and quiz the
child on assigned school materials. In this manner, children are far more likely to perform
adequately in school and thus increase their level of self-esteem and status in nondelinquent ways. Clearly, many children are not being helped properly with their schoolwork
by their parents and consequently do poorly in school. Poor school performance is a pre-
dictor of juvenile behavior. "The literature linking delinquency to poor school performance and inadequate educational facilities is extensive. Youths who feel that the teachers
do not care, who consider themselves failures, and who do poorly in school are more
likely to become involved in a delinquent way of life than adolescents who are educationally
successful. Research findings based on studies done over the past two decades indicate
that many school dropouts, especially those who have been expelled, face a significant
chance of entering a criminal career. In contrast, doing well in school and developing

attachments to teachers has been linked to crime resistance" (Siegel et al. 2003, 120). At many schools, children are more afraid of becoming a victim of physical violence than they are of doing poorly in school. Among the more threatening behaviors confronting youths are the presence of gangs that hang out in or around the school.

As children age, their associations with peers become increasingly important. Children begin to value the company and opinions of their friends more than of their parents or families. A **peer group** consists of individuals who are roughly the same age. For some youths, the peer group becomes a primary agent of socialization. This occurs when the influence of the peer group has led an individual to become more independent of adult authorities, when the individual has embraced the concept of group loyalty, and when friendship and group norms are valued over societal expectations. When peer groups distance themselves from societal and parental expectations, they have freed themselves for delinquent behavior. As explained in Chapter 3, gangs tend to evolve from peer groups—what Thrasher called the "spontaneous" gang. When youth peer groups embrace deviant and antisocial behavior, they begin to cut themselves off from conventional associations and institutions. Chronic juvenile delinquents surround themselves with peers who share their antisocial attitudes and behavioral mannerisms. "People who maintain close relations with antisocial peers will sustain their own criminal behavior into their adulthood. When peer influence diminishes, so does delinquent activity" (Siegel et al. 2003, 120). As the children in a peer group age, they may be tempted to join, or start, a gang.

Reasons to Join a Gang

The composition and the purpose of the gang have changed radically over the years. The early street gangs usually consisted of young members who eventually outgrew the gang affiliation by the time they reached their late teens or early 20s. Today, many gang members are in their late 20s and 30s, and they stay in the gang for more years now as well. As Moore (1991, 47) explained, in the early cliques of the 1950s almost no boy over the age of 15 joined the gang, but in the recent cliques, almost a third of the men joined at age 16 or older. More than a decade later, gang members are often much older, especially those in prison gangs. Furthermore, turf protection and ethnic pride have disappeared as the primary or sole reason for the gang's presence.

Padilla (1992, 78–90) cited a number of reasons why the members of the Diamonds joined the gang (and these reasons are common to many gang members' decision to join):

1. **Peer influence**—Many youths are directly recruited by a friend whom one thinks highly of and may already belong to the gang, or is thinking about joining the gang. The youth is led to believe that this is the cool thing to do, or the right thing to do.

2. **Protection**—In many neighborhoods, trying to stay out of a gang by claiming to be neutral leads to attacks from members of a number of gangs. Thus, by joining one gang, the youth has protection from his own gang and allies against the other gangs.

3. **Revenge**—When an individual is picked on by bullies or a gang, there is generally little that he or she can do alone. Joining a gang, however, allows for the youth to gain revenge against others for past injustices.

4. **Police treatment**—A constant complaint among the Diamonds (as with most gangs) is the manner in which they are treated by the police. From the perspective of gang members, the police are out to harass them. The Diamonds recounted personal stories of how the police "dissed them in front of their girlfriends." Accusations against the police that they planted drugs on them to make an arrest were also common complaints.

5. **Family problems**—Turmoil, in any shape or form, at home often led many of the Diamonds to seek out a place that felt more like home and group that felt more like a family. The gang often serves this function for troubled youths.

Martin Jankowski (1991) provides six primary reasons why youths join a gang. He points out that many youths in the low-income inner cities of the United States face a situation in which a gang already exists in their neighborhood and therefore they don't really have a choice in joining a gang.

1. **Material incentives**—The gloomy economic reality of many urban neighborhoods leads many youths to seek their economic fortune in nonconventional ways. These youths believe that the gang will provide them with a chance to make big money, quickly. Some even believe that they can make enough money to help support their families. "It was also believed that less individual effort would be required in the various economic ventures in a gang because more people would be involved" (Jankowski 1991, 41). The most attractive method of making money usually involves the sale and distribution of illegal drugs. The reality, of course, is that few gang members make money, and eventually they get caught and go to prison, or they are shot and killed by rivals. Most gang members leave the gang as poor as they entered.

2. **Recreation**—Since gang members spend most of their time just hanging out, the gang provides opportunities for entertainment, recreation, fun, partying, and women. "The gang provides individuals with entertainment, much as a fraternity does for college students or the Moose and Elk clubs do for their members" (Jankowski 1991, 42). The gang will also provide the drugs and alcohol that youths desire for recreational purposes. Moore (1991) described this same reality with the barrio gangs that she studied. Moore found that gang members like to "party." For gang members (as with many American adolescents) "partying" was generally associated with getting high.

3. **A place of refuge and camouflage**—"Some individuals join a gang because it provides them with a protective group identity. They see the gang as offering them anonymity, which may relieve the stress associated with having to be personally accountable for all their actions in an intensely competitive environment" (Jankowski 1991, 44). In other words, individual gang members can sometimes blend into the greater group, making a clear identification by police and other social control agents difficult. The gang, then, provides the individual

members a place to blend in, as if wearing camouflage. It also provides a place of refuge until the heat goes away.

4. **Physical protection**—As most researchers have identified (including Padilla in the previous listing of reasons gang members join a gang), the gang provides protection to its members. In certain neighborhoods, gang members and nongang members alike risk becoming victims of urban violence. Joining a gang gives them some measure of self-defense (or offense). Providing a stereotypical outlook on gangs, Jankowski (1991, 44) states, "Individuals also join gangs because they believe the gang can provide them with personal protection from the predatory elements active in low-income neighborhoods."

5. **A time to resist**—Gang members from poorer neighborhoods hope to avoid living in poverty like their parents had. The high degree of economic deprivation combined with a sense of hopelessness lead many urban youths to believe that gang life represents an improvement on the alternative endured by their parents. "Most prospective gang members have lived through the pains of economic deprivation and the stresses that such an existence puts on a family. They desperately want to avoid following in their parents' path, which they believe is exactly what awaits them. For these individuals, the gang is a way to resist the jobs their parents held, and, by extension, the life their parents led" (Jankowski 1991, 45).

6. **Commitment to community**—"Some individuals join the gang because they see participation as a form of commitment to their community. These usually come from neighborhoods where gangs have existed for generations" (Jankowski 1991, 46). Gangs with a history are especially concerned with protecting turf. This dedication bestows upon the gang member the status of a type of local patriot. Such status in the community is equated to earning great respect, the critical component to the gang member's ego.

Many youths want to join the gang because one of their friends had recently attained membership. The simple fact that so many youths find turning to a gang more commendable than turning to society is a sure sign that there are flaws in the social system.

Curry and Decker (2003) argue that the key issue regarding joining a gang is whether individuals are *pulled* or *pushed* into a gang.

Young people who are pulled into membership join their gang because of the attractions if offers to them—the promise or expectation of friendship, opportunities to make money, or the ability to provide something for the neighborhood. Being pushed into the gang conveys a very different motivation for joining the gang. Individuals who see themselves as pushed into gang membership join the gang out of fear for physical consequences if they do not do so, or because they see themselves as powerless to resist the temptations of gang life (Curry and Decker 2003, 68).

Gang members who are pulled to the gang join voluntarily and are more likely to evolve into hard-core members. Gang members who are pushed into a gang had generally tried to remain neutral but found themselves being victimized by all the rival gangs. These members are less likely to evolve into hard-core members.

Recruitment

As the preceding has outlined, there are many reasons why a youth may want to join a gang. Eventually, these wannabe gang members will be recruited by the local gang(s). The method of recruitment will vary depending on the type of gang. Street gangs, for example, may take the *fraternal* approach by convincing the recruit that gang membership is about companionship and brotherhood (or sisterhood) and that it is the cool thing to do. Street gangs may also attempt to recruit wannabe members by selling them on the concept of an *obligation* to the local community. The recruit should want to join a gang for patriotism, community honor, and local respect. In other cases, street gangs may use a *coercive* approach to recruitment through intimidation. Coercion and intimidation tactics may include both physical and psychological tactics (Jankowski 1990; Shelden et al. 2001).

Prison gangs have their own techniques for recruiting wannabes. The Texas Syndicate uses a comprehensive and lengthy recruiting process that includes meeting the "homeboy connection" requirement. A thorough background check is conducted on the recruit to make sure he is "clean" (i.e., that he is not a police informant). Upon successful completion of the background check, the entire membership must cast a unanimous vote before admittance is granted. If membership is denied for any reason, the recruit risks being coerced into paying the gang for protection or being used as a prostitute by the gang (Fong 1990). Recruitment into the Mexican Mafia is not nearly as strenuous. If the recruit meets the "homeboy connection," passes a poorly conducted background check, and receives a simple majority vote of the entire group, he is granted membership. This loosely structured recruiting procedure is the major factor in the dramatic growth in Mexican Mafia membership found throughout state prisons such as those in Texas and California (Fong 1990).

Initiation

Gangs not only do not share consistent recruitment patterns, they have also developed different rites of passage, or initiation ceremonies, that recruits must pass in order to gain membership. Gang initiation rites, fighting, and drinking are behaviors that are encouraged because they allow young males an opportunity to prove their manhood (machismo) (Vigil and Long 1990). Initiation ceremonies have become increasingly ritualized since the 1950s and 1960s. Moore (1991) reported that few gang members were initiated in the original cholo gangs. The gang asked a youth to join and that was it. Gang initiations have become far more ritualized in the contemporary gang era. "Nearly every documented gang in the United States has an initiation process, and there is variation in how initiation rituals occur. Most are rather crude with few formal aspects to them and involve some form of violence, typically by current members of the gang directed against the initiate" (Curry and Decker 2003, 71). Most gang members, males and females, are "jumped" into the gang to test the recruit's ability to stand up in a fight. Specific initiation requirements vary from gang to gang. Some gangs (e.g., the Crips) will require new members to commit a crime in front of a gang witness. This process is called "loc'ing in." Most gangs have rituals in which they "beat-in" a member—a literal beating—to test the bravado and toughness of the recruit.

Padilla (1992) provides one of the more comprehensive reviews of the physical "beat-in" in a process that he called the "violation ceremony." Padilla stated that the violation ceremony can take place on three separate occasions:

1. **the "V-in"**—the initiation beating that a recruit receives when first joining the gang
2. **the "V-punishment"**—used when a gang member violates the rules and is punished for such infractions
3. **the "V-out"**—used when the member wants to leave the gang

The **V-in** ceremony involves the recruit taking an extreme beating with fists and feet. This is done in order to test the toughness of the recruit and to make sure that he will not run or panic during times of a gang crisis. Usually a time limit is set in which the inductee will be beat on by a number of gang members. The gang members are allowed to kick and punch. In some gangs, there are rules against blows to the head of the recruit, for the reason that the beating will be easier to hide. The inductee is to "willingly" take the beating and is not allowed to fight back. If the inductee survives, he (or she) is accepted into the gang. Recruits who already have a reputation for being tough and getting in fights usually receive a more lenient initiation. The violation ceremony is more than a physical beating, however. Padilla (1992, 59) explained that "although these young people agree to the physical punishment embodied in the V-in ceremony, it is important to regard it as the culmination of a process through which their attitudes and views have been shaped." The **V-punishment** will be implemented when gang leaders determine that certain violations of gang regulations warrant a severe punishment in a ceremonial fashion. Violations that may lead to a physical punishment include stealing from the gang, violating a gang-ordered truce on a rival gang, disrespecting gang leaders, disobeying orders, and so on. The **V-out** ceremony involves a physical beating as well. It is especially brutal under two conditions: when the exiting member possesses a great amount of information about the gang—to remind him of loyalty priorities—and when the exiting member was a troublemaker who caused problems of some sort for the gang during his tenure.

There are times when gang initiation beat-ins are so brutal that the inductee may die as a result. In September 2004, six teenagers, aged 13 to 15, were charged with homicide in the beating death of an eighth-grader who agreed to the fight as part of his gang initiation. The blows taken by Tarus DeShawn Williams, 15, were so severe that blows to his chest crushed the left chamber of his heart (*Syracuse Post-Standard*, 2004D).

Leaving the Gang

Despite the "considerable mythology" (perpetrated primarily by the media) that surrounds the topic of "leaving a gang," it *is* possible to do so (Curry and Decker 2003). The mythology that Curry and Decker refer to includes reports that in order to leave the gang one must commit a particularly heinous crime (e.g., kill a parent). "Interviews with former members document that most of them simply quit their gangs in the same way they ended other affiliations" (Curry and Decker 2003, 77). The reasons provided by ex-gang members for leaving the gang range from concerns over violence (they may have inflicted, witnessed, or been victimized by it) to other obligations of life (e.g., becoming a parent, getting older, having a job). Leaving the gang may be accompanied by a physical beating. The primary reasons for the beating are to remind the gang member of the link to the gang and/or because wanting to leave is perceived as a sign of disrespect the exiting member is directing toward the gang. High-ranking gang members who leave the gang run the risk of forever being a target of rival gang members, especially those hoping to make a name for themselves.

In the contemporary era, however, many members are choosing not to leave the gang. Instead, they are remaining in the gang throughout their adult life. This is generally a very costly decision, as the more years that a gangbanger remains in the gang, the greater the likelihood of being a homicide victim or of being caught for committing a criminal offense. Criminal conviction, of course, leads to incarceration. The tremendous increase in the numbers of gang members in prison has led to a continuation of street gang affiliation behind prison walls. Active street gang members who manage to escape arrest and/or criminal prosecution run an increased risk of eventually facing their own mortality on the streets. Death on the streets will result in a memorial tribute—the more famous the gang member the more elaborate the tribute. Tupac Shakur's death illustrates this dreary reality. A memorial was set up for Tupac outside Club 662 shortly after his death. "Aerosoled in red and blue on the side wall was the title of a Tupac song, 'Shed So Many Tears,' with R.I.P. written backward. The paint was still wet, and there was an overpowering smell of cheap beer on the ground below it: This was a traditional ghetto memorial, poring out tribute to a dead brother. There was amazingly little glamour here, just a sad, ugly feeling, very creepy, very hollow. No art, no life, just ashes" (Solotaroff 2002, 267). Tupac may have a mythical status, but he no longer has life. A physical beating, or the V-out, may actually represent the easy way out of a gang.

CODE OF THE STREET: RESPECT

Without question, the subcultural value that carries the highest value for all gang members is **respect**. Any sign of disrespect shown toward a gang, or gang member, will result in retaliation with extreme prejudice (a militaristic response). The gang subculture becomes a *lifeway* for youths (Vigil 1988), and this lifeway, or way of life, is learned on the streets. Young children (those who are too young to the join the gang) in tough urban environments learn early on that violence is generally the method of choice used to settle disputes. They may learn this by observing domestic violence in the home, fights at school, and violent events (e.g., robberies, gun battles, police pursuits of suspects) in the neighborhood. Padilla (1992, 62) recounted the story of Tito, a Diamonds' gang member, who stated that "growing up among the local youth gang meant witnessing various fights and hearing the different explanations offered by gang members to justify their behavior." After witnessing a gang fight as a 7th-grader, Tito said that he learned that gang members settled their differences by *throwing down* (fighting). Gang members believe that it is their responsibility to protect their turf from other gangs and criminals. The local gang would justify its behavior by saying things like, "This is my hood. If I see you here again, I'm going to kick the shit out of you" (p. 62).

Gang members like Tito learn two important lessons from examples like this. First, you protect your neighborhood, with violence if necessary. This is done because the perception is that these rivals have disrespected you simply because they came into your neighborhood (the neighborhood boundaries include all shopping stores, movie theatres, and so forth that are found within the protected territory). Second, if one finds oneself on enemy territory, one better be ready to fight. The Diamonds' gang member Tito stated, "We want our neighborhood for us, so we have to protect it. So, when I was in grade school, I saw these guys doing things that I thought were necessary to do, like protecting their section of the neighborhood from other gangs. And, you know what, ask any of these guys around here what they think about their neighborhood, they all going to tell you that that is the most important thing for them. So, learn to care for the neighborhood—that's really important" (Padilla 1992, 63).

Entering a rival gang's territory is just one way of disrespecting a gang member. Looking at a gang member the wrong way or stepping on his shoes are among the hundreds of violations deemed disrespectful and offenses deserving of some sort of physical beating. The importance attached to respect is not limited to the street environment; it also extends to the prison setting. Journalist Leon Bing spent four years in the late 1980s interviewing members of the Bloods and Crips in prison. Those conversations formed the basis of her 1991 book *Do or Die*. Portions of this book reappeared in Donohue's *Gangs* (2001). In an interview with gang inmate Monster Kody, Bing inquired about the importance of respect in prison. Kody responded by stating:

> Respect is not negotiable. You get and you give, but you don't get respect unless you give it. In prison you learn one of the virtues of life, and that's reciprocity. You learn to give and you learn to take. It's nothin' one-way about it, it's nothin' about lookin' out for number one. That's individualism, and that mentality disappears in prison, because prison's not about *you*. It's about survival of your unit, your people. There's no star system in prison, but the hierarchy exists. It's just not as apparent as it is on the street. . . . Now, dreadfully so, even prison settings are being overturned by rambunctious gang members. The same erratic behavior you see in the streets is beginning to be the norm inside. Flaggin.' Saggin.' Braggin.' Lettin' people know you're part of something that is powerful. Is mysterious. Is deadly (Bing 2001, 218–219).

So the street sensitivity to anything remotely considered disrespectful has extended to inside prison walls. The obvious disadvantage of having enemies in prison is the fact that the hunted have no place to hide, and, therefore, it is simply a matter of time before the perceived violator is victimized.

The Gang Mentality

Gangs value respect, but they also value other core beliefs that constitute their subcultural identity. "There appear to be several core beliefs and values that tend to be most important in the lives of gang members. These include honor, respect, pride (in oneself and in one's neighborhood), reputation, recognition, and self-esteem, such as having courage, heart, and loyalty. Not unlike as with soldiers or comrades, one must prove oneself worthy to be a gang member" (Shelden et al. 2001, 76). Jankowski (1990) articulated the difference between respect and honor. Respect is something that must be earned and then protected (common with African-American gangs). Honor is something that is automatically bestowed upon a person (common with Chicano gangs, which believe honor has been earned as soon as the youth enters the gang).

Consistent style of dress among members of a gang is another behavior that unifies the group. The unification of a gang helps to establish a "we" feeling. The "we" feeling is overtly displayed by wearing the same colors or style of clothes. The category of "they"—the rival gangs—becomes easily identifiable because "they" will be sporting different colors or styles. Racial and ethnic groups have a history of identifying themselves based on their distinctive "we-ness." The creation of the "we" category provides a sense of community. For street gangs, "we-ness" plays an integral role in the daily lives of gang members. Rival gang members become the "they" group. The designation of one group as a "they" group implies that confrontations between the two are inevitable. Since conflict is inevitable for gang members, they must be willing to fight. Physical strength and prowess in the field of battle are behaviors worthy of automatic respect among gang members.

Gang mentality is better understood from Nawojczyk's (1997) description of the "Three Rs" of gang culture:

1. **Reputation/Rep**—This is of critical concern to gang members. A rep extends not only to each individual but to the gang as a whole. In some gangs, status (or rank) is gained within the gang by having the most "juice," based largely on one's reputation. The manner in which one gains "juice" is also important. Stories of bravado are often embellished in an attempt to enhance the feeling of power. Committing crimes and causing physical harm (including murder) to rivals are especially important in creating a reputation.

2. **Respect**—Every gang member wants to be respected. Respect is sought for not only the individual but also one's set, or gang. Some gangs require, by written or spoken regulation, that the gang member must always show disrespect to rival gang members—to "dis" the rival. If a gang member witnesses a fellow member failing to "dis" a rival gang through hand signs, graffiti, or a simple "mad dog" or stare-down, they can issue a "violation" to their fellow posse member (the V-punishment ceremony as discussed earlier in this chapter). When a gang member properly disses a rival, the third "R" becomes evident.

3. **Retaliation/Revenge**—A major part of the gang subculture value system involves the belief that no challenge can go unanswered. Many times, drive-by shootings and other acts of violence follow an event of perceived disrespect. A common occurrence is a confrontation between a gang set and a single rival gangbanger. Outnumbered, he departs the area and returns later with his "homeboys" to complete the confrontation and to keep his reputation intact. This may occur immediately or follow a delay for planning and obtaining the necessary equipment (e.g., weapons) to complete the retaliatory strike. Many retaliatory acts of violence are the result of bad drug deals or infringement on drug territory.

The beliefs and values held by gang members are inconsistent with the ones shared by conventional society. Gang members live by their own code, the code of the streets.

The Code of the Street

As Elijah Anderson (1999, 9–10) explained,

> In some of the most economically depressed and drug- and crime-ridden pockets of the city, the rules of civil law have been severely weakened, and in their stead, a "code of the street" often holds sway. At the heart of this code is a set of pre-scriptions and proscriptions, or informal rules, of behavior organized around a desperate search for respect that governs public social relations, especially violence among so many residents, particularly young men and women. . . . The code of the street emerges where the influence of the police ends and personal responsibility for one's safety is felt to begin, resulting in a kind of "people's law," based on "street justice."

Anderson shares his years of observations of Philadelphia ghetto street life in his book *Code of the Street: Decency, Violence, and the Moral Life of the Inner City* (1999), which grew out of the ethnographic work he conducted for his previous book *Streetwise: Race, Class, and Change in an Urban Community* (1990). According to Anderson, one of the most salient features of urban life is the relative prevalence of violence. Anderson used Germantown Avenue as a natural continuum of the conduct found in Philadelphia. One end of the avenue is characterized largely by a code of civility, with conventional citizens of society, whereas the other end is regulated by the code of the street. On the "street" end of Germantown Avenue, "people watch their backs and are more careful how they present themselves. It isn't that they are worried every moment that somebody might violate them, but people are more aware of others who are sharing the space with them, some of whom may be looking for an easy target to rob or just intimidate" (Anderson 1999, 21). Intimidation and violence are constant reminders to street residents that they face a different daily reality than conventional residents.

> Of all the problems besetting the poor inner-city black community, none is more pressing than that of interpersonal violence and aggression. This phenomenon wreaks havoc daily on the lives of community residents and increasingly spills over into downtown and residential middle-class areas. Muggings, burglaries, carjackings, and drug-related shootings, all of which may leave their victims or innocent bystanders dead, are now common enough to concern all urban and many suburban residents. The inclination to violence springs from the circumstances of life among the ghetto poor—the lack of jobs that pay a living wage, limited basic public services (police response in emergencies, building maintenance, trash pickup, lighting, and other services that middle-class neighborhoods take for granted), the stigma of race, the fallout from rampant drug use and drug trafficking, and the resulting alienation and absence of hope for the future (Anderson 1991, 32).

Youths who are raised in such a violent environment learn early in life the value of being "streetwise." They must learn to handle themselves in a street-oriented environment.

> This is because the street culture has evolved a "code of the street," which amounts to a set of informal rules governing interpersonal public behavior, particularly violence. The rules prescribe both proper comportment and the proper way to respond if challenged. They regulate the use of violence and so supply a

> rationale allowing those who are inclined to aggression to precipitate violent encounters in an approved way. The rules have been established and are enforced mainly by the street-oriented; but on the streets the distinction between street and decent is often irrelevant. Everybody knows that if the rules are violated, there are penalties. Knowledge of the code is thus largely defensive, and it is literally necessary for operating in public (Anderson 1999, 33).

Families who are located in "street" neighborhoods and try to teach their children the conventional rules of society find it reluctantly necessary to also teach them how to negotiate the inner-city environment.

A great deal of violence on the streets is the direct result of someone being disrespected by a rival. The importance of respect has already been discussed in this chapter, but Anderson also described its importance to the code of the street.

> At the heart of the code is the issue of respect—loosely defined as being treated "right" or being granted one's "props" (or proper due) or the deference one deserves. However, in the troublesome public environment of the inner city, as people increasingly feel buffeted by forces beyond their control, what one deserves in the way of respect becomes ever more problematic and uncertain. This situation in turn further opens up the issue of respect to sometimes intense interpersonal negotiation, at times resulting in altercations. In the street culture, especially among young people, respect is viewed as almost an external entity, one that is hard-won but easily lost—and so must constantly be guarded. The rules of the code in fact provide a framework for negotiating respect. With the right amount of respect, individuals can avoid being bothered in public. This security is important, for if they *are* bothered, not only may they face physical danger, but they have been disgraced or "dissed" (disrespected) (Anderson 1999, 33–34).

From a middle-class, or conventional, perspective, the many forms (maintaining eye contact for too long, for example) of dissin' appear to be very petty and certainly not worth fighting over. Anderson argued that the code of the street can be traced to the profound sense of alienation from mainstream society that many inner-city black people, especially the young, experience. "The code of the street is actually a cultural adaptation to a profound lack of faith in the police and the judicial system—and in others who would champion one's personal security. . . . The code of the street thus emerges where the influence of the police ends and where personal responsibility for one's safety is felt to begin. Exacerbated by the proliferation of drugs and easy access to guns, this volatile situation results in the ability of the street-oriented minority (or those who effectively 'go for bad') to dominate the public spaces" (Anderson 1991, 34). The alienation that inner-city residents experience is attributed to their financial struggles.

The search for some sort of financial security ties back to one's need for respect. "In the inner-city environment respect on the street may be viewed as a form of social capital that is very valuable, especially when various other forms of capital have been denied or are unavailable. Not only is it protective; it often forms the core of the person's self-esteem, particularly when alternative avenues of self-expression are closed or sensed to be" (Anderson 1991, 66). By the time inner-city street youths become teenagers, most of them have internalized the code of the street, or at least learned to comport themselves in accordance with its rules.

> The code revolves around the presentation of self. Its basic requirement is the display of a certain predisposition to violence. A person's public bearing must send the unmistakable, if sometimes subtle, message that one is capable of violence, and possibly mayhem, when the situation requires it, that one can take care of oneself. The nature of this communication is determined largely by the demands of the circumstances but can involve facial expressions, gait, and direct talk—all geared mainly to deterring aggression. . . . Even so, there are no guarantees against challenges, because there are always people around looking for a fight in order to increase their share of respect—or "juice," as it is sometimes called on the street (Anderson 1991, 72–73).

The code of the street is the street life from which many gang members evolved; it is an environment of hopelessness and great alienation. These subculture values of gang members underlie gang structure and process.

SUMMARY

Gangs vary a great deal in terms of their organizational structure. Some gangs are so highly structured that they resemble the military. At least one researcher believes that gangs are so violent that they could be compared to a violent, murderous Amazonian tribe. Gangs may be categorized by a number of different typologies: age, degree of criminality, degree of attachment to and involvement in the gang, type of activity, and racial and ethnic distinctions. The processes of recruitment and turning to the gang are also quite various. Initiations can be brutal and highly violent. Most gang members are expected to be members for life. The most cherished desire and need of gang members is to be respected. Any form of disrespect can be met with extreme prejudice.

CHAPTER SIX

Street Gangs: Local, Regional, and Super-Sized

Gangs come in all shapes and sizes. Estimates of the true number of gangs are hampered by the fact that so many gangs are local, regional, and relatively unstructured, often slipping below the research and law enforcement radar screen. Local gangs tend to be small in membership. Small gangs are tied to specific neighborhoods and generally are short-lived. Regional gangs are longer-lasting and show signs of expansion beyond the immediate neighborhood. Large gangs, or super-sized gangs, have spread beyond the immediate neighborhood and their influence extends across cities, states, and in some cases even countries. Some researchers refer to such super-sized gangs as "nations" or "super gangs." Examples of super-sized gangs include the Bloods, Crips, People, Folks, and the Asian Triads and Tongs.

GANG DENIAL

In smaller jurisdictions, gangs are social and fiscal burdens on the local community and law enforcement. Resources are tight in all municipalities, but this is especially true in smaller cities. Money cannot be taken from some other sector of the allocated budget to deal with the rising gang-related costs because the operating budget is so small in the first place. Consequently, some communities suffer from **gang denial** (this was the case, for example, in Syracuse—to be discussed later in this chapter). When a community suffers from gang denial, ineffective prevention of gang growth and development is often a consequence. Local leaders and politicians are sometimes reluctant to acknowledge the presence of gangs in their jurisdictions because they worry about causing undue concern and fear among the citizens. Unfortunately, by the time some communities and institutions acknowledge that they have a gang problem, the situation may have already accelerated. Gang denial generally begins in the families of the gang members. The mother of a gang member is especially likely to deny that her child belongs to a gang. Often, the mother is the central figure of the gang member's family; she will deny that there is a problem and will attempt to protect the youth from accusations of criminal, delinquent, or gang behavior. Denial of gang activity in small cities and towns is also the result of a general belief among townspeople that such activities cannot occur in their hometown. Such people understand how gangs are a problem in cities like Los Angeles, New York, Chicago, and Detroit but question their existence in smaller cities. Public denial of the existence of gangs and a lack of proactive community efforts to control them are major contributing factors to the alarming increase in the number of gangs. When the local media outlets (especially newspapers) and politicians fail to acknowledge the existence of gangs, resources will not be put aside to deal with the problem.

Gangs flourish in areas where they are allowed to conduct their illegal activities by the lack of police intervention or surveillance. The lack of police involvement may be the result of unawareness of a gang problem in certain neighborhoods because the local citizenry failed to report an emerging problem. Adopting a zero-tolerance policy is the most effective way for small communities to combat gangs (in larger cities it is nearly impossible to enforce a zero-tolerance policy in all neighborhoods because there simply are not enough resources available and gangs will move from one neighborhood to the next). To be effective, a zero-tolerance program needs the assistance of local citizens' watch groups and individuals who are willing to get involved (by performing such basic tasks as placing anonymous phone calls to the police to report crimes and the need to remove graffiti). The schools need to get involved as well. Many youth gangs form in school; consequently, teachers and administrators should be able to identify those youngsters "at risk" or already active in gangs. Training programs can be designed to help school officials with this task of identification. The schools and local law enforcement agencies can work together on policies related to curbing delinquency and gang activity. The community infected by gang-related crime needs to take a stand against gangs by establishing an even higher community profile than the gang. Community involvement coupled with police intervention (on a local, state, and national level) will help to slow the growth of gangs and may deter gang activity altogether.

In larger cities, gang denial is not an issue, as citizens and law enforcement officials are all too aware of the reality of gangs as quasi-institutional fixtures of the landscape. The gangs of larger cities have a choice. They can remain relatively small with the primary purpose of protecting turf, or they can merge with the larger gang and claim nation affiliation. Los Angeles and Chicago are the home base of the largest nation coalitions, with the Bloods and Crips having formed in Los Angeles and the People and Folks in Chicago. These gangs have acquired super-sized categorical status and are known generically as super gangs. According to the National Alliance of Gang Investigators Association (NAGIA), certain criteria must be met in order to qualify as a super gang. Among them are

- Membership exceeds 1,000 members.
- The gang can be documented in multiple states.
- The gang maintains extensive drug networks.
- The gang exercises aggressive recruiting strategies.
- The gang has advocated an ambition for power and massive membership.

There are both advantages and disadvantages in a local gang's decision to join a nation coalition. A decision to remain small and independent may lead to constant battles with a great number of rival gangs. Remaining independent may adversely affect a gang's desire to expand a criminal enterprise, such as selling drugs. Smaller gangs risk dissolution and may eventually disappear completely. Additionally, joining a nation coalition often means that a local gang loses its unique identity. On the other hand, a decision to join a nation coalition has its perks. With a national backing, the former small gang is now a force to be contended with in its local neighborhood because it will always have allies to go to war with them. It still has rivals—in fact all the rivals of the nation coalition are now the enemies of this former small gang—but its attempt to keep independent status made it a target anyway. It is easier to expand a criminal drug operation through the assistance of the coalition. Furthermore, the lost former identity of the gang will simply be replaced by a more "respected" super gang identity (*Note*: Many of the former small gangs still maintain a degree of localized identity and the local gang can abandon the national alliance and/or join a rival alliance).

Padilla (1992) described the Diamonds' alliance with the Folks nation and what it meant in regard to their expected behavior. "Gangs belonging to the same nation were expected not to engage in fights and squabbles. It was expected that relations between nation-member gangs were to be nonviolent. If fights were to erupt, they were to be directed at opposition gangs—that is, against gangs from the other nation. . . . Theoretically, the nation approach was directed at significantly reducing the degree of intergang violence. . . . Organizing various gangs into a nation was good for business: It contributed immensely to solidifying the business operation of the gang" (Padilla 1992, 100–101). Local gangs are always expected to make their presence known within their neighborhood to warn off rival gangs. However, gangs from the same coalition are expected to leave each other alone. In an interview conducted by Padilla (1992, 100) with one of the Diamonds, Rafael, the nature of the respect toward nation affiliates is revealed. "Gangbanging is nothing really hard to do. In my neighborhood you have to hang out a lot. Our chief wants us out there a lot so nobody else would try to take our neighborhood from us. And we have boundaries, and a little bit of the neighborhood we have to share with others from the same nation but of a different affiliation. And we have our territory, and, if they were to come into our territory, we wouldn't start trouble by getting loud and stuff like that. We all respect each other pretty much, and it's alright." National allegiances are tenuous at best, as general agreements among affiliates often break down, and intergang fights are not rare.

A further description of the differences between small gangs and nation coalitions is presented in the remainder of this chapter. Discussion begins with the often ignored American rural gangs. Analysis continues with a few examples of local and regional urban gangs and finishes with a review of super-sized, or nation gangs.

AMERICAN RURAL YOUTH GANGS

In small, rural towns across the United States sounds of serenity and/or farm field machinery are being replaced by gang gunfire. For example, in Caldwell, Idaho, a town of 30,000 halfway between Boise and the Oregon line, police have responded to more than 100 reports (from July to October 2004) of shots fired. "Two young men have been killed and several more wounded by drive-by shootings. Police believe that most of the violence is gang-related" (*The Citizen*, 2004). Residents of places with small-town conservatism and the farming work ethic are alarmed by the "big-city" violence that has infested their quiet slice of America. Authorities in Caldwell claim that most of the gang members come from Hispanic farm working families who have, in increasing numbers, settled in Caldwell year-round instead of working the rotating seasonal schedule. (The recent economic upturn in Caldwell is cited as a reason for this.) A number of poor white youths in Caldwell have also formed gangs in an attempt to combat the growing Hispanic gangs.

National Youth Gang Surveys have shown that gang problems occur in communities of all sizes, including rural towns. Law enforcement agencies were contacted in rural jurisdictions in an attempt to chronicle gang presence. The 1997 survey revealed that 23% of the jurisdictions reported persistent gang problems; 57% reported a persistent absence of gangs; and approximately 20% reported transitory or temporary gang problems. Fourteen percent of the reporting agencies in towns of less than 2,500 residents reported gangs.

There is speculation as to whether urban gang members migrate to rural areas or whether only the symbols and culture of the gang are exported to rural communities. In their analysis of the 1997 survey results, Weisheit and Wells (2004, 5) found that in "most rural areas reporting gang activity, the majority of gang members were local youth. Yet, in many jurisdictions, the impact of migrating gang members was substantially greater than their limited numbers alone would suggest; they became an important conduit for the movement of ideas and symbols into these areas." Most of the gang members who move to rural areas and form gangs are, ironically, from families who moved there to escape the urban street gang life. Most rural agencies reported that they are prepared to deal with gangs as most departments had at least some officers with gang training. Most agencies that report having a gang problem indicated that they have adopted a zero-tolerance policy of suppression. Nearly all agencies also stressed the importance of prevention and community involvement as means of combating the growth of gangs. (*Note*: Various prevention, suppression, and treatment efforts will be discussed in Chapter 9.)

So, just how prevalent is gang activity in rural America? Results from the 1997 National Youth Gang Survey indicate that "despite reports of drugs, assaults, drive-by shootings, and even homicides, only 43 percent of those reporting gangs described the gang problem in their community as 'serious.' . . . Although drug use and drug sales were common among gang members and periodic violence was evident, most of the observed gang problems (such as graffiti, parties, and alcohol consumption) were of a type that would, indeed, frequently be viewed as minor" (Weisheit and Wells 2004, 3).

LOCAL AND REGIONAL GANGS

As we have already learned, all municipalities, no matter how small, are potentially susceptible to gang formation and therefore gang-related problems. Larger cities such as Los Angeles, San Diego, Chicago, and New York generally receive the most attention from gang researchers and the media. Many people across the nation might be quite surprised by the level of gang violence that is running rampant in the upstate New York cities of Syracuse, Rochester, and Buffalo (technically, these cities are in central and western New York). The growing incidence of violent crime and homicide attributed to street gangs in Syracuse, Rochester, and Buffalo proportionately rivals that of the more "traditional" gang cities. Because of gang mayhem, these Thruway Cities (they are linked by Interstate 90) have some of the highest homicide rates in the country. Buffalo's homicide rate in 2001 was 4 times the national rate, the 2002 homicide rate for Syracuse was 3 times the national average, and Rochester's homicide rate in 2003 was almost 5 times the national average. The primary cause of gang homicide in these cities is drug trafficking.

The study of gang research along the "Thruway corridor" represents an important contribution to the overall understanding of gang activity. Since the majority of gangs develop spontaneously, most gangs are made up of local youths. Although cities such as Syracuse, Rochester, and Buffalo have nation gang affiliates, a great deal of the gang-related crime is committed by locally based gangs.

Syracuse Gangs

Syracuse is New York's fourth-largest city (population of 145,164 in 2002) and is known for its university's sports (which include national championships in football, basketball, and lacrosse) and long, snowy winters (average annual snowfall is 114 inches). As with any city of significant size, Syracuse has its rough, urban sections where violence is common and drug deals sometimes end with murder. In fact, the homicide rate in Syracuse (2001) was 15.7 per 100,000, almost 3 times the national average. There were 25 homicides in Syracuse in 2002 (up 2 from the previous year), the most ever for the city. Loosely organized street gangs have existed in Syracuse for decades. As with most other cities, the crack epidemic of the late 1980s spearheaded the creation of drug enterprise street gangs in Syracuse. These organized gangs attempted to control the illegal drug market. By the mid-1990s, many local Syracuse gangs had pledged allegiance to various nations, including the Latin Kings and the Bloods. At the turn of the century, the local **Boot Camp** gang flexed its collective muscle to gain control of the tough streets of Syracuse's South Side.

The presence of the **Almighty Latin Kings and Queens Nation** can be traced in Syracuse at least as far back as the mid-1980s. The Latin Kings insist that they are not about violence and that they care more about community service and serving as a family for those who need them. They see themselves as a "nation of people." Members of the Kings must abide by a large number of formal rules, or codes of conduct. Among their rules: pee wees (young gangsters) must stay in school, obey curfews, and achieve good grades; married Kings must remain faithful to their wives; homosexuality is prohibited; and members must support each other when outsiders give them trouble. If a King disobeys a rule, he faces a violation ceremony. Membership size is information shared only among Latin Kings. Secret handshakes and phrases help the Kings to identify one another.

The Spanish Action League estimated that King membership in Syracuse in 1996 was about 100 local men and boys (Duffy 1996). Local officials view the Latin Kings as a gang and not a community provider. Syracuse police reports linked the Kings to at least three shootings during the summer of 1996 in the city's south and near west sides. According to the police, the Latin Kings were involved in a feud with a local gang called the **Gracetown Boys**, who reside on Grace Street and claim Grace Park as their turf. Some Gracetown Boys claimed that members of the Kings tried to kill them in a drive-by shooting. They identified the shooters as Latin Kings because of the beads they wear around the neck. New Kings receive black and yellow beads that they treat with reverence. The colors have special meaning; for example, black is a reminder that Hispanics share a common ancestry, as most Latinos descend from African, Spanish, and Taino Indians—this is especially true for natives of Puerto Rico. "In Syracuse, many Latino immigrants and Puerto Ricans new to the mainland settle on the near west side . . . the neighborhood was ranked the 12th poorest predominantly white neighborhood in the country by *U.S. News & World Report* in 1994" (Duffy 1996, A16). Despite the information provided by the Gracetown Boys, the police could not identify the Latin Kings as responsible for the shootings or any of the city's murders that year. Presently, the Latin Kings remain as a gang in Syracuse.

In 1997, increased gang activity in Syracuse caught the attention of many civic leaders. In the first ten months of 1997, 46 of the city's 53 assaults with a firearm or handgun occurred on the city's south and near west sides. The two most prominent gangs to claim this area are the **110 Gang** and Boot Camp. The 110 Gang claimed the area around Bellevue Avenue, including most of the southwest side; Boot Camp, the primary rival of 110, claimed turf around the corner of Midland Avenue and Colvin Street. These two vicious gangs fight over turf, girls, appearances, and glares that are perceived as a sign of disrespect. The numerous confrontations between the two gangs have led to murder, retaliation murder, and a vicious cycle of continuous revenge shootings. "No one can put an exact number on their size, but community members who work with youths say the gangs usually range from 12 to 15 members or more. The violence wrought by this relatively small group is taking its toll on the community's peace of mind. . . . Both Onondaga County Judge Joseph Fahey and Assistant District Attorney Michael Price say they have noticed an alarming increase in the number of cases involving teen-agers, gangs, and guns" (*Syracuse Post Standard* 1997, A8).

Both of these gangs, 110 and Boot Camp, are strictly local gangs with no nation affiliation. These gangs care as much about controlling turf as they do about making a profit selling drugs. In 1996, David Kennedy, a researcher at Harvard University, declared that the 110 and Boot Camp gangs were not highly organized drug business enterprises and that they posed no real threat to the stability of the neighborhood. "Kennedy was among a team of experts who visited Syracuse last summer, at the request of the grassroots Youth Violence Task Force of Syracuse and Onondaga County, to help local officials develop a collaborative approach to reducing juvenile gun violence" (*Syracuse Post Standard* 1997, A8). Kennedy's research in Boston led to the creation of the Operation Cease-Fire Program, which was aimed at curtailing juvenile-related gun violence. Kennedy's conclusion about Syracuse's Boot Camp gang was inaccurate. By 2003, Boot Camp had become so notorious and well organized that law enforcement officials used the RICO Act to issue numerous arrest warrants against this drug cartel.

Boot Camp was formed in 1994 by Tyree "Cav" or "Caviar" Allen as **Fernwood Boot Camp**. Allen supplied crack cocaine to gang members, who, in turn, sold it on the streets for a profit. Allen named his gang after the rap band Boot Camp Clik, a loose congregation of hard-core underground rappers. In 1995, a group of younger and much more aggressive delinquents (Little Boot Camp) from the neighborhood attempted to join Allen's gang. Allen did not want these youths in his gang because they were too violent. He referred to them as "young guns" because they always carried guns. By mid-1995, Karo Brown emerged as the leader of the "young guns." After Brown initiated a shootout between the young gangsters and the original gangsters, Allen merged the two groups into Boot Camp. The Boot Camp hierarchy includes the Original Gangsters (O.G.) at the top tier, with the "soldiers" ranked below them and the "flunkies" at the bottom. Allen sold crack to Brown at a reduced rate.

On June 23, 1996, Lee Scott, a member of the **East Side** gang, was shot to death on Midland Avenue and Colvin Street (Boot Camp turf). No one was ever charged with the death and the proud members of Boot Camp began to refer to their turf as "Murder Capital." From that point on, Boot Camp gangbangers would cross their middle and ring fingers and spread their index and pinky fingers. They hold the hand with fingers pointed down, to form an "M," which represents both Midland (street) and Murder. Boot Camp may also flash the letter "C" for Colvin Street. (Midland and Colvin is the epicenter of Boot Camp's turf.) Another normal pose for Boot Camp members involves one fist outstretched with a curled finger sticking out, as if they were firing a gun ("Bust your gun" is the expression they use; it means to fire your gun). On June 29, 1996, Allen and fellow gang member Orson Starling were killed in a car crash. Allen was out celebrating the birth of his son. Current Boot Camp gang members pay homage to Allen by stating "Word to Cav" as they place their hands over their hearts (O'Brien 2004b). With Allen's death, the Boot Camp gang, led by Karo Brown, became increasingly violent and orchestrated war against rival gangs that attempted to profit from selling drugs on the South Side.

The events leading up to the RICO arrests of Boot Camp in August 2003 reveal an acknowledgment of the growing gang problem in Syracuse and the commitment level of law enforcement officials to do something about it. As *Syracuse Post Standard* staff writer Maureen Sieh (2003, A1) reported, "For years, the Syracuse Police Department denied there were gangs in the city: Teens calling themselves Boot Camp and Elk Block were 'wannabes,' authorities said, or 'loosely organized' groups claiming certain street corners on the city's South Side as their turf. But last year, Police Chief Dennis DuVal and other officials admitted there are gangs in Syracuse and created a gang task force to root them out." It was revealed during the 2004 RICO (Racketeer Influenced Corrupt Organization) trials of Boot Camp members that Syracuse police were ordered not to use the G-word in their reports. "Investigators could not write 'gang' in crime reports until a policy change in 2002 when the city hit an all-time high for homicides, Detective Steven Stonecypher testified in the racketeering trial of accused Boot Camp gang leader Karo Brown" (O'Brien 2004a, A1). Syracuse is a prime example of what can go wrong when city officials engage in gang denial.

In 2002, Syracuse Police Chief DuVal declared war on gang members, warning "They know we are coming" (Weibezahl 2003, A1). Authorities were especially targeting members of Boot Camp and **Elk Block** (from Elk Street on the South Side), gangs suspected of running highly organized operations selling guns and drugs on city streets (Sieh 2003). The **1500 gang**, which claimed South Avenue and West Colvin Street, was also alleged to be selling and distributing drugs on Syracuse streets. The Syracuse police department's full-time gang task force filed 10,849 charges (from the time of its inception, April 29, 2002, to April 15, 2003) against a total of 5,566 different people—some of them known gang members. The police department reported that it confiscated 187 guns, a major step in combating street gangs. The courts have assisted in the prosecution of violent offenders through the technique of "fast-tracking"—a process designed to streamline a defendant's trip through the criminal justice system and keep him off the streets at the same time (O'Hara, 2003).

Despite these numbers, some residents and store owners of the gang-ridden neighborhoods report that they have not noticed a difference. This belief is borne out by the fact that most of the arrests were for minor infractions (e.g., loitering, open containers, noise ordinance violations) with fewer than 3% for felony violations (e.g., grand larceny, weapons, attempted murder). Residents also wonder what took authorities so long to acknowledge the growing crisis on the city's South Side. As Sieh (2003, A1) explained, "these arrests raise questions: How does a group of youths hanging out on the corner become a criminal enterprise in just a few years? When should authorities recognize these groups as gangs? Does a delay in that recognition cause the problems to get worse?" Residents in neighborhoods such as East Division Street on the North Side wonder if the growing level of delinquency among juveniles there indicates the formation of new street gangs. North Side district councilor Steve DeRegis believes that the city should pay close attention to children who drop out of school and hang out on street corners, because these status offenses lead to an increased probability of a youth joining a gang and selling drugs. DeRegis argued that "anytime you're in denial about something, you're not addressing the issue" (Sieh 2003, A8). Malcolm Klein, a foremost authority on gang research and professor at the University of Southern California, notes that Syracuse was not alone in denying gangs. In fact, Klein (1995) reported that 40% of all cities go through a denial stage. Residents of gang neighborhoods notice the problem first and then report it to the police, but the police, politicians, and school officials are often slow to admit to the problem.

On August 8, 2003, two members of Boot Camp were indicted by a federal grand jury on charges of violating the RICO act by using their membership in Boot Camp to engage in drug possession and murder. Demetrius Elmore, a member of the Elk Block gang, was gunned down in a drive-by shooting by Leonard Holbdy (the driver of the car) and Christian Williams (the shooter), members of Boot Camp, because Elmore was riding his bicycle to see his grandmother who lived in Boot Camp turf. On June 28, 2004, Williams pleaded guilty to shooting Elmore. One month earlier, Holbdy's brother Christopher was among 26 Boot Campers indicted on RICO charges of using systematic violence to control their turf and their drug trade (O'Brien 2003, A5). In September 2003, a reward was offered for help in capturing seven members of Boot Camp who were not apprehended when the indictments were served. Among the missing was Karo Brown, the leader of Boot Camp (within months all 26 Boot Camp members were apprehended). Police determined that Brown was the leader by intercepting the letters members of Boot Camp were sending to each other inside and outside prison. According to authorities, Boot Camp called themselves "Gambinos" after the notorious New York City Mafia family. They labeled some of their letters to each other as "War Report." "Police intercepted the letters as part of a federal investigation that led to the incitement of 26 suspected Boot Camp gang members in June. Those gang members are charged with running a criminal enterprise for eight years by using systematic violence to control the gang's drug trade on the city's South Side" (O'Brien 2003, A1).

By August 2004, 24 Boot Camp members arrested under RICO had pleaded guilty and one had the charges dismissed before going to trial. On August 3, 2004, a federal court jury found Karo Brown guilty of federal racketeering charges (RICO) and that he was responsible for at least two murders or attempted murders. Defense attorneys argued that a federal law designed to bring down mobsters should not apply to street gangsters. They also argued that Boot Camp was not a criminal enterprise as defined by the RICO Act. However, RICO had been used successfully to convict street gang members as criminal enterprises in Los Angeles, Chicago, New York City, Atlanta, Columbus, and Salt Lake City. RICO convictions against Boot Camp have stood as of early 2005.

Boot Camp had grown from a gang that was not considered to be a serious threat and that was lacking in the organizational skills necessary to carry out a criminal drug enterprise (in 1997) to a highly structured organization worthy of federal investigation. Boot Camp was just a local gang, with no nation-coalition affiliation, and yet it developed into a gang capable of controlling a highly profitable drug market. It used acts of intimidation, violence, and murder to enforce its presence and control a neighborhood. Authorities have linked more than 43 crimes to Boot Camp in the period 1995 to 2003. "The gang's crimes include two murders, several attempted murders, drug-trafficking and witness tampering. . . . Boot Camp made a profit of between $350,000 and $1 million" (O'Brien 2003, A4). "The Boot Camp case may be the first in the country in which the RICO violation was based on geography rather than hierarchy against a street gang" (O'Brien 2003, B5). Other street gangs have been prosecuted under RICO, but apparently not for using systematic violence to protect turf. The lesson provided by Boot Camp should not be lost on local agencies and officials who attempt to deny the presence, and impact, of local gangs in their jurisdiction: Ignoring the growing presence of gangs in the community can lead to damaging repercussions.

The indictments and convictions of the Boot Camp gang members have had positive results in Syracuse. Early 2004 crime reports indicate that criminal activity has dropped in Syracuse (14% in the first six months compared with the same period in 2003. There were 17 total homicides in Syracuse in 2004, the same number as in 2003. Police calls and criminal charges were cut in half since the 2002 RICO arrests of Boot Camp members. Despite this evidence, grassroots organizations such as "Families Against Injustice (FAI)" criticize the use of federal racketeering laws that lead to incarnation of disadvantaged youths. The FAI believes that social policies should be created that prevent the social conditions that lead to crime. Gang activity still persists in Syracuse as new gangs attempt to fill the void left by the dismantling of Boot Camp. In March 2004, gang members from the 110 Gang and Lexington Avenue fought a gang member from the Brick Town Gang at the Syracuse Renaissance Academy at Carnegie School. Five members of the Bloods street gang were arrested by a federal-state gang task force in late 2004 in Syracuse. The gang members were arrested on charges of selling crack cocaine in the city over the previous two years. Thus, authorities need to keep an eye on all the existing and emerging gangs in Syracuse.

The Syracuse/Onondaga County Law Enforcement Coalition on Youth Violence (which includes federal law enforcement agencies, county departments, city police, and some county police departments) identified 900 gang members in Onondaga County. The coalition estimates that about 200 to 300 of those gang members are hard-core. Boot Camp and Elk Block are considered especially dangerous. Members of these gangs are often chronic offenders—arrested repeatedly. Syracuse gang members can also be found in the local prisons. "More than 900 Onondaga County Justice Center jail inmates have claimed affiliation with more than 100 street gangs during the past five years, according to a confidential list kept by sheriff's deputies. The 19-page list includes seven or eight groups that authorities have identified as gangs engaged in serious crimes on city streets" (O'Brien and Sieh 2003, A1). Between 200 and 300 of those identified as gang members are considered hard-core gangsters. Information gathered by the Onondaga County Sheriff's Office in a January 2002 report, and published by the *Syracuse Post Standard* (O'Brien and Sieh 2003), revealed that the gangs with the most inmates claiming affiliation were

1. Bloods—141
2. Boot Camp—98
3. 110 Gang—79
4. Brighton Brigade—75
5. Bricks (or Bricktown)—42
6. Crips—28
7. Lexington Boys (Lex or Lex Diamonds)—22

Nearly 70% of the inmates were black, 9% were white, 2% were Hispanic, and the other 19% were other race/race not listed. Not surprisingly, most of the inmates claiming gang affiliation were young. Fifty-eight percent of the inmates were between the ages of 20 to 25 and another 11% were under age 20.

Rochester Gangs

Rochester, with a population of 219,773 (2001 Census), is the third-largest city in the state of New York. This city enjoys a white-collar image and attempts to portray itself as more glamorous than its western (Buffalo) and eastern (Syracuse) neighboring cities. Unfortunately for Rochester, especially its citizens, this city has the highest homicide rate in the state. In 2003, Rochester had a total of 57 homicides, 16 more than in 2002. This figure equates to a whopping homicide rate of 25.9 per 100,000 people (almost 5 times the national rate), by far the highest in the state. The national homicide rate was 5.6 per 100,000 in 2002, and New York City's was 7.3 per 100,000. According to the FBI's Uniform Crime Report, the national homicide rate for young black men aged 14–24 is 125 per 100,000. In Rochester, the rate is about 520 per 100,000, compared to the rate of 16 per 100,000 for white males of the same age category (Dobbin 2004).

The high homicide rate in Rochester is directly attributed to street gangs. An impoverished area of the city known as "The Crescent" (home to 27% of the city's residents) is the location of 80% of Rochester's homicides. There is no specific neighborhood called "The Crescent"; rather, the high-crime neighborhoods together form a crescent (think of the ecological/Chicago School theory described in Chapter 3) when the locations of murders and violent crimes are plotted on a map of Rochester. Thus, the high-crime areas of inner-city Rochester are commonly collectively referred to as

"The Crescent." Facing a $50-million budget gap, Rochester City School Superinten-
dent Dr. Manuel Rivera announced that the city would have to cut funding to the
schools unless there was an increase in state aid. In light of the gloomy economic
picture facing Rochester's school district and referring to the concentrated poverty in
the city's "crescent" neighborhoods—site of the majority of Rochester's 57 homicides
in 2003—Rochester Mayor Bill Johnson stated that the problem was like "a noose
around our necks" (Oliveiri 2004, 8).

Officials have been aware of the street gang problem in Rochester for years. Information provided by the Federal Bureau of Investigation's (FBI) *Law Enforcement Bulletin* reveals that "a 5-year study (1990 through 1994) conducted in Rochester, New
York, attributed 86 percent of youth violence in that city to individuals involved with
the gang subculture. The same study contended that gangs controlled the majority of
drug trafficking within Rochester" (Federal Bureau of Investigation 2001). Most of the
gangs found in Rochester are local gangs but some, such as the Latin Kings, who operate
in the Clinton section (especially around Avenue D) of Rochester, have nation affiliation. The dominant gang in Rochester is **Dipset** (a local gang). They have been linked
to 8–10 homicides from mid-2002 through 2003. Dipset is also the largest gang in
Rochester, with an estimated total membership of 80, most of whom are between the
ages of 15 and 21. As with most of the Rochester gangs, Dipset consists of youths who
have grown up together (spontaneous gangs) and as they got older began to engage in
criminal acts such as drug dealing, robbery, and homicide. The name Dipset comes
from the "Dipset Anthem," a rap song by The Diplomats (Flanigan 2003B). The lyrics
for this song (available on the Internet) are filled with references to gangsters, drugs,
drive-bys, and homicide. The word *dipset* may be a code word for "run," or it can be
used as a term for a person who is a sexual play toy.

In late December 2003, police arrested 12 members of this northeast Rochester
gang. Police Chief Robert Duffy's goal was to make "the Monroe County Jail the largest
gang clubhouse in western New York" (Flanigan 2003, 8A). The suspects were placed on
a "fast track" in the criminal justice system (similar to the approach used in Syracuse),
with indictments coming just days after an arrest. Six assistant district attorneys along
with several police investigators were assigned to make sure that the charges against the
Dipset members stuck. Chief Duffy also stated that Rochester gangs appear to be a
loose confederation of youths who conspire to commit such crimes as drug sales, robbery, and various acts of violence and lack the formal hierarchy of national gangs, such
as the Crips and Bloods. Another sign of their loose alliance was demonstrated by how
quickly members of Dipset were willing to provide information to police in exchange
for a reduction in sentences. Nation coalition gang members would never sell out their
comrades. Regardless, the members of Dipset were extremely violent. Police believe
that they had committed at least 20 "executions"—planned murders.

Dipset competes with such rival gangs as **Thurston Zoo** (operating on Thurston
Road) and **Plymouth Rock** (which operates on Plymouth Avenue) for control of the
lucrative drug market. Plymouth Rock is also known as Plymouth Roc, as in, "Roc"-
hester. Dipset is so large that its claimed turf includes Hudson, Clifford, and Joseph
Avenues, along with Avenue A and North Street (Flanigan 2003a). These gangs are
local and have no affiliation with national gangs. They exist as a confederation of
youths who conspire to commit such crimes as drug sales, robbery, and physical

assaults. They are neighborhood kids who grew up together. Residents of the crescent area of Rochester are well aware of the presence of Dipset and their rivals as their graffiti can be found throughout the area.

For the past decade Rochester's street gangs have been responsible for a great deal of violence. Law enforcement officials hope that if they can dismantle the gangs, the high homicide rate in their city will be dramatically reduced. Suppression efforts to control gangs include the 1997 **Youth Violence Initiative**, a coordinated multiagency organization designed to reduce the violence committed by youth between the ages of 13 and 21. The initiative, which became fully operational in July 1998, involves the co-operation between a number of law enforcement and juvenile justice agencies. The Youth Violence Initiative employs a two-pronged approach:

1. concentrating enforcement efforts on the small percentage of youth who are responsible for the vast majority of violent crimes

2. identifying those youth who may be at risk of becoming violent offenders and providing them with the appropriate intervention and prevention services (*Source*: Rochester's 1999 State of the City Report)

Approximately 14 city and county personnel staff were hired to work on this initiative full-time. One of these agencies, called **Cease Fire**, is a multiagency effort that brings together representatives from local law enforcement, human service agencies, government, and the community to deliver a zero-tolerance message to juvenile offenders and adult gang members who have been identified as most active in youth violence. Offenders are warned of the serious consequences of their continued gang activity and are offered a variety of alternatives that include education, job training, or job placement assistance. This agency meets with local gangs or gang-affiliated individuals on the streets and at the Monroe County Jail. Another component of the Youth Violence Initiative led to the creation of **School Resource Officers**, who are essentially police officers assigned to every middle and high school in the City of Rochester. Although controversial, their presence has greatly reduced incidents of crime, particularly violent crime. The **Truancy Intervention Program** is another of the 14 programs established by the initiative. As in most cities, the idea of enforcing truancy laws is guided by the realization that youths cannot commit crimes during school hours on the streets if they are in the schools where they belong (*Source*: Rochester's 1999 *State of the City Report*).

Some community members fear that suppression efforts alone fail to address the root of the high crime rate in Rochester. Sister Grace Miller, executive director of the House of Mercy, a homeless shelter and community outreach center on Hudson Avenue, believes the reason there are so many gang members is because of poverty and hopelessness. Her belief that intervention strategies are also necessary to combat the growing presence of gangs is shared by many community leaders throughout the nation and is echoed by gang researchers as well. In Rochester, the city developed a program consisting of 11 distinct campaigns to enhance the quality of life for all of its citizens. Collectively, this program is a part of **Rochester's Urban Renaissance** program. Campaign number 3, "Rochester as a City of Compassion and Caring," addresses the issue of street gangs and their impact on the quality of life experienced by Rochesterians. In an effort to improve the physical and mental well-being of its citizens, as well as a sense of pride in the community, the city has developed a number of key strategies. First, reducing the need for human services by increasing the health, safety and welfare of its citizens; reducing the number of citizens who experience the problems of homelessness, teen pregnancy, alcohol/drug abuse and poverty; establishing neighborhood resource centers; and reducing public tolerance of drug use, violent behavior, drunkenness, and gangs (*City of Rochester Comprehensive Plan* 1999).

The city of Rochester is firmly committed to winning the war against gangs and increasing the quality of life for its citizens. Time will tell if Rochester is successful in this worthy goal, although it certainly saw improvements in 2004, when Rochester's murder rate dropped by 39%. There were 35 criminal homicides in 2004, the lowest number since 1999. Law enforcement officials attribute this decline to two initiatives that were started in 2003. The first involved creating a gang task force that increased the number of uniformed and undercover police officers on the city's streets. The second initiative involved a "get tough" on gang members stance by which the worst offenders are not granted any leniency from the court. Training and other services are offered to non-hard-core members.

Buffalo Gangs

Buffalo, with a population of 287,698 (2002 Census), is the second-largest city in the state of New York. Following national patterns, Buffalo gangs are racially segregated. There are at least 35 street gangs in Buffalo with an estimated total membership of 450–500. Most of these gangs are neighborhood gangs and are named after the neighborhood streets. The greatest numbers of gangs are found on Buffalo's impoverished East Side. The most notorious African-American gangs include the **Fruit Belt Posse**, **Bailey Street Posse**, **Fillmore Street Boys**, **New Burgh Crew**, **Townsend Boyz**, **Good Year Crew**, **Downtowners**, **Uptowners**, **Loepere Street Crew**, **Michigan Street Posse**, and the **Genesee Street Posse**. Many of the local projects have their own gangs: **Langfield**, **Perry**, and **McCarley Gardens**. The Vice Lords, Gangster Disciples, Crips, and Bloods have affiliation gangs in Buffalo as well.

The number of Crips and Bloods continues to increase in Buffalo. Cheektowaga (a Buffalo suburb) police believe that there are about 100 Blood members in the Buffalo area (*Cheektowaga Times* 2003). The Crips in the Buffalo area have the following gangs among their affiliates: **Shot Gun Gangster Crips**, **Rolling Gangster Crips**, **KB Deuce Crips**, **Loso Crips**, **Central Park Crips**, and the **8-Ball Crew Crips**. Many of these gangs have female auxiliary gangs (e.g., **8-Ball Girls**). Among the independent female gangs in Buffalo are the **Mama Thugs** and the **Baby Thugs** (Ernst 2002). The **Hillbillies**, a new all-female gang on Dodge Street emerged when many men in the Dodge Street Posse were jailed and the gang recruited young women to take over the drug business (Thomas 2004). Hispanic gangs in Buffalo are smaller in number and less notable than black gangs. They are generally found on the West Side of Buffalo, with the **10th Street Gang** and the **14th Street Gangs** as the most notable. These gang members are mostly Puerto Rican.

Street gangs have existed in Buffalo for nearly a hundred years. The early Buffalo gangs were similar to other gangs of this era in that they were primarily involved in petty crime and delinquent activities. As in larger urban cities, the rise of contemporary Buffalo gangs had its roots in the general 1960s "civil disobedience" movements. In the 1960s, a gang known as the **Mad Dogs** claimed most of the East Side. The Mad Dogs used drugs (marijuana, heroin, and cocaine) and wore jackets with Mad Dogs printed on the back. They were involved in petty crime, such as theft, and fought over turf. Most battles were settled by hand-to-hand combat with the traditional weapons of bats, rocks, bricks, and switchblades. After nearly ten years in existence, the Mad Dogs' reign over the streets of Buffalo ended. Most of them got factory jobs, as there were plenty of factory jobs in Buffalo in those days (e.g., Bethlehem Steel).

In the early 1980s, the Fruit Belt Posse (FBP) emerged, mostly as an offshoot of the Mad Dogs. The Fruit Belt Posse is a gang from a neighborhood that centers on the intersection of High Street and the Kensington Highway (the 33) with side streets named after fruits (grape, peach, orange, and lemon). For the most part, members of the neighborhood accepted them because they were primarily a cohort of adolescents who attended the same local public school (Future's Academy School #37 on Carlton). As the years went by, the FBP became increasingly violent. School #37 was experiencing a great deal of disruptive behavior, resulting in several gang members being transferred or expelled. In the 1980s and early 1990s, the Fruit Belt Posse was age-graded by three distinct levels:

1. Senior Posse: ages 16 and over
2. Junior Posse: ages 11–15
3. Baby Posse: younger than 11

To become a member of the FBP, recruits had to be initiated by means of a physical beating. Anyone who ran away during the initiation ceremony was a "marked" man. These disgraced recruits would be subject to gang beatings because they were considered a "punk bitch" or "cur" (a person who is scared to fight).

The FBP were known to sell drugs for profit. They fought with rival gangs on the streets and at neutral sites such as the East Ferry New Skating Land. FBP members would walk in packs through the crowd of youths chanting "Fruit Belt, Fruit Belt, Fruit Belt" as a means of drawing attention to themselves and calling out rival gangs and nongang members alike. They were known to dance in a circle as a crew to intimidate others and they danced with girlfriends from rival gangs to start fights. With the escalation of weaponry, gun battles replaced fist fights as a means of settling disputes. The FBP died out in the early 1990s due to the deaths of many members and the incarceration of most of the remaining members. There is evidence that the FBP has reemerged in the 2000s.

The **M&B Crew** rose to power in the early 1990s under the leadership of Donald "Sly" Green and Darryl "Reese" Johnson; the M&B refers to gang members from Marshall Street and Barthel Street. The level of violence committed by this infamous Buffalo gang is legendary—the homicide rate hit an all-time high during the early to mid-1990s, with a modern record high of 92 in 1994. A large number of these murders were committed by the M&B Crew as they attempted to control the distribution of crack cocaine in Buffalo. Green and Johnson routinely ordered the executions of rival gang members. A massive law enforcement effort by federal and local police resulted in the arrests of Green, Johnson, and numerous other gang members. Green and Johnson are currently serving multiple life sentences on multiple charges, including murder and drug trafficking. After Green and Johnson were sent to prison, the M&B Crew was led by Calvin Cornelious, who immediately took control of drug distribution. Cornelious followed the same pattern of murder and drug trafficking as Green and Johnson. In 1999, he was arrested on 60 counts of federal racketeering and murder. He was already in federal custody for unrelated drug trafficking and rape charges (*Buffalo News* 1999).

In the period 1997–2000, Buffalo averaged 40 homicides a year, a relatively low number for this city compared to the era that preceded it. However, at the turn of the century, the Bloods and Crips had found their way to Buffalo. The Blood and Crip recruiters in Buffalo came mostly from New York City (the Bronx) rather than directly from Los Angeles. The signs of renewed street gang activity became quite apparent. There were 66 homicides in 2001, and there were 19 murders alone in the month of May when gangs were fighting over the control of drug trafficking. As of January 2002, there were only 26 arrests for the 66 slayings (Michel 2002). Buffalo's homicide rate for 2000 was 22.55 per 100,000, a figure that is 4 times the national average of 5.6 per 100,000 (FBI statistics). The high homicide rate in Buffalo is a common trait that it shares with fellow upstate cities Syracuse and Rochester.

It is important to note that there are a large number of shootings that do not result in murder. However, these shootings may result in injury to gang members and innocent civilians. Gang shootings terrorize community members who are forced to live in gang territories. In 2001, there were 820 shootings in Buffalo, with most of the victims in their late teens and 20s. A majority of the shootings occurred on the city's East Side, but a handful occurred on the West Side (Thomas and Pignataro 2003). Most of Buffalo's gang homicides occur on the East Side and the victims are generally African-Americans. Buffalo Police Department Lt. Jake Ulewski, when describing a rash of shootings in Buffalo in late July 2003, stated, "It's like a wild west show" (Weibazahl 2003, A1).

While local street gangs like the Downtowners (from the Clinton-Jefferson area) and Uptowners (from the Bailey and Minnesota area) continue to have an influence on the street gang scene, involved in such criminal acts as murder and drug trafficking, it is the presence of the Crips and the Bloods that commands the greatest concern. Most of Buffalo's gangs are local and neighborhood-based; some are affiliated with such national gangs as the Bloods and Crips. The Bloods and Crips recruit Buffalo's youth to help in the highly lucrative drug trade found in Buffalo. Elsie B. Fisher, the principal at Buffalo's Alternative School, reported in the early 2000s that there were many signs of Bloods and Crips recruiting schoolchildren into their gangs. Some students at the Alternative High School on Oak Street and the Junior High on Fulton Street have tried to wear gang colors to school. As in Los Angeles, the Buffalo Blood gangs wear red plaid handkerchiefs, known as **soldier rags** (do rags), wrapped around their heads; the Crips wear blue plaid handkerchiefs. The flashing of gang signs and the use of gang graffiti and symbolism are other shared traits between these local Bloods and Crips and their LA-based brothers and sisters. Officials at the Alternative stepped in immediately and banned the wearing of gang colors to school.

In my own interviews with members of the 8-Ball Crips and the Central Park Crips, it became quite apparent that these Crips have many similarities with those of Los Angeles. The 8-Ball Crips are all expected to know their gang history, including such things as the LA origins and leaders, past and present. These Crips abide by the nation rules and have an alliance with the Folks, whom they consider "cousins," as opposed to fellow Crips who are treated like brothers. The right-left distinction is also abided by, with the Crips slanting to the right out of respect to the Folks. The six-point star is also respected as are Gangster Disciples' pitchforks. Thus, the 8-Ball Crew will chant "6 poppin', 5 droppin'" revealing allegiance to the six-star nation and death to five-star-nation gangsters—a six-star member shoots (pops) a five-star gangster (he is going to drop). One of the gang members ("Sam") told me that they generally wear black, especially black bandannas (which is symbolic of a "war flag") when they go into battle. Gang members are never to leave their flag behind—it is the ultimate embarrassment and sign of weakness in battle. Returning to the home base without your flag is met with extreme prejudice among gang members and a violation ceremony will follow. On the other hand, bringing back a rival's flag is usually proof that you killed an enemy and the member is received with great honor. The flag is extremely important to gang members. As one gang member told me, "It is your heart, you keep it, and you show it off."

Crips refer to Bloods as Slobs as a sign of disrespect. The Crips have a saying, "See a Slob, Kill a Slob." K-Swiss is favorite attire worn by these Crips because the KS is interpreted as "Kill Slobs." Joining the 8-Ball Crips involves an initiation process. One of the most common forms of initiation involves brands and burns on the upper right arm. Many preteens begin their indoctrination into the gang by getting gang burns on their arms. A six-pointed star is burnt into the arm and then a pitchfork is burnt into the leg later. (*Note*: Buffalo Blood gangs initiate recruits with burn marks in the arm as well.) The 8-Ball crew has a hierarchal organizational structure:

1. godfather (and sometimes a simultaneously reigning queen)
2. superiors
3. original gangsters (OG)
4. generals
5. commanders
6. foot soldiers
7. riders

The godfather is the reigning power. As revealed in the typology, women may gain high levels of respect; the queen, the highest-ranking female gangster, commands a great deal of esteem. She is just below the godfather but above most males. This is rather unusual for most gangs, as a woman generally has little authority over males. Superiors are next in the line of command and have status and authority over the OG because of some past or present demonstrated prowess. Original gangsters are the oldest active members of the gang. The generals are active on the streets overseeing operations. Generals may sometimes leave the original gang in order to start their own set. This is permissible because they still answer to the godfather. The commanders are the go-betweens between the generals and foot soldiers. The foot soldiers do all the dirty work (petty theft, robberies, serving as "watches," etc.) and the riders are really wannabes and are only semiactive in the gang.

The primary reason for the very high homicide rate in Buffalo is tied directly to gang activity in drug trafficking. The Buffalo area has become increasingly used as a drug corridor for illegal drugs entering the United States via Canada. Huge amounts of cocaine, heroin, marijuana, and methamphetamines are smuggled into the Buffalo distribution point by gangs and organized crime syndicates in New York City. On November 26, 2003, New York Senator Charles E. Schumer issued a press release stating that the "Buffalo area is smack in the middle of an illegal drug pipeline." Schumer added that Buffalo's proximity to New York City and Canada creates a perfect storm for the convergence of drugs and gangs in western New York. Despite the efforts of local law enforcement officials, Schumer agreed with Buffalo Mayor Tony Masiello and Police Commissioner Rocco Diina that the federal government needed to get involved to combat the threat of gangs and drugs plaguing the area. Schumer referred in his press release to Buffalo and western New York as a distribution point for drugs and stated that the increased federal funding would be used to fight drug trafficking. If Buffalo becomes designated by the U.S. Office of National Drug Control Policy as a "high intensity drug trafficking area (HIDTA)" as Schumer wants, then western New York cities will be eligible to receive millions in federal money to help local law enforcement clamp down on the illegal drug trafficking that is so prevalent (Schumer 2003).

In addition to the deadly violence and drug trafficking of the African-American gangs and to a much lesser extent of the Hispanic gangs in Buffalo, there are Chinese gangs who have committed a number of "traditional" Asian gang-related crimes. These Asian gangsters are generally from New York City and come to the Buffalo area to target Chinese restaurants and businesses. They are also known for their brutal home invasion robberies. Special agents from the Asian Organized Crime Task Force in New York City state that these types of crimes are a common means for Asian gangs to make money (Herbeck 2000).

Gang violence and homicide represent a constant threat to many citizens of the Buffalo area. Law enforcement personnel have done the best they can to fight the growing presence of street gangs in Buffalo. As previously stated, Senator Schumer hopes to find federal funding to help assist the suppression efforts of local officials in Buffalo. The city already receives $5.1 million in federal money from a COPS grant, which helped to provide about 25 officers for community policing (Thomas and Pignataro 2003). The Buffalo police have established an intelligence unit to share information among police in the region regarding gang-related activity. Buffalo, like crime-plagued Niagara Falls, has enlisted the help of state troopers and county officers in its attempt to cope with the high rate of violence, due to the reality that many gangs transcend police-district boundaries. Members of the **Buffalo Gang Suppression Unit** coordinate efforts with the **Major Case Squad** and **Flex Unit** and **Narcotics Bureau Detectives**. Suburban police, such as those in Cheektowaga, have joined in the information and intelligence effort to combat gangs. Cheektowaga has witnessed a reemergence of gang members, shootings, and thefts in the western end of the town. **Project Exile** was created, in part, to provide training to local police officers in federal criminal gun charges that sometimes carry more severe prison sentences than state laws. Also assisting Buffalo police with gang information is the **Violent Crime and Career Criminal Task Force**, which includes federal law enforcement agents and police from area municipalities.

Despite the fact that the number of homicides dropped to 44 in the year 2002, it would appear that the Buffalo gang problem is escalating. In 2003, Buffalo had 60 criminal homicides, and in 2004, there were 51 criminal homicides, with investigators solving just 39% of them. The weapons being used range from .22- and .25-caliber handguns to shotguns and AK-47s. Many of the shootings are drive-bys. The Bloods and Crips have received much of the blame for the increased level of gang violence in Buffalo in 2004 and 2005. The Bloods claim territory on the East and West sides, including Central Park and the Bailey-Delevan neighborhoods (Thomas 2004). Bloods recruit young, local Buffalo kids while inside juvenile detention centers and the Erie County Holding Center, in the malls, and in local schools. Among the emerging gangs in Buffalo are the **Young Blood Thugs**, described by some officers as Blood gang members in training.

The motives for gang violence are multiple and include attempts by one gang to establish itself in a neighborhood, individual gang members trying to make a name for themselves, a perceived lack of respect, turf, or women. However, one factor sticks out above all else for gang homicides: control of the drug trade and turf. Selling drugs as a means of earning money reflects the socioeconomic realities of a depressed Buffalo region. The lure of quick money from drug trafficking, the lack of enough properly funded community programs for urban youths, and the overall poor economic condition in Buffalo, specifically, and upstate New York, in general, indicate that more and more youths are likely to turn to gangs. Close attention to the rising Buffalo gang problem is advised.

18th Street Gang (Los Angeles)

In the street gang capital of the world, Los Angeles, it might seem hard for any one gang to stick out, especially in light of the fact that Los Angeles serves as the home base for the country's two largest nation coalitions, the Crips and Bloods. The **18th Street Gang** (a regional gang) is such a gang. The 18th Street Gang is the largest gang in Los Angeles County, with an estimated membership of 20,000 (although some estimates put the number as low as 8,000). Most of the members are Mexican and Chicano, although there are some Salvadorians and blacks. The 18th Street Gang is actually a collection of smaller gangs, but it is not large enough to be considered a nation. It is also confined to a limited region—Los Angeles County. Individual sets are dispersed throughout the county in the San Fernando Valley, the San Gabriel Valley, the South Bay, South Los Angeles, and Downtown. Their stronghold, and oldest barrio, is located east of the Staples Center (home of the Los Angeles Lakers, Kings, and Clippers) between the Harbor Freeway (east) and Hoover Avenue (west). Two of the more significant barrios of the 18th Street Gang are in South LA, with one between Vernon (north) and Slauson (South) along Vermont Avenue, and the other between Florence (north) and 91st Street (south). The biggest rival of the 18th Street Gang is **Florencia 13**, a

Hispanic gang that is large both in terms of membership and turf size. Florencia 13 has a turf that extends from Western Avenue (west) to Compton Avenue (east) (Alonso 2002). (See Figure 6.1.)

The formation of the 18th Street Gang can be traced back to the 1960s and has its origins in racial prejudice. During this time, the Clanton Street Gang, a second-generation Hispanic street gang, limited membership to those who were American citizens from a pure Hispanic background. Thus, youths who were undocumented immigrants or of mixed ancestry were not allowed to join the Clanton Gang. These juvenile delinquents, although turned down by Clanton, were committing crimes that led to their arrest and incarceration in local juvenile detention facilities. While incarcerated, their membership was still denied. As an inevitable result, these rejected youths decided to bond together and form their own gang to rival the Clantons. A youth nicknamed "Glover" did most of the recruiting and purposely targeted mixed-race youths to join the gang. Glover and most of these youths came from 18th Street (just four blocks away from Clanton gang turf), located in the Rampart district of Los Angeles, a notoriously tough area, but they originally called themselves the "Clanton Street Throw-aways." These delinquents became the original members of the 18th Street gang.

The 18th Street gang was the first Hispanic gang to break the racial membership barrier. Because of the lax membership criteria, the 18th Street gang grew very rapidly. It was largely composed of immigrants and multiracial youths. Most of the members are Hispanic, but some cliques include African-Americans, Asians, Caucasians, and Native Americans. Youths who have developed a reputation for violence are especially recruited and welcomed. Although the 18th Street Gang is primarily turf-oriented in its structural design, it has, over the years, sent members out of California to set up new cliques of the gang.

The 18th Street Gang is involved in a wide variety of criminal activities: auto theft, carjacking, drive-by shootings, murder, murder for hire, extortion, arms trafficking, and drug sales and distribution. Various intelligence and law enforcement agencies have

SC represents South Central, a specific clique of the 18th Street Gang. *XV3* represents 18 for 18th Street Gang. *W* at the end represents West Side.

F at the front and *13* at the end represent the Florencia 13 street gang, a rival of the 18th Street Gang. *Eight 5* in the middle is for the 85th street clique.

FIGURE 6.1 18th Street Gang and Florencia 13

indicated that the gang has established ties with the Mexican and Columbian drug cartels, which have a big impact on the Southwest border states. The respect that the gang command on the streets extends inside prison walls, as the 18th Street Gang has ties with both the Mexican Mafia and black prison gangs. The 18th Street Gang not only controls a great number of streets in the drug trade, it also makes a great deal of money through extortion. These gangsters approach local vendors and threaten them unless they pay a "protection tax." If people refuse to pay the tax, they risk bodily harm and death. The gang has also learned to make money in the white-collar world as well by committing such crimes as forging identification cards and immigration papers, cloning cellular phones, and stealing credit cards, bus passes, and food stamps.

Because it is known to recruit elementary and middle-school youths, the 18th Street Gang is sometimes referred to as the Children's Army. The gang attempts to recruit members early on in life by intimidation, including the threat of death (including the deaths of their loved ones) if the recruit attempts to leave the gang. 18th Street Gang members can be identified by their tattoos. They will have ink done all over their bodies, such as on their foreheads and above their eyebrows. The most common tattoo is the number 18 or XVIII, and they sometimes have 666 tattooed on their bodies as well. Popular folklore, along with some religions, considers the number 666 to represent the devil. For example, *Revelation* 13:16-18 states, "And he causeth all, both small and great, rich and poor, free and bond, to receive a mark in their right hand, or in their foreheads: And that no man might buy or sell, save he that had the mark, or the name of the beast, or the number of his name. Here is wisdom. Let him that hath understanding count the number of the beast: for it is the number of a man; and his number is six hundred threescore and six." The early Christians attempted to link Julius Caesar to the devil beast. Caesar, the first Roman persecutor of the Christians, penned the phrase "VENI VIDI VICI." This phrase, when reduced to Roman numerals, converts to VIVIVI, or 666. From this, Caesar came to be viewed as the devil. In gang reality, when the numbers 666 are added together they equal 18, thus, the connection of 666 to the 18th Street Gang. As for identification based on clothing, the 18th Street Gang members generally wear brown or black pants with a white T-shirt. The use of graffiti is also common. The 18th Street Gang can be found throughout South Central Los Angeles and has a strong presence in such high schools as Manual Arts, Washington, Dorsey, Crenshaw, and Freemont. It is, for the most part, a regional gang, but as its drug cartel continues to expand, its presence is being felt in many surrounding states. Law enforcement officials are very aware of the power of the 18th Street Gang. As we will see in Chapter 7, **judicial injunctions** have been used in an attempt to control this powerful street entity.

Mara Salvatrucha (MS, MS-13)

The gangs discussed so far in this section are either of the local or regional variety. **Mara Salvatrucha (MS)** serves as a transition to a discussion of super-sized gangs, as MS is larger than a regional gang but not quite big enough to qualify as a "nation." The roots of this American street gang can be traced back to El Salvador and its civil war. Many refugees from this war-torn country fled to the United States. Some of these refugees were former members of such military organizations as the Farabundo Marti National Liberation Front and were trained as guerrillas, known as Salvatruchas. These rebels had attempted to overthrow El Salvador's government during the civil war. Former California State Senator Tom Hayden attributes the rise of Salvadorian gangs to U.S. military intervention in the El Salvador civil war and President Reagan's misguided use of the military:

> The sudden emergence of these *pandillas* (gangs) was due entirely to U.S. military intervention in El Salvador in the eighties. The same neoconservatives who promoted the wars on gangs and drugs at home were champions of the military policies, which, ironically, would import those wars to the streets of Los Angeles and other cities. When Ronald Reagan was elected in 1980, the civil war in El Salvador was stalemated, with Jimmy Carter's ambassador reporting that Salvadoran leaders wished a political and economic settlement instead of further war. . . . The incoming Reagan administration ignored Jimmy Carter's negotiations-oriented [approach] . . . announcing a doubling of military aid to El Salvador in March 1981. . . . By most estimates, 75,000 Salvadorans died in the conflict, mostly at the hands of soldiers trained or supplied by the U.S. military (Hayden 2004, 200–201).

The Salvadorian refugee youths in Los Angeles started calling themselves the *la mara loca*, which roughly translates to "the crazy neighborhood." "Soon they were known as *mara Salvatrucha stoners*, and finally *mara Salvatrucha*, the 'Salvadoran neighborhood,' or simply MS. In a larger sense, they were *las frutas de la Guerra*, the fruits of the war, a description that would become a rap anthem of Homies Unidos a few years later" (Hayden 2004, 203). The MS-13 gang first formed in the Pico Union section of Los Angeles in the early 1980s (Kelleher and Gonzales 2004). MS 13 and the 18th Street Gang of Los Angeles had a loose confederation until 1992. Salvadorians were welcomed by 18th Street and they formed a very powerful multicultural super gang. No one is exactly sure what led to the split between these two power gangs, but MS 13 has been independent for over a decade now (Hayden 2004).

Rejected by Hispanic gangs, the vast majority of Mara Salvatrucha gang members are therefore of either first- or second-generation Salvadorian descent. The rest of the members come from other Central American countries such as Costa Rica, Honduras, Ecuador, and Guatemala. MS quickly received recognition for its level of violence and organization. Mara Salvatrucha is also active in Central America, Mexico, and Canada. The Mara Salvatrucha gang is commonly referred to as MS-13, MS standing for *Mara Salvatrucha*, which translates to "Forever Salvador" or, more loosely, "Long live El Salvador." As mentioned, MS-13 is well organized and efficiently run. Each local branch is divided into cliques, or **cliclas**. There is not much of a hierarchy within local cliclas except for local leaders and treasurers who answer to the leaders of MS-13. During group meetings, members of MS-13 stand in a circle, signifying that all members are equal. The members will then display the two-handed "M" hand sign and say aloud "La Mara," which is slang for the gang. Group members are allowed to voice their opinions and discussion leads to group decisions. At the end of all meetings, MS-13 members again flash the two-handed "M" and yell "La Mara." Large-scale meetings—those involving multiple cliclas from all regions—are called "universal meetings."

These meetings are held yearly on the thirteenth day of a predetermined month. When the members gather for a universal meeting, they stand in a circle in order to maintain each clicla group's integrity (Rozanski 2003). The number 13 is significant for MS-13 because the letter "M" is the thirteenth letter of the alphabet. Thus, when using graffiti, or getting tattoos, the letter "M" and the number 13 are popular expressions of gang affiliation. The letter "S" stands for both Salvador and **Sureno**, a Spanish word for "Southerner." The colors of MS-13 are the same as those used in most Central American national flags: blue, gray, white, and black. Blue and white beaded necklaces are also common. Sports jerseys with the number 13 are among the favorite items of clothing worn by members of MS-13. (See Figure 6.2.)

Females are allowed to join MS-13 and must go through an initiation similar to the males', which involves a violation ceremony where several members of the gang beat the recruit to test his or her ability to take a beating. If a recruit fails the initiation rite of passage, he or she is then murdered for lack of courage and spirit. Females serve as gun and drug runners because the police generally pay more attention to male MS-13 members. Males and females alike must attend local meetings and are expected to pay membership dues. Members of MS-13 consist of both adults and youths as young as age 12. The older members are expected to teach the younger ones in weapons use—especially explosives and explosive devices—car theft, and gang rules and protocols. Much of the advanced military-style training is deemed necessary in order to conduct criminal activities. Because MS-13 maintains ties to El Salvador, it has easy access to sophisticated military weapons and often traffics weapons throughout the United States, but only to people of similar Central American descent and never to whites or blacks. Stealing cars is another important moneymaker for MS-13. Vehicles are regularly stolen by organized groups of MS-13 and then sold to specific junk yards and "chop shops" or sometimes shipped to South America.

The MS-13 gang can be found in New York City, Los Angeles, Washington D.C., and in such far-away places as Kodiak, Alaska. In 1998, Los Angeles Superior Court Judge Patricia Collins issued an injunction against the Hollywood clique of MS-13. Members were prohibited from gathering in public, blocking sidewalks, and other

The most commonly used identifier for the Mara Salvatrucha gang is *MS*, which represents Mara Salvatrucha along with the number 13 (the letter *M* is the 13th letter of the alphabet).

FIGURE 6.2 Mara Salvatrucha (MS, MS-13)

activities. The injunction also placed a curfew on members under age 18. County Supervisor Zev Yaroslavsky claimed that the gang uses "murder, rape, robbery and extortion" to terrorize residents in the Hollywood area. Local officials believe that the level of violence associated with this drug-trafficking gang is second only to that of the 18th Street Gang. MS-13 is known to have ties with La Eme, the notorious Mexican prison gang (The Associated Press 1998). La Eme appreciates and respects MS-13's level of violence and commitment to protecting drug markets; on the other hand, La Eme considers MS-13 to be a "loose cannon" because of its unwillingness to follow organizational rules.

In the New York City area, the Port Washington police department reported that the MS-13 gang had earned a reputation for violence and drug trafficking by the late 1990s. It estimated that there were several hundred members of MS-13 in Nassau and Suffolk Counties alone (Port Washington News 1998). In 2004, federal prosecutors announced the indictment of 30 gang members from across Long Island, claiming that they were responsible for five murders and multiple stabbings, shootings, and a fire-bombing. Investigators said that the 30 defendants were members of three different gangs: the Bloods, based in Nassau; the Murder Unit, which operates in Greenport; and Long Island's largest gang, MS-13, based in Nassau. Members of MS-13 in Nassau are affiliated with the growing national MS-13 gang. Law enforcement officials are convinced that gangs and gang violence are "out of control" on Long Island. According to Assistant United States Attorney Andrew C. Hruska, MS-13 has more than 300 members in Nassau and Suffolk Counties (Healy 2004) and are found in such suburban villages as Bethpage, Baldwin, and Valley Stream.

MS-13 is a huge problem in Charlotte, North Carolina. It is considered the most violent of the city's gangs, being suspected of seven of the nine gang-related homicides in 2003 (Campo-Flores 2003). In Charlotte, as in other American cities, MS-13 is a recent gang phenomenon that has developed as a result of a wave of immigration which dramatically increased the number of North Carolina's Latinos (Campo-Flores 2003).

The criminal activities of MS-13 in the Virginia suburbs of Washington D.C. caught the attention of U.S. Attorney General John Ashcroft in 2004. Ashcroft expressed concern that gangs were threatening several communities a short drive from the nation's capital (Johnson 2004), and in fact MS-13 has been identified as responsible for a number of violent crimes in the capital district. For example, in May 2004, a suspected MS-13 gangster was charged in a machete attack on a 16-year-old boy in Alexandria, Virginia. The geographic distribution and growing membership indicate that MS-13 is on its way to becoming a national gang.

SUPER-SIZED GANG NATIONS

There are a large number of local and regional street gangs, although the exact count is hard to determine. Many local gangs have an affiliation to larger, super-sized gangs, known as nation coalitions. The largest of these nation coalitions are the Crips, Bloods, People, and Folks. Discussion of super-sized gangs begins with the Los Angeles-based Crips.

The Crips

The Crips are believed to be the largest of all the gangs found in the United States. Their home base and origin are on the mean streets of South-Central Los Angeles. (South-Central LA is now called Southern LA.) The history of the Crips can be traced to the late 1960s and early 1970s. Some people believe that the formation of the Crips was the direct result of the FBI's crackdown on the Black Panther Party in the late 1960s, when activism and political organization in the black community were viewed as threats to national security by the FBI and the LAPD (Chambliss 1993). The Black Panther party was a progressive political organization that sought social change. The Panthers were founded by Huey P. Newton, who viewed the party as a means of meeting the needs of oppressed African-Americans under the party slogan of "survival pending revolution." Its first program was the Free Breakfast for Children Program started at a Catholic church in the Fillmore district of San Francisco. The program was so successful it spread to every city in which the Panthers had chapters. The federal government quickly modeled its own version of this program for the public schools. The Panthers ran a number of other programs within communities as well, and its example influenced future gang attempts to provide social services to the local people. In accordance with partywide rules, chapter members were required to attend political education courses regularly, learn how to use firearms (training was conducted in the Mojave Desert), and learn to perform emergency medical techniques (Black Panther Party 1999).

The Southern California chapter of the Black Panther Party (BPP) was formed in 1968, in Los Angeles, by street gangster Alprentice "Bunchy" Carter (Black Panther Party 1999). Carter (1942–1969), known as the "Mayor of the Ghetto," was the former head of the 5,000-strong Slauson Gang and its hard core, the Slauson Renegades. While spending four years in Soledad prison for armed robbery, Carter became a Muslim and a follower of Malcolm X. Carter met BBP Minister of Defense Huey Newton in 1967 and became a Panther on the spot. He was given the title of Deputy Minister of Defense when he took over the Southern California chapter in 1968. By April 1968, the Southern California chapter was gaining 50–100 new members each week, although not all stayed. As the chapter grew, so did the attacks (from the police) against it. FBI Director J. Edgar Hoover believed the BPP to be the greatest threat to the internal security of the country. Carter began attending UCLA. On January 17, 1969, he was gunned down at Campbell Hall on the UCLA campus—some say by the FBI, others say by rival members of the BPP. Huey Newton proclaimed the FBI to be behind Carter's execution, either directly or indirectly (by hiring/blaming members of the cultural nationalist U.S. organization led by Ron "Maulana" Karenga). By the end of the decade, 28 Los Angeles Black Panthers had been reported killed by the police. Youths (such as Raymond Washington and Stanley "Tookie" Williams) who were too young to join the Panthers and who were upset by their grim socioeconomic realities, began to form their own groups (gangs).

The crackdown on the politically active Panthers upset many blacks, who are generally upset with the political system because they feel they never receive justice. This view gains some credence when looking at the pattern followed by civic projects. Civic leaders considering projects like freeway expansion put a great deal of time and effort into assuring the wealthy and "connected" people that they will not be "harmed" by the construction. As a result, it is the politically weak who are. The construction of the Century Freeway in Los Angeles, for example, caused the destruction of numerous homes in South-Central Los Angeles and led to the building of housing projects. A number of small gangs formed in these projects, among them the **Avenues**. The Avenues, who date back to the early 1960s, became the first dominant African-American gang in Los Angeles. They claimed the areas around Central Avenue.

A 15-year-old high school student named Raymond Lee Washington wanted to join the Avenues but was denied because of his young age. Undaunted, Washington got together with a few of his friends and formed a gang called the **Baby Avenues**, in line with the older Avenues gang. Washington and his crew attempted to preserve the Black Panther aura by forming a quasi-political street gang to represent a new generation of African-Americans. Because blacks had long experienced the negative effects of oppression and lack of political influence in American society the Black Panthers had been a sign of hope to many young blacks, especially in Los Angeles. At the same time that Washington was organizing a powerful gang of young teenagers, Stanley "Tookie" Williams was earning great status as a vicious street gang fighter. Williams had moved to Los Angeles from Louisiana when he was 9 years old and learned quickly that the only way to survive and, more importantly, dominate was to fight. Williams never backed down to anyone, and no one was tougher. Inevitably, Williams and Washington met one another. Their great mutual respect led to an immediate alliance and commitment to make their collective gangs more powerful than any other and to become a more political and intimidating force than the Panthers. Neighborhood gangs merged with the Baby Avenues rather than risk fighting them.

Around 1970, the Baby Avenues changed their name to the **Avenue Cribs**. The word *crib* was used to describe their youthfulness. Soon after, *crib* got changed to *crip*, for reasons no one knows for certain. Some suggest that Williams's handwriting was so poor his "b's" looked like "p's" and after a while everyone started to think *crib* was *crips*. Others suggest that Washington, who was a poor speller, wanted to change the name of his gang to "crypts" but spelled "crips" instead (Crip History 2003). A television show *Tale of the Crypts* was popular at that time. A more plausible explanation is the statement by one of the original members of the Baby Avenues that the word *crip* stood for "Continuous Revolution in Progress" (Davis 1992, 299). The early Cribs wore black leather jackets, walked with canes, and wore earrings in the left earlobe. On one occasion in 1971, several Crib members assaulted a Japanese woman and were described as young "cripples" who carried canes. The local media picked up on this description and named the group the Crips (*Los Angeles Sentinel*, February 10, 1972). This story provides yet another explanation as to how the Cribs came to be called the Crips. The term can be used as a verb, *crippin*, which means to steal, but also describes a way of life. Regardless, by the early 1970s, the Avenue Cribs became known as the **Crips**. It was Washington's intent to link his Crip gang to other African-American gangs in an attempt to unify the "movement." He worked hard in the early 1970s to organize a number of crib **sets**—gangs that maintained individuality but were linked to the greater nation coalition. Washington and Williams initiated black teens throughout the inner city into their Crip gang, starting up the East Side Crips, West Side Crips, Avalon Garden Crips, and the Inglewood Crips. Crip gangs emerged around the Fremont, Locke, and Washington high schools.

The process of gang expansion was explained by Sanyika Shakur (born in 1963 as Kody Scott) in his book *Monster: The Autobiography of an L.A. Gang Member*. Shakur joined the Crips at age 11, and by 17 was one of the most feared gangsters in Los Angeles. Shakur (2002, 199) explained the process of gang expansion as follows:

> The mechanics involved in taking a street, or territory, is not unlike any attempt, I would assume, on behalf of early Euro-American settlers. Send in a scout, have him meet the 'natives,' test their hostility level, military capabilities, needs, likes, and dislikes. Once a military presence is established, in come the 'citizens'—in this case, gang members. Those who are not persuaded by our lofty presences *will* be persuaded by our military might. All who are of fighting age become conscripts. The set expands, and so does our territory. Sometimes there is resistance, but most of the time our efforts are successful.

As the Crips expanded, they came upon other gangs that were less willing to give up their claims to specific neighborhoods. The **Piru Street Boys** was one of the gangs the Crips came across that were uncooperative. During the summer of 1972, the Crips from Compton fought with the Compton Piru Street Boys, who, outnumbered, were beaten badly by the Crips. Looking for revenge, the Pirus turned to the Lueders Park Hustlers for backup, and they agreed. A member of the **L.A. Brim** gang had been murdered by a Crip earlier that year, so the Pirus asked them as well to join in a meeting to discuss a revenge battle. The **Denver Lanes** and **the Bishops** also joined the Pirus. All of these gangs were greatly outnumbered by the Crips, so they decided to form a permanent alliance. The Crips were known for wearing blue bandannas, so the Piru alliance decided to wear red bandannas. Eventually they came up with the name **Bloods** for their new gang. Other gangs would join the Blood and Crip alliances until the predominantly African-American neighborhoods of Los Angeles were dominated by one gang or the other. Over the years, political issues became totally irrelevant and making money and gaining respect on the streets became the primary goals of the Bloods and Crips.

The amount of attention in the press that the early Crips received enticed younger boys, who became eager to join a group that provided black teenagers with raw power. For marginalized male youths, joining the Crips was a sign of manliness. Each inductee had to go through the initiation ritual of beating-in by members of the gang. The beating includes fist punches and body kicks, and the recruit is not allowed to fight back—he must simply take the beating willingly. Many modern Crip gangs initiate members by having them commit a crime in front of gang witnesses, a process called "loc'ing in." Chapters 3 and 4 explained some of the many reasons that individuals choose to join a gang. For the Crips, gang activities represent an opportunity to earn an income. Most Crips are involved in such criminal activities as murder, armed robbery, and selling illegal contraband in the underground economy—especially drugs and weapons. The Crips have been involved in the sale and distribution of crack cocaine since it first came on the drug scene in the early 1980s. Attempts to control the distribution of drugs is what led the Crips to sets throughout the nation.

The Crips are notoriously violent and do not hesitate to use extreme methods to protect their turf against rival gangs and the police. Crip gang members are generally members for life, whether they are incarcerated in prison or have become rich and famous in the legitimate society. Stanley Williams is an example of the former and

Calvin Brodus (aka Snoop Dogg) the latter. Williams, the cofounder of the Crips with Raymond Washington, has been on death row at San Quentin State Prison since 1981 for his conviction in the 1979 murders of four people during robberies at a convenience store and a motel in Los Angeles. California prison authorities believe that Williams runs the Crip inmate population. In July 2003, authorities at Corcoran State Prison locked down 1,300 African-American general-population inmates in their cells as they investigated whether incarcerated members of the Crips were conspiring to attack prison staffers in retaliation for the anticipated execution of Williams (Warren and Morain 2003, B1). Prison officials had uncovered notes from prisoners indicating that Crips were going to attack and kill high-ranking prison staff members. Prison officials admit that any time a Crip attacks a staff member they look for a link to Williams. Tookie enjoys much acclaim among young African-Americans because of his accomplishments since incarceration. "Enjoying mythic status among young-generation Crips, Williams won a different kind of fame two years ago when a member of the Swiss parliament nominated him for a Nobel Peace Prize for a series of children's books he co-wrote" (Warren and Morain 2003, B1). In the following year, Williams was nominated by a Brown University professor for the Nobel Prize for Literature. Calvin Brodus, better known as rap artist Snoop Dogg, helped to transform a criminal lifestyle and a childhood spent in a hostile environment into a style of music known as gangster rap (see Chapter 4 for a discussion on this musical genre). Snoop Dogg claims to have given up his days of *crippin*, but he openly pays homage to the nation coalition of the Crips by immortalizing his criminal past in his rhymes. In one of his songs, "187," Snoop makes numerous references to firearms and praises the killing of police. In his musical videos, Snoop often employs members of his Crip crew, who openly flash gang signs and wear the blue gang color.

The blue bandanna is symbolically the Crips' "flag." The flag is always to be respected and never left behind during the heat of battle. Crips identify themselves by gang-related tattoos and by wearing other "gang-related" clothing, for example, clothes representing various sports teams such as the Dodgers because their team color is blue or the Chicago Cubs because of the letter "C" for Crips and British Knights because their initials—BK—represent "Blood Killers." Even Burger King (BK) is preferred over other fast-food restaurants. Since the Bloods are the sworn enemies of the Crips, any time a Crip can wear something that disrespects the Bloods, he will do so. Because of their allegiance to the Folk nation, Crips may represent by using a six-pointed star and the number 6 (represents "F," for Folks, the sixth letter in the alphabet). Crips may use the number 3 (for "C") in graffiti as well.

Gang graffiti is one of the most prevalent ways a gang identifies itself. Among other functions, graffiti is used to mark turf, make certain pronouncements, commemorate the dead, and issue challenges. Gangs generally use their specific colors when spray-painting graffiti. However, because most gang members are poor they will use any color they can get their hands on. **Scratchiti** is another form of graffiti. Scratchiti involves using a sharp object like a knife to scratch painted surfaces, wood, and glass windows. Scratchiti is very common on buses, subway trains, and bathroom stalls. The Crips refer to Bloods as "Slobs" (in graffiti the letter "b" is crossed out) and will use such graffiti slogans as: Crips 187 Slobs. The "187" refers to part of the California penal code for homicide; thus, Crips murder Bloods. (See Figure 6.3.)

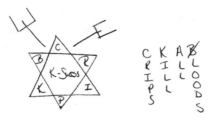

The Crips, as "cousins" to the Folks, will often present a six-point star and Gangster Disciples pitchforks as signs of respect to the Folks. The letters *C, R, I, P*, denote that it is a Crip gang; and the letters *B* and *K* are used for Blood Killer. Note that the letter *B* is crossed out on the graffiti on the left as a sign of disrespect to the Bloods.

In the Crip graffiti, the six-point star and pitchforks are used to respect the Folks. The misspelled *6 poppin' 5 droppin'* is a common chant among Crips. *King Huva* is a tribute to Larry Hoover, the founder of the original Folk gang.

This hand sign is shaped like the letter *C*, for Crips.

FIGURE 6.3 The Crips

The Crips also use the following chant as a means of disrespecting the Bloods:

> Ashes to Ashes
> Dust to Dust
> In Crips We Trust
> In Bloods We Bust
> Kill a "Slob" Win a Prize
> Kill a Crip and Your Family Dies

Today, the Crips are among the most violent street gangs in the world. They are most likely the largest of all the street gangs. They have extended their reach to nearly every large city in the United States (they are also found outside the United States).

They make money through the distribution and sale of drugs, gun trafficking, and a number of other violent and property offenses. The Crips are highly feared because they readily cause harm to anyone who interferes with their goals. It should be pointed out that not all the Crip factions are unified; they are known to fight each other nearly as often as they fight Blood gangs. But despite their growth and spread over the decades, the franchising of Crip gangs (and Blood gangs as well) is nothing like the process of franchising retail stores—they are not *that* organized.

As a point of interest, as of July 2004, Tookie Williams was still in prison and Raymond Washington was shot and killed in gang violence in the 1970s.

The Bloods

It is estimated that the Crips outnumber the Bloods by 3 to 1 (Shelden et al. 2001). The ability to stand up to the mighty Crips with such a disadvantage in numbers is a testamony to the strength and potential brutality of the Bloods. The Bloods hold an elevated status in the gang world. As mentioned, the Bloods originated in and around the Piru Street area in Compton, California. Because the original Blood gang was the Piru Street gang, the Bloods are often referred to as Piru gangs. They are primarily an African-American gang; however, unlike the Crips, the Bloods have accepted other racial groups into the gang: Hispanics, whites, and Chinese members have been identified.

The Blood nation formed as a protective alliance against the forces of the Crip nation. The rivalry between these two super gangs has been responsible for a great deal of violent crime in Los Angeles, dating back to the early 1970s, and as the years went on, the degree of violence escalated. The sharp increase in assaults and homicides attributed to gangs is directly related to the increased use of firepower by gang members and the tactic of drive-by shootings. The Crips claim that the Bloods were the first to use guns in gang fights. This would seem logical, considering they were generally outnumbered by Crips. Like the Crips, the Bloods protect their neighborhoods at all costs. The Bloods share a common philosophy of all for one, one for all and have a true devotion to their set and nation. To keep presence in any neighborhood that has a Crip set, the Bloods have expanded to all corners of the country. Bloods in the northeast generally identify with the **United Blood Nation**, which originated at the Riker's Island prison in New York in the early 1990s. According to New York authorities, Omar Portee (known on the street as O.G. Mack) formed the United Blood Nation (usually, simply called Bloods) while he was an inmate at Riker's Island in 1993; he continued to lead the Bloods on the streets of New York City after his release. Portee's Bloods were the largest street gang in New York, and by 2000, the Bloods were known as the most violent gang on the East Coast (Savelli 2000). In August 1997, in a three-day sweep, New York City police arrested 167 alleged members of gangs, most of whom were Bloods. Police attributed 135 slashings to the gang initiation rituals (Tyre 1997). Two Blood members would approach a stranger on the street or subway, pull out a box cutter, and slash the victim's face. The NYPD launched the sweep in an attempt to stop the slashings and the gang's expansion. The NYPD named this operation "Red Bandanna." Executed by the Citywide Anti-Gang Enforcement (CAGE) unit, Red Bandanna was a multiagency drug-and-gang initiative set up to dismantle street and other violent drug gangs in targeted areas of the city. "The operation was focused in precincts in Upper Manhattan, Southern Queens, Northern Brooklyn, and on Riker's Island. Criminals arrested during this operation were accused of selling drugs, committing armed robberies, weapons' possession, and murder. With 'Red Bandanna's' strategic arrests, we dismantled seven sets of Bloods and one set of Crips and achieved the purpose of the sweep, which was to stop the gangbangers from expanding their activity" (Safir 2003, 181). On April 14, 2003, a federal judge in Manhattan sentenced Portee to 50 years in prison. When Naomi Reice Buchwald of the United States District Court sentenced the Blood gang leader, she noted the amount of violence and lawlessness that he was responsible for and the lack of anything on the positive side of the ledger (Weiser 2003).

Howard Safir (former NYPD commissioner) recounted the epidemic of gang-related crimes attributed to the Bloods in New York City:

> The Bloods were an active and violent gang, and we began seeing a violent trend of gang-related incidents: random slashings and stabbings, mostly on subways, with box cutters and knives, that we associated with initiations. The gang lived by their code of "Blood in. Blood out." To be initiated you had to spill someone's blood; and to get out of the gang your own blood was spilled. Because of the NYPD's enforcement of low-level crimes, many of the gang members had stopped carrying guns, and so slashings and stabbings with box cutters fulfilled most initiation rites and solved some of the disputes that in the past would have involved shootings (Safir 2003, 180).

According to intelligence sources, the Bloods were believed to number around 500 gang members with 16 subsets in New York City in the early 2000s (Safir 2003).

Among the codes of the Bloods is a lifetime allegiance to the gang. Blood gangs have a strict set of rules that members must abide by or otherwise face punishment ordered by the gang leaders. Gang members must follow all orders given to them by their leaders or risk a violation ceremony. Violation punishments may range from menial tasks and physical assault to (in some extreme cases) death. The philosophy of punishment varies from one set to another, with Blood gangs in New England having a reputation for being more structured and rigid than sets in California.

Recruitment into the Bloods is usually done aggressively and involves an initiation, which generally takes the form of "jumping in." In this ritual, the new member is required to take a beating and is not allowed to fight back. The most common form of initiation involves the recruit "walking the line," which means walking between two lines of gang members with hands behind while the members beat and kick them. The goal is to get to the end of the line without falling to the ground; otherwise, the recruit must start all over. To gain acceptance into the gang, the individual must "Blood-in," meaning that they must spill someone's blood or have their own blood spilled. Among the various ways to go about this is to fight, slash, or assault a law enforcement officer or regular citizen. Committing robberies and rape can be another way to "Blood-in." Women recruits may be obligated to participate in group sex. As with all other gangs, the initiation process is conducted so that the new member can demonstrate loyalty to the gang. New recruits are also expected to memorize the nation history, organization, and symbolism.

Much of the Blood's criminal activity consists of drug distribution and sales. The Bloods distribute such drugs as marijuana, LSD, PCP, heroin, and cocaine and make a great deal of money from the sale of crack cocaine, powder cocaine, and heroin. Profits from drug sales allow the gang to prosper and grow. As the Crip nation expanded its turf to increase both its membership and its share of the drug market, the Bloods grew with them. In the early 1980s narcotics trafficking was considered a minor activity of the Bloods and Crips in Los Angeles. But by 1983, both of these gangs had established criminal networks throughout California. Today, they have drug markets throughout the country. The Bloods also have connections with drug lords and traffickers in South America and other drug-producing countries. They are also known to engage in violent activity against rival gang and nongang members. They regularly participate in such illegal activities as robberies, car thefts, extortions, rapes, and murders. These crimes are committed for a variety of reasons: initiation, general acceptance, to raise money for dues, or for personal benefit. In the Northeast, the Bloods regularly slash victims across the face with little or no warning of the attack.

The Bloods also enjoy a reputation as a vicious prison gang. Incarcerated Bloods are responsible for a great deal of violence inside prisons and jails, primarily stabbings and slashings. In prison, they fight with rival gang members and nongang inmates and work to eliminate any threats or competition to business inside the prison setting. Going to prison elevates the status of gang members on the street. When inmates are released, they usually gain O.G. ("original gangster" or "old gangster") status.

Bloods can be identified in a number of ways, especially by color (red), graffiti, and signs. The color red is the main identifier; they wear or carry a red bandana and treat it as if it is their "flag." During a battle, a Blood can never leave the fight without his flag; Bloods are willing to risk death to retrieve it. On the other hand, returning from battle with an enemy's flag/rag will result in great honor, as it usually means that a rival has been killed. Some Bloods may use other colors, such as the Lime Street Pirus, who of course wear lime colors. Although most gang members maintain a level of individuality by adopting a nickname or street name (e.g., Killer Dog, 12-Gauge, and Cop Killer), the Bloods have gang-related tattoos to identify themselves. Other forms of identification include gang-related bling-bling and certain types of clothing. Calvin Klein's are popular with Bloods because the CK is understood to mean "Crip Killer." As usual with all gangs, they have adopted certain sport team logos. Some Bloods will wear a Pittsburg Pirates ball cap because of the logo "P" on the cap. The "P" stands for Pirus (it is also used by the Bloods ally, the People Nation). Kansas City "Chiefs" hats are very popular with Bloods because they are red and the letters CHIEFS spell out "Crips Hated in Every F***ing State." East Coast Bloods are particularly fond the FUBU clothing line. To them, FUBU means "Forever Us Bloods United." When the Bloods paint graffiti they prefer the color red and will never use the letter "C" because of their hatred for the Crips (thus, they will not wear a Cincinnati Reds ball cap for the letter "C" even though the team color is red). Bloods will often draw three round circles to form an upside-down triangle, which represents a dog's paw, and they will paint the word *Crabs* as a sign of disrespect toward the Crips. Although the specific signs that Bloods flash and the symbolism in their graffiti change constantly, their practice is a constant. (See Figure 6.4.)

The Bloods remain a real threat on the streets of numerous American cities both to rival gangs and civilians alike. They continue to grow in number and expand the size of their territory, an expansion fueled by the sale of drugs. Generally, Blood members consider the gang their family and their loyalty to it is very strong. By all accounts, the Bloods look to be a formidable force for years to come. Their competition with the Crips and other gangs will guarantee that blood will continue to spill.

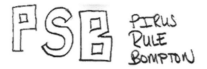

PSB represents Piru Street Bloods. The Pirus were the original Blood gang and hail from Compton, California. The Bloods do not acknowledge the letter *C* so they spell *Compton* as *Bompton.*

A five-point star is a tribute to the People, who are "cousins" of the Bloods. The pitchfork is upside down as a sign of disrespect to the Folks. *ECB* represents East Coast Bloods. The letter *C* is crossed out to disrespect the Crips. As an added insult, the letter *K* appears within the letter *C* to spell out *CK*, or Crip Killer.

Graffiti of the Denver Lane Bloods features a five-point crown on top. *CK* is for Crip Killer.
FIGURE 6.4 The Bloods

The People

The next two super-sized gangs to be discussed are the **People Nation** and the **Folks Nation**. The Chicago-based People and Folks are far more diverse than the predominantly African-American, Los Angeles-based Bloods and Crips in at least two major ways. First, there is a greater ethnic and racial mix among the gangs aligned to the People and Folks. Second, whereas the Bloods and Crips consist of individual sets of gangs by the same name (Blood or Crip) the People and Folks nations consist of a number of distinct gangs with their own unique names. Thus, these two umbrella groups are not gangs in and of themselves, but represent a collection of individual gang factions. Using a sports analogy, the People and Folks are like conferences (Big East and Big Ten or the National League and American League). For example, the Folks include such gangs as the **Black Gangster Disciples**, **Latin Disciples**, **Simon City Royals**, **C-Notes**, and the **Spanish Gangsters**. The People include such gangs as the **Latin Kings**, **Vice Lords**, the **Almighty Conservative Vice Lords**, **Insane Vice Lords**, **Black P-Stone Nation**, and the **Almighty Gaylords**. It is not uncommon for some gangs to change nation allegiance, nor is it uncommon for a gang to rejoin a nation after declaring itself independent. Thus, any listing of gangs belonging to nations is subject to change. The People and Folks are found predominantly in the upper Midwest, especially in Milwaukee and Chicago, and throughout the East.

The People and Folks distinguish themselves in a number of ways. The People use a five-point star as a gang insignia and the Folks use a six-pointed star. Thus, the People use in their drawings a 5-pointed crown or 5-pointed star. The Folks represent their affiliation with the number 6 and/or the 6-pointed Star of David. The People and Folks abide by the "left" and "right" rule of dressing, writing, wearing tattoos, and so on in order to show alliance to the gang. The People gangs wear their identifiers to the left side of the body, including, but not limited to, hats, bling-bling, a rolled-up left pant leg, or hand inside left pocket.

Among the more significant gangs that make up the People are the Latin Kings. The Latin Kings are one of the oldest and largest Hispanic (predominantly Mexican and Puerto Rican) gangs in existence. They were founded by Hispanic inmates in Chicago during the 1940s to protect themselves against other prison gangs (Safir 2003). In 2002, the estimated Chicago membership of the Latin Kings was 18,000 (Main and Sadovi 2002). "The Almighty Latin King Nation began in Chicago in the forties, one of dozens of street-and-prison gangs in the city. What made the Kings different was their mixture of intense discipline and revolutionary politics with a home-made religion called Kingism, adding idealism and a boot-camp rigor to the usual gang camaraderie—a potent mixture for troubled ghetto kids whose lives lacked structure and hope" (Richardson 1997, 32). The Latin Kings developed slowly in Southeast Chicago and the Humboldt Park area throughout the 1950s. There were numerous gangs in Chicago in the 1950s, including many white ethnic gangs. During this time, the Humboldt Park community was a very strong and thriving Jewish community with nearly 75 Jewish temples. By the 1960s, Latinos and blacks were moving into Humboldt Park and South Chicago, effectively dissolving the Jewish community and the local white ethnic gangs. The Latin Kings rose to power as their turf protection skills increased. They also learned to form alliances with other gangs, like the

Vice Lords, who shared with them common enemies, and thus began a nation coalition. The Latin Kings are generally Mexican or Puerto Rican but are also known to recruit white youth. It is estimated that there are as many as 25,000 Latin Kings.

In an attempt to expand their territory, the Latin Kings began to expand to other Eastern cities during the 1980s. They can be found in New York, Connecticut, New Jersey, Iowa, Indiana, Ohio, Florida, and Massachusetts as well as in Illinois and Wisconsin. In fact, wherever there is a sizable Hispanic community, it is likely that the Latin Kings have recruited there. The Latin Kings' presence in New York can be traced back to the mid-1980s. "The New York branch of the Kings was established in 1986 by Luis Felipe, or 'King Blood,' who is currently serving a life term in solitary confinement for ordering hits on several Latin King members in the early 1990s" (Safir 2003, 181).

The Latin Kings are highly organized and well structured and live by a charter constitution. Most sets have a hierarchical structure with military-style titles (high-ranking soldiers are called lieutenants and lower-level ones are known as sergeants). Foot soldiers are used to sell drugs and are required to pay a "street tax" of more than half their drug profits to higher-level gang members (Main and Sadovi 2002). The primary leaders are known as the High Holy Incas, secondary leaders as Supreme Caciqua, and leaders third in command are called the Royal Crown. Female members are known as **Latin Queens**. The gang members function in a cooperative manner and work under the ideal of one body, mind, and soul. New recruits are initiated. Current members who violate the gang's rules are subject to "physicals" (a violation ceremony, or punishment). Most Latin King gangs, and especially the **Almighty Latin King Nation (ALKN)**, have the mentality of "Once a King, always a King." The Latin Kings participate in all the regular gang criminal activities: drug and weapons sales and trafficking, assault, robbery, intimidation, property damage, murder, and so on. The Latin Kings are generally considered to be the most violent of the Hispanic gangs. They are notorious for fighting in packs and implement a "911" tactic—the Kings call to battle (Richardson 1997). This inevitably results in constant disputes with rivals, which leads to a high level of violence.

Criminal activity and religious mysticism are intertwined in this street gang. As mentioned, the Kings employ a religious philosophy. The ALKN commonly use a fist over the heart to represent, "I will die for you, for you are the flesh of my flesh, blood of my blood, son of my mother who is the universal nature and follower of Yahve, who is the Almighty King of Kings." This passage is found in the book of Genesis in the Bible. The primary symbol of the Latin King is the five-pointed crown. As Latin King members explain, slogans and prayers used by the Latin Kings reflect both a secular and religious flair. Latin Kings pay homage to each other and to God by stating, "Almighty Father, King of Kings, hear us as we come before you, one body, mind, and soul, true wisdom, knowledge and understanding. Give us strong brown wisdom, for we realized you are the best, and the wisest of all seeing eyes." The Latin Kings consider January 6 to be "Kings Holy Day," and the first week of March as "Kings Week." These occasions are celebrated by gang members hanging out and consuming drugs and alcohol. The private notebooks that King members use are referred to as "Bibles" of Kingist teachings.

The Latin Kings are responsible for a great deal of crime and violence. In an attempt to combat the criminal presence of the Latin Kings in New York City, the NYPD worked with the FBI on "Operation Crown," a 19-month undercover investigation that ended with simultaneous citywide raids. "The 1998 sweep by one thousand federal, state, and local law officers began before sunrise and netted close to one hundred gang members, including Antonio Fernandez, a Brooklyn man known as 'King Tone,' who was the gang's leader. Until then the Latin Kings had been approximately three thousand strong, and Antonio 'King Tone' Fernandez was their guru" (Safir 2003, 181). In the raids, the police seized drugs, weapons, and cash. Law enforcement officials were convinced that "Operation Crown" was successful in curtailing the growth of the Latin Kings in New York. The Latin Kings are responsible for so much crime in New Jersey that U.S. Attorney Chris Christie stated that they "represent the new organized crime in the state of New Jersey" (*Buffalo News* 2002, A8). Forty-five members of the Latin Kings were arrested in October 2002 on charges that included attempted murder and drug distribution. This suburban-based New Jersey Latin King gang recruits new members from high schools, primarily from the tri-state area (New York, New Jersey, Pennsylvania).

Another important gang aligned to the People nation is the Vice Lords. The Vice Lords are an African-American gang with a 2002 estimated Chicago membership of 20,000 (Main and Sadovi 2002). The Vice Lords are said to have been begun in 1958 in the St. Charles Juvenile Correctional facility by a group of youths from around 16th Street on the west side of Chicago. These early gangsters agreed to pool their gang affiliations so as to become one of Chicago's toughest gangs. "There were 66 original Vice Lords when the gang formed. In about two years, membership grew to over 300 in five branches. In the 1960s they incorporated as a nonprofit organization with around 8,000 members in 26 divisions" (Shelden et al. 2001, 16). Today, the Vice Lords can be found all over the Midwest and in some Eastern cities. They continue to maintain a stronghold in many Chicago neighborhoods.

The Vice Lords possess a rank structure within individual factions that includes general, minister, lieutenant, and foot soldiers. This structure is similar in all sets of the Vice Lords; however, each set's leadership is unique and has no power over members of other factions. A Vice Lord leader's power is not exercised through force, but, rather, through influence. Members of the Lords follow a leader out of respect. The strength of an individual's power is subject to constant fluctuation. Power is based on the number of one's followers, and the following is constantly changing.

There are a number of Vice Lord factions. Among them are the Conservative Vice Lords, Imperial Insane Vice Lords, Renegade Vice Lords, Gangster Stone Vice Lords, Ebony Vice Lords, and Four Corner Hustlers. The Conservative Vice Lords were especially prominent in the 1960s as a gang attempting to organize legitimate job opportunities for members of deprived urban communities (the nonprofit organization mentioned previously). They worked to eliminate crime and violence in the community, but they were not successful. Local officials did what they could to undermine the authority of the Conservative Vice Lords. Like the Latin Kings, the Vice Lords developed in Chicago communities experiencing rapid social and racial change. Communities such as these are not conducive to producing normally functioning social institutions designed to meet the needs of the people.

The Simon City Royals, a mostly white street gang that was well known for its burglary rings in Chicago, is generally credited for the formation of nation alliances in Chicago in the 1970s. As Simon City Royal (SCR) members began to get arrested, prosecuted, and incarcerated, they quickly realized how outnumbered they were in the Illinois prison setting. The SCR agreed to provide drugs to fellow inmates who belonged to the Black Gangster Disciples in exchange for protection from the Latin Disciples. The alliance between the Simon City Royals and the Black Gangster Disciples led to the formation of the Folks. The Latin Disciples aligned themselves with other gangs and formed the People. On the streets, the SCR also provided guns to allied gangs in order to secure the Folk alliance. Presently, there are over 30 different gangs that claim allegiance to one of these two nations.

As for why the Almighty Gaylords, another gang affiliated with the People nation, did not choose to join the SCR and the Folks, the Gaylords had their own history of fights against most of the individual gangs that made up the Folks alliance. On the other hand, their biggest rivalry was against the Latin Kings, the primary member of the People. Latin King members had killed Almighty Gaylord members in the 1970s, 1980s, and 1990s. The Gaylords are a white, Chicago-based street gang, and the alliance to the People nation was a tough thing for many Gaylord members to accept (in fact, many wonder why the white gangs do not form a national coalition of their own). They were always on guard against their alliance partners the Latin Kings because of the way the Kings had pushed fellow alliance member the Insane Deuces too far. The choice to join the People really came down to the fact that the Gaylords had more enemies within the Folks, including the SCR, who had also killed a member of the Gaylords. But their decision to join the People nation has not really benefited them, because the Almighty Gaylords automatically gained all Folks gangs as enemies. It should be noted that the Folk nation is larger than the People nation, and the Gaylords, as a white gang, is already small. Its territories around Palmer Street have now been overtaken by Folks.

Members of the People nation can be identified in a number of ways beyond the five-pointed star and the "left-right" rule. The predominant colors of the People are red, black, and white. However, the primary colors of the Latin Kings are black and gold, and they wear black and yellow clothes. Many members of the People wear Chicago Bulls clothing because of their black and red colors. The Latin Kings will wear beads with their gang colors as a necklace and also wear LA Kings apparel. Tattoos for Latin Kings are often symbolic: A teardrop in red means the gangster has killed someone, and a teardrop without color means the gangster has lost someone. The Vice Lords wear Bulls clothing but also always wear a playboy bunny emblem or tattoo. Sports teams such as the Pittsburgh Pirates and the Philadelphia Phillies, because of the prominent letter "P," are favorites among People gangsters. The Vice Lords like to wear the University of Nevada-Las Vegas (UNLV) clothing because of the red-and-black color scheme and because the UNLV letters can be rearranged to read "Vice Lords Nation United." The Vice Lords wear Louis Vuitton hats because they choose to read the initials backwards. Primary symbols of the Vice Lords include a pyramid with a crescent moon, the letters "VL," a bunny with a top hat, cane, and gloves, and a crescent moon. The Latin Kings can be identified by such symbols as a three-pointed crown (as well as a five-pointed crown), five dots, cross necklace, a king's head with a crown, lions, and the letters "LK." When tagging, they always cross out the "C's" (for Crip) and X-out the "O's" (for Hoover). They refer to Folks and Crips as "Craps"—it is meant as a sign of disrespect to the word *crip*. Since the Folks often use a pitchfork as a major identifier symbol, the People will paint upside down pitchforks as a sign of disrespect toward Folks. (See Figure 6.5.)

L and *K* represent Latin Kings. A five-point crown is utilized by the People. The pitchfork is upside down to disrespect the Folks.

A three-point crown (and star, not shown) is also used by the People as an identifier.

The Vice Lords are represented by a bunny and cane. The right ear is pointed down to disrespect the Folks. A five-point star is in the background.

FIGURE 6.5 The People

The Folks

As the previous discussion on the People revealed, the Folks are the other dominant super-sized Chicago-based gang. The Folks are larger in number and equally as brutal as the People. The Folks have aligned themselves with the Crips to counterbalance the alliance between the People and Bloods. The original Folk gang (Gangster Disciples) was started by **Larry Hoover**, and that is why the Folk nation is sometimes referred to as the **Hoover Nation** gang. Larry Hoover, currently serving a life term in prison, is still considered the Chairman of the Folks. Folk gang members display a six-pointed star, which is symbolic of the core beliefs of the Folks: Life, Loyalty, Love, Wisdom, Knowledge, and Understanding.

The most prominent of the Folk gangs is the Black Gangster Disciples. These gangsters use an upright pitchfork as their primary symbol in graffiti. To disrespect the People (especially the Vice Lords), the Folks draw, in graffiti, a cane handle upside down. The Black Gangster Disciples are an African-American gang with a 2002 estimated Chicago membership of 30,000 (Main and Sadovi 2002). The Disciples have their roots in the Chicago streets (the Englewood neighborhood) dating back to the 1960s.

In the mid-1960s Jeff Fort united the leaders of some 50 area street gangs into a single alliance called the Black P-Stone Nation. The gang was controlled by a 21-man commission, self-titled the "Main 21." The ideal of this gang was to create a socially active organization designed to empower poorer members of the community (similar to the Conservative Vice Lords, who ran a teen center and job-training classes for youths on the West Side). This organization received $1.4 million in federal antipoverty funds, which were actually used to fund the illegal activities of the gang. The misappropriation of funds was discovered and a federal grand jury convicted Fort of the mismanagement of funds and he was sent to federal prison.

Many other gang organizations surfaced and attempted to secure money as the Black P-Stone gang had managed. Two very influential gangs, the Black Gangster Disciples, led by David Barksdale, and the Gangster Disciples, led by the aforementioned Larry Hoover, followed Fort's example and unified their gangs to form the Black Gangster Disciple Nation. The Black Gangster Disciples wear the six-pointed Star of David (the Jewish star) as a tribute to their leader, David "King David" Barksdale, who was seriously wounded in an ambush in 1969 and died of kidney failure in 1974. A gentile, Barksdale wore the medallion because it was his namesake and because he considered himself a star. Throughout the 1970s the Black Gangster Disciple Nation controlled the drug trade and became bitter rivals of the Black P-Stone Nation. Their wars were brutal and left many dead or imprisoned. The Gangster Disciples continued their war with the P-Stone Nation inside prison walls. Their war was another major contributor to the formation of the People and Folks Nations in the 1970s. The P-Stone Nation ended up with the People and the Black Gangster Disciples with the Folks.

Recruitment and initiation into the Folks nation are similar to that of the other nations. Recruitment is highly encouraged and actively pursued because of the simple premise of there being strength in numbers. The most common initiation is "The Line," which involves the prospective member walking a line between fellow gangsters from whom he takes an extreme beating. The gang has a constitution and a hierarchical structure, with all underlings expected to strictly abide by rules and codes of conduct.

Violations result in a physical beating. The Black Gangster Disciples are "cafeteria-style" criminals—their crimes include murder, drive-by shootings, robbery, auto theft, home invasions, weapons sales and distribution, and, of course, the sale and distribution of drugs. The Black Gangster Disciples, like other gangs, utilize "false-front" businesses to run their drug distribution syndicate. Music stores, car washes, ice-cream shops, barbershops, and apartment buildings are the traditional locations of either "market places" or money laundering. When Larry Hoover was convicted in 1997, prosecutors estimated that the Disciples were netting an estimated $100 million a year. In fact, (all) gangs have become such a major economic force in Chicago, it is estimated that their annual profit from the sale of drugs is a half-billion dollars. Federal officials in Chicago estimate that the figure is closer to 1 billion dollars—more than 1% of Chicago's gross domestic product (Main and Sadovi 2002).

The basic gang identifiers of a six-point star and raised pitchforks utilized by the Folks are illustrated above.

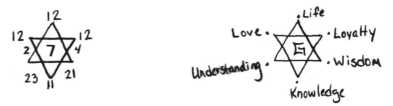

Gangs often use numbers in place of letters. The numbers *12, 12, 21, 11, 23,* and *12* at the tip of each point on the star represent the first letters of the core beliefs of the Black Gangster Disciples: life, loyalty, wisdom, knowledge, understanding, and love. The numbers *2, 7,* and *4* written across the middle of the star represent Black Gangster Disciple.

SC represents the Simon City gang. The raised pitchfork indicates that they are aligned with the Folks. The graffiti on the right is that of the Latin Disciples.

FIGURE 6.6 The Folks

Members of the Folk nation can be identified in a number of ways in addition to the six-pointed star and the upright pitchfork. The Folks are dedicated to "right" identification, as in wearing articles of clothing to the right (caps, bandannas, belt buckles, etc.), wearing jewelry to the right, rolling up the right pant leg, putting one hand in the right pocket, and so on. The primary colors of the Gangster Disciples are blue and black. Black Gangster Disciple members may wear any of the following types of clothing: apparel with the letter "D" (for example, the Detroit Tigers cap) for Disciple; the letter "G" for Gangster (especially the "G" on Georgetown apparel); Duke sweatshirts (the letters are read as "Disciples Utilizing Knowledge Everyday"); Denver Broncos clothing (switch the letters to BK—for Black Disciples); and clothing with the University of Indiana logo (because the IU emblem looks like a pitchfork). The Folk Nation really likes the Georgetown Hoya emblem, not just because the letter "G" is prominent, but also because the collar worn by the dog has six studs and is tilted to the right. Other factions of the Folk Nation abide by "the right" rule and the six-pointed star. The **Satan Disciples** have black and canary yellow for their colors, a devil with a pitchfork for a symbol, and wear clothing with the letter "D." **Orchestra Albany** has gold and brown for its colors and the letter "O" over the letter "A" as its symbol and wear Oakland A's and California Angels apparel. **Latin Lovers** have red and yellow as colors and the double letter "L" inside a heart as their symbol and wear Kansas City Chiefs apparel and Chicago Bulls clothing (minus the "BU" in Bulls). The **Black P. Stone** gang also wears Chicago Bulls clothing but interprets the lettering to mean "Boy U Look Like a Stone." (See Figure 6.6.)

As with the People, the Folks have extended their territory far beyond the limits of Chicago. Some faction of either the People or Folks can be found in nearly all Eastern cities. Their involvement in drug sales and distribution provides them with over a billion dollars with which to enforce their territories.

ASIAN GANGS

Asian gangs are something of a mystery to researchers, civilians, and law enforcement personnel. Of all the street gangs, Asian gangs tend to be far more secretive. They are generally clean-cut, act with respect toward law enforcement, and victimize members from their own culture. They seldom represent gang affiliation with visible colors, clothing, and tattoos. Before 1975, Asian gangs were mostly limited to delinquent youths living in the "Chinatowns" of larger cities. "Prior to the departure of American forces from Vietnam in 1975, the stereotypical American concept of Asian gangs derived largely from the image of San Francisco tongs or triads of an earlier era. Since that time, the image of Asian gangs has changed to include new immigrant groups, such as Vietnamese, Vietnamese-Chinese, Laotian, Cambodian and Hmong gangs, which can now be found in communities across the nation where recent Southeast Asian immigrants have settled" (Kodluboy 1996, 1). Recent Asian immigrants are frustrated by their lack of instant success in the United States. Some disenchanted youths turn to gangs as a means of escape from their economic deprivation.

Traditional Asian Gangs

Review of the traditional Asian gangs begins with the Chinese **triads** and **tong** gangs. Triads are secret societies that originally formed during the 1600s in China. Modern-day triads are generally viewed by law enforcement as criminal organizations. "Triads are secret societies, originally formed in China in the early 17th century as resistance groups to the Ching Dynasty. They are patriotic and nationalistic organizations formed for various reasons, for example, as religious groups, peasant rebellion groups, and political groups. But some also exist mainly as criminal groups in Hong Kong and Taiwan" (Kenney and Finckenauer 1995, 257). Among the more prominent triads are the **Green Pang** and the **Hung Pang** (Chin 1986). Other major triad gangs include the **Sun Yee On**, the **Sung Lian**, **Tian Dao Man**, **Four Seas**, and the **United Bamboo** (Posner 1988). The triads have over 80,000 members, with Sun Yee On as the largest (over 25,000). The name *triad* came about as a result of the society's triangular symbol, which consisted of three dots, two on the base and one on the top (thus forming a triangle).

Originally, the triads were known as the "Men of Hung." The word *Hung* was so sacred and secret that it was rarely used aloud or in public. The Men of Hung were separated into three divisions: the Tien-ti Hui, the San Tien Hui, and San-ho Hui. Collectively, these three distinctions represented the "Three Harmonies Society" (Booth 1999). This secret society, or *hui*, was made up of ruthless outlaws—merciless robbers, pillagers, kidnappers, and murderers. The *hui* attacked government offices, barracks and prisons (in order to release fellow triads), imperial supply convoys, and cargo junks. Many Chinese civilians supported the "cause" of the triads, believing it to be an honorable one. Their mix of Confucian, Taoist, Buddhist, and pagan thinking, and goal of eternal happiness attracted many young people to the triads. Their goal was to right the imperial wrongs and address imperial injustice by any means necessary. By the mid-nineteenth century, the triads had become institutionalized into the subculture of Chinese society.

Perhaps the most honored of all the ancient Chinese triads are the Shaolin. The Shaolin Temple trained warriors and housed sacred scrolls, writings, and books. Shaolin monks trained at the temple learned philosophy and meditation techniques to help them achieve enlightenment. Naturally, the Emperor viewed the Shaolin as a challenge to him and ordered his soldiers to kill the monks and destroy the temple and all the documents and records (Booth 1999). Five young monks survived the slaughter and carried on the tradition of Shaolin. Today, many of the Shaolin traditions are upheld in martial arts training, thus preserving the ancient culture through triad ceremonial positions and beliefs.

By the year 2000, in both China and the United States, the triads had begun to act and function more as urban gangsters than as political idealists seeking social justice. Considering that over 60 million Chinese live outside China, the possibility for increased numbers of triad organizations is very real. Furthermore, Chinese communities are often very secluded and closed off to Westerners. The secretive nature of triad gangs reflects the greater Chinese communities' (e.g., American Chinatowns) efforts to distance themselves from the outside world. Chinese officials consider membership in the triads a criminal offense, but because of the secretive nature of the gangs, it is extremely difficult for law enforcement to penetrate them.

Triads are found in most American cities that have a sizable Asian community. Members of triad gangs in the United States are usually between the ages of 13 and 35 and are almost exclusively male. About two-thirds of America's triad gang members are immigrants, the rest are native-born (Chin 1996). Like most gangs, the triads operate in a hierarchical manner, with the "Dai-Lo" as the "big brother" and the "Sai-Lo" as the "little brother." The various sets of triads all use a numbering system beginning with the number 4, which represents the four oceans that were believed to have surrounded China in ancient times and so signifies the universe as a whole. The initiation of new members involves the recruit taking a number of oaths of privacy and respect. Current criminal activity involving triads includes arms smuggling, credit card fraud, counterfeiting, software piracy, smuggling of aliens, prostitution, gambling, loan-sharking, home invasion robbery, high-tech theft, and trafficking in endangered animals and plants. Extortion is the most common crime committed by the triads and other Asian gangs. Triads extort money from businesses and wealthy members of the Asian community in the form of a "protection" racket. Home invasions and burglary remain as trademarks of the triads and most Asian gangs (Huston 1995). Smuggling of illegal immigrants has become so lucrative and commonplace that the triads and their rival gangs often abduct these aliens and hold them for ransom (Chin 1996).

Chinese social clubs are known as *tongs*. These traditional Chinese secret clubs have long been suspected by law enforcement agencies to be fronts for violent gangs. "The word *tong* refers to a hall or gathering place. The groups called Tongs function as benevolent associations, business associations, ethnic societies, and centers of local politics in Chinese communities in the United States. They engage in a number of activities, including political activities and some protest activities" (Kenney and Finckenauer 1995, 257). The FBI believes that the tongs are used as fronts for vicious Chinese organized crime groups. Crimes associated with tongs are illegal gambling, extortion, drug trafficking, robbery, and prostitution for pornography (Keene 1989). The first American-based tong was the Leong Merchant's Association founded in 1849 in San Francisco. **On Leong** is the original tong in New York City, having formed in Manhattan's Chinatown during the 1890s. On Leong ran a lucrative empire of gambling houses, brothels, and opium dens. **Hip Sing**, the primary rival tong of On Leong, also dates back to the 1890s in New York City. Hip Sing was first led by the notorious Mock Duck, who is mentioned in Herbert Asbury's *The Gangs of New York* (1927). A particularly violent confrontation between On Leong and Hip Sing in 1909 left more than 50 dead (Century 2004).

The **yakuza** are associated with traditional Japanese gangs. "Yakuza is actually the collective name for some 2,500 different crime groups operating in Japan and elsewhere, including Hawaii and the U.S. West Coast. The Japanese word *yakuza* is said to describe a worthless hand in a card game. Thus, the Yakuza call themselves 'worthless persons and social outcasts'" (Kenney and Finckenauer 1995, 260). The Japanese National Police refer to them as the *Boryokudan*, or the "violent ones." It is estimated that there are more than 200,000 yakuza members worldwide, making them perhaps the largest of all the gangs. The yakuza trace their roots back to the fourteenth century, when outcasts of the prevailing feudalist society banded together for mutual protection. The name comes from a popular Japanese card game called *Sammai Karuta*. A yakuza leader is known as an *oyaban* and the general members as *kobun*. The **Yamaguchi** represent the largest faction of yakuza in Japan with nearly 10,000 members. They are all men, as the yakuza do not believe women should be involved; instead, they should be wives and mothers.

Yakuza gangs in the United States are heavily involved in weapons trafficking, with the guns being sold in Japan. Unlike the United States, the Japanese have very strict gun laws; consequently, there is a flourishing black market for guns. Handguns are in especially high demand. "U.S. handguns valued at $100 to $200 in the United States can be sold in Japan for $1,000 or more. . . . The FBI believes that Yakuza activity in the United States has increased in the last 15 years because we are a source of weapons because we serve as an excellent investment source for excess capital generated by the drug business, and because of the tourist business, particularly in Hawaii and California where the Yakuza active in the United States are located" (Kenney and Finckenauer 1995, 261). The yakuza are especially active in Southern California, the San Francisco area, and in Nevada. Prostitution is a lucrative business for them. They provide underage girls at sex clubs for wealthy businessmen. In addition to their numerous illegal businesses, the yakuza have financial interests in a number of legitimate American businesses. "In the United States, the President's Commission on Organized Crime (1986) found that the yakuza had financial interests in legitimate import-export businesses, real estate, oil, nightclubs, gift shops, and tour agencies. One yakuza entity, the Rondan Doyuki Company, was said to own shares in General Motors, Bank of America, Atlantic Richfield, Chase Manhattan, Citicorp, IGN, Sperry, and Dow Chemical. The commission indicated that yakuza members attended stockholders' meetings of these corporations" (Kenny and Finckenauer 1995, 262).

The yakuza are an efficiently run organization that uses violence whenever necessary as a means of normal operating business procedures. In the United States, the yakuza have become similar to their triad counterparts. They are a secretive gang and generally commit crimes within their own communities. The yakuza have an interesting way of dealing with members who have offended the gang leader or violated protocol. Violators are not killed; instead, they go through a ritualistic ceremony called a *Yubizume* in which the offender cuts off his little finger and presents it to the person he is apologizing to. If the offering is accepted (as it generally is), then the violator is kicked out of the yakuza permanently.

Contemporary Asian Gangs

Most of the contemporary youths who join Asian gangs do so because they feel overwhelmed, lost, depressed, and angry as they try to adjust to living in the United States. They are experiencing the same angst, alienation, and anomie as their Irish, Italian, Jewish, and Hispanic counterparts felt before them. They are new immigrants to a land where their lack of sufficient and relevant job skills, low levels of education, and language deficiency hamper their goals of success. This is especially true among many Vietnamese, Cambodian, and Laotian immigrants. They often feel as though they are victims of racial/ethnic prejudice and discrimination on the part of the greater society, similar to what many in the black and Latino communities feel. Blocked opportunities to success and learned helplessness lead to feelings of frustration. Expecting instant (economic) gratification and lacking the patience to acquire the necessary skills, many deviant youths turn to gangs. There is growing evidence that Asian youth are turning to street gangs in increasing numbers. It is also common for many Asian gang members to have ties to the larger and more formal Asian organized crime groups (e.g., the triads and yakuza).

The makeup and purpose of Asian gangs vary by ethnicity, but nearly all engage in drug trafficking, prostitution, and extortion. Their specialty, however, is "home invasion." Home invasions occur when the gang breaks into the home of a wealthy family, or family-owned business (especially restaurants), tie up the family members, and terrorize them until the family produces valuables or money. Common tactics include beatings, torture, and the raping of female family members. Asian families are targets because they are less likely to report such crimes to the police because they fear reprisal by the gang. Recent immigrant families from Asia do not trust the U.S. police, believing that they may work with the gangs. Furthermore, it is common for Asian immigrants to keep their valuables at home rather keeping them in a bank.

Contemporary Chinese-American gangs have their genesis in the late 1960s and early 1970s. "Youth gangs started to emerge in Chinatown in the sixties and seventies, and they have a distinctive culture—a bizarre mixture of traits borrowed from the Hong Kong triads (secret criminal societies) and the clichés of American and Chinese gangster movies" (Dannen 2002, 298–299). The passage of the Immigration and Naturalization Act of 1965 opened the door for numerous new Asian immigrants to enter the United States. Most of these people were poor and some of the youths joined gangs. They often served as "muscle" for the existing triads and other Chinese crime organizations. Playing the role of foot soldier was viewed by the immigrant gang members as a step toward admittance to the more established organized crime syndicates. Chinese gangs can be found in Los Angeles, Boston, Chicago, Toronto, Buffalo, New York, Vancouver, and especially in San Francisco. The Chinese gangs in Chicago have evolved out of two old and historic community organizations, the Hip Sing and the Tong. The Hip Sing is active in the Uptown community along the lakefront of Chicago. The **Tong** gang members are a South Side group prominent in the more traditional Chinatown at 22nd Street and Wentworth Avenue (Lindberg 2003).

Gregory Yee Mark (2004) stated that the first nationally known American Chinese gang was the **Hwa Chings**, which means "young Chinese," who originated in San Francisco's Chinatown in 1964. "Eventually, branches of this group and other similar types of gangs spread throughout America's Chinatowns. Since the 1970s, due to escalating violence and expanded criminal activities, Chinese gangs have been increasingly viewed as a major social problem in the Chinese American community and as a menace to society-at-large. In government reports and popular media, these gangs are blamed for the increasing violence in Chinatowns, shiploads of undocumented Chinese immigrants, and the massive smuggling of illegal drugs to the United States" (Mark 2004, 142). The Hwa Chings consisted of mostly teen-aged immigrant youths, the majority from Hong Kong. By 1967, the Hwa Ching were committing violent crimes in and around Chinatown. Two years later, they made national news because of a 1969 issue of *Esquire* magazine, which referred to the gang as "The New Yellow Peril." Other dominant Chinese gangs emerged in the late 1960s, and most of them identified with a tong. "By the end of 1968, the **Tom Tom** gang, the youth gang affiliated with the San Francisco **Suey Sing Tong**, emerged as the strongest gang" (Mark 2004, 146).

The Hwa Ching were never seriously challenged until 1989 when the **Wo Hop To** triad from Hong Kong began moving into the San Francisco Bay area. In recent years these two gangs consolidated (English 1995). Various factions of Chinese gangs have aligned themselves with either the Bloods or Crips as a means of protecting their turf and guaranteeing revenue from criminal activities. Chinatown gangs were formed primarily for protection and street survival from outside rival gangs. "Even today, thirty years later, young immigrants still join Chinese gangs, Samoan gangs, Cambodian gangs, and Filipino gangs for mutual protection" (Mark 2004, 151).

Among the more visible contemporary Chinese gangs found in New York City's Chinatown and nearby Flushing is the **American Eagles** (or **Asian Empire**). The American Eagles (AE) claim the streets of Chinatown and Flushing (especially around Mulberry Street in Chinatown and Main Street in Flushing) and travel in packs armed with knives. Members wear satin jackets and sport tattoos with dragons on their biceps (McPhee 2003). Local law enforcement consider AE the newest Asian gang since the **Flying Dragons** and **Ghost Shadows** were busted up and sent to jail. According to Century (2004, 88), the Ghost Shadows favor "tight straight-leg black jeans, satin jackets and little kung-fu slippers. And the dead giveaway: Hair tips dyed blond." The American Eagles have 50 confirmed members, who are mostly immigrants from China's Fujian province or ABCs (American-born Chinese). At the end of 2003, the American Eagles were primarily involved with assaults and petty crime.

New York City's Chinatown has recently become home to a growing hip-hop Chinese gang presence. Chinese-American rapper Christopher Louie, aka. L.S., is among the leading hip-hop gangsters. Bragging about being shot and run-ins with the law are just a couple of the similarities between Chinese rappers and black rappers. The lyrics of L.S. parallel the meanings of black rappers as well. Infusing Cantonese slang into their hip-hop, Chinese rappers use the word *chink* the way other rappers drop the word *nigga* (Century 2004). As documented in *Blender* magazine, Century (2004) provides examples of the lyrics used by L.S.:

> Every time they harass me
> I want to explode
> We should ride the trains for free
> We built the railroads.

Promoted as the Chinese answer to rapper 50 Cent, L.S. has a bullet-scarred torso and gangsta taunts (e.g., "**** kung fu—we know *gun*-fu"). L.S. uses the term "yellow slums" to reflect the life of urban poor Asian youth, especially the Chinese.

American Vietnamese gangs are the result of the traditional factors that lead recent immigrants into gangs. According to U.S. Census data, more than 900,000 Vietnamese migrated to the United States between 1975 and 1997. During that same period, another 400,000 Vietnamese-Americans were born here. These Vietnamese immigrants were mostly undereducated, underskilled, and usually unable to speak English. There was no history of organized crime in Vietnam, but the U.S.-sponsored South Vietnamese government and military were riddled with corruption, so recent immigrants had had experience with bribery, corruption, extortion, and violence. "The thousands of Vietnamese who came to the United States in the late 1970s and 1980s did not come from a country with a tradition of organized crime to a great extent; their involvement in organized crime in the United States developed out of their experiences as immigrants here. It was, however, very much shaped by who they were and where they had come from" (Kenney and Finckenauer 1995, 266).

Vietnamese gangs appear to be the most secretive of all the Asian gangs and therefore have a certain intrigue. They are often considered the most violent of all Asian gangs. They have a stronghold in Southern California, especially in Orange County, where the city of Westminster is known as "Little Saigon" because of the huge Vietnamese population—there are more Vietnamese there than anywhere outside Vietnam. The city has over 2,500 Vietnamese-owned restaurants, malls, hair salons and professional offices in the commercial Westminster community. These businesses are automatic targets for Vietnamese gangs. Among the common criminal activities committed by Vietnamese gangs are extortion, armed robbery, home invasion, prostitution, auto theft, arson, and gambling. The longevity of Vietnamese gangs is often brief. They are known to form a "hasty gang"—a loose, quickly formed, mobile, nomadic gang that forms and disbands following a brief crime spree such as home invasions or burglaries of occupied dwellings (Kodluboy 1996).

Filipino gangs are found mostly in Los Angeles, San Diego, and San Francisco but can also be found in Las Vegas. The largest gangs include the **Santanas**, **Taboos**, and **Temple Street Gang**. Filipino gangs began in the 1940s in the California prison system, but contemporary Filipino gangs have their roots in the immigration of Filipinos to the United States during the 1970s (Shelden et al. 2001). William Sanders in his research on Filipino gangs in San Diego traced the Filipino population in San Diego to the military establishment and the nursing profession. "A large contingent of Filipinos who served in the U.S. military, especially during the Vietnam War, was allowed to immigrate to the United States during the 1970s. Likewise, a large number of Filipino nurses immigrated to the United States during the 1970s when a nursing shortage generated a more liberal immigration policy for nurses" (Sanders 1994, 153). These relatively high-paying jobs placed the Filipino immigrants in the middle class, where they were generally accepted by their white neighbors. The Filipinos were politically and socially conservative like much of San Diego suburbia. Not surprisingly, "throughout most of the 1980s the Filipinos were not only low in crime statistics, but no Filipino gangs were recognized by the police. However, by 1988, about 14 percent of all gang-related incidents recorded by the police department's gang detail involved Filipino youths, and by 1991, 18 percent of the drive-by shootings were by Filipino gangs" (Sanders 1994, 153). These Filipino gangs were involved in drug sales, robberies, car theft, and drive-by shootings.

As previously mentioned, Asian gangs are very secretive and will deny that they are gang members if apprehended by police. However, they do use scarring or mutilation to create gang markings (Chin 1996), often burning themselves in strategic places. For example, Filipinos burn their hands, the Vietnamese and Cambodians burn the forearms, the Chinese burn their upper arms, and female gang members have burns on their ankles or feet (Chin 1996). These burns and burn patterns have significant relevance and importance within the gang. A single burn generally means that the individual is willing to engage in criminal activity. Some Cambodian and Hmong gang members in several American cities have adopted the style, dress, slang, nicknames, hand signs, and names of black and Hispanic gangs of the West Coast and Midwest.

Recently, a number of Asian gangs have begun to get tattoos. For example, a member of the **Ninja Clan Assassins**, a Vietnamese gang, will be inked with "NCA." Generally, the tattoos are not visible. Although Asian gang members generally maintain a clean-cut image, they are increasingly adopting the style of the Bloods and Crips.

Asian gangs represent a minority among the diverse types of American street gangs. However, the American-Asian population is a rapidly growing one. The U.S. Bureau of the Census predicts that the Asian population will more than triple to 33 million by 2050. If these estimates hold true, Asian-Americans would comprise 8% of the total population in 2050; it is at 4% presently (*Syracuse Post Standard* 2004, A12). Only time will tell if this rapidly growing population will translate into an increase in gang activity among Asian-Americans.

SUMMARY

This chapter closely examined gangs of all sizes. As we know, gangs are virtually everywhere in the United States. Some are small and localized; others are larger and regionalized; and some gangs are so large they extend from one coast to the other, forming nation alliances with numerous sets of individual gangs. The evolution of gangs into much larger, stronger, and more powerful entities has made them an economic force, due to their sale and distribution of drugs and other black market items. There are still many communities in the United States that remain relatively free from the threat of gang violence; on the other hand, some people live in areas where the threat of gang violence is an ever-present reality. In some smaller jurisdictions, local law enforcement and civic leaders fall victim to "gang denial"—the belief that they are immune to gangs and associated criminal activities. Underestimating the lure and power of gangs can be dangerous for localities that do not currently have a gang presence. For those jurisdictions and communities beset by gangs, their task is a daunting one.

CHAPTER SEVEN

Female Gangs and Gang Members

Women have been involved in criminal activity for nearly as long as men, only never to the same extent. Historically, however, little attention has been given to female gangsters, unless their crimes were related to violations of codes of morality (e.g., prostitution, witchcraft). During the 1800s, women like Belle Starr carried guns, robbed stagecoaches, and cavorted with men who were just as devious. Starr was a fearless, guilt-free murderer and bragged about it. At age 18 (1866), Belle ran off with outlaw Cole Younger, who was a cousin to Jesse James and a member of the Younger-James gang. Starr took part in numerous crimes with Younger. Likewise, Pearl Hart was infamous for robbing stagecoaches with her outlaw boyfriend Joe Boot. Hart was eventually sent to Yuma Territorial Prison (Arizona). Kate "Ma" Barker, born in 1871, gained notoriety for being a bank robber and kidnapper. The Barker gang often engaged in daring robberies that captivated the American public during the Depression. Banks had instituted high interest rates and often foreclosed on mortgages when people were at their economic lowest. Thus, bank robbers such as Ma Barker gained "Robin Hood" status. During the twentieth century, Bonnie Parker and Virginia Hill would gain fame for their criminal activities and immoral activities (Belknap 2001). Bonnie Parker, born in 1910, formed a romantic and criminal relationship with gangster Clyde Barrow. Bonnie once smuggled a gun to imprisoned Clyde, allowing him to escape. The criminal escapades of Bonnie and Clyde, coupled with Parker's ability to write poetry, made them both folk heroes during the Depression. Virginia Hill, born in 1918, dated Joe Epstein, an accountant for the Mafia in Chicago. She moved on to other key Mafia men, including Frank Nitti and Benjamin "Bugsy" Siegel. Hill became a "Mafia queen." In the 1950s, after years of working for the Mafia, she was called before the Kefauver Committee in Washington D.C. to testify regarding organized crime in interstate commerce. At age 48, she was found dead of a drug overdose—some suspect it was the Mafia's way of keeping her quiet because she knew too much.

Despite these examples of high-profile and notorious women, little attention overall has been paid to female criminals. This is also true of female street gang members. Thoughts about gangs provoke stereotypical images of males committing extreme forms of violence, such as drive-by shootings, and who are involved in the use and sale of drugs, graffiti, rap music, and instilling fear within the communities where they are found. Since these activities are generally viewed as masculine traits, it was therefore presumed that females did not take part in these behaviors (Moore and Hagedorn 2001). However, as this chapter will reveal, the number of females participating in gangs has been increasing steadily for years. Furthermore, female involvement in gangs accelerates the decay of the family structure.

FEMALE GANG PARTICIPATION

A number of extensive studies have been made of street gangs but they generally addressed females as satellites, or auxiliaries, of male gangs, due in part to the belief that female involvement in gangs has historically been considered less important than male involvement (Taylor 1993). But female participation in gangs dates to the inception of gangs (Covey, Menard, and Franzese 1997). In Thrasher's (1927) famous study of gangs, he referred to females as auxiliaries. Of the more than 1,000 gangs he identified, he classified only six as female. In fact, his definition of gangs excludes females as potential participants—"the spontaneous efforts of *boys* to create a society. . . ." Female gang members were usually described in reference to their sexual role. Female gangsters were assumed to be just "sex toys," "objects," or "tomboys" to the male gang members, an assumption that has carried over to contemporary stereotypes of female gangsters. Whether these stereotypes of female gang members as "tomboys and sex toys" are accurate is difficult to confirm because often these stereotypes do not come from reliable sources (Moore and Hagedorn 2001). A great deal of information on female gang members does not come from gang researchers, but instead from journalists and social workers, who may have their own agenda and motives when reporting on female gang members. In addition, it is important to realize that the way females are treated by male gang members varies a great deal from gang to gang.

After Thrasher's studies of gangs, there was little interest in female gang members until Miller's study in the 1970s. Miller found fully independent female gangs but stated that they represent less than 10% of all gangs (Sheldon et al. 2001). A decade later, Moore found that one-third of Hispanic gang members in Los Angeles were female. He acknowledged that the literature on girl gangs is very limited because much of it assumes that girl gangs are "auxiliaries" to the tightly bound boy gangs and found, on the contrary, that in the late 1930s and the early 1940s girl gangs (e.g., the **Black Legion**, **the Cherries**, **the Elks**, **the Black Cats**, and the **Vamps**) in Maravilla were not only free from association with the boy cliques, they were also not bound to the neighborhoods in the Maravilla barrios. Preceding Moore's findings on female gang participation were two significant studies done in the 1980s, a brief review of which is presented next.

John Quicker's *Home Girls*

The first in-depth look at female gangsters was conducted by John Quicker. In 1983 he published a very short book titled *Home Girls* based on research he had begun in the early 1970s. The title of Quicker's book comes from the gang terms common with Hispanics. "Chicana gang members use the affectionate terms 'homegirl' and 'homeboy' (sometimes shortened in speech to simply 'homes') to refer to other gang members. These terms take on the same affect as 'brother' and 'sister,' reflecting the family-like structure of the group" (Quicker 1983, 6). In *Home Girls*, Quicker examined the role of female gangsters in East Los Angeles. He interviewed girls from 12 different gangs in the notoriously violent barrios of East L.A. and concluded that the Chicana gangs were predominantly auxiliaries to the boy gangs. As Quicker (1983, 9–10) explained:

> The homegirls never achieve complete independence from the boys; however, their relative autonomy does vary from group to group. The type of affiliation they have found (and indeed if they are to affiliate at all) is worked out with the boys. I have not encountered any instance of a girls' gang existing independently of a boys' gang, though there are some boys' gangs that do not have associated girls' gangs. However, in general, the overwhelming majority of gangs do have these auxiliaries. As an indication of this close association, the girls' group always derives its name from the boys' name. . . . There are also age differentiated cliques within the groups that share names, such as "chicos" for the older boys and "chicas" for the older girls, or "locos" for the younger boys and "locas" for the younger girls.

Quicker noted that the boys appreciated the help and assistance provided by the chicas (the girls will often conceal weapons used by the boys) but felt, for the most part, that girls do not belong in gangs and that gangs are for males. As for the girls, they generally believed that the boys liked them hanging around even though they knew that the boys were against female gang members. "Boyfriend/girlfriend relationships further confound these ambivalences. The boys, almost categorically, do not want their girlfriends to join the gang, while making exceptions for other girls. However, if the girlfriend joins, the boy makes little effort to convince her to leave" (Quicker 1983, 12).

The girls that Quicker interviewed reported that they generally dated only the boys from their own cliques and that they were allowed to date boys in other gangs as long as the gangs were not fighting each other. "Dating practices are strongly influenced by the cohesiveness of the gang. That is, the closer the gang, the more likely it is that exogamous dating patterns are restricted. . . . Where girls are on the periphery of a weakly organized gang, exogamous dating patterns are not as traumatic" (Quicker 1983, 13).

Quicker found that the girls joined the gang primarily because of their socially marginal status, negative experiences in school, the search for fun and excitement, respect, and the simple fact that they wanted to be close to the boys from their barrio. As Quicker (1983, 80) concluded, "To be in a gang is to be a part of something. It means having a place to go, friends to talk with, and parties to attend. It means recognition and respected status." As for membership, Quicker stated that the gang was not open to all who desired to join it. There were three requirements:

1. The girl must not be interested in joining solely for protection (i.e., to have the gang fight her battles for her).

2. There must be some indication that the girl will not fold under pressure but will support the banner of the gang even under adverse conditions (i.e., she must be willing to acknowledge her affiliation).

3. She must be able to "throw" down (to fight). Girls who are physically weak or unable to defend themselves are not an asset to the gang and often will not be allowed to join (Quicker 1983, 14–15).

Once these requirements were met, she was ready for the initiation—being "jumped in." The recruit must take a beating from a group of gang members, although in some cases, a girl might be allowed a "fair fight" by going up against a skilled member of the gang. Leaving the gang is more complicated than entering. Quicker found that there were two basic types of departure, the active and passive.

> In the active mode, either the girl herself or the other members initiate procedures that will unequivocally remove her from the group. The passive mode occurs when the girl gradually stops "hanging around" with the gang, or when the gang itself begins to slowly disintegrate. Active departures are the most violent kind. The ordeal is generally significantly more difficult than the initiation. If the girl decides to leave, she will have to "throw" with a number of girls—a battle which she can expect to lose . . . she will be thoroughly beaten, often suffering some kind of injury (Quicker 1983, 17–18).

The beatings are so severe that the girl risks permanent injury or scarring. The gang's initials are often carved on her back. One girl that Quicker spoke with told him that she was raped by eight boys from the gang that she was leaving. In most cases, the girls never really leave the gang. Those that get pregnant have the easiest escape because they are allowed to leave the gang without a beating or being raped.

Anne Campbell's *The Girls in the Gang*

In 1984, Anne Campbell published a more substantial book on female gangs titled *The Girls in the Gang*. Campbell began her two-year study of girl gang members in New York City in 1979. She found that at that time there were around 400 gangs with a total membership between 8,000 and 40,000 in the city, with most of the female gangs being auxiliaries to the male gangs. Campbell concluded, as Miller had 10 years earlier, that approximately 10% of gang members were female. According to Campbell:

> Ten percent of those members are female, ranging in age from fourteen to thirty. Some are married and many have children. They are blamed as the inciters of gang feuds; they are described as "passive, property and promiscuous." They are accused of being more vicious than any male; they are praised for being among the few with enough power to curb male gang crime. For some they represent the coming of age of urban women's liberation, for others the denial of the best qualities of womanhood. The contradictions of their position have provoked speculation among the police, the media, and public about their reasons for joining, their roles and way of life. Despite the volumes written on male gang members, however, little is actually known about the girls, the standard reason being that girls constitute such a small number of gang crimes (1984, 5).

Campbell found that, like boys, gang girls sought out excitement and trouble because it breaks the monotony of a desperate life that offers little hope for the future.

> They admire toughness and verbal "smarts." They may not be going anywhere, but they make the most of where they are. Authority, in the shape of school, parents, and police, is the enemy but a welcome one since it generates confrontations and livens things up. Because these girls accept a lower-class value system, they are represented in the literature as "bad girls" . . . their undisguised interest in sexual relationships has led them to be branded as Sex Objects by many writers . . . Some "bad girls" choose to compete with males on their own

terms and are therefore considered in the literature as Tomboys. . . . Sex Objects and Tomboys have much in common. Both have romantic and sexual relationships with the boys in the gang. . . . Both will use their femininity in the service of the gang by acting as spies with other nearby gangs, by luring unsuspecting male victims into situations where they are robbed or assaulted by the boys, and by carrying concealed weapons for the boys since as females they cannot be searched on the street by male officers (Campbell 1984, 7–9).

Campbell's conclusions about gangs were that they exist not because they represent a counterculture, but because they represent a microcosm of American society—a distorted mirror image in which power, possessions, rank, and role are major concerns, but within a subcultural life of poverty and crime. According to Campbell, "Gangs do not represent a revolutionary vanguard rejecting the norms and values of a capitalist society that has exploited them. When gang members talk of politics, they talk of the American Dream, of pride in their country. . . . Girl members as women want to be American, to be free, to be beautiful, to be loved. These girls subscribe to the new woman's dream, the new agenda: No more suffering or poverty" (1984, 267). This is a highly romanticized and politicized viewpoint of gangs—as contributors to the numbers of American patriots!

Anne Campbell's study, as Miller's before, agreed with most studies of female gang participation that set the rate at, or around, 10%. This number may be an underestimate, however, because many police agencies are reluctant to identify females as gangsters due to their relatively low levels of criminality (Curry 1998). Nonetheless, the 10% figure is quite consistent. "Agencies responding to the 1996 National Youth Gang Survey reported that females accounted for eleven percent of gang members" (Interagency Task Force 2003, 1). As Moore and Hagedorn (2001) reported, two other nationwide surveys of law enforcement agencies, conducted in 1996 and 1998, estimated, respectively, that 11% and 8% of all gang members were female. Schmalleger (2004) states that nationally, 8% of gang members are females. Data provided by the Office of Juvenile Justice and Delinquency Prevention (OJJDP) (2000) indicated (based on law enforcement responses to a 1998 survey) that 8% of gang members were females. As for a geographic breakdown of female gang members,

> Female gang members were least prevalent in large cities (7 percent) and most prevalent in small cities (12 percent) and rural counties (11 percent). . . . Female gang members were more prevalent in the Northeast (13 percent) than in other regions. Their representation was lowest in the Midwest (5 percent), far lower than in the Northeast . . . . Survey responses indicated that less than 2 percent (1.76 percent) of all gangs in the United States in 1998 were female dominated. . . . Of the 171 jurisdictions reporting female-dominated gangs, 143 reported that these gangs represented only 14 percent or less of total gangs in their jurisdictions (OJJDP 2000, 17–18).

There is no consensus on the exact number of females currently participating in gangs. Some researchers believe that female gang membership is increasing; others believe it remains around the 10% figure. According to a 1999 *Chicago Tribune* article, 16,000 to 20,000 of the 100,000 gang members in Chicago were female (O'Brien 1999), which would be greater than 10%. According to information compiled by the

Detective Support Division of the LAPD in February 2000, there were 8,076 female gang members in California, with 6,007 living in LA County (Bing 2001). This figure falls far short of 10% of the total number of estimated gang members overall in California. It is also consistent with researchers' accusations that police authorities tend to underestimate female participation rates. Hunt, MacKenzie, and Joe-Laidler (2004, 49) insist that "estimates of female membership today range from 10 to 30 percent of all gang members." Regoli and Hewitt (2003, 318) reported that "recent studies suggest that girls may comprise anywhere from 4 to 38 percent of all gang members." When one considers that there is a lack of consensus on the true number of gang members overall, it is no surprise that there is a lack of agreement on the number of female gang members.

FEMALE GANGSTERS

We may not know how many female gangsters there are, but we do know they exist. But why do they exist, what do they look like, and what type of activities are they involved in? Females join gangs for many of the same reasons as males: economic considerations, protection, lack of a stable family background, and respect. Female gangsters engage in the same types of criminal and noncriminal activities as boys. They can be very violent as well. According to Huizinga (1997), female gang members account for more violent crimes than do nongang boys. "The stereotype of the girl as primarily a sex object, with limited participation in the delinquent activity of the gang, apparently requires reexamination" (Esbensen, Deschenes, and Winfree 2004, 76).

Reasons for Joining the Gang

According to the National Alliance of Gang Investigators Associations (NAGIA), young women are taking active roles in gangs and female gangsters are being incarcerated in increasing numbers. There are many reasons why the number of girls joining gangs is increasing, but the most common one is that girls join a gang for protection—not from other girls, but from the physical and/or sexual abuse of their fathers or other family members. "A gang serves as a refuge for young women who have been victimized at home. High proportions of female gang members have experienced sexual abuse at home" (Moore and Hagedorn 2001, 3). Generally, abused girls run away from home; sometimes, they run to the neighborhood gang, which offers them the protection they seek. Other female gangsters come from families that are dysfunctional in other ways (e.g., absentee parents); still others join simply to rebel against their parents. The desire to rebel is common among most teenagers, nongang members included. All adolescents want freedom from the rules of their parents. A small percentage of these rebellious youth turn to gangs. Females are more likely to turn to a gang if their boyfriends are already in the gang. "About half of all female gang members report that their boyfriend is also a member of the same gang" (Knox 2001, 16). Female gang members generally report that they feel independent when they belong to a gang.

The economic reality facing many youths of lower socioeconomic status remains a critical motivator for turning to a gang. Male gang members make huge sums of money selling drugs; the girl gangsters hope to accomplish the same thing. The underground black market in drugs offers ambitious and aggressive gang members plenty of opportunities to make money and until such drugs are legalized, this will obviously remain true. For many youths, the underground economy is viewed as the *only* economy. If there were legitimate job opportunities for impoverished youths, that would help deter many of them from turning to gangs. But the huge growth of gangs and gang members can be directly tied to the closing of numerous factories and the sending of American business and production overseas, a failure of U.S. political leaders. Unskilled labor has been unable to find employment in the new service economy. Moreover, many inner-city youths lack the job skills necessary to survive in the changing economic system because of the poor quality of education provided in many inner-city school districts, where schools are generally and drastically underbudgeted and teachers are forced to work under conditions that are far from "ideal"— not even equal to those of most suburban schools. The continued deterioration of the inner city has formed an underclass that breeds hopelessness.

The NAGIA (2002) summed up that females most likely to join a gang are between the ages of 12 and 18 who have low self-esteem, come from dysfunctional families, and have a history of victimization. Girl gang members are very likely to have been victims of physical and sexual abuse. The gang provides friends, money, drugs, power, excitement, and perhaps most important of all, a sense of family. In other cases, gangs have become so institutionalized in some communities that some girls have been raised in a gang culture in which their families have been members for generations. The NAGIA also reports that females with friends, boyfriends, or siblings in a gang are most likely to be in a gang themselves.

Recruitment

The girls who join gangs are looking for a strong support system. Gangs provide support through friendship and mutual understanding. Girls who feel lost at home and at school, thus lacking any trusted adult to turn to, look up to the older girl gang members and bond with their peers. Feeling "lost" is especially difficult for adolescent girls, who experience major biological and emotional changes. Gang girls learn that the only people they can trust are each other. If a gang is not available, a number of girls may decide to form their own gang. Thus, many gangs are formed out of normal friendship groups; they develop spontaneously. Thus, girls are not generally "recruited" in the normal sense of the term, nor are they pressured or coerced. Members come from existing friendship groups in the neighborhood and/or through family ties (Harris 1988). Joe and Chesney-Lind's (1995) study of Hawaiian gangs supported this common understanding that many, if not most, gangs form gradually among youths from the same neighborhood (Chesney-Lind and Shelden 2004). In her study of Hispanic female gangs in California, Mary Harris (1988) found that girls were not pressured or coerced into joining a gang but did so because of friendships and family ties.

Initiation

After a female has decided to join a gang, she is typically initiated. Gang initiation processes vary and a few gangs may not use the process at all. Generally, initiation is completed in one of three ways: being "jumped in" (beaten), "born in" (being naturally accepted because of familial ties), or "trained in" (raped or forced to have sex with several male gang members at once) (Portillos 1997). The first form of initiation, the beating, can include two variations. The first involves the recruit taking a physical beating from the gang members. This is especially important for violent female gangs who routinely engage in fights. The recruit needs to prove that she is tough and is as willing to receive a beating as she is to administer one. The second variation involves the recruit committing some sort of violent or criminal act against a rival gang member or person of authority (law enforcement personnel). Females may be required to participate in robberies or muggings or commit a drive-by shooting. As Taylor (2001) explained, a potential gang recruit may have to show her toughness and willingness to commit criminal acts by participating in such activities as face slashings or, if they are in prison, the killing of an inmate or warden.

Females who are "born in" to the gang may escape the physical beating and the humiliation and degradation experienced from the "train in." Females who are "born in" may get away with just being tattooed with gang symbols. Another variation of the "born in" initiation is being "blessed in" by gang members praying over the girl (Regoli and Hewitt 2003). For example, the Latin Queens may "bless in" a recruit, who needs only to promise dedication to the Nation's rules and adhere to the five points of the Nation crown, which stand for respect, honesty, unity, knowledge, and love (Taylor 2001). Many gang members are now second-, or even third-, generation members; they are the ones who are able to take advantage of the "born in" variation of initiation. Clearly, the "born in," especially the "bless in," is a much kinder form of initiation.

A third general category of initiation into female gangs is the "train in." This form of initiation almost always leads to a loss of respect for the girl. Any young woman who is "trained in" has a difficult time shedding the negative stigma that is attached to her. It is also highly likely that she will always be viewed as a sexual object, will never have the respect of most of her fellow female gang members, and rarely will gain the respect of the male gang members. "Girls who are sexed into a gang are at much greater risk for continued sexual mistreatment and exploitation and are generally viewed by male and female gang members as weak, promiscuous, and subject to contempt and disrespect" (Regoli and Hewitt 2003, 320). The "train in" initiation involves a girl having intercourse with multiple male gang members. "Some gangs have what are called *roll-ins*, in which a female initiate rolls a pair of dice and whatever number appears determines how many males have sex with her. In addition, there is a rumored 'HIV initiation' in which females have sex with an HIV-infected male—there is, however, no data to support this claim" (Chesney-Lind and Shelden 2004, 81). The rank of the male in the gang determines who is the "engine, the caboose, or somewhere in between" in this type of initiation (Sikes 1997, 103). The female gang members seldom accept those who choose to be "trained in" over "jumped in" because they displayed submissiveness in sacrificing their bodies instead of fighting (Portillos 1997).

TYPES OF FEMALE GANGS

Female gangs can be placed in general categories according to their level of affiliation with male gangs and by class and race. "There are three types of female gang involvement: (1) membership in an independent gang, (2) regular membership in a male gang as a coed, and (3) as female auxiliaries of male gangs. Most girls are found within the third type" (Chesney-Lind and Shelden 2004, 71). Supporting this categorization scheme, Regoli and Hewitt (2003, 318) add, "While the majority of gang boys are in all-male gangs, most girls who join gangs join mixed gangs (which tend to be dominated by boys), female gangs affiliated with male gangs, or independent female gangs."

Affiliation with Male Gangs

Raised in an environment of broken or abusive homes that offered little hope and incentive to achieve, most gang girls experience low levels of self-esteem. Negative family relationships lead many to seek personal relationships elsewhere. Gang girls find these needed friendships with their fellow gang members. Their sense of loyalty to each other is very strong. Often lacking a loving relationship with their fathers and consequently seeking to replace that missing love with empty sexual relationships, it is very common for gang women to have children at a young age; many times they have children by multiple fathers. When girls join a gang it is usually already affiliated with a male gang, meaning that it is an auxiliary gang. Even newly formed female gangs are almost always preceded by a male gang.

> Auxiliaries usually form after a male gang comes into existence and, as noted earlier, usually take a feminized version of the boys' gang name. They often reflect the age grouping found in male units. They have no formal leader but usually have some members with more clout than others. Girls are not coerced to join. Rather, they come into the gang through regular friendships and families (Chesney-Lind and Shelden 2004, 70).

Many auxiliary girl gangs have some control over their own gang. They do not exist simply to support male gang members. "They collect dues, hold meetings, expel members for violating rules, and so on. Strong normative control is exerted over members of the gang" (Chesney-Lind and Shelden 2004, 70).

There are female gangs that are completely independent of any male gang. Historically, these gangs have been short-lived. More recently, however, there appears to be a growing number of independent girl gangs. Campbell (1984) interviewed females from independent girl gangs and Taylor (1993) described a number of independent girl gangs in Detroit. Females who form independent gangs do so for the same reasons as males: They seek a way out of ghetto life, respect, and association with "like-minded" people who share the same values and norms as they possess.

In some cases, girls and boys are integrated into the same gang. Girls in these gangs usually enjoy higher levels of respect from male gang members than girls in auxiliary gangs. On the other hand, they have less freedom than if they had their own independent gang.

Class and Race

Gang members, male and female alike, generally come from lower socioeconomic social classes. Harper and Robinson (1999) found that 96% of girl gang families were receiving unemployment or welfare benefits, 56% were receiving food stamps, 7% received reduced-cost or free lunch at school, and 48% were from single-parent families. As described in Chapter 3, economics plays an important role in an individual's decision to join a gang. When young people become disheartened by their bleak financial futures, the gang often appears to be an appealing alternative to struggling in conventional society. Minority members are disproportionately found in the lower economic strata, which accounts for their higher participation rates in gang activity. Residing in high-crime urban areas increases the opportunities for youths to join.

Since a great number of gangs develop spontaneously, it is easy to conclude that many girl gangs developed as a result of girls who grew up together in the same neighborhood or housing project. Chesney-Lind and Shelden (2004, 73) reviewed the research study conducted by Laidler and Hunt (1997), who "found that most of the girl gang members either grew up in the same housing project or knew a relative associated with their group." People who grow up in poverty have two choices: They can work hard, earn an education, and hope to find a good job; or they can adopt the role of victim and respond in nonproductive ways (i.e., do nothing/collect unemployment and/or welfare, or turn to a criminal lifestyle that may or may not include gangs). Thus, poverty often leads directly, as well as indirectly, to gang participation.

Campbell (1984) linked the effects of poverty to the formation of the girl gangs that she studied in New York City. These girls were worried about their dismal conventional futures and believed that joining a gang offered them an alternative that would provide economic success. These girls wanted economic success and freedom from a life destined for unfulfillment. Campbell (1984, 267) concluded:

> These expectations were unrealistic. . . . They want better welfare and health benefits, they want more jobs, but they don't want revolution. . . . Girl members as women want to be American, to be free, to be beautiful, to be loved. These girls subscribe to the new woman's dream, the new agenda: No more suffering or poverty. No more lonely, forced "independence," living alone on welfare in a shabby apartment. First, a good husband; strong but not violent, faithful but manly. Second, well-dressed children. Third, a beautiful suburban apartment. Later for the revolution.

Thus, according to Campbell, American gangs do not represent a revolutionary force in society that seeks political and economic change; they are reflections of America's materialism. Gang members seek material success, not a political overthrow of the government. Girl gang members also seek financial success. Unfortunately, they view the gang as the best route to this desired goal. This speaks volumes about the current economic-political state of affairs in American society.

Race is another critical variable in gang participation. As reported by the OJJDP (2001), the 1998 National Youth Gang Survey revealed that Hispanics were the predominant racial/ethnic group among all gang members nationwide. Forty-six percent of all gang members were Hispanic, 34% were African-American, 12% were Caucasian, 6% Asian, and 2% were some other category (e.g., Native-American). The vast majority of female gangs are also either Hispanic or black. The primary reason cited by researchers for why minority females are more likely to join a gang than white girls is racism. "Kitchen's study in Fort Wayne, Indiana, revealed some strong feelings about race and racism. Her respondents had some very strong feelings about the society they lived in; expressing the belief that racism was fundamental. . . . Kitchen's study demonstrates the dual problems faced by African American women: racism and sexism. The world they inhabit does not afford many legitimate opportunities to succeed. It is a world filled with poverty on the one hand and the ready availability of drugs on the other hand" (Chesney-Lind and Shelden 2004, 71).

As discussed earlier in this chapter, Quicker's study (1983) of girl gangs was exclusively of Hispanics. He found that poverty, sexism, and racism were all common reasons that led girls to join a gang. The barrio represented a safe haven from the outside world, which was perceived as out to get them. A study of gang members in San Francisco found that nearly 80% of girl gang members were Latina (Lauderback, Hansen, and Waldorf 1992). Miller (2001, 93) studied gangs in Columbus and St. Louis and found that both class and race were important factors in gang participation. In St. Louis, with its high rate of poverty, 89% of the girl gang members were African-American; the rest were other minorities. In Columbus, a city with a lower poverty level, 25% of the girl gang members were white. Joe and Chesney-Lind (1993) found that girl gang members in Hawaii were minority members, the majority of them being either Filipino or Samoan.

CRIMINAL ACTIVITIES

Female gang members spend a great deal of their time just hanging out. Nonetheless, girls who join gangs are delinquents by implication, and they are often criminal in behavior as well. Bjerregaard and Smith (1993) reported that female gang members had a higher rate of delinquent offenses than did nongang females. Regoli and Hewitt (2003, 318–319) agreed, adding

> Gang girls are much more likely to be involved in delinquency, especially serious delinquency, than are nongang females. In general, gang girls commit fewer violent crimes than gang boys and are inclined to commit property crime and status offenses. And like males who join gangs, girls' involvement in crime increases with gang membership and tends to decline after leaving the gang. . . . Gang girls are much less likely to be victims of violence than are gang boys, although much more likely than nongang females. Their lower rates of violent victimization are attributed to a number of factors: Gang boys tend to exclude them from potentially violent activities, girls' peripheral status as gang members reduces the likelihood of their being targets of violence by rival gang members, and girls are protected by male gang members against predatory males in the community.

Growing evidence indicates that some female gang members are as violent as male gang members. For example, Fagan (1990) found that gang girls in Chicago, Los Angeles, and San Diego were heavily involved in serious violent offenses. In general, however, female gang members commit fewer violent crimes than male gang members, but girls are 3 times more likely than boys to be involved in property offenses and larceny (*Female Gangs* 2003). In short, female gang members may be involved with all the same types of criminal activities as males.

Crime

Information about girl gangs and their criminal activities generally comes from three major sources: law enforcement agency reports, surveys of at-risk youths, and field studies. Law enforcement reports are limited to actual arrest statistics available on female gang members. This information does reveal that female gang members in jails or prisons usually make up only approximately 5–10% of the total inmate population (*Female Gangs* 2003). (Contrast this to the dramatically increasing number of male gangsters found in jails and prisons.) Police reliance on arrest statistics is one of the leading contributors to the perceived underreporting of female gang membership, however. In many cases, female gangsters' involvement in crime is understated so as not to reflect the presence of female gangs. Some agencies "as a matter of policy" do not report female gang crimes as gang-related crimes. Furthermore, jurisdictions often differ in the labeling of offenses as "gang-related" (Moore and Hagedorn 2001, 4).

Surveys of at-risk youths provide a much different perspective on female gang participation in criminal acts. The questionnaires ask youths about their involvement in a gang and whether, and how often, they have committed certain criminal offenses. But these surveys are anonymous, therefore making them difficult to verify. The statistics generated from these types of surveys generally indicate a higher rate of crime than do police agency reports.

Field studies provide the most in-depth analysis of gang life. "Many of these studies, however, do not raise the issue of criminality, and most are confined to one time and one place, making it difficult to generalize from findings" (Moore and Hagedorn 2001, 4). Additionally, the limited research on female gangs makes it difficult to come up with any reliable generalizations. It should be noted, however, that getting to interview female gangs is more difficult (for a variety of reasons, including lack of entry to the gang, the small number of female gangs, and the dominant nature of male gangs). All texts written on gangs rely heavily on field studies conducted by other researchers; this book is no different—although it does contain original research on gangs from a city generally neglected by field researchers.

Female gangsters may commit a variety of different offenses, ranging in severity from the mild (status offenses such as running away from home and truancy), the moderate (property offenses), to the extreme (assault, kidnapping, and murder). Although the amount and degree of criminal acts committed by female gang members vary from one gang to the next (some may not commit any crimes), the violence is disproportionate to that of nongang females. Furthermore, female gang members are more likely to engage in violent behaviors and be victims of violent crimes than nongang girls (Deschenes and Esbensen 1999).

Among the specific crimes committed by girl gangs are theft, robbery, and acts of physical violence (fights, stabbings, assaults, drive-by shootings, and murder). These activities serve to generate money for the gang and to protect its turf. They are also perceived as methods of obtaining respect and initiating new members. In Miller's study (2001) of girl gangs in St. Louis and Columbus, he found, "when comparing male and female gang members, there were no significant differences in their levels of crime: girls were about as likely as boys to steal things, joyride in stolen cars, damage or destroy things, intimidate or threaten people, attack with the intent to seriously hurt them (62 percent of males and 55 percent of females participated in this offense), and sell drugs" (Chesney-Lind and Shelden 2004, 74). Sikes (1997) found that female gang members do not seek out violence; rather, it is an activity that is taken for granted and has become commonplace. Sikes found that Los Angeles female gang members equate money with power. Equating money with power follows Campbell's conclusion that gangs embrace capitalism, that they have internalized American culture. Unfortunately, they seek the desired goal of economic success by illegitimate means. Female gang members justify this behavior in a number of ways. (*Note*: These techniques will be discussed later in this chapter.)

There are times when male gang members will use female gang members to "set up" rival gangs. In her research on female gangs in Los Angeles, San Antonio, and Milwaukee, Gini Sikes (1997) was told repeatedly how the girls would seduce rival gang members in secluded areas so that the males could jump them and either beat or murder them. Female gang members might be required to have sex with rival gang members in order to gain information. Rival gang members usually realize that they are being set up because they do the same thing.

Female gang members are capable of committing murder but their homicide rate is much lower compared with males. Less than 1% of the 1,072 gang-related homicides documented in Curry's study (1998) were committed by females. Research conducted by Loper and Cornell (1995) led to the revelation that "girls' homicides are more likely to grow out of an interpersonal dispute with the victim (79%), while homicides committed by boys are more likely to be crime related (57%); that is, occurring during the commission of another crime, such as robbery" (Chesney-Lind and Shelden 2004, 68). All evidence clearly indicates that female gang members do not commit a great number of homicides. "Gang girls are much more at risk of being killed than killing" (Hagedorn 1999, 2).

Kitchen (1995) found that gang girls do not want to participate in the conventional job market that most likely would relegate them to lower-paying, menial jobs. Instead, they see dollar signs flashing before their eyes when they consider selling drugs like crack on the street. He pointed out that females who sell drugs must be particularly aggressive and violent. The very nature of the underground drug market necessitates the willingness to fight, even with deadly force. Female gangs that sell drugs have to be tough enough to fight against males in order to protect their market. Laidler and Hunt (1997) suggested that female gang members must be tough because they are challenging the traditional gender roles, where even on the streets, toughness is measured by patriarchal norms. Many of the female gang members in Hawaii studied by Joe and Chesney-Lind (1995) had extensive arrest records, with about 25% having ten or more arrests. "Their offenses were mostly property offenses, but many (about one-third of the girls) had been arrested for violent offenses. Not surprisingly, girls were about equally likely to have committed status offenses as any other type of offense" (Chesney-Lind and Shelden 2004, 77).

In research conducted by Miller and Decker, 85% of the girls reported having hit someone with the idea of hurting them. In a study conducted by Finn-Aage Esbensen and his colleagues, 39% of gang girls revealed that they attacked someone with a weapon; 78% had been involved in gang fights; 65% had carried weapons; and 21% said that they had shot someone (Regoli and Hewitt 2003, 319). Gearty and Hutchinson (2001) conducted field research on the Bloodettes, a female auxiliary to the Bloods in New York. They found the Bloodettes to be "as criminally cunning and ruthless as the Bloods." The Bloodettes were used by the Bloods as a source of income for the gang. The girls would dupe nongang citizens by obtaining credit cards and/or credit card information in order to conduct such crimes as credit card fraud and identity theft schemes. The Bloodettes are also accused of a number of violent offenses, including the 2000 pipe beating of a woman in the Bronx. Leon Bing, author of *Do or Die*, a book written about the rival LA gangs the Bloods and the Crips, conducted research on female gang members in Los Angeles. Some of his research was made available in his *Rolling Stone* article "Homegirls" (2001). In this article, Bing recounts his interview with Claudia, a former Crip member who retired after being blinded in a shotgun attack. Claudia was living with her mother and two children—Nelson, 13, and Kaleesha, 10—who were already getting in trouble at school for fighting and hanging out with known gang members. Bing described how, in the hard-core gang areas of Los Angeles, Watts, Compton, Inglewood, and Baldwin Hills ("the jungle"), school girls with gang affiliation spell out their allegiance to a Blood or Crip set in fancy block lettering on their denim notebooks. These girls were ready to fight any other girl who professed loyalty to a rival set, and this was just the beginning of the violent and criminal activities that LA gang girls engage in.

> A homegirl might carry a homeboy's weapon, or she might man the wheel for a drive-by shooting, but it was as fighters—with fists, not guns—that these girls excelled. I heard legends about one or two female gangsters (sometimes referred to as gangsta-lettes) who were said to be "riders," an expression of respect used to describe fiercely active gang members. In the main, however, girls were perceived as trophies, conveniences or troublemakers. One of the longest-standing (and lethal) internecine battles between two Crip sets kicked off in a schoolyard when a girl broke up with one boy to go out with a kid from another neighborhood. . . . They're living in an environment where they know things are a certain way, and they do what they have to do to survive. Things happen to them in their environment: There are one or two shootings in South Central every day, and they're trying to deal with pregnancies and raising their kids and just trying to survive as females (Bing 2001, 80).

In this violent environment, Kaleesha became one of the 66 gang-related homicides in Watts. She was shot and killed while sitting on the front porch of her mother's house (Bing 2001).

Bing conducted interviews with a number of female gang members and it is clear that they were actively involved in violent criminal offenses. They robbed and beat people up. And when one of their members is killed, they seek out their own revenge instead of having their homeboys take care of it. They participated in drive-by shootings and face-to-face murders. In these neighborhoods of Los Angeles, despair is commonplace. The lack of high-paying, low-skill jobs limits the opportunities of gang members, who are generally poorly educated. This is especially true for inner-city minority females. One interviewee stated:

> I'm a black female gangbanger. No education, no trade, no experience with anything except gangbanging. I can't tell you how to work no computer. I can't make up no payroll. I can tell you how to load a gun and shoot it, how to sag yo'

pants and tie yo' blue rag. I thought about getting a GED, but in the situation I am—single, young, black and the mother of two kids—I don't have time to go back to school. I got some welfare, and I'm tryin' to find work (Bing 2001, 85).

This quote reflects a general feeling shared by many females in the inner city. Economic hopelessness leads many people to the underground market, where street-smarts are the valued job attributes. Among the most financially attractive underground economic opportunities believed to lead to riches is drug trafficking.

Drugs

Many female gangs are involved with drugs for both recreational purposes and for profit via drug trafficking. Drug violations are among the most common offenses committed by female gang members along with violent offenses. Females may sell drugs to raise enough money so that they can "party," or they may sell drugs for profit. "Most female dealers are working for someone else, although there are a few powerful female career dealers" (Moore and Hagedorn 2001, 5). A study conducted by Moore and Mata in the 1980s found that nearly 20% of all Mexican-American female gang members dealt heroin at some point during their time with the gang. Within any gang, the younger members are generally the ones sent out to sell drugs for the higher-ranking gang leaders. Some male gangs have girls sell drugs for them as well. Many female gang members begin to sell drugs when their husbands (or boyfriends) go to prison because they need the money to support themselves and their families.

Moore (1991) described in detail the common occurrence of drug use in the families of the gang members she interviewed. Heroin was always the drug of choice for these cholo gang members, even during the crack cocaine "epidemic" of the late 1980s. Moore referred to this phenomenon as the **tecato lifestyle**. (A **tecato** is a term for heroin addict.) Moore stated that very few of the women in the earlier cliques (1950s and 1960s) used heroin; in fact, most of the gang members did not use heroin until they joined the gang. "Even then, it was primarily men, not women, who used heroin. (Almost half of the men, but less than a quarter of the women were using heroin by the age of 20)" (Moore 1991, 107). Mere membership in the gang meant that the label *tecato* would be placed on all gang members whether they used heroin or not. Heroin was so important to some gang members that when asked what was the major happening of their teens, "a full 39 percent of all of the men and 16 percent of the women named 'heroin, drugs, narcotics'" (Moore 1991, 197). Moore found that female gang members who used heroin were likely to have come from a family where heroin was used in the house. "Women were also much more likely to have their heroin use bracketed by a mate: They tended to start heroin use with a boyfriend or husband, and, even though each liaison might be short-lived, the street world almost dictates that a tecata's next boyfriend will also be a heroin user. To some extent, then, women's heroin use is enacted in a familial context. It might be seen as a twisted version of the usual Mexican emphasis on family roles for women" (Moore 1991, 109). Lauderback and associates (1992) found that drug use among girl gang members in San Francisco was nearly as common as among male members, with marijuana being the most popular among the females.

A study of African-American and Latina female gang members in Milwaukee during the 1990s found that approximately 50% of the female gangsters dealt drugs, especially cocaine (Moore and Hagedorn 2001). There was a significant difference between these two racial groups, as 72% of the Latina females sold drugs compared to just 31% of black female gang members. As a rule, males were found to be more heavily involved in the sale of drugs than females. In 1993, Taylor conducted an extensive study of female drug offenders, focusing on Detroit's corporate gangs—gangs designed for profit (Moore and Hagedorn 2001). He concluded that female gangbangers became involved with the drug trade in the early 1990s and predicted that the role of females in drug trafficking would increase as a result of decreased economic opportunities. Miller (2001) found that girls sold drugs in both St. Louis and Columbus, although to a higher degree in St. Louis. The girls reported that "most of the proceeds of drug selling were used to 'party.'" Also, the drug selling was sporadic rather than a daily event. Kitchen (1995) found that female gang members sold crack cocaine because it was such a profitable business enterprise. Selling crack cocaine is not only lucrative, it is dangerous. The girls that sell rock must be willing to act aggressively and violently to protect their stash and money, let alone their very lives. In their study of San Francisco gangs, Lauderback and associates (1992) found that the girls had an easier time selling drugs than their male counterparts because they generally did not wear their gang colors and were therefore less likely to be harassed by the police. Crack cocaine sales were handled differently. "Most of their crack sales are conducted in rock houses. These houses are usually a neighbor's residence that is rented in exchange for drugs" (Chesney-Lind and Shelden 2004, 77).

Female gangsters generally face the world with a sense of hopelessness. They do not want to be poor and suffer through a life of misery. Lacking the necessary education and job skills needed to advance in the current socioeconomic system, these girls have learned to justify their violent and criminal behaviors through such techniques as neutralization and an overall lack of a guilty conscience. Sykes and Matza's analysis of neutralization was discussed in Chapter 3, but we will now briefly apply it to female gangsters.

Denial of responsibility is a common neutralization technique used by gang members and nongang members alike. It is the most common response heard from the guilty—"I didn't do it!" Female gang members will often deny their involvement in criminal activities. *Denial of injury* is a common defense for property crime and vandalism. Gang members believe that "marking" their territory is an acceptable form of behavior—it meets the standards of their norms. *Denial of a victim* is common among females who get into fights with other girls over boys. Fighting a rival is deemed appropriate behavior, especially if one can claim that she was the original victim. *Condemnation of the condemners* is similar to the tactic of the best defense being a good offense. Rather than take the defensive approach of proving one's innocence, some gang members attempt to turn the tables on their accusers by claiming they were beaten by the police or that the police planted drugs on them. Female gang members can accuse male police officers of inappropriate sexual contact. *Appeal to higher loyalties* is an essential technique of neutralization for female gang members. The higher loyalty can be both to the gang and the family that she has created with a male gang member. The mother status is highly respected by gang members.

As with many criminals, female gang members may not feel the need for any neutralization technique because they lack a guilty conscience. As we have seen, female gang members are capable of committing a wide range of criminal offenses, and they may not feel any guilt about them. For female gang members, this lack of conscience developed within the gang subcultural context. If someone honestly doesn't believe that she is guilty of committing a crime or violating a societal norm, she will not feel remorse for such behavior. Furthermore, some theories (see Chapter 3) suggest criminals are born as "bad seeds" and therefore are incapable, or unwilling, to feel remorse for criminal activities.

Violating the laws of society may lead to incarceration. Believe it or not, incarceration may be the best thing to happen to a gang girl. She is less likely to die in prison than she is on the streets. In addition, female prisons are not dominated by gangs as male prisons are beginning to be. Once a female gang member is incarcerated, she is generally forgotten by the rest of her gang as they move on with business as usual. While in prison, the female gang member speaks of leaving the gang forever. This seldom occurs. When a female gang member is released from prison, she generally returns to the old neighborhood and resumes friendships with old acquaintances that draw her back into the gang lifestyle. Frustrated by the lack of legitimate job opportunities for ex-inmate female gang members, the lure of the gang becomes even stronger.

RELATIONSHIPS WITH MALES AND SCHOOL

The relationship that female gang members have with their male counterparts varies a great deal from gang to gang. As for their school experiences, nearly all girl gang members had experienced a number of problems while they attended school.

Relationships with Males

As we have said, females and males appear to join gangs for similar reasons: a sense of belonging, family, identity, protection, economic success, and respect. There are, however, several differences between male and female gang members. First, females tend to drop out of the gang at an earlier age than males, mostly because of pregnancy. "Females leave gangs at the end of their teens, as opposed to less than 25 percent of men in male gangs. The reasons why females left varied: most of them said they grew out of gangs; others said that their parents left the neighborhood, ending their membership. Two-thirds of the women became teen mothers and more than 90 percent were mothers before their mid-twenties" (Tonry and Moore 1998, 388).

Another difference between female and male gang members is the fact that generally women are less violent than men. Males often use guns; women are more likely to engage in fist fights and use knives. And although males and females are equally affected by the economic shift (and the loss of high-paying factory jobs), women were affected far more severely by cuts in welfare than were men. "In 1990, welfare reforms were introduced that reduced or eliminated welfare payments. Because female gang members often face significant barriers to legitimate employment, it is unclear what they will do to replace welfare support" (Moore and Hagedorn 2001, 3). It appears that many female gangsters have decided to sell drugs and engage in more violent criminal activities as their response to welfare reform.

As mentioned several times earlier in this chapter, historically, female gangs have been auxiliary to males. The very term *auxiliary* implies a secondary role and is defined in terms of "providing help" and "functioning in a subsidiary capacity." Furthermore, when considering the fact that most males report that they prefer their girlfriends not to be in a gang, it is easy to understand why, for the most part, female gang members are not well respected by males. For example, Fishman (1995) described how the Vice Kings reported that their primary relationship with the Vice Queens was sexual. The Queens were expected to have sex with the Kings. The girls interviewed by Laidler and Hunt (1997) reported that their boyfriends were "possessive, controlling, and often violent." All of the male gang members that Totten (2001, 163) interviewed admitted that they committed some form of abuse against their girlfriends, with many admitting that they used sexual force. The "sexing in" initiation practice highlights the subordinate role that women play to men in the gang world.

Thus, just as is sometimes found in the general society, female gang members find themselves victims of sexism. Males do not deny their sexist position and often report that they consider female gang members as "possessions" (Moore and Hagedorn 2001). Sometimes, females are treated as sex objects within the gang. Traditionally, gangs have used their female counterparts: "Girls were useful to them because the police were less suspicious of them. Girls could stand on street corners and serve as decoys while boys committed robberies. Girls could hold weapons or drugs in their clothes, knowing the police would be less likely to frisk them. Gang members often treated girls like guns or knives, passed along from member to member" (Goldentyer 1994, 52). Females themselves affirm their secondary status to male gangs when they take feminized versions of their names. However, as noted earlier, there are currently more female gangs existing independently of male gangs and that are autonomous, as well as being allied with a male gang. Moore's study (1991) of Mexican-American gangs in Los Angeles found that two-thirds of women, both older and younger, denied being treated like a possession. However, "more of the men—especially the younger men—agreed that the boys treated the girls like possessions (41 percent of the older men and 56 percent of the younger men, reflecting the increase). Among those who denied such sexism, the keynote was that the gang was like a family" (Moore 1991, 53).

Many females, especially minority women, claim that they are not respected in the legitimate job market and believe that, despite the sexism found within the gang world, they have a better chance of survival in the underground market. "Sexism was a topic that Kitchen explored with her respondents. Women (especially African American women) do not appear to get much respect within the legitimate business world, but in the informal economy of drug dealing, they command respect as long as they are tough and do not sell themselves" (Chesney-Lind and Shelden 2004, 86). Girls who sell themselves for drugs or money are not respected. The girls are aware of this double standard and told Kitchen that it is easier for a male to get respect because all he has to do is beat someone up, commit a crime, or have sex with lots of women. Female gang members will not be respected if they have a lot of sex (Kitchen 1995). "These types of roles tend to suggest a no-win situation for gang girls. As Sex Objects they are cheap women rejected by other girls, parents, social workers, and ironically often by the boys themselves. As Tomboys, they are resented by boys and ridiculed by family and friends who wait patiently for them to 'grow out of it'" (Campbell 1995, 70).

Sex comes into play in other ways as well. Gang members may rape the girlfriends of rival gang members as a form of intimidation or retaliation. Equally disturbing, if a female gang member breaks up with her boyfriend, the male may instruct members of his crew to sexually violate her. Thus, rape is a big part of the female gang member's life. She may have been raped by her male gang counterparts as part of her initiation, she may be set up as a decoy by trading her body for information from rivals, she may be raped by rival gang members, and she may become victimized by her own boyfriend and gang affiliation. Many studies of female gangs reveal that girls admit to being raped by gang members, family members, or boyfriends. Female gang members will not report these heinous crimes to authorities because they know that they risk death (Sikes 1997). Often, female gang members who are victims of rape do not even receive sympathy from the rest of the girls in the gang. They blame the victim and believe that she should have defended herself better. Female gang members particularly loathe women who "cry rape" (those not really raped but falsely accuse someone of rape) (Sikes 1997).

There are still other issues related to sex for the female gang member. For instance, they assume that their boyfriends will cheat on them. The girls place all the responsibility for these types of occurrences on the other girls rather than their boyfriends. The gang girls interviewed by Sikes (1997) stated that they believed that it was up to them to keep their boyfriends happy. They believed that if they flaunted themselves in front of guys, guys would respond. And if that guy already had a girlfriend, she would have to fight to keep him. This low expectation of men was obviously learned—most likely in the home and especially in single-parent households. And although the threat of HIV/AIDS has been around for decades now, these gang girls run a relatively high risk for acquiring this disease (along with any other STDs), considering the likelihood of rape, promiscuity, and drug and alcohol use. The risk is high primarily because the males engaging in sexual behavior with the gang women generally do not wear protection.

Moore (1991) also described how girls who are raped by male gang members are in a bad position because if they complain to the police they are labeled a "rat" or "snitch" and also their own homegirls will not support them against the accused rapist. "The entire gang—girls included—go all out to protect their homeboy. One Maravilla woman commented that it was particularly important for the gang girls to go court to back up their homeboys, because it helps the defense lawyer make the rape victim 'look like a tramp'" (Moore 1991, 56). So seemingly, the males have all the power in the gang. But once again, just as often occurs in general society, the female is capable of manipulating males to behave in the manner they wish. "There are many stories about how gang girls manipulate their homeboys' possessiveness to incite gang fights" (Moore 1991, 56). Intergang dating is a leading cause of fights among the gangs that Moore studied. This common occurrence led to many wars between rival gangs. Female gang members can also be successful in convincing males not to fight rival gang members. However, while in the gang, both males and females prefer dating gang members rather than nongang members ("squares" or conventional people). Those lucky few who get out of the gang generally prefer to date nongang members, but people who are not too "square." They prefer those labeled "hip-square" (street-smart, but not gangbanging).

In Gini Sikes' study of the Lennox-13 El Salvadorian female gang in Los Angeles, she found that the relationship between boys and girls varied over time. "The level of girls' involvement in the Lennox cliques went in cycles over the years. At times the boys' gangs welcomed girls, at other times they pushed them aside, denigrating them as whores, bitches, snitches, and spies. Girls frequently found themselves in a catch-22: male leaders would order the prettiest to infiltrate an enemy party to set up or lure a rival—at high risk to herself—only to resent her and all females for making men vulnerable" (Sikes 2001, 244). The male gang members also had an interesting viewpoint toward lesbians:

> Many male gang members welcomed lesbians in their ranks with an acceptance that extended beyond anything I'd witnessed in mainstream society. Though at first this surprised me, in time it made sense. Both boys and girls in gangs prize aggressive masculinity above nearly any other trait. Extremely butch homosexual women win respect precisely because they appear almost indistinguishable from men, favoring the same clothes, right down to their boxer shorts. They stay active far later in life than straight women because usually they do not have kids (Sikes 2001, 248).

Since masculine attributes are the most highly valued in the gang, terms like *bitch*, *girl*, or *faggot* are considered the worst insults that one can sling at a man (Sikes 2001).

Thus, the feminine role in gangs is complicated. "Although some feminine girls secure a role beyond that of seductive informer or spy—I have encountered petite, frail girls who could reduce many men to a pulp, their seemingly innocent faces an effective surprise weapon—inevitably their biology holds them back. Sooner or later, most become pregnant and in Latino gangs a woman on the street who has children at home is an object of scorn" (Sikes 2001, 248). Ultimately, girls, like boys, seek respect, and they fight hard to keep it. Fighting is something that the Lennox-13 gang is good at; after all, "their native country's civil war prepared them well for the streets of LA" (Sikes 2001, 250).

Relationships with the Schools

It is common for gang members to have had problems with schoolwork. They are classic underachievers and generally lack the stable family environment that would support academic pursuits. Youngsters who enter school unprepared (lacking basic skills) risk falling behind at an early age and being placed in "special" classes—and consequently, they run the risk of negative labeling. Students who do not have family members, primarily parents, to help them with their daily homework fall even further behind. Eventually, the child becomes frustrated and loses interest in schoolwork. If the child is from a gang neighborhood, the disinterest in academic knowledge is often replaced by a thirst for a street education. In short, problems with school are a high risk factor for turning. Furthermore, as researchers like Joan Moore have indicated, many individuals join a gang because the gang has a presence in the school. Thus, the school itself is a risk factor for turning.

Minority children often believe that they are victimized in school because of their race or ethnicity. "Ethnic identity confusion has been identified as a problem for Chicanos in all kinds of communities, and it is by no means confined to youngsters who join gangs or have other kinds of problems" (Moore 1991, 85). Some of the gang members in Moore's study revealed how they discovered their "Mexican-ness" while in school: White kids generally brought sandwiches with them to school for lunch; Mexicans brought tacos. And as Mexican-Americans, these kids struggled with their English skills, which also hurt them in their pursuit of academic knowledge. Moore cautioned, however, against reading too much into the school experience as a factor for ethnic minorities turning to gangs. "It is easy to make too much of such identity confusion. It was undoubtedly shared by other youngsters in the barrios: these gang members were by no means unusually Mexican for their times" (Moore 1991, 85).

Felix Padilla also examined the role of the school environment as a factor for youths joining gangs. Many of the "Diamonds" reported to him that they were routinely negatively labeled by teachers, especially in elementary school. Those who were so labeled began to associate with each other, creating for themselves "a distinctive subculture within which they could examine and interpret what was going on in their lives and in school as well as determining the most appropriate set of activities for dealing with these conditions" (Padilla 1992, 69). In essence, the early seed of future ganghood was planted for these youths in elementary school. Padilla (1992, 69) blamed the teachers and staff for the negative feelings experienced by the Diamonds in school, stating that they "refused to understand and respect their cultural and socioeconomic class background." Padilla also pointed out the influence of the self-fulfilling prophecy. These youths were told repeatedly by their teachers that they were no good. Over time, these youngsters began to internalize these negative labels and also started to act like deviants (by getting into fights, not doing their homework, etc.); thus, they turned out to be deviants. "For members of the Diamonds the disparaging treatment by teachers and peers dampened their interest in school and led them to conclude that it was far better to stay out of school than to be victimized by their teachers' constant verbal assault and sometimes physical punishment. These young people lost interest in school and stopped attending. . . ." (Padilla 1992, 75).

Negative feelings toward school experiences are generally a more important contributing cause of joining a gang for males than for females. Girls have an easier time in school, for they are less likely to receive the negative labels of "deviant" and "troublemaker" than are boys. Even so, many minority females become equally disenchanted by the whole school experience. "Many have noted that school is often deemed irrelevant to the lives of gang members and presents a motivation to drop out and become part of a gang" (Chesney-Lind and Shelden 2004, 94). Davis (1999, 257) reported that gang girls considered school as "a road that leads to nowhere." Harris (1997) found that none of the chola gang girls in her study graduated from high school. In his study of the Vice Queens in Chicago, Fishman (1988) reported that most of the gang members attended school only occasionally, eventually just dropping out. Kitchen (1995) found that even though 70% of the gang members he interviewed had graduated from high school, most of them felt unprepared to compete in conventional society. They felt that the teachers did not care about them and that, in general, school was a waste of time.

Considering that most gang members are likely to drop out of school by the tenth grade, one has to wonder if teachers' predictions of such behavior by certain children are not warranted. After all, risk factors are easy to identity as early as elementary school. The key, then, is to find some way to keep these youths interested in school. Interest in school begins with individual motivation and responsibility, followed by a supportive family, qualified teachers, and proper funding of all schools.

GANG FAMILIES

Ideally, the family is a social institution that provides a nurturing and safe, loving environment in which children are raised. Unfortunately, this is not always the case. Many children are brought into the world by people who are unwilling or unprepared to raise them properly. Currently, the family social structure appears to be in peril. At the very least, it is changing dramatically, and some of these changes have led to negative consequences. For example, broken homes and single-parent families are a leading contributor to the increased numbers of gang members (although, certainly there is not a cause-and-effect relationship). Some point to the existence of female gangs as further evidence of the decline of the family. "Young women's involvement in gangs is disquieting precisely because females in gangs are perceived to be outside the traditional arena of family control. More specifically, female gang participation generates alarm because it signifies, yet again, fears about the decline of the 'traditional family'" (Hunt et al. 2004, 49). If the family cannot fulfill its traditional role as an "ideal" socializing and control agent, and females, along with males, feel the need to join the gang to gain a substitute family, then the family as an institution is indeed in turmoil.

The Dysfunctional Home Family

Hunt and associates (2004) believe that "normal" girls do not become involved in gangs and that therefore the reasons certain young females join a gang must lie within deeply troubled families. "Accordingly, the female gang member is viewed within the larger framework of family disintegration and violence. From this viewpoint, aggression and violence in the family are regarded, by definition, as dysfunctional and deviant forms of family disintegration. Consequently, young gang women adopt a lifestyle of violence only as a result of an early and damaging experience, and in compensation for such an experience" (Hunt et al. 2004, 50). The gang, then, provides for the troubled girl a substitute family that is more nurturing than the one in which she was raised.

As a general rule, females who turn to gangs have either been victimized at home or witnessed victimization and abusive relationships at home. These girls may have experienced verbal, sexual, and/or physical abuse. "Females most at risk for gang involvement come from homes in crisis" (Chesney-Lind and Shelden 2004, 90). The majority of the girls interviewed by Totten (2001) indicated that they saw their mothers being abused by both their biological fathers and by "social father-figures" (stepfathers, boyfriends). One common form of abuse suffered by girls who turn to gangs is incest.

Moore (1991) found that 29% of the female gang members she interviewed reported that some member of the family had raped them. She speculated that more gang girls had actually been victims of rape than reported it. Moore (1991, 96) described how incest is fairly common in traditional Mexican families:

> Incest is generally associated with patriarchy, and there are indications that the more patriarchal homes were in fact more likely to be incestuous. Fathers of incest victims were more likely to beat their wives, and they were more likely to be strict with and depreciatory of their daughters. Incest victims were also more likely to see their fathers as alcoholics, but they were not significantly more likely to feel that their fathers were trying to set themselves up unequivocally as heads of the household or to control their mothers' visitors—other indicators of patriarchy. In most cases the assailant was the father, but uncles, brothers, and grandfathers were among the culprits. And the experiences occurred at all ages, ranging from 5 to 17, with a median age of about $11\frac{1}{2}$. In about 40 percent of the cases, only one approach was made, but the remainder reported repeated sexual encounters.

Alcohol and heroin abuse were additional problems found in the homes of the gang members interviewed by Moore. These and other drugs are commonly abused in the families of girl gang members.

Research conducted by Joe and Chesney-Lind (1993) found that the majority of both girls and boys lived with both parents, but most of them (55% of the boys and 62% of the girls) reported being physically abused. A significant difference was that 62% of the girls indicated that they had been sexually abused or sexually assaulted (Chesney-Lind and Shelden 2004, 92). Flowers (1995, 181) stated, "Girls join gangs for all the things their families haven't given them: devotion, support, acceptance and love." The gang becomes a refuge for young women who have been victimized at home. These abused girls run away from home and join a gang in order to obtain protection from abusive families. He further explained that joining a gang can be an assertion of independence not only from family, but also from cultural and class constraints. The gang may provide them with a sense of meaning and identity, a place that they can call "home." In summary, the females most likely to join a gang are those who witness physical violence between adults in the family, were abused by a family member, lived in a house with alcohol and drug abuse, whose family had multiple problems (violence, criminality, a family member in jail), and had a family member already in the gang (Miller 2001).

It should be mentioned that some gang members retain a relatively solid relationship with their family members. The families disapprove of their activity but nonetheless still accept them as family members. Geoffrey Hunt and associates (2004, 67) offer this conclusion about the relationship between gang females and their families:

> In our analysis we have tried to illuminate the relationship and meaning of family among homegirls. In doing so, we have tried to dispel popular conceptions about the disintegration of contemporary inner-city families of color, and about the pushing of young minority youths onto the streets. Family relationships, particularly homegirls' ties to mothers, sisters, grandmothers, and other extended kin, are based on reciprocal and mutual forms of emotional and practical support. Not surprisingly, we have found . . . that although homegirls make

a heavy investment of time in gang friendships, related activities, and loyalty to the gang, almost all of the women named family members as the most important people or role models in their lives. . . . Many of the other women whom the homegirls admired were to be found in their immediate and extended families and among their homegirls. In their accounts, these two groups were frequently intertwined: Blood sisters, female cousins, and aunts doubled as homegirls and "gang sisters." Such loyalties and bonds call into question the standard and traditional notions about what constitutes family. In the homegirls' formation of their domestic and family units, we may be witnessing a pragmatic process encouraging survival in what may be less than ideal environments and situations.

This conclusion raises an interesting question: Is the gang a "legitimate" form of the family? As more and more gang women have children and raise them in a gang environment, the gang may in fact take on the role of an extended family, which is quite common in many cultures according to the concept of "It takes a village to raise a child." What if this village consists entirely of gangbangers?

Pregnancy and Starting One's Own Family

Nearly all female gang members eventually get pregnant, something that is, of course, true of nongang females as well. These children are almost always fathered by male gang members, who typically do not take responsibility for them. The struggle and burden of raising these gang children is generally left to the mother. Sometimes she can depend on her extended family. "The Latino cultural emphasis on extended family may play an important role in the support system for these gang members as they negotiate womanhood in a patriarchal environment at home and on the street. Scholars have shown that African American families develop strong real and fictive kinship networks for both emotional and practical support" (Hunt et al. 2004, 52). The gang becomes an extended kinship system that can assist in the raising of the next generation.

There are some advantages to pregnancy. The female may now gain a new status and sense of purpose. "A large part of her identity is provided by the baby under her care and guidance, and for many street-oriented girls there is no quicker way to grow up. Becoming a mother can be a strong play for authority, maturity, and respect, but it is also a shortsighted and naïve gamble because the girl often fails to realize that her life will be suddenly burdened and her choices significantly limited" (Anderson 1999, 148). The gang girl who is now a mother must try to break the cycle of ganghood, or her child will face the same negative environment growing up that she did.

When the gang woman has her baby she realizes that the father is likely not to stick around. Generally, she would prefer to have a family man in her life who would help to raise the child. "Aware of many abandoned young mothers, many a girl fervently hopes that her man is the one who will be different. In addition, her peer group supports her pursuit of the dream, implicitly upholding her belief in the young man's good faith. When a girl does become engaged to be married, there is much excitement, with relatives and friends oohing and ahhing over their prospective life. But seldom does this happen, because for the immediate future, the boy is generally not interested in 'playing house,' as his peers derisively refer to domestic life" (Anderson 1999, 152).

The boy does not want to be labeled a "square." His male counterparts try to convince him that he was "tricked" into getting married because his girlfriend got pregnant on purpose. "Up to the point of pregnancy, given the norms of his peer groups, the young man could simply be said to be messing around. Pregnancy suddenly introduces an element of reality into the relationship. Life-altering events have occurred, and the situation is usually perceived as serious" (Anderson 1999, 156).

Even when the father sticks around and starts a family, it is common for him to rejoin gang activities whenever he gets bored hanging around the house. Lauderback et al. (1992) found in their study of girl gang members that the gang fathers almost never got involved in the lives of the children. Obviously, gangbanging activity is not conducive to a fully functioning family. The father/husband maintains his relationship with the gang for many reasons. His loyalty is often stronger to the gang than to his wife and child and the gang may not allow him to leave. "Hanging out with the gang led to problems for the family, because the gang remained of central importance to the man, even more than the marriage. Also, when there were problems in the marriage, the gang became a convenient escape" (Chesney-Lind and Shelden 2004, 92). It has become increasingly common for women to maintain their allegiance to the gang as well. But when both the mother and father are actively gangbanging, the family and marriage are in big trouble. In short, gang marriages do not last.

SUMMARY

Female gangs have been around for nearly as long as male gangs. Despite the growing evidence for independent female gangs, most of them remain auxiliary to male gangs. Most researchers believe that 10% of all gang members are females. These estimates vary depending upon who collects the data. Female gang members are very capable of committing violent criminal acts but not in the same proportion as male gang members. Female gang members join gangs for the same reasons as males, the primary ones being to seek economic success, a substitute family, and respect. Over the years, research on female gangs has been increasing but much more is needed in order to gain a greater understanding of this social phenomenon.

The criminal justice system will have to develop new methods for dealing with the increasing number of female gangs. Law enforcement officials need to acknowledge the existence of female gangs and police officers need to be trained in identifying female gang members. Few police departments have developed programs to specifically deal with female gang members.

The single fact that so many female gang members come from abusive and sexually exploitive environments is a strong reason for considering female gang membership a serious social problem. Most female gang members have children, and since the fathers generally refuse to take family responsibility, the fiscal burden is often shifted onto society in the form of welfare programs. As gang children age, they inevitably become active in gangbanging themselves. Thus, another generation of gang members is guaranteed and their numbers will continue to increase for some time.

CHAPTER **EIGHT**

Criminal Activities of Street Gangs

istorically, gangs have formed to ensure the basic survival of their members and to protect their neighborhoods from outsiders who intended to cause harm to local residents. Gangs have also always been known for their criminal activities and their high degree of violent behavior. The focus of this book is on street gangs in American society. It is important to note, however, that street thugs are a problem in many nations of the world. France, for example, had a higher crime rate than the United States in 2001. The primary reason for this high crime rate is the violence caused by immigrant gangs from northern and sub-Saharan Africa, Romania, and the former Yugoslavia. In 2001, "more than 25,000 cars were burned in French cities. (An average of six cars a night are torched in the historic city of Strasbourg.) Thefts in the Paris subway average 1000 a week" (*Parade Magazine* 2002). Firefighters and rescue workers refuse to go into many French ghettos for fear of their lives. Gangs in Haiti terrorized storm victims of Hurricane Jeanne in September 2004. They mobbed aid convoys, broke into homes to steal food, and shot anyone who got in their way. The failure of Haiti's U.S.-backed government to disarm gangs has created a climate of insecurity that jeopardizes lives, according to an AP report (*Syracuse Post-Standard* 2004e). The presidents of Honduras and El Salvador claim that street gangs in their countries are as big a threat to national security as terrorism is to the United States. In Honduras, gang members are known as "maras," after a species of swarming ant. Authorities estimate there are 70,000 to 100,000 gang members across Central America and Mexico, where gangs are alleged to have killed thousands of people in the last decade (Thompson 2004).

NORMAL ACTIVITIES OF GANG MEMBERS

American street gang members spend the bulk of their time engaged in "normal" activities, such as sleeping, eating, and hanging out. In that regard, gang members are not so different from most people. They play ball, go to movies and ballgames, hang out with their friends, date, become parents, and so on. If their behavior was restricted to these activities, society would not have to worry about street gangs. However, as we all know, gang members do participate in criminal activities and these are the actions that concern society in general, gang victims, and especially law enforcement officers. The amount of time gang members spend on committing criminal acts is not important. What is important is the fact that gang members are involved in a large number of serious delinquent and criminal acts. Gang members are responsible for greater levels of crime and violence than nongang members, and gang-related delinquency is far more violent than nongang-related delinquency. The type of criminal activities committed by gang members varies from gang to gang; some are involved in a "cafeteria-style" pattern of offenses and others are engaged in acts of violence or the sale and distribution of drugs. Generally, gangs are involved in four major categories of **criminal activities**: the use, sale and distribution of drugs; violence; homicide; and other crimes.

Often, all of these criminal activities are intertwined. "Few phenomena have been stereotyped as easily as gangs, violence, and drug use, especially when they are taken in conjunction. Drug and alcohol use have always been a part of gang life, as has peddling of small quantities of whatever street drugs are popular at the time. Alcohol and marijuana have always been, and continue to be, the most widely used substances among both gang and nongang youth" (Fagan 2004, 237–238). In fact, drinking is most likely the second most popular activity among all gang members (hanging out would be number one) (Fagan 2004). Even the pursuit of "legitimate" activities such as partying may entail criminal action. "Partying tends to increase the likelihood of crime because, first, it corresponds with heavy drinking and drug use, both related to crime. Also, there is a need to obtain drugs for parties, costing money, which in turn brings gang members into contact with the illegal drug world. Because most gang members are without work (either because it is unavailable or because they have never been socialized into good work habits), crime becomes a part-time job. The most common crimes tend to be robberies (because they can produce money fairly quickly) and drug dealing" (Shelden et al. 2001, 101).

DRUGS: USE, SALE, AND DISTRIBUTION

The research on the relationship between gangs and drugs is mixed. Are gangs really beginning to take control of the drug market, as many in law enforcement believe? Or has gang involvement in drugs been overstated? A study by McCorkle and Miethe (1998, 2001) suggested that it is a myth that gangs have taken over the drug market. The researchers found that gang members represented only 2 to 8% of all felony drug defendants. It is fairly common knowledge that most gang members do use drugs recreationally, especially marijuana, ecstasy, PCP, speed, crack cocaine, and heroin. It is also quite commonly known that many gangs sell drugs. Perhaps what is most unclear is their level of participation in the distribution of drugs. Furthermore, there is no evidence to suggest that gangs are responsible for shipping drugs into the country from foreign markets (e.g., Colombia for cocaine or Thailand for high-grade marijuana and heroin). It is true, though, that many gangs are capable of creating their own drugs in "methamphetamine labs," which can operate as a distribution center.

Biker gangs are more likely to be involved in the distribution of drugs. The Hell's Angels, in particular, have been targets of international law enforcement agencies for decades because of their involvement with the drug trade. The Hells Angels are responsible for importing drugs from Canada into the United States through border cities like Niagara Falls. In eastern Canada, the Hells Angels are at war with their rivals the **Bandidos.** In June 2002, Montreal police arrested 27 people, including the leader of the Hells Angels and Bandidos president Alain Brunette. Computers, weapons, and drugs were confiscated during dozens of searches in Quebec and Ontario. "The battle for control of the drug trade between the Bandidos, previously called the Rock

Machine, and the Hells Angels has claimed more than 150 lives in the past decade" (*Buffalo News* 2002).

Drug Use

Gang members **use drugs** for a variety of reasons. As mentioned, drugs are generally consumed recreationally. Drugs such as marijuana and crack cocaine are welcome party favors for gang members who are hanging out. They serve as a social "lubricant" during times of collective relaxation (Vigil 1988). "Research conducted in the 1980s and 1990s has documented extensive youth and adult gang member involvement in drug use and generally higher levels of use compared with nongang members" (Howell and Decker 1999, 2). Drugs may also be consumed for ritualistic reasons (e.g., "toasting" a fallen comrade or smoking pot at 4:20 PM). Drugs will also be used in conjunction with acts of aggression. Vigil found that Chicano gang members often prepared for imminent fights with other gangs by drinking and smoking PCP-laced cigarettes. The drug PCP makes the user feel invincible and the adrenalin rush that the user experiences makes him (or her) a much better fighter. (Think of Rodney King withstanding the repeated blows of the LAPD—he was so high on PCP the baton blows could not hurt him or bring him down, causing the officers to use excessive force.) Hispanic gang members in Los Angeles smoke marijuana joints laced with PCP, commonly referred to as "dusters." It is interesting to note that the gang members studied by Vigil were able to use PCP with alcohol for both relaxation when hanging out and as a way to "amp-up" for battle. "Evidently, gang members had substantial knowledge about the effects of alcohol (and its reactivity to PCP), and they had developed processes to adjust their reactions to the mood and behaviors they wanted" (Fagan 2004, 238). Of course, marijuana smokers do the same thing. They can smoke weed to get high or to "veg-out," a fact research on the effects of marijuana often fails to address. Alcohol users can also control the effects of the drugs. Sometimes the alcohol user drinks to get high; other times, to unwind or relax.

It is important to note that in some gangs drug use is forbidden. Spergel (1995) described how gang members who used heroin were forced out of gangs because they could not be relied on in fights with other gangs. Research conducted by Chin (1990) revealed that New York City Chinese gangs disallowed the use of drugs and alcohol, especially when they could interfere with conducting gang business. Gang leaders do not want their drug sellers high when they sell because they might mess up business.

Drug Sales

The **sale of drugs** has been a source of income for gangs for a long time, and many indications point to a large number of gangs resorting to the selling of drugs for profit in order to operate the gang. "Selling small amounts of drugs, especially marijuana . . . has been a common feature of gang life for decades. But the cocaine and crack crises of the 1980s created opportunities for gang and nongang youth alike to participate in drug selling and increase their incomes" (Fagan 2004, 239). Decker (2004, 264) stated that "most research has demonstrated that gang members sell drugs as individuals, and that gangs exert little instrumental control over the patterns of sales and the profits made by their members." (Note that this directly contradicts Padilla's discussion of the Diamonds, who pooled their money to purchase more drugs, the profits from which went back into a general fund.) Responses to the 1996 National Youth Gang Survey conducted by the National Youth Gang Center and published in the Office of Juvenile Justice and Delinquency Prevention (OJJDP) *Juvenile Justice Bulletin* (1999, 3), revealed the following:

> On average, respondents estimated that 43 percent of the drug sales in their jurisdiction involved gang members. Rather than using the average response, it was determined that more meaningful observations could be made by aggregating responses into groups and referring to the percentage of all responses within each group for analyses in this Bulletin. Gang member involvement in drug sales was divided into three response ranges: low (0–33 percent), medium (34–66 percent), and high (67–100 percent). This classification of responses revealed that 47 percent of all drug sales involved gang members at a low level, 26 percent at a high level. While the average for the entire response range (0–100 percent) was 43 percent, this division shows that the preponderance of responses fell into the low range (33 percent or less).

Research one year later revealed that the percent of gangs involved in the sale of drugs remained stable (though down slightly).

> According to respondents to the National Youth Gang Center's 1997 survey, it is estimated that 42 percent of gangs were involved in the street sale of drugs and 33 percent were involved in drug distribution for the specific purpose of generating profits for the gang. More than 90 percent of the jurisdictions reporting gang activity in the *National Drug Intelligence Center (NDIC) National Street Gang Survey Report—1998* stated that their gangs were involved in local drug sales, while 47 percent reported gang involvement in interstate drug trafficking (National Alliance of Gang Investigators Association 2002, 3).

As anyone who has taken a statistics class can attest, "statistics never lie, but their numbers are up for interpretation." Thus, the percentage of gangs involved in the sale of drugs may seem alarming. However, it is also clear that gangs are responsible for far less than half of all drug sales; consequently, the "problem" of selling drugs does not rest solely with gangs. "There is little evidence that gang members have become involved in drug selling more than nongang adolescents. Klein and his colleagues, based on police arrest reports following the appearance of crack in Los Angeles in 1985, found no evidence that gang members were arrested more often than nongang members for crack sales or that drug-related homicides were more likely to involve gang members than non-gang members" (Fagan 2004, 239–240). It should be noted that studies Fagan refers to (Klein, Maxson, and Cunningham 1991; Maxson and Klein 1989) took place 15 years ago. The fact remains, however, that many gangs are actively involved in the sale of drugs. The increased participation rate is directly attributable to the decline of the American industry, which no longer employs unskilled labor to the extent that it had prior to the 1980s. The decline of manufacturing jobs was especially harmful to minority males who were mainly concentrated in specific geographic areas. "Drug markets provided 'work' for displaced workers, and the growing popularity of crack cocaine opened new opportunities for youth to make money. Traditional pathways from gang life (jobs, marriage, starting a family) were constricted by the changed economy, prolonging gang involvement and making drug trafficking more attractive" (Howell and Decker 1999, 3). Gang members are among these adolescents who are taking advantage of the American public's desire for drugs and the government's refusal to provide them legally.

One might wonder just how much money gang members make selling drugs. The answer varies dramatically from gang to gang and by individual "pusher." It was determined during the RICO trial of Syracuse's Boot Camp gang leader Karo Brown that each gang member made between $400 and $2,000 a week selling crack cocaine. An average of 15 gang members were dealing drugs at once. Thus, the gang's annual profit was between $312,000 and $1.6 million (O'Brien 2004c).

The increasing number of gangs involved in the sale of drugs has led to formation of **drug gangs**. According to the OJJDP, drug gangs are organized specifically for the purpose of trafficking in drugs. Klein (1995) suggested nearly a decade ago that it was necessary to make a distinction between street gangs and gangs designed to sell drugs. "Unfortunately, youth gang studies have not revealed much about management and control of drug-trafficking operations versus street-level distribution systems. Most studies of youth gangs that are involved in drug trafficking describe their involvement in street-level distribution only . . . . Information on the prevalence of youth drug gangs has only recently become available" (Howell and Decker 1999, 4). In 1998, the OJJDP attempted to remedy this lack of distinction between street gangs and drug gangs:

> Survey respondents were asked to estimate the percentage of youth gangs in their jurisdictions that were drug gangs. A total of 34 percent of all youth gangs nationwide were reported to be drug gangs. Nearly 100 jurisdictions (99) reported that all their youth gangs were drug gangs. More than 300 jurisdictions (343) said that none of their youth gangs were drug gangs. . . . Surprisingly, drug gangs were most prevalent in rural counties, where 38 percent of all youth gangs were said to be drug gangs. . . . Drug gangs were most common in areas with very small populations (less than 10,000), where 40 percent of all gangs were reported to be drug gangs (p. 33).

The concept of a "drug gang" is relatively new and its parameters appear to be quite ambiguous. The lack of clarity on what constitutes a drug gang is understandable when one considers that the very definition of a "gang" is often difficult to pin down. As Howell and Gleason (1999) explained, when police jurisdictions are unclear about what constitutes a drug gang, the statistics become compromised.

> Whether or not respondents included drug gangs in their youth gang definition greatly affected the distribution of responses on gang involvement in sales. Respondents who included drug gangs in their youth gang definition reported a much larger proportion of drug sales involving gang members than did respondents who did not include drug gangs in their definition. In jurisdictions that did not include drug gangs in their definition, two-thirds of the respondents said that as much as 33 percent of their drug sales involved gang members. In contrast, in jurisdictions that included drug gangs, two-thirds of the respondents said that as much as 70 percent of their drug sales involved gang members (Howell and Gleason 1999, 3).

A further complication in accurately assessing the number of gangs involved in drug sales and whether or not a gang is a drug gang is that "not all gang members sell drugs even in gangs where drug selling is common. Drug-selling cliques within gangs are responsible for gang drug sales. These cliques are organized around gang members who have contacts with drug wholesalers or importers" (Fagan 2004, 240).

In sum, it is important to distinguish between gangs that sell drugs primarily for personal benefit—that is, so that they have enough money to party—and those who traffic in drugs to make a profit. The OJJDP (1999) reported that only 42% of the jurisdictions reported gangs that sold drugs for the purpose of generating profits for the gang. In other words, the vast majority of gangs are not drug traffickers.

Drug Trafficking and Drug Distribution

Some gangs *do* engage in **drug trafficking** and **drug distribution**. Drug distribution is generally defined as "the purchase or transfer of large quantities of drugs which are divided into smaller quantities to be sold on the street" (OJJDP 1999). Drug trafficking involves the transport of drugs from one jurisdiction to another. It is not surprising that street gangs have become actively involved in drug trafficking; after all, drug trafficking is the number-one criminal enterprise in the world (followed by weapons trafficking and art theft) according to Interpol (*Parade Magazine* 2003). As far as gang members are concerned, the sale and distribution of drugs is like any other business enterprise. One of the most comprehensive pictures of a street gang involved in drug trafficking was provided by Felix Padilla in *The Gang as an American Enterprise* (1992). In this book, Padilla described the entire evolution of the fictitiously named Diamonds. The Diamonds, a Puerto Rican gang, started off as a musical group that performed in local Chicago nightclubs. In 1971, one of the members was mistaken for a gang member and killed by gunshot fired by a rival gang. The incident sparked the reorganization of the group into a violent criminal youth gang. For six years, the Diamonds were on a course of vengeance and retaliation, often provoking fights with other gangs. Throughout the early years, the Diamonds' involvement with drugs was strictly recreational. By the late 1970s, however, the gang decided that it could make money by selling drugs. The Diamonds set up numerous **puntos** (a number of street-corner marketplaces; translated, *punto* means "points") and took control of their neighborhood by running off the previously established drug dealers. They created a hierarchical structure with the distributors at the top; the thieves were at the low end of the hierarchy. Above the thieves were the runners and then the street dealers, who reported directly to the distributors. As in any business enterprise, members of the Diamonds hoped to climb the ranks, as each level represented more income and respect. As Padilla clearly illustrated, the Diamonds had become a criminal enterprise with a highly entrepreneurial spirit.

Skolnick (1990) concluded that the entrepreneurial gang is the one most likely to be involved in drug trafficking. He argued that black gangsters in Los Angeles had also undergone an evolutionary change, what he called a shift from cultural to entrepreneurial gangs. This change was fueled by the availability of crack cocaine in the 1980s and the quick money the distribution and sale of crack represented to the street gang. Skolnick attributed the very ambition among so many urban youth to join a gang to the perceived opportunities to make money selling drugs. The existing gang, in turn, looked at new recruits in terms of their ability to sell drugs.

Moore (1991) reminds us that adult criminal organizations were involved in drug trafficking before the crack cocaine epidemic of the 1980s. The Office of National Drug Control Policy's (ONDCP's) *Pulse Check* reports describe high-level drug distribution organizations that are not youth gangs. "The typical organizational structure uses franchise operators to control an area and delegates street-level sales to others. Only a few of ONDCP's ethnographers report that cocaine sellers are organized in youth gangs" (Howell and Decker 1999, 4). Nonetheless, there is growing evidence that street gangs are increasingly taking control of both the sale and distribution of drugs. The National Alliance of Gang Investigators Associations (NAGIA 2002, 3) reported that "most gangs have members who are involved in drug trafficking to some extent. However, the level of drug trafficking by gang members varies regionally. . . . Gang involvement in drug trafficking ranges from street-level sales to wholesale distribution. The typical scenario of gang participation in drug trafficking involves the entrepreneurial gang member who shifts a retail drug trafficking operation into an adjoining community or state. This move could be either temporary or long-term." The Black Gangster Disciples, for example, had an organized interstate drug trafficking gang that extended its network to over 40 states. "In 1997, seven leaders of the gang were convicted of a drug conspiracy that the U.S. Attorney alleged took in over $100 million a year in cocaine and heroin sales" (NAGIA 2002, 4). Data provided by numerous law enforcement agencies has led the NAGIA to conclude that some gangs involved in wholesale drug distribution have connections to major international drug-trafficking organizations.

A great number of unusual alliances have occurred due to gang drug trafficking as gangs continue to migrate from city to city. The LA-based Crips and Bloods have established drug markets throughout the California region, the Northwest, and eastward to such states as New York and Connecticut. Lawton, Oklahoma police reported that gangs have migrated from California into their city to set up a narcotics ring. Police report the same thing in Oklahoma City and Wichita Falls, Texas. In some cases, the Bloods and Crips have joined forces to sell drugs in Portland, Oregon, according to police reports. They are overlooking their allegiance to red and blue for green (money). Arlington Heights, Illinois, reported the aligning of the Folk and People gangs with each other to benefit their narcotics trafficking (NAGIA 2002).

The NAGIA (2002, 4) reported that "drug trafficking by gangs primarily involves cocaine and marijuana. However, gangs in California, the upper Midwest, and New England are increasingly involved in heroin trafficking. Methamphetamine trafficking by gangs is common in the western half of the United States and appears to follow the eastward migration of Hispanic gangs. Drug trafficking drives, binds, and reinforces gang culture by the criminal activity itself, as well as providing lucrative profits for the gang and individual gang members." The OJJDP has also reported differences in drug trafficking patterns based on geographic region. According to its *Juvenile Justice Bulletin* (1999), the Northeast had the highest percentage (50%) of youth gangs involved in the street sale of drugs, followed by 45% for the Midwest, 38% for the South, and 30% for the West. These differences were found to be statistically significant. The correlations of geographic location and drug sales included the findings that the percentage of crack cocaine and heroin sales conducted by street gangs was higher in large cities and suburban counties than in small cities and rural counties, and the percentage of street sales by youth gangs of crack cocaine, heroin, and methamphetamine varied substantially by region. Crack cocaine sales involving youth gang members were most prevalent in the Midwest (38%), heroin sales were most prevalent in the Northeast (15%), and methamphetamine sales were most prevalent in the West (21%). There was very little variation between regions for sales of powder cocaine and marijuana (*Juvenile Justice Bulletin* 1999).

Generally speaking, law enforcement agencies reported to the OJJDP that most gangs do not control or manage most of the drug distribution in their jurisdictions. "More than two-thirds of the respondents reported gang control of drug distribution at none to less than half; nearly half (47 percent) of the respondents said that gangs 'control or manage' less than one-fourth of all drug distribution in their localities. In contrast, less than one-third of respondents said gangs controlled more than half of the drug distribution in their jurisdictions" (*Juvenile Justice Bulletin* 1999, 3). Reporting agencies also indicated that female gangs controlled a significantly smaller percentage of the drug markets in their jurisdictions.

VIOLENCE

By design, gangs are violent groups. **Violence** in the gang begins with the initiation process in which new recruits are supposed to demonstrate their willingness to take a beating for the gang. The gang engages in violence with rival gang members, nongang members, law enforcement officers, and often among themselves. Gangs will use violence to protect turf and to acquire turf. And when the turf represents a profitable marketplace (i.e., for selling drugs), the level of violence involved often escalates to murder. The use of violence by youth street gangs to protect their turf is not unique; the use of violence for this purpose by non–street-gang, adult criminal organizations (e.g., the Mafia) is well established, and many "youth" street gangs are dominated by adult members. As Howell and Decker (1999, 4) explained, "The relationship between drugs and violence is widely accepted in adult criminal organizations such as drug cartels and prison gangs; in some instances, however, it is difficult to distinguish these adult criminal organizations from youth gangs." The very concept of a "youth" street gang seems to be disappearing, as most gang members are in for life now, and it is common for gangs to have active members well into their adult lives. Additionally, as described earlier in this chapter, since the advent of crack cocaine, a number of drug gangs have come into existence. A drug gang is as much a criminal organization as the American or Russian Mafia.

Some researchers have concluded that the introduction of crack cocaine to the streets has led to increased levels of violence (Taylor 1989). Fagan (1996) found that the level of violence increased with the sale of crack for a number of reasons: "Violence associated with crack cocaine was linked to organizational competition for market share and profits; protection of drug-trafficking territory; regulation of employees in the new selling organization; the urge among habitual users for money to buy crack; its liquid value among the poor; and, for a small group, its psychoactive effects"

(Howell and Decker 1999, 4). Goldstein (1985) detailed three possible relationships between drugs, drug trafficking, and violent crime:

1. The "pharmacological" effects of the drug on the user can induce violent behavior.

2. The high cost of drug use often impels users to commit "economic compulsive" violent crime to support continued drug use (e.g., robbery for the purpose of securing money to buy drugs).

3. "Systematic" violence is a common feature of the drug-distribution system, including protection or expansion of the drug distribution market share, retaliation against market participants who violate the rules that govern transactions, or maintenance of the drug trafficking organizations (Howell and Decker 1999, 5).

More recent data have shown that Goldstein was correct that gangs would establish systematic drug distribution networks. It should be noted, however, that there is little or no evidence to support the claim that drug use, aside from alcohol and PCP, leads to violence. The opposite would be expected for marijuana users. But the *NDIC National Street Gang Survey Report—1998* revealed that many law enforcement agencies say that drugs contribute to gang violence. The Phoenix Police Department, for one, reported that most of the violent crimes involving gangs are the result of their drug trafficking. The Akron, Ohio, Police Department stated that gangs are heavily tied to the drug trade in their city and that this involvement has led directly to an increase in violence and gang-related shootings (NAGIA 2002). Because of the high cost of illegal recreational drugs, it is clear that the economically poor will often engage in petty crimes to raise enough money to purchase the desired drugs. If most recreational drugs were legalized, street crime and violence should be dramatically reduced.

The violence associated with drug trafficking is primarily directed at law enforcement officers but is not limited to the police. Border Patrol agents on both the Mexican and American sides risk attack by individuals with ties to the Mexican drug cartels. There are reports that drug cartels have offered rewards up to 10 thousand dollars for the home addresses of Border Patrol agents and have also offered bounties on the lives of agents on duty. The U.S. Drug Enforcement Agency estimates that Mexican-based gangs and their connections (usually from Colombia) are responsible for the estimated 770 tons of cocaine, 5.5 to 6.5 tons of heroin, and 7,700 tons of marijuana that enter the United States annually. Once the drugs enter the country, a wide variety of people, including street gangs, become responsible for their distribution.

Gangs are also involved with a great deal of violence unrelated to drugs. They are the cause of much violence in America's schools and streets. It has been established that most gangs develop naturally or spontaneously from friendship groups formed in schools or local neighborhoods. School officials often miss or ignore (gang denial) the early warning signs that gangs are developing in their schools. They may view certain delinquent behaviors committed by students as simply a part of "growing up"; since most students will not become involved in gangs, there is some validity to this idea. At other times, school officials mistakenly label juvenile delinquents as "wannabes" (Thump 1996). As a result, nongang students usually notice the presence of gangs before school officials do. "Once a gang problem has developed, it is usually too late to simply put a stop to it. In many cases, by the time officials begin to recognize the existence of a gang problem within their school and attempt to respond to it, the gangs have already established a foothold of power. Students know long before school officials whether there is a gang presence within their school" (Thompkins 2004, 196). When school officials acknowledge the existence of a gang in their school, they typically create an "us-versus-them" relationship, "which paradoxically, leads to many gangs' gaining a level of credibility and increased power. As real and suspected gang members are singled out and punished for what is determined to be gang behavior, students may come to fear the gangs even more. Moreover, the 'us versus them' relationship has the potential to draw some students to the gangs precisely because they want to be recognized as outsiders, as someone who breaks the rules and challenges authority" (Thompkins 2004, 196). As the gang gains in strength in the school, the environment becomes increasingly violent because the gang is driven by a desire for power and respect. Innocent students become the unwilling victims of the gangs and marginalized students are drawn to the aura of the gang. There have always been bullies in school; gang members have become the new ones.

> As gangs begin to appear on school campuses, they become the bullies, and the level of fear and violence escalates. Gang members commit both individual and group acts of violence, and students know, or at least they believe, that if they retaliate against an act of aggression committed by one gang member, they will have to deal with the entire gang. This can lead to students' suffering increased levels of fear and stress, which not only disrupt their learning process but can also lead to the formation of new gangs. Previously unaffiliated students have been known to come together or "clique up" and form their own gang for protection against other gangs (Thompkins 2004, 197).

Once rival gangs develop within a school, the level of violence escalates even further. Rival gangs fight for space and respect and students who are in school to learn are faced with even bigger challenges in their desire to earn a quality education.

Gangs are also responsible for a great deal of violence on the streets, especially in certain urban neighborhoods. Innocent citizens in these neighborhoods are always at risk of being victimized by gangs. Young males who remain neutral to gangs, for example, may find themselves victims because of misidentification. The greatest risk of violence, however, is to gang members. Just by identifying themselves as gang members makes them a target. Being in a gang increases the probability that one will either be victimized by violence or commit violence to another. As described in Chapter 4, some gang members simply love the idea of violence. They get a rush from inflicting pain on others. Those who were victimized by violence in the home find gang activity a catharsis, a release of pent-up frustration. Many members feed off this adrenaline rush. In short, many gang members are attracted to gang life because of the violence. Studies have consistently shown that, overall, violence is more common among gang adolescents than nongang adolescents.

When gang members confront rivals, violence is nearly inevitable, but there are many reasons for gang violence: invasion of turf, dating rivalries, chance meetings between rival gangs in neutral locations (e.g., a shopping mall), sporting events, and personal issues in which the gang is brought in as reinforcement to back up an individual gang member. The level of violence varies from one gang clique to another and by situation. For traditional gangs, violence is a sign of masculinity or machismo. Getting into a fight is a coming-of-age rite for young boys, especially among the lower socioeconomic classes. "Violence is an important part of the gang experience. It is the motivation for many young people to join their gangs, it is typically part of the initiation, and is ever present in the lives of most gangs" (Curry and Decker 2003, 76). There are a number of ways to categorize the general types of violence committed by gang members. The following classification system comes from Shelden, Tracy, and Brown (2001, 112–113):

1. **Violence Between Members of the Same Gang**—The first act of violence against a member of the same gang begins with the initiation process. It may occur again as part of a violation ceremony when one member disobeys gang rules or shows disrespect toward the gang. Fights between members of the same gang are often quite brutal and more serious than fights with others. This is because any sort of betrayal by one gang member against his or her crew is frustrating and disappointing. After all, gang members expect the worst from their rivals but the best from their homies.

2. **Attacks on Members of Other Gangs**—These occur for a number of reasons, primarily out of fear. "Fear is an important trigger for one gang attacking another. This usually happens in a neutral area (e.g., members of rival gangs happen to be at the same mall, football game, or party)" (p. 113). Another reason for an attack on rivals is personal ambition. "Attacking members of other gangs is used to try to advance within the organization. Yet another reason is to test how strong they and others really are, often to test the reputation of another gang" (p. 113).

3. **Attacks on Residents in Their Own Community**—"This usually involves gang members acting on their own. There are most often two reasons for this: (1) fear of being reported to the police and (2) a threat to one's respect or honor by a resident (e.g., an insult) or by someone going after one's woman or someone trying to restrict the gang member's activities" (p. 113).

4. **Violence Against People Outside Their Community**—This violence occurs because of a threat of some sort or to show off one's fighting skills.

5. **Attacks on Property in the Community**—These are crimes such as arson and spray painting graffiti on buildings and nature (trees, rocks).

6. **Attacks on Property Outside the Community**—These are attacks on the property of people who have refused to do business with them or those who might have disrespected them somehow.

Whether drug-related or not, gang violence is a real presence in many U.S. communities. "As gangs and the gang subculture spread across the country, the gang-related violence that was previously limited to urban areas now reaches into suburban and rural communities. The National Institute of Justice estimates that the financial costs of violent crime to American society are well over $400 billion a year. Adding pain and suffering, as well as the reduced quality of life, the total climbs to $450 billion each year—roughly $1,800 for each man, woman, and child in the country. The figures do not include the cost of running the criminal justice system or private actions taken to cut crime—such as hiring guards or buying security systems" (NAGIA 2002, 4–5). Street gangs and their violence thus represent a high cost to American society, both in terms of money and in quality of life.

HOMICIDE

Homicide represents the epitome of violent crimes. According to former California State Senator Tom Hayden (2004, vii), "over 25,000 young people—nearly all of them African-American and Latino—have been slain in street wars during the past two decades." The number of homicides committed by gang members has increased from decade to decade. Nearly all gang researchers, law enforcement agencies, and gang members themselves attribute the rise of gang homicide to the increased availability and firepower of weapons. The weapons used by gangs in the 1970s were almost archaic compared to the high-powered assault weapons used by gangbangers today. The mere presence of firearms increases the likelihood of murder. "The Uniform Crime Reports indicate that about half of all murders and a third of all robberies involve a firearm. Handguns are the cause of death for two-thirds of all police killed in the line of duty. The presence of firearms in the home has been found to significantly increase the risk of suicide among adolescents, regardless of how carefully the guns were secured or stored" (Siegel 1995, 298). Miller (1992) reported that the routine use of guns in gang conflict began in the early 1980s. "The growing use of firearms in gang assaults is a major contributor to the growth of gang murders. The proportion of all youth gang homicides committed with a firearm has been increasing so that at the present time almost all are the result of firearm use" (Howell 2004, 212).

Gang members have numerous ways to acquire guns, both legally (at a variety of gun shops and on-line) or illegally (they may steal guns from homes or other places) or through any number of street methods. High-powered weapons have dramatically changed the lethality of violence and have become the primary method of settling disputes and challenges to respect and honor (Klein 1995). The use of guns has become so intertwined as a subcultural norm that gang members now assume rivals are packing and therefore feel it necessary to pack a gun as well. Thus, it is fairly common that in any given gang, all will be heavily armed wherever they are, in private or in public. The possession of a gun gives the holder a feeling of power and invincibility— until he runs into someone else who is also "carrying" and who makes the drop on him first. "Skewed conceptions of power and masculinity have developed in these contexts, fueling a violent response to disputes" (Fagan 2004, 237). Recent studies have shown that firearms are prevalent in nearly all youth gangs today, and gang members of any age are capable of blasting away an enemy for something as simple as perceived disrespect. Using data collected from interviews in 1995 with arrested juveniles in the Drug Use Forecasting (DUF) study, Decker and colleagues (1997) found that gang members are much more likely than nongang juveniles to carry guns most or all of the time (31% versus 20%). In addition, percentages of arrestees who reported using a gun to commit a crime were higher among adolescents who sold drugs (42%) or belonged to a gang (50%) than among other juveniles (33%) (Howell and Decker 1999, 6).

Youth gang homicides are characterized by periodic spurts and declines but have been increasing overall nationwide. Evidence indicates that this trend will continue, especially in certain cities (Maxson 1998). The spurts are usually explained by disputes between warring gangs (Block and Block 1993), for gang homicides do not occur throughout a city but are usually confined to specific neighborhoods. Gang battles that lead to homicide generally take place within small, fairly intimate local neighborhoods (Reiner 1992). Most victims of gang homicides are gang members (as opposed to innocent civilians). In fact, some marvel at how accurate gang hits are. Gang members show no remorse and will often stand over their victim. If they have the chance, they will take their victim's flag and maybe rob him of any drugs and money.

A number of characteristics distinguish gang homicides from nongang homicides. Decker and Curry (2003, 76) provide these distinctions:

1. Gang violence is more likely than other crimes of violence to involve firearms, particularly handguns.

2. The victims of gang homicides resemble their killers; that is, the victims of gang homicide are more likely to be in the same race, age, sex, and neighborhood where they live as the people who kill them.

Decker and Curry (2003) also indicate that most gang homicides are not tied to drug trafficking, but are instead motivated by revenge or battles over turf. Klein and Maxson (1989, 223–234) focused on additional characteristics of gang homicides as distinct from nongang homicides:

1. Gang homicide is more likely to occur on the streets (as opposed to most other homicides, which occur inside people's homes).

2. Gang homicide is more likely to involve a gun and less likely to be committed in conjunction with a robbery.

3. Gang-related homicides involve more participants than nongang ones.

4. Gang-related homicides have a much higher rate of youth suspects than nongang homicides.

Gang homicides are also more likely to involve minority males and the use of automobiles and to take place in public places. Gang-related homicide perpetrators and victims are much younger than in nongang-related homicides (Spunt 2002).

It is very difficult to determine the total number of gang homicides for a number of reasons. First, many gang homicides go unreported. Second, some police agencies choose not to respond to surveys on gang homicide. Third, some agencies report a gang homicide only if it is committed in relation to a gang function (e.g., a street battle or drugs). Fourth, some agencies choose not to identify certain crimes as gang-related—for a variety a reasons, including gang denial (OJJDP 2000, 26). In an attempt to gain some statistical knowledge regarding gang homicides, Curry and colleagues analyzed gang homicide data reported in the National Youth Gang Survey during 1996–1998:

> More than one-half (55 percent) of the cities that experienced gang problems in at least 1 year during the 1996–98 period did not report any gang homicides, but almost all (93 percent) of these were cities with populations less than

200,000. Of the cities that experienced gang problems in the 3-year period, nearly one-half (45 percent) reported a gang homicide in at least 1 year. The overwhelming majority of the cities with populations of 25,000 or more that reported gang homicides in the 1996–98 period (88 percent) reported a maximum of 1–10 homicides in any given year of the 3-year period. Ten percent (45 cities) reported a maximum of 11–50 homicides, and 2 percent (8 cities) reported a maximum of more than 50 homicides. Among the 237 cities that reported a gang problem and provided a homicide statistic in all 3 years, 49 percent reported a decrease in gang homicides over the 3-year period, 15 percent stayed the same, and 36 percent reported an increase (OJJDP 2000, 27).

There were an estimated 3,340 gang-related homicides committed in the United States in 1997. Large cities accounted for 64% of the total estimated number of gang homicides (OJJDP). According to the FBI, the national homicide total was 18,210 in 1997; consequently, street gangs were responsible for 18% of all homicides. Chicago has the distinction of being the homicide capital of the United States. According to Hayden (2004, 10), "Chicago remained the country's overall per capita murder capital in 2002, with 658 deaths, up from 646 the year before, the thirty-fifth consecutive year that the toll exceeded 600." As Hayden points out, the percentage of these homicides that are gang-related is hard to determine and he underlines the difficulty of finding accurate statistics on gang homicides: "Police experts sometimes alleged in the media that over half of the city's death toll was related to drug-dealing street gangs, a body count higher than the percentages revealed in their internal data" (Hayden 2004, 10).

Homicide is often accompanied by a number of other crimes. For example, Anthony Copeland, a Buffalo gang member who shot his friend because he suspected him of being an informant for local police, was convicted on the rarely used charge of felony gang assault. He was also convicted of first-degree gang assault, felony assault, conspiracy, and criminal facilitation, but was acquitted of attempted murder (*Buffalo News* 2003).

A specific category of gang homicide, the **drive-by shooting**, involves the use of automobiles. Variations of **drive-bys** can be traced back to the 1920s, the era of Al Capone and other gangsters. These incidents were sporadic, however, and never caught on among all criminals in the decades that followed. Klein (1971) stated that early drive-bys were called *japing*, after the hit-and-run tactics of Japanese soldiers in World War II. (*Japing* is considered a racist term today and would not be used by academic researchers. Bill Parcells, head coach of the Dallas Cowboys, got into trouble when he used the term *Jap plays* in a 2004 press conference to describe the "sneaky" plays he uses in football games.) Miller (1966) referred to mobile attacks as "forays." The victim of a drive-by shooting may be walking the streets, riding in another automobile or bus, or at home (Howell 2004, 210). Most drive-by shootings involve assailants shooting at intended victims from a moving car. However, gang members may also use a different variation of the drive-by. In these cases, the gang will drive to a specific location, find the target, jump out of the car and chase the victim down, shoot the victim, and then escape in a fleeing automobile. Beyond the obvious act of killing an enemy, the drive-by shooting serves as a very powerful act of intimidation to promote fear.

By the 1980s, drive-by shootings had become fairly common in most major urban cities. Drive-by shootings have replaced the idea of a fair fight. The "old-school" gangs always maintained a "fair-fight" mentality; that is, they fought with fists and knives and stopped fighting when a victor was clearly established. Furthermore, they fought face-to-face; anything else would be considered an act of cowardice. They would never utilize a "drive-by shooting" because it violated gang norms that dictated the "honorable" fair fight. The introduction of *mobile gangs* violated this concept. Contemporary gangs do not follow the fair-fight concept—they have a win-at-any-cost mentality—a primitive way of thinking that often has deadly consequences and demonstrates a blatant disregard for human life. Often, when drive-bys are conducted, innocent bystanders—nongang youth, children, and old people—are victimized. Without fair warning, these people have no chance of defending themselves. Contemporary gangs view drive-by shootings as a means toward an end. The shootings serve many purposes:

1. They provide individual members an opportunity to prove themselves.

2. They may be used as part of an initiation rite for a new member.

3. They are a means of resolving arguments.

4. They can be viewed as preemptive attacks to intimidate rival gangs not to try the same thing.

5. They are used to eliminate competition in illegal businesses.

6. They are used to settle turf fights.

7. They are used as a means of retaliation against rivals for a previous attack.

This is not meant to be an exhaustive list, but it does demonstrate that today's gangs view the drive-by shooting as a reasonable way of dealing with rivals. The fact that innocent citizens may be harmed or killed is of little concern.

Economics is correlated with gang homicides. In a study of the staggering number of homicides in Los Angeles, researchers found that employment and per capita income were more closely associated with the city's gang homicide rate than any other variable—including demographic factors (e.g., race), level of education, or the proportion of single-parent family households. "In communities where unemployment ran highest, between 14% and 16%, there were 125 to 175 gang homicides per 100,000 population— about 15 times the killing rate compared to communities where unemployment ran a more modest 4% to 7%. Similarly, gang homicides in the city were almost entirely confined to communities where the per capita incomes were less than $10,000 annually, where the homicide rate ranged from 75 to 175 people per 100,000 population. And in communities where the per capita income was $25,000 or more, the homicide rate was less than 10 per 100,000 residents" (Krikorian 1997, B1). Age is also an important factor in homicides as the highest gang homicide rates were recorded in communities where the population under 20 years of age was a sizable 40%. The lowest murder rates are found in communities where a quarter or less of the population fell below the age of 20.

According to the NAGIA, there is an additional cost of up to $2 million dollars per homicide when four suspects are arrested, a figure determined by adding up trial cost, crime scene investigation, medical treatment, autopsy, and incarceration costs if the four suspects are convicted and serve 20 years. These costs are a burden on taxpayers, and, more importantly, derive from an activity that detracts from the overall quality of American life.

OTHER CRIMINAL ACTIVITIES

Most gang violence is directed toward rival gang members. However, gangs are involved in a great deal of **criminal activity** other than violence and homicide. These criminal acts are generally directed toward nongang members. For example, gang victims of robbery and extortion are almost always nongang members. This introduces an interesting point; whereas gang-against-gang violence is mutually understood and expected by all the participants, gang-versus-nongang assaults include a reluctant participant.

Assault and Battery

Many people believe that the terms **assault and battery** refer to a single act, when actually they are two separate crimes. "*Battery* requires an offensive touching, such as slapping, hitting, or punching a victim. *Assault* requires no actual touching but involves either attempted battery or intentionally frightening the victim by word or deed" (Siegel 1995, 312). Generally these offenses are treated as felonies, especially when the perpetrator uses a weapon or if they occur during the commission of a felony (assaulting a victim during a robbery). Gang members commit a large number of violent acts against nongang members. "Many assaults and fights have involved gang members attacking non-gang members. While most of the cases involve clear instances of gang members initiating the violence, some cases do not involve gang initiation" (Sanders 1994, 116). As a rule, people who are not gang members go to great lengths to avoid contact with gang members. However, there are times when the gang forces itself upon innocent victims and conflict becomes inevitable.

The OJJDP (2000) compiled data on law enforcement responses to youth gang involvement in criminal activity that reveal gang members are responsible for a great number of assaults. Twelve percent of the respondents reported that gangs are responsible for "most/all" assaults, 43% reported that gangs are responsible for "some" of the assaults, 40% said "few," and just 6% reported that gangs are responsible for "none" of the assaults.

Robbery

The common-law definition of the term **robbery** is derived from the FBI: "The taking or attempting to take anything of value from the care, custody or control of a person or persons by force or threat of force or violence and/or by putting the victim in fear" (Siegel 1995, 316). A robbery is a serious crime and a crime of violence because it puts the victim's life in jeopardy. Most robberies occur on the streets as opposed to inside the home. Siegel (1995, 317) created a typology of robberies:

1. Robbery of persons who, as part of their employment, are in charge of money or goods. For gang members, convenience stores and banks represent easy targets for quick cash.

2. Robbery in an open area. These robberies include street offenses, muggings, purse snatching, and other attacks. In urban areas, this type of robbery constitutes

about 60 percent of reported totals. Street robbery is most commonly known as muggings.

3. Robbery on private premises. This type of robbery involves robbing people after breaking into homes. The FBI reports that this type of robbery accounts for about 10 percent of all offenses.

4. Robbery after preliminary association of short duration. This type of robbery comes in the aftermath of chance meeting—in a bar, at a party, or after a sexual encounter.

5. Robbery after previous association of some duration between the victim and offender.

The gangs most likely to commit a "robbery on a private premise" are Asian gangs (see Chapter 6). These crimes are described as "home invasions." The most common type of robbery committed by gang members is known as a "jacking" or mugging. **Jackings** are street robberies against innocent individuals (Sanders 1994). Jackings are generally not planned, but rather are crimes of opportunity. Even so, gang members put themselves in places where such opportunities present themselves. For example, gang members will loiter near ATMs in order to rob people who have just taken cash out of the machine or near bars where they can take advantage of drunken patrons. Convenience store robberies have continued to rise ever since these stores came into existence. The phrase "stop and rob" has become synonymous with convenience stores because of their high incidence of robberies. Gang members are highly visible and draw the attention of store clerks. "Since they are often seen taking goods from stores, they are challenged by the clerk or store owner. When this occurs, they threaten the clerk and transform a petty theft misdemeanor into a felony crime" (Sanders 1994, 115). As someone who once, long ago, worked as a cashier at Los Angeles convenience stores (c-stores or "stop and robs" as we called them even then) during the "graveyard" shift, I realized that the graveyard reference has more than one meaning! During my years in management at Los Angeles c-stores, I learned of many horror stories about cashiers who were brutally victimized by robbers, gang members and nongang members alike. There are few jobs scarier than being a convenience store cashier late at night in certain neighborhoods.

According to the statistics compiled by the OJJDP (2000), gang members are responsible for "most or all" robberies in just 3% of jurisdictions, 30% of the jurisdictions reported that gangs are responsible for "some" of the robberies, 49% reported a "few" robberies, and 19% reported that gangs are responsible for "none" of the robberies in their jurisdictions.

Burglary/Breaking and Entering

In common law, **burglary** used to be defined as "the breaking and entering of a dwelling house of another in the nighttime with the intent to commit a felony within" (Siegel 1995, 342). Because the potential threat to home occupants (even if they were not home at the time of the initial break-in) is so high, most jurisdictions punish burglary as a felony. The legal definition of burglary has changed considerably. Most states have removed the nighttime element from the definition. Furthermore, "it is quite common for states to enact laws creating different degrees of burglary. In this instance, the more serious and heavily punished crimes involve a nighttime forced entry into the home; the least serious involve a daytime entry into a nonresidential structure by an unarmed offender. Several gradations of the offense may be found between these extremes" (Siegel 1995, 343).

Gang members are well equipped to commit this particular crime. Breaking into and entering someone's home, especially while they are home, takes a certain amount of courage. The risks are high and the payoffs are sometimes low. On the other hand, the payoff can be very beneficial from the financial standpoint of the burglar. According to the OJJDP (2000), gang members are responsible for 13% of burglaries in "most/all" jurisdictions, 45% in "some," 36% in a "few," and "none" in just 6% of the jurisdictions. Interestingly, rural jurisdictions reported the highest percentage of gang members who committed "most/all" of the burglaries (21% compared to 11% in large cities).

Larceny/Theft and Motor Vehicle Theft

One of the original English common-law crimes was an act that led to one person taking or using the property of someone else. "At common law, larceny was defined as 'the trespassory taking and carrying away of the personal property of another with intent to steal'" (Siegel 1995, 337). Larceny generally refers to such crimes as shoplifting, passing bad checks, and other acts that do not involve force, threats to a victim, or forcibly breaking into someone's home or place of business. For example, the Latin Kings of Chicago have been involved in counterfeiting documents. In 1998, the U.S. Immigration and Naturalization Service seized nearly 40,000 counterfeit identification documents. Slightly more than half of these documents were green cards. Social Security cards, driver's licenses, birth certificates, travel documents, and identification cards were other items apprehended by law officials (Marx and Puente 1999). Larceny itself is usually divided into two separate subcategories: petit (or petty) larceny and grand larceny. Petty larceny involves small dollar amounts, usually leading to a misdemeanor sentencing; grand larceny involves merchandise of higher dollar value and is considered a felony punishable by prison.

Motor vehicle theft is a common type of larceny offense. However, because of its frequency and seriousness, it is treated as a separate category in the Uniform Crime Reports. According to the FBI, more than 1 million vehicles are stolen in the United States each year—about one every 27 seconds. As a general rule, the more popular (or, in a few cases, the rarer) the vehicle, the more likely it is to be stolen (because there is a lucrative market for replacement parts). In 2000, the most popular-selling car was the Toyota Camry, and, not surprisingly, it ranked number one in the United States as the most stolen. Interestingly, thieves' tastes vary by region. According to the National Crime Insurance Bureau, in Los Angeles and Buffalo, Japanese cars are the most frequent targets, pickup trucks are at the top of the list in Texas, and domestic vehicles lead the list in Detroit (Glynn 2002, B6). Auto theft is attractive to a number of people. Gang members may steal a car to use it in a crime, to sell it on the black market or for parts at "chop shops," for their own personal transportation (for example, to take their girlfriends out on a date or a road trip), or for the simple thrill of stealing a car.

Carjacking is a type of auto theft that involves the armed robber approaching a car and forcing the owner to give up the keys. In many cases, car owners make the mistake of reacting too slowly and end up dead.

According to the OJJDP (2000), gang members are responsible for a great deal of larceny/theft offenses. The percentage of gang members to nongang members (in the "most/all" category) arrested for larceny/theft (17%) is second only to drug sale offenses (27%). Survey respondents in suburban counties reported the highest levels of gang involvement in motor vehicle theft, larceny/theft, and drug sales.

Vandalism

Vandalism involves damaging or defacing property. Recklessly damaging property is called **criminal damage**. As defined by Arizona state law (A.R.S. 13-1602A&B), criminal damage may be defined as a misdemeanor or a felony depending on the amount of damage. Defacing property, which includes the scratching or painting of property (including buildings, furniture, vehicles, cemeteries, signs, and freeway overpasses), is also considered criminal damage. One of the more common forms of vandalism involves the use of graffiti by gang members. In the state of California, vandalism up to $400 may result in up to less than 1 year in county jail and a fine of no more than $5,000. If the amount of damage exceeds $400, the consequences may include time in prison or county jail for no more than 1 year and a fine of $10,000.

Graffiti in the community is often the first sign that gangs are taking over a neighborhood. For gangs (and those who can read the language, including law enforcement and street-smart residents) graffiti is like a newspaper, containing messages about turf boundaries and advertising gang exploits. Some even view their work as "art." Graffiti appears in many forms, but all the same, it's not on the artist's property. The costs of graffiti are immense. Schools, businesses, local governments, and property owners spend millions of dollars each year to clean graffiti, repair buildings, or replace vandalized equipment. Local governments pass the costs on to taxpayers, and businesses pass the costs of vandalism on to customers through higher prices. According to the Metropolitan Transportation Authority, graffiti costs New York City residents $50 million a year (Carter 1999). Graffiti announces gangsters' power in a neighborhood but it is also a major form of disrespect directed toward the local residents. Graffiti lowers property values, heightens fear among residents, and diminishes a community's quality of life.

Graffiti is also used by nongang members. The most common nongang members to utilize graffiti are **taggers**. A tagger does not (necessarily) belong to a gang; instead, he or she enjoys defacing the property of others by "tagging" their "name" (an alias is common) on numerous forms of property. Tagger crews exist. They typically lack the relatively formal organization of gangs, but some carry weapons for protection against rival tagger crews. Regardless of who creates it, graffiti is a scourge against humanity.

Extortion

Gangs may be involved in two types of **extortion**. The first involves schoolchildren. Gang members who are still in school may extort lunch money and articles of clothing from other students in school or other youths outside school. Beyond the monetary benefits of extortion, it also serves the valuable function of instilling fear of the gangs (Sanders 1994). A second type of extortion by gangs is extortion against businesses. In this scenario, gang members demand "protection" money from shop owners. If they refuse to pay for the gang's "insurance," the proprietors risk property and personal harm. Generally, the shop owners who end up paying for this protection are in high-crime areas and realize that they will fall victim to someone; therefore, they don't mind paying one gang protection money because that alleviates their fear of attack from other gangs. Asian gangs often commit extortion crimes against members of their own community.

Rape

Rape has existed throughout human history. Often, it is associated with war.

> In early civilization, rape was a common occurrence. Men staked a claim of ownership on women by forcibly abducting and raping them. This practice led to males' solidification of power and their historical domination of women. . . . During the Middle Ages, it was a common practice for ambitious men to abduct and rape wealthy women in an effort to force them into marriage. The practice of "heiress stealing" illustrates how feudal law gave little thought or protection to women and equated them with property. It was only in the late fifteenth century that forcible sex was outlawed and then only if the victim was of the nobility; peasant women and married women were not considered rape victims until well into the fifteenth century. . . . Throughout recorded history, rape has also been associated with warfare. Soldiers of conquering armies have considered sexual possession of their enemies' women one of the spoils of war . . . [this has been true] from the Crusades to the war in Vietnam" (Siegel 1995, 298).

In common law, rape was defined as "the carnal knowledge of a female forcibly and against her will." It is one of the most loathed crimes of humanity, surpassed, perhaps, only by murder. There is no excuse for this horrible behavior and yet it continues to happen. Most sociologists consider rape to be a violent, coercive act of aggression against individuals as a means of forcible dominance having little or nothing to do with sexual attraction. Although one might think, since any rape is sex with an unwilling person, that all rapes are forcible, the Uniform Crime Reports (UCR) "distinguishes among three categories of rape: (1) forcible rape, (2) statutory rape, and (3) attempted forcible rape. Some jurisdictions draw a distinction between forcible rape with the use of a weapon and forcible rape without the use of weapon. . . . Other types of rapes include spousal rape, gang rape, and homosexual rape" (Schmalleger 2004, 54).

As described in Chapter 7, female gang members are often victimized by rape. In some cases, it is used as a form of initiation, and in other cases, it is used as a method of punishment. Many male gang members treat women as possessions and therefore easily justify their behavior. When rape is committed, a number of other crimes may also occur. For example, in New York City in May 2003, two male gang members who had sex with three 14-year-old girls as part of the girls' initiation into the Crips street gang were eventually arrested for rape and aggravated sexual assault, possessing and creating child pornography, child endangerment, and initiation into a criminal street gang (*New York Post* 2003). Gang members may also rape innocent victims as well. In especially horrific examples, a large number of gang members will attack a female (e.g., a female jogging alone in a park), taunt her, and then take turns raping her. This is known as a **gang wilding**.

Witness Intimidation

Gangs thrive on creating an environment of fear and intimidation. It has been well documented by this point that gangs are very violent and willing to murder their enemies. Apprehending gang members who commit crimes presents a challenge to law enforcement officials. Criminal prosecutors often have trouble convicting gang members because of **witness intimidation.** "President Clinton announced during his weekly radio broadcast on January 11, 1997, 'One of the most difficult problems facing law enforcement is the power of gang members to thwart the criminal justice system by threatening and intimidating the witnesses against them'" (NAGIA 2002, 5). Gang members did not create witness intimidation; it is a problem that has confronted law officials throughout the era of civil law. In a Justice Department survey on gang and drug-related witness intimidation, "192 prosecutors found that intimidation of victims and witnesses was a major problem for 51 percent of prosecutors in large jurisdictions (counties with populations greater than 250,000) and 43 percent of prosecutors in small jurisdictions. An additional 30 percent of prosecutors in large jurisdictions and 25 percent in small jurisdictions considered intimidation a moderately serious problem. Several prosecutors estimated that witness intimidation occurs in up to 75 to 100 percent of the violent crimes committed in some gang-dominated neighborhoods" (NAGIA 2002, 5).

Witness intimidation occurs at many levels. A juror who is glared at by a gang member during court may feel threatened or fear for the lives of loved ones. Outside the courtroom, fellow gang members of the accused may intimidate family members of jurors. Many people fear jury duty when it involves a violent, gang-related crime. An example of gang witness intimidation is the case of Trevis Ragsdale, a Blood member from Brooklyn who was sentenced to 25 years to life for killing a witness less than 48 hours before the victim was to testify against the half-brother of a reputed gang leader. Ragsdale received orders from a local Bloods leader to kill witness Bobby Gibson (*Syracuse Post-Standard* 2004F).

SUMMARY

As we have learned in this chapter (as well as in previous chapters), gang members are involved in a great number of criminal activities. These crimes include drug use, the sale and distribution of drugs, violent assaults, homicide, robbery, burglary and breaking and entering, larceny theft and motor vehicle theft, extortion, forcible rape, and witness intimidation. Although arrest statistics reveal that gang members are not responsible for a majority of crimes in any of these crime categories, they do, however, commit a great number of them. In addition, there are indications that gang members are slowly taking over the drug trade in the United States. Juvenile gang members are far more likely to engage in criminal activities than nongang adolescents, and although most gang activity is directed at rival gang members, a great number of innocent people are also victimized by gangs. For example, targets of gang robberies are typically people who live in gang neighborhoods.

Law enforcement officials have their hands full given the amount of crime committed by street gangs. Legislators are working to create new laws to combat gang crime. But community and national leaders will need to address the many complicated socioeconomic factors that lead to the formation of gangs in the first place. These issues are addressed in Chapter 9.

CHAPTER NINE

Gang Prevention, Suppression, and Treatment

This chapter discusses various intervention techniques designed to fight the power of gangs in society. It is important to remember that there are numerous reasons why individuals decide to join a gang and therefore a variety of efforts to combat gangs must also be utilized. The techniques implemented by various policy makers are determined by their ultimate goal. Prevention efforts are those methods designed to stop youths from joining a gang in the first place. Suppression efforts are attempts by law enforcement and judicial bodies to punish existing gang members. Treatment programs are designed to help rehabilitate gang members so that they can become positive members of society. Considering the fact that the number of gangs and gangbangers continues to escalate, it is fair to conclude that most of these programs have failed miserably. Howell (2004, 318), for one, paints a very bleak picture:

> The history of efforts to solve the youth gang problem in the United States is largely filled with frustration and failure. Early in our nation's history, youth gang work emphasized prevention. These programs were followed by interventions designed to reintegrate particular gangs into conventional society. Then a major shift occurred as programs, led by the police, aimed to suppress youth gangs. Currently, a mixture of approaches is being tried across the nation. . . . None of these approaches has been demonstrated conclusively through rigorous research to be effective. Two factors appear to account for this: the difficulties associated with gang intervention work and the complexity of program evaluation in this area.

A review of gang intervention programs begins with prevention strategies, which are designed to prevent youths from joining a gang.

PREVENTION STRATEGIES

The many reasons why youths choose to join a gang were discussed in Chapters 3 and 4. The goal of prevention strategies is to identify the warning signs that indicate a youth has shown an interest in joining a gang and to combat the many socioeconomic factors that lead to the view that the gang is the most suitable option for economic success. In essence, **prevention strategies** are the various techniques used to steer youths away from the temptations of "turning" to gangs and on the straight path toward "conventional" lifestyles. As Travis Hirschi articulated, youths need to form a social bond to family, community, and society. Providing troubled youths with viable long-term goals is an important ingredient informing a successful bond with society.

A number of programs have been initiated to steer children away from gangs. For example, the Montreal Preventative Treatment Program was designed to "prevent anti-social behavior among boys of low socioeconomic status who displayed disruptive problem behavior in kindergarten" (Howell 2000, 7). Targeting kindergarten-age youths as potential gang members might seem extreme to most readers. The Montreal intervention program provides parent training and childhood skills development, in the hope that antisocial children will be steered away from gangs. Intervention programs are designed to reduce the criminal activities of gangs by coaxing youth away from gangs. Unfortunately, as Malcolm Klein (1995) found, intervention programs some-times backfire. When youths are told to stay away from specific gangs, the attractive-ness of these gangs is enhanced and the solidarity felt among the targeted gangs also increases. Despite the potential pitfalls of prevention programs, "the early history of gang programming in the United States emphasized preventing both gang emergence and joining" (Howell 2004, 317).

Prevention strategies, in general, fall into two categories: community programs and national programs. Discussion begins with a brief review of the history of commu-nity prevention strategies along with a number of examples of community programs.

Community Prevention Programs

The origin of gangs is in local communities—communities that, for the most part, have failed to provide youths with hope for a positive future. The community, then, becomes the cornerstone for the existence of gangs and is the focal point of attempts to prevent youths from joining a gang in the first place. As described throughout this book, factors such as poverty, unemployment, and the absence of meaningful jobs contribute to the presence of urban street gangs. Although it is clear that gangs may form in any social en-vironment (e.g., the suburbs, rural areas, prisons, and Native-American reservations), for the most part it is true that "the traditional image of American youth gangs is character-ized by urban social disorganization and economic marginalization; the housing projects or barrios of Chicago, Los Angeles, and New York are viewed as the stereotypical homes of youth gang members" (Esbensen 2000, 5). Many youths are born into social environ-ments filled with violence and hopelessness. "Further, large numbers of America's youth, especially in public housing and inner city areas, are slipping into a quagmire from which return is extremely difficult" (Pope and Lovell 2004, 355). In short, a number of inner-city youths are "at risk" simply because they were born into certain neighborhoods.

The lives of those nongang citizens who live in neighborhoods dominated by gangs are filled with fear. In addition to the direct costs to victims resulting from vio-lent and property offenses, "the community as a whole" suffers, as all taxpayers pay significant monies for law enforcement, trials and other judicial proceedings, secure confinement, and correctional programs (Thompson and Jason 1988). Thus, all citizens benefit from gang intervention programs directly or indirectly. Gang intervention pro-grams are designed to improve the quality of life for both "at-risk" youths and citizens of affected communities.

The history of gang intervention programs can be traced back to Chicago and the creation of the **Chicago Area Project (CAP)** in 1934 by Clifford Shaw and colleagues. Shaw had endorsed the "social disorganization" approach that was popular with the Chicago School explanation of gang formation (see Chapter 3 for a review of this theoretical perspective). From this perspective, the disorganization found in many of Chicago's communities was explained in terms of the rapidly changing environment. The core poverty areas were plagued by a number of social problems, including poor schools and a lack of social services.

> CAP is representative of a community change approach and is perhaps the most widely known delinquency prevention program in American history. CAP was based on the theoretical perspective of Shaw and McKay and is summarized in their 1942 publication. Its intent was to prevent delinquency, including gang activity, through self-help committees based in preexisting community structures such as church groups and labor unions. Consistent with the research findings of Shaw and McKay, it was believed that the cause of maladaptive behavior was the social environment, not the individual" (Esbensen 2000, 6).

As Howell (2004, 319) further explained, "CAP was designed to involve local community groups, that is, indigenous community organizations, in improving neighborhood conditions that Shaw believed permitted the formation of youth gangs. . . . CAP invented 'detached workers' (agency representatives detached from their offices and assigned to communities). CAP also originated the community gang worker role." It was in the 1940s that CAP introduced its detached worker program, which focused on either at-risk youth (secondary prevention) or, in some instances, current gang members (tertiary intervention). Hundreds of community committees were formed, resulting in numerous local programs that sponsored such activities as recreation, mediation services, advocacy assistance with probation and parole, and school reforms. The CAP program was massive—it extended throughout the city of Chicago, making evaluation difficult. Howell (2004) suggests that the only effective way of measuring the success of such a huge "community" program would be by comparison to another city.

The success of CAP's detached-worker component led to many other community-based programs. In New York City in the late 1940s, for example, community organizations designed to prevent youths from joining gangs relied almost exclusively on detached workers and led to eventual formation of the New York City Youth Board (1960). "Created to combat the city's growing number of fighting gangs, this city-run program relied on detached workers to transform youth gangs from fighting groups into prosocial ones. Most of the transformation was to be accomplished in the streets where gangs met, played, and hung out. Worker activities included securing health care for gang members, providing employment counseling, doing advocacy work with the police and courts, and taking almost any other action that might transform gang values" (Howell 2000, 15). Even though the effectiveness of this program was never evaluated, it served as the forerunner of such later detached-worker programs as the Mid-City Project in Boston.

The Mid-City Project was a community-wide project that consisted of three major program components: community organization, family service, and gang work. Established in the Roxbury section of Boston in 1954, the Mid-City Project staff worked with 400 members of 21 street corner gangs, providing intensive services to 7 gangs. Miller's (1962) rigorous evaluation of the Mid-City Project concluded that the project was ineffective. "All of his measures of delinquency—disapproved actions, illegal behavior, during-project court appearances, before-during-after court appearances, and control group court appearances—provided consistent support for a finding of 'negligible impact'" (Howell 2004, 325).

Although the benefit of a community-involved intervention program as an effective means of combating gangs seemed "obvious," the detached-worker programs appeared to be ineffective across the nation. In Los Angeles, a detached-worker program begun in 1961 with the emergence of African-American gangs in South-Central was designed in such a way that workers were to employ "group guidance" as a means of intervention. Staff members of The Group Guidance Program (of the Los Angeles Probation Department) created such activities as tutoring, individual counseling, and advocacy with community agencies and organizations as means of providing "guidance" to a nongang way of thinking about and dealing with adverse conditions. Klein (1995) found, however, that the number of official arrests actually increased during the period of time that the Guidance Program operated. In the 1960s, he had conducted the Ladino Hills Project, a carefully designed implementation and evaluation of the detached-worker program. Klein found that the detached workers created an unintended outcome: increased gang cohesiveness, which resulted in increased gang crime. "Klein's research focused on detached workers targeting gang members (tertiary prevention), but the overall effectiveness of the CAP model remains in question. . . . To date . . . the evaluations of this strategy have not reported a reduction in gangs or gang activity" (Esbensen 2000, 7). An evaluation of Boston's Mid-City Project had similarly documented that the program failed to reduce delinquency and gang activity.

In the 1970s, The House of Umoja community-based gang program was started in Philadelphia and modeled after CAP. The Umoja Project consisted "of a residential and nonresidential program for gang and other delinquent youths, providing a sanctuary for them from street life while assisting target youths through a comprehensive program that included educational development, career development, employment assistance, and individual counseling. The House of Umoja is a unique grassroots program initiated by community residents" (Howell 2004, 322). The program was often able to negotiate gang summits and truces that were instrumental in reducing the gang homicides in the city during the late 1970s. The truces were generally short-lived.

Beginning in the 1970s, **crisis intervention** was a service commonly provided by detached workers. "Philadelphia's Crisis Intervention Network (CIN), established in 1974, pioneered the assignment of gang workers to work in specific areas rather than with specific gangs. They were to patrol hotspots in radio-dispatched cars, attempting to defuse potentially violent situations" (Howell 2000). The CIN program was never evaluated but CIN officials declared it a success. Gang researchers such as Klein (1995) and Spergel (1995) disagreed. A variation of Philadelphia's CIN program, named the Community Youth Gang Services (CYGS) program, was used in Los Angeles. Like CIN, the CYGS used such suppression tactics as dispatching patrol teams in specially marked cars, social intervention, group programming and outings for gang members, and truce meetings (Klein, 1995). "Preventing gang wars by means of truces is an intervention that has not been systematically evaluated. Reports indicate that some truces have been successful but others have failed" (Howell 2000, 19). During the 1990s, emergency room intervention and victim programs were established in many high-crime communities. Emergency room intervention programs for injured victims may help curtail the cycle of gang violence. Other intervention programs have involved providing counseling for victims of drive-by shootings to reduce the traumatic effects of victimization and to discourage retaliation (Groves et al. 1993; Hutson et al. 1994, 1995).

In most major urban cities there exists a proliferation of programs designed to prevent delinquency and gangs. "Despite the presence of enough agencies, coalitions, partnerships, committees, initiatives, programs and task forces to suck up all the letters of the English alphabet" yet another program was recently started in Syracuse (Case 2002, A8). In the early 2000s, Julius Edwards started the "Syracuse Partnership to Reduce Gun Violence." (By December 2003, Edwards had left the Partnership to become an assistant director at Hillbrook Detention Facility.) The Partnership has eight outreach and case workers and has attempted to involve various churches and local businesses to help with its intervention tactics and goal of reducing gun-related violence. Edwards accused the city of Syracuse of not doing all that it could to help eliminate gang violence at the grassroots level. Edwards was quoted as saying, "What does it say about coordination and cooperation that the city has sold the lot on Cannon Street out from under the grassroots group, Community United to Rebuild Neighborhoods (CURN)? Right when we need a successful small program like that grabbing kids off the street?" (Case 2002, A8). The Partnership became the center of a growing controversy in Syracuse when three staff members were arrested on RICO violations because of their past association with the notorious Boot Camp street gang. Edwards had hired the three men (Antonio Owens, Ridwan Othman, and Cheiron Thomas) after asking the Partnership's steering committee if there was any reason not to employ them. This committee included representatives of the Syracuse Police Department and the Onondaga County district attorney's office. Owens was hired as a peer counselor at an alternative high school for students with behavioral problems and Othman and Thomas as recreation aides at an evening program run by the Boys & Girls Club at Danforth School and the former St. Anthony's School (O'Brien and Sieh 2003). Thus, the actual employer of the three men was the Partnership and not local schools. As it turns out, the police were already investigating the three former Boot Camp members but failed to inform the Partnership. "Edwards said he knew the three men were involved with Boot Camp, but he didn't know they were involved in a major drug enterprise" (O'Brien and Sieh 2003, A23). The Partnership had initially planned on not hiring anyone with a criminal record. However, as community members of the Partnership pointed out, the only way an outreach program would have any success with troubled youths would be by using counselors who had been in trouble and had turned their lives around. Former gang members have street credibility and the respect of at-risk youths, which are critical assets for counselors who hope to reach these youths. Therefore, banning former gang members (as some Syracuse citizens had demanded) is not advisable. The most successful counselors are those who have experienced firsthand the troubles these youths face. An extensive background check should be conducted, however, to ensure that they are no longer actively involved in gang or criminal activities (including outstanding warrants, etc.).

Thus, the overall effectiveness of the detached-worker approach to community intervention is mixed at best, and unsuccessful in most cases. Community-based programs alone do not appear to be the solution in turning at-risk youths away from gangs. Because the reasons that gang members join a gang are complicated, such a "simple" approach to gang intervention as detached-worker strategies and other community-based programs cannot succeed because they merely address the symptoms of the problem. Most gang researchers today agree with Spergel's (1995) idea that "a detached worker strategy by itself is inadequate to deal with the complex problems such as remedial education, job preparation and development, and community issues" (Howell 2004, 326). Detached-worker programs should include other forms of intervention as well, such as temporary shelters for low-income youths, mentoring programs, activity centers, postsentencing social services, drug treatment programs, and intergang mediations (Spergel and Curry 1990; Howell 2004, 326).

The OJJDP officially promotes the Spergel Comprehensive Gang Model as a means of responding to the threat of gangs. This model consists of five strategies:

1. Mobilizing community leaders and residents to plan, strengthen, or create new opportunities or linkages to existing organizations for gang-involved or at-risk youth.

2. Using outreach workers to engage gang-involved youth.

3. Providing or facilitating access to academic, economic, and social opportunities.

4. Conducting gang suppression activities and holding gang-involved youth accountable.

5. Facilitating organizational change and development to help community agencies better address gang problems through a team "problem-solving" approach that is consistent with the philosophy of community-oriented policing (Burch and Kane 1999; Howell 2000).

Community interventions, then, must include other aspects of the community, such as the family, schools, and local businesses (as well as the police and suppression intervention efforts to be discussed later in this chapter).

Families, Schools, and Local Business

The role and influence of the family in gang life has been discussed throughout this book. Clearly, all individuals are ultimately responsible for their own behaviors, but in many cases the options available are so limited that joining a gang seems like the best option. But before society can be blamed for "disappointing" the individual, the family must be held responsible for failing to keep the youth out of the gang. The first line of defense in fighting against youths joining a gang, then, is the family. Many community organizations such as preschool/Head Start programs and parent training/support programs have been designed to assist parents with at-risk youths. Most troubled youths have problems at school and most gang members are high school dropouts and so families with school-aged children can find assistance from programs that generally come under the collective umbrella of **compensatory education**.

"Compensatory education programs are designed to encourage the development of healthy study habits and appreciation for learning—usually at an early age in a pre-school setting such as the Head Start program" (Farley 1998, 339).

Although evaluations of the effectiveness of compensatory education programs are mixed, reviews of the **Head Start** program are very positive. "In general, children who receive compensatory education score higher on IQ and achievement tests, are less likely to be placed in special education classes or to fail a grade, have better achievement self-images, and get more encouragement from their parents to get a good education than similar children who have not received compensatory education" (Farley 1998, 339). Unfortunately, not nearly as many children who qualify for Head Start programs have been enrolled by their parents/guardians. Additionally, in many communities the demand for Head Start programs by needy families is unmet because of a lack of federal funding. It has been my experience, from interviewing at-risk youths and young adults in Buffalo, that the Head Start program there is highly respected and has served as an effective gang prevention mechanism, even though it is not such a program, but an example of compensatory education, which is designed to help all needy children.

School-based intervention is a very important factor in the war against gangs. The days of student-related problems being confined to the occasional playground fight or someone playing hooky are long gone. "Today, we are seeing the problems of crime, violence, gangs, guns and drugs spilling over from the streets into our schools. These criminal activities are not exclusive to the inner city schools. They are occurring in rural and suburban areas as well" (Illinois State Police 2002). The schools, especially public ones, can spearhead efforts to prevent youngsters from "turning" to gangs. Among the school-based intervention programs that are available are social skills training programs, law-related education, classroom management programs that focus on ways of strengthening the bond between teachers and students, alternative schools, cooperative learning programs, and antidrug education programs. The need for schools and families to work together to intervene between youths and gangs is fundamental. The very success of any school program is contingent on reinforcement from the family. But if it is the family that is the cause of the youth's delinquency, effective social programs may identify and correct this problem. Program advocates (teachers and other professionals) in school-based programs can work with youths and family members to improve communication and educate them in an attempt to deter youths from gangs and other deviant pursuits.

By middle school, many at-risk youths have been clearly identified by school teachers and administrators. Many educational problems become quite evident by middle school as well. Some children inevitably begin to struggle with classwork. They may have trouble understanding the material (as a result of a non- or misdiagnosed learning disability), lack family support in reviewing the school material at home, or have ineffective teachers or teaching methods. Many of these students are held back because of their poor academic grades, which lowers their self-esteem. Of course, the much more harmful option (than failing a student) is passing a student who has not met the course requirements—this is known as "social promotion." Social promotion serves no redeeming purpose in education. Youths who struggle at the lower level will most assuredly struggle and fail at a higher level because they are not prepared to handle the progressively more difficult course material. If they are passed along then, too, the problem will only continue. As a result, the socially promoted child will suffer an even greater blow to self esteem and self-image. The disgruntled student will seek solace outside the school. For some, the gang becomes a welcoming social group, as gang members warmly accept another convert. It is also not acceptable for administrators, in hopes of keeping academically marginal students in school, to resort to policies that force teachers to "dumb down" the curriculum just because a few students cannot handle the material. By doing so, they are cheating the rest of the students out of their right to a quality education. It is up to school officials to find a course curriculum that is right for students who do poorly in school, for whatever reason (e.g., vocational training, skills improvement programs). Once youths become school dropouts, their chances of finding a quality job disappear, further dooming them to lives that potentially involve deviance, criminality, and gang membership.

Because the vast majority of American youths attend public schools, it has become very common in recent years for the schools to lead the way in gang prevention programs. "The average middle school provides 14 different violence, drug, and other social problem prevention programs (Esbensen 2000, 7). Among the most effective and recognized gang-specific prevention programs is **Gang Resistance Education and Training (G.R.E.A.T.).** G.R.E.A.T. was first introduced by the Phoenix Police Department in 1991. Its purpose was to provide students with real tools to resist the lure and trap of gangs (Esbensen 2000, 7) and it was modeled after the Drug Abuse Resistance Education (DARE) program. The G.R.E.A.T. program, a school-based intervention gang program, is designed to prevent youth crime, violence, and gang involvement, while developing a positive relationship among law enforcement officers, families, and youths. The slogan of this antigang program sums up its intended goal: "No Violence is G.R.E.A.T." Uniformed law enforcement officers provide a wide range of structured, community-based activities and classroom instruction for school-aged children.

They teach a 9-week curriculum to middle school students concerning conflict resolution skills, cultural sensitivity, and the negative aspects of gang life. Each of the weekly sessions addresses a specific theme:

1. Introduction—The students become acquainted with the G.R.E.A.T. program and the presenting officer.

2. Crime Victims and Their Rights—Students learn about crimes, their victims, and their impact on the school and neighborhood.

3. Cultural Sensitivity and Prejudice—Students are taught how cultural differences affect their school and neighborhood.

4. and 5. Conflict Resolutions (two lessons)—Students learn how to create an atmosphere of understanding that would enable all parties to better address interpersonal problems and work together on solutions.

6. Meeting Basic Needs—This lesson involves teaching students how to satisfy their basic social needs without joining a gang.

7. Drug Neighborhoods—Students are taught how drugs affect their school and neighborhood.

8. Responsibility—Students learn about the diverse responsibilities of people in their school and neighborhood.

9. Goal Setting—This lesson involves teaching students the need for personal goal setting and how to establish short- and long-term goals (Howell 2004, 323).

"As evidenced by the curriculum, the intent of the G.R.E.A.T. program is to provide life skills that empower adolescents with the ability to resist peer pressure to join gangs. The strategy is a cognitive approach that seeks to produce a change in attitude and behavior through instruction, discussion, and role-playing. Another notable feature of the program is its target population. In contrast, to suppression and intervention programs, which are directed at youth who already are gang members, G.R.E.A.T. is intended for all youth" (Esbensen 2000, 7). After students complete the program they are acknowledged in a graduation ceremony. According to Esbensen (2000) two evaluations of the G.R.E.A.T. program have shown small but positive effects on students' attitudes and their ability to resist peer pressure to join a gang. In one evaluation, Esbensen and Osgood (1997) found that "students who completed the G.R.E.A.T. program reported lower levels of gang affiliation and self-reported delinquency, including drug use, minor offending, property crimes, and crimes against the person" (Howell 2004, 324). The G.R.E.A.T. program is so highly regarded that it has been adopted in all 50 states and several countries.

Another school-based prevention program of note is **Broader Urban Involvement and Leadership Development (BUILD)**. The prevention component of BUILD consists of a gang prevention curriculum and an afterschool program. Students selected for this program attend 12 sessions of instruction over a 12-week period and are taught about gang violence, substance abuse, gang recruitment strategies, and consequences of gang membership. "Most classroom sessions were led by project staff; others were led by a prosecuting attorney and by ethnic minority guest speakers who held various positions in the community. The curriculum was taught to eighth-grade students in Chicago middle schools located in lower- and lower-middle-class areas with high levels of gang activity. Following the completion of the curriculum component, youths from the classrooms considered to be at high risk for joining a gang were invited to participate in an afterschool program" (Howell 2004, 322). The afterschool program provides recreational activities, job-skills training workshops, educational assistance programs, and social activities. Rigorous evaluation (Thompson and Jason 1988) of this program has shown it to have promise in keeping targeted youths out of gangs.

In response to the increasing incidence of gang violence in Illinois schools, the Illinois State Police have developed a school-based gang prevention program called **Violence Education & Gang Awareness (VEGA)**. "VEGA was designed to meet the needs of all communities regardless of the level of school violence and gang involvement. VEGA's goals are to stress the importance of resolving conflicts without the use of violence, and to provide young people with a better understanding of the consequences they face when joining gangs and participating in acts of violence" (Illinois State Police 2002). The program is taught to fifth- and sixth-graders and is meant to complement any existing gang prevention program taught in individual school districts. The program curriculum consists of police officers teaching five lessons over five consecutive weeks emphasizing cooperative learning strategies. The lessons deal in a straightforward manner with the tough situations youths are experiencing. The five VEGA lessons are the following:

1. Gangs are a Matter of Choice—This lesson helps to teach children the basic facts about gangs and the destructive consequences of gang membership.

2. Violence and its Victims—This lesson helps the students discover what causes conflict and why violence is not a constructive solution. This lesson emphasizes that gang life is not glamorous.

3. The Circle of Violence—The third VEGA lesson continues to investigate the sources of violence and conflict by discussing how different ideas and feelings cause people to disagree. This lesson emphasizes how violence not only fails to solve conflicts with others, it actually escalates the problem.

4. Peacemakers, Not Peacebreakers—This lesson focuses on problem-solving skills and pro-social skills which can help people evaluate the risks involved in a situation. Students are taught how to apply these skills in order to resolve conflicts.

5. Thinking Ahead—A Look at Tomorrow—The fifth VEGA lesson helps students to understand and be empathetic to the effect people have on one another. Children learn to take the perspective of others (Illinois State Police 2002).

The police invite parents and community members to become actively involved in the VEGA program. Students and attendees are asked to share their ideas on how to combat gangs and these ideas are then discussed in an open environment.

There are numerous other school-related gang prevention programs, for example, the **School Development Program** in New Haven, Connecticut, which is based on parental involvement and multidisciplinary mental health teams to aid staff in managing student behavior problems, and **Project CARE** in Baltimore, Maryland, which involves a team approach to classroom management techniques and cooperative learning (Shelden et al. 2001, 217–218). The LAPD developed the **Jeopardy** program for boys and girls ages 8 through 17 and their parents. Jeopardy combines the influence of the community, neighborhood schools, and the police department to effect positive, lifelong attitudinal changes in youths to have a positive impact on the community.

Time and space do not allow for a review of all the worthwhile school-based programs designed to keep youths out of gangs. Furthermore, since nearly all community-based prevention programs involve **local businesses** in their efforts to prevent youths from joining a gang—due to the simple fact that many youths choose to join a gang for economic reasons—time and space limitations makes it equally impossible to provide any sort of comprehensive review of all the programs that involve businesses. It can be said that there are businesses that "give back" to the community in nearly all cities across the United States. But how effective are the contributions from local businesses in keeping at-risk youths out of the gang? The initial involvement of businesses is met with much fanfare, including press releases, photo ops, and praise from local politicians and media. But what happens when the initial funding disappears? Do local businesses continue to contribute? We don't really know because comprehensive evaluation programs are nonexistent.

To provide one example of a program sponsored by local businesses, the **Syracuse Choice** program is discussed here. Local businesses raised nearly a quarter-million dollars ($230,000) to start Syracuse Choice. The program is responsible for hiring "youth advocates" to provide one-on-one attention to at-risk youths, even on weekends and days off. Advocates help pupils with homework and school projects. "While the program works with city school district students, Contact Community Services administers most of the money for the program. Workers, which Syracuse Choice officials call youth advocates, are paid about $21,000 a year" (Perez 2004, B8). Even at this low salary, the original funding ended after just one year (on August 31, 2004), jeopardizing the whole program. "The reason behind local businesses contributing money to Syracuse Choice was in direct reaction to the violence that has gripped Syracuse in the past few years. Those leaders wanted to help at-risk youths before their behavior turned violent, landed them in trouble with the law and made Syracuse a tougher place to do business" (Perez 2004, B8). Helping at-risk youths, then, indirectly helps business. But if funding disappears, the hopes and dreams of many youths disappear with it.

Most reviews of the role of business in gang prevention center around the job-training programs they provide, trainee positions for at-risk youths, and computers and other material goods that they give to local schools and youth centers. However, many businesses have taken a proactive approach in their fight to prevent gang behavior, and, more specifically, to prevent their becoming victims of gang-related crimes. They have advocated for the use of **curfews**. It may seem odd to think of curfews as a form of gang prevention, but in many ways that is appropriate. In many cases, preventing gang behavior is simply a matter of preventing an opportunity and location for gang members to congregate. Among the most common places for juvenile delinquents to hang out (as gang members generally do) are shopping malls. In large cities like Los Angeles, it is fairly common for rival gang members to go to battle after a chance meeting at a mall. Shopping malls are an easily accessible geographic location for gang members and other delinquents to meet. As a result, all across the United States, shopping malls have instituted various forms of curfew in an attempt to cut down on juvenile delinquency in general and gang activity specifically. At Syracuse's famous Carousel Center mall, a policy was enacted in the summer of 2003 requiring that anyone younger than 18 be accompanied by a parent or guardian who is at least 21 after 4 P.M. on Fridays and Saturdays. (The age-restriction policy is known by its slogan "MB-18"—must be 18 years old.) Merchants report a significant difference in mall clientele on weekends. Before the curfew, the mall had been dominated by teenagers walking through (not shopping) hooting and hollering (Kulkus 2003). The policy has been so successful adult shoppers would like to see it extended to every evening. Frustrated youths seek out other malls that have yet to implement this crime prevention technique. The Carousel Center was certainly not the first mall to install a curfew designed to prevent juvenile delinquency and gang behavior. Buffalo's Walden Galleria instituted a curfew policy in September 2002 that requires youths 17 and under to be accompanied by a parent or adult 21 years or older after 4 P.M. on Fridays and Saturdays. A large number of gangs had been loitering in the mall, prompting business merchants to institute the curfew. "The policy has been devised in response to continual incidents where teens have been pushing and shoving shoppers, using foul language and creating an overall intimidating atmosphere in the mall" (Pendolino 2002, 2). Customers and merchants agreed that measures needed to be taken to curtail the gang activity in the mall, but both expressed a desire that nongang youths should be allowed in the Galleria unescorted. The McKinley Mall in Hamburg (a Buffalo suburb) instituted such a policy in 1991 but had since dropped it. Buffalo's Main Place Mall has had in effect since 1998 a ban on unescorted youths 18 or younger on weekdays from 8 A.M. to 4 P.M. (Pendolino 2002). Youths, of course, are upset with such policies, claiming that they have no place else to go. Business owners, obviously, do not view their stores as recreational facilities for youths looking for trouble.

National/Broad-Based Prevention Strategies

More and more, community-based intervention strategies have turned to the federal government for assistance, especially when local programs involve drug prevention and education. Drug treatment programs are almost entirely dependent upon federal financial assistance. The poor families from which at-risk youths primarily come are generally incapable of providing adequate health and mental health coverage for their children, and local social services are generally ill-prepared to take on such a financial responsibility. Gang members are also often victims of, or witnesses to, domestic violence and abuse. Local communities often rely on the federal government for assistance in providing shelters and counseling. For any community, providing jobs is the most important task, but finding jobs for underskilled, at-risk, and former gang members is extremely difficult. Many reformers have called for an increase in the minimum wage to make lower-paying jobs more attractive. In general, there needs to be a federal job creation program designed to keep people employed and, thus, positive contributors to society. The federal government also needs to be involved because many gangs have ties outside of the immediate community and some have a national allegiance (e.g., Crips and Bloods), which implies that multiple police agencies need to be involved when dealing with local gangs.

An example of a national program designed to address the issue of family violence as a contributor to gang involvement is the National Center for Neighborhood Enterprise (NCNE) and its development of **Violence-Free Zones**. Conceptually similar to "drug-free school zones" (which involve increased penalties for drug violations within a certain distance from a school), Violence-Free Zones represent grassroots community intervention through federal assistance. Specifically,

> The Violence-Free Zone model is based on the premise that the breakdown of the family structure is a key risk factor for gang involvement and a major contributor to destructive behavior. In many cases, gang members come from fatherless homes in which mothers struggle to meet the economic and individual needs of their children. Consequently, they find it difficult to provide the necessary guidance. Violence-Free Zone implementers fill this void, taking on the role of mentor and engaging in reparenting. Job training and work opportunities also are provided for youth's social, personal, and economic development to help them make the transition from gang life and criminality to violence-free lives and productive citizenship" (Howell 2000, 17).

Youths who have successfully gone through the program often assist other youths in other communities to expand Violence-Free Zones.

The gang world is increasingly becoming a drug world, as we have seen. Historically, gang members have used drugs recreationally, but, as illustrated in Chapter 8, gangs have become increasingly involved in drug trafficking and distribution. Many federal programs have attempted to prevent youths from taking drugs, one of them being **Operation Weed and Seed**. "Operation Weed and Seed has involved a multidimensional strategy with a primary emphasis on addressing the problems of gangs, drugs, violence, crime and community recovery from drug problems and violent gang activity. The thrust of the overall strategy was based upon an awareness that in various communities a coordinated comprehensive approach was needed" (Pope and Lovell 2004, 356). This program attempted to integrate governmental and private organizations' efforts to reduce criminal activity (the "weed" part) and stimulate community recovery (the "seed" part). As explained by Pope and Lovell (2004, 356–357), the Weed and Seed program includes four strategies:

1. Suppression—enforcement, adjudication, prosecution, and supervision of those who account for a disproportionate percentage of criminal activity.

2. Community-oriented policing—providing a "bridge" between law enforcement activities and neighborhood reclamation and revitalization activities.

3. Prevention, intervention, and treatment—focusing on youth services, school programs, community and social programs, and support groups.

4. Neighborhood reclamation and revitalization—focusing on economic development activities designed to assist legitimate community institutions.

Operation Weed and Seed provided the resources for local communities in designated areas to help eliminate gang activity and reduce the number of at-risk youths who turn to gangs.

Perhaps the most well-known national gang prevention program is the **Boys and Girls Clubs of America (BGCA)**. The BGCA was officially founded in 1906 and is a national network of affiliated clubs that assists about 2.2 million boys and girls. "Of the approximate 1,700 clubs across the country, 270 are in public housing areas. The clubs have also extended their outreach efforts to military families and Indian reservations. Its national headquarters is located in Atlanta with regional service centers in New York, Chicago, Dallas, Los Angeles, and Atlanta (Trojanowicz et al. 2001, 258). The BGCA works cooperatively with other existing programs. For example, it was an ideal partner to Weed and Seed efforts. The Boys and Girls Clubs "typically provide recreational programming for youth as well as other services such as tutorial programs; field trips; craft programs; mentoring positive enhancements, such as SMART MOVES (a programming strategy which provides focused group discussion tailored to teens concerning such topics as drug use, sexual relations, and other matters); and the like" (Pope and Lovell 2004, 357). The BGCA aggressively attempts to reach with its programs at-risk youths as well as those currently involved in gangs. It performs a needs assessment on all referrals (youths who were referred to BGCA by school officials, parents, police, probation officers, and others) to determine what program is best suited for specific youths. For example, the **Gang Prevention Through Targeted Outreach** program is directed toward youth who are at risk of becoming involved with gangs. The program provides structured recreational, educational, and life skills activities geared toward enhancing the communication skills, problem-solving techniques, and decision-making abilities of at-risk youths, seeking to alter their attitudes and perceptions while at the same time improving their conflict-resolution skills (Esbensen 2000, 8).

An overriding mission of Boys and Girls Clubs is to serve youth from disadvantaged backgrounds. It attempts to build the self-esteem of youths, while instilling honest values and a desire to pursue productive futures. To achieve these goals, the clubs provide the following resources:

- A safe haven away from the negative influences of the street.
- Guidance, discipline, and values modeling from caring adult leaders.
- Constructive youth development activities and programs in supervised supportive environments.
- Access to comprehensive, coordinated services that meet the complex needs of youth at risk.
- Educational support, increased awareness of career options, and goal-setting skills.
- A comprehensive violence prevention initiative.
- A future vision of life beyond public housing (Trojanowicz et al. 2001, 259).

Essentially, the BGCA is designed to prevent youths from joining a gang by providing alternatives to gang life, especially through education and employment. The BGCA also provides life-skills development and works to establish truces among rival gangs and to reduce the incidence of gang violence. The BGCA has been very successful in providing young people jobs as outreach workers in a variety of programs. Evaluation of the Boys and Girls Clubs of America has led to positive conclusions. Pope and Lovell conducted an extensive study and analysis of 33 Boys and Girls Clubs from April 1991 to February 1992. "The overall conclusion of this evaluation effort was that the youth gang prevention and early intervention initiative of the Boys and Girls Clubs of America was both sound and viable in its approach. The neighborhoods and communities where many of the 1,450 Clubs are located, as well as the nature of the Clubs' programming, place them in position to serve the needs of youth at risk of gang involvement. . . . The level of attendance and involvement served as a clear indicator of the ability of Clubs to provide viable programming and activities which attract at-risk youth, bring them into the Clubs, and maintain their interest and participation in regular Club programming" (Pope and Lovell 2004, 366).

Padilla (1992) described the impact of the Boys and Girls Clubs of Chicago on the "Diamonds." The Chicago programs began in 1948 to serve the youth and families of "Suburbia" and were geared toward improving the academic backgrounds and needs of Latino youth. It was hoped that once these disadvantaged youth sustained an interest in academics, they would also show an interest in nonacademic programs. In the early 1980s, the Boys and Girls Club established an alternative high school program, which was modeled after the NYS Alternative High School. The program was built around one teacher who was responsible for teaching most of the subjects in the curriculum and coordinating participation by assistant teachers from the students' traditional home schools. The students who attended the alternative school were those who could not make it in regular high school, whether it was because of general delinquency, gang activity, or poor grades.

SUPPRESSION STRATEGIES

The dramatic increase in the shear numbers of gangs and gang-related crimes has led to numerous suppression strategies in the war against gangs. Many prevention/intervention programs have failed miserably in their attempt to curb gang violence and most of the programs that do work take an extended period of time to be effective. Meanwhile, many innocent (along with not-so-innocent) citizens fall victim to gang violence. Alarmed community members and concerned politicians have sought a more immediate intervention strategy in the form of various **suppression strategies**. "Intervention and suppression programs share the common goal of reducing criminal activities of gangs. Suppression programs use the full force of the law, generally through a combination of police prosecution and incarceration, to deter the criminal activities of entire gangs, dissolve them, and remove individual gang members from them by means of prosecution and incarceration" (Howell 2000, 21). Suppression strategies generally come in two forms: law enforcement responses and judicial/legislative responses.

Law Enforcement Suppression

The primary tactic employed against youth gangs is **suppression**. The dramatic increase in the number of gangs in the past two decades has led to the reality throughout the nation of local police battling with gangs on a daily basis. In a national survey (in 1988) of youth gang programs, Spergel and Curry (1993) found that suppression techniques were the most common strategy employed by police (Webb and Katz 2003). "Police gang suppression strategies involve a variety of activities. According to a Bureau of Justice Assistance report on urban street gang enforcement, the key elements in police gang suppression involve understanding the nature and scope of the community gang problem, gathering information and intelligence into a comprehensive database, and developing strategies that will ultimately incapacitate gang leaders and the most violent and criminally involved members and associates" (Regoli and Hewitt 2003, 321).

William Sanders (1994) described police suppression efforts against gangs in terms of *proactive strategies* and *reactive strategies*. **Proactive strategies** entail intelligence gathering. Investigators attempt to document gang members, make contacts with them, learn their names, identify gang tattoos and graffiti, and cultivate informants. Gathering this information allows the police an opportunity to prevent illegal gang activities and to catch those involved in such activities (Sanders 1994). A typical fact-gathering strategy employed by police is to go to a place where several gang members are known to hang out, search them for weapons and/or drugs, and if illegal weapons or drugs are found, make an arrest. If no arrests can be made, the police attempt to gather information about the gang and its activities through interrogation.

Reactive strategies involve the everyday interaction between the police and gang members who are actively committing a crime. The efficient flow of information from a caller reporting a crime to a police dispatcher to a police officer is critical in the reactive fight against gang crime. At other times, the police come across crimes in progress and pursue the perpetrators on foot or via a car chase. Unfortunately, as the foot soldiers in the battle against gang crime, the police are blamed for social injustices that they did not create and held accountable for labeling citizens as criminals. Social critics view the police as oppressors who protect the privileged at the expense of the poor, disadvantaged, and politically disenfranchised. The police view themselves as practical crime fighters caught in a web of political intrigue (Sanders 1994, 178). As important as proactive policing is, the fact remains that most police work is reactive. "Overall, most of the work the police do is reactive in that their options are limited unless the gangs act criminally" (Sanders 1994, 179). The reactive strategies are the ones that interest the media and the public's curiosity, whereas information gathering isn't likely to excite people. As Webb and Katz (2003, 27) explained:

> Suppression and enforcement gang unit activities are those likely to capture the imagination of the public and the media as well as the police officers looking for action on the streets. Whereas the intelligence function and the sharing of information gives value to gang unit activities and legitimizes the existence of the unit from the perspective of many departmental stakeholders, it is suppression/enforcement that legitimizes the unit in the eyes of the public and the media, and gives them confidence that the unit is actively engaging in enforcement efforts directed at gangs and gang crime.

There are a variety of law enforcement suppression techniques, but one of the most common ones is the neighborhood "sweep." A **sweep** involves a large number of officers who enter (sweep) a specified area (generally a specific neighborhood, house, or building), arresting and detaining known or suspected gang members. Successful sweeps are hyped by the media, which, in turn, makes a large number of citizens and politicians feel better about themselves. A sweep is evidence that something is "being done" about the gang problem. Another suppression tactic involves "hot-spot targeting" of known gang members and their hideouts. "Police select certain gangs for intensive or saturated surveillance and harassment in an effort to apply pressure and send a message of deterrence" (Regoli and Hewitt 2003, 321–322). Klein (1995) identified some other police suppression tactics:

- Saturation—to cover an area with police
- Special surveillance—using modern technology
- Zero tolerance—police do not give out warnings, arrests are made for even minor offenses that would otherwise be ignored
- Caravanning—cruising neighborhoods in a caravan of patrol cars (Howell 2000, 22).

Typically, police patrol certain known gang areas (e.g., minority public housing districts with high crime rates, parks, specific parking lots) where gang members are likely to be hanging out (Webb and Katz 2003). Simply patrolling an area allows the police an opportunity to gather information, intervene against visible criminal activity, and make their presence know to the gangs. Police can also crack down on youth gangs and other violence by setting up roadblocks and questioning people who act in a suspicious way. Syracuse police have utilized this tactic through **the Gang and Violent Crime Task Force**, which has marked and unmarked cars policing high-crime areas of the city. According to Deputy Police Chief Gary Miguel, the task force is comprised of 27 police officers and detectives and has its own roll call each day (Weibezahl 2002). The task force targets the city's South Side because that is where the greatest number of gang-related problems occur. The task force is an example of a trend in law enforcement suppression efforts over the past decade or so—the majority of police departments have created specialized units to focus specifically on gangs and the crimes that they commit. "Results of the 1995 National Youth Gang Survey indicated that 64 percent of police departments and 50 percent of sheriff's departments had some type of specialized unit to address the gang problem" (1997 National Youth Gang Survey 1999). The data from this survey also revealed that large cities were the most likely (77%) to have a specialized gang response unit, and rural counties were the least likely (34%). Data provided by the Bureau of Justice Statistics (1999) revealed "that among large agencies with 100 or more sworn officers, special gang units existed in 56 percent of all municipal police departments, 50 percent of all sheriffs' departments, 43 percent of all county police agencies, and 20 percent of all state law enforcement agencies. . . . These findings lead to an estimate of approximately 360 police gang units in the country" (Webb and Katz 2003, 21). Eighty-five percent of these gang units were formed in the past 10 years (Katz, Maguire, and Roncek 2000).

Gang units depend on intelligence information. "Both police officials and researchers have identified intelligence gathering and the development and maintenance of gang tracking systems and databases as one of the most important functions carried out by specialized gang units" (Webb and Katz 2003, 26). However, it should also be noted that "although nearly every gang unit engages in some form of intelligence gathering, the importance of this function to the gang unit and to its respective department varies from one department to the next" (Webb and Katz 2003, 26). The intelligence function of the gang unit merely allows it the opportunity to perform its primary function—suppression and enforcement. Making arrests and confiscating illegal contraband is the best way for a gang unit to "quantify" and "justify" its existence (to politicians and taxpayers). The various law enforcement agencies all have their own criteria for determining who gets added to a gang database and/or tracking system. The Los Angeles Sheriff's Department instructs its officers to enter a name in the gang database only if the suspect meets at least two of the following gang criteria (O'Connor 2000, A23):

- Professes to be a gang member.
- Is deemed a gang member by a reliable source, such as a trusted informant, teacher or parent.
- Is called a gang member by an untested informant with corroboration.
- Has gang graffiti on his personal property or clothing.
- Is observed, by an officer, using gang hand signs.

- Hangs around with gang members.

- Is arrested with gang members.

- Identifies his gang affiliation when brought to county jail—something authorities say suspects do to avoid being jailed with enemy gang members.

The LA Sheriff's Department attempts to be very careful about whose name is added to a gang list but insists that gang databases are a critical tool in the fight against gang activity. This cautious approach reflects these of other police agencies that seek to avoid violating privacy rights. In Tulsa (Oaklahoma), a city with a rising gang problem, officials designate people as possible gang members based on a range of factors (e.g., criminal records, tattoos, brands on skin that claim an allegiance to a specific gang, frequent associations with known gang members). Tulsa's database (2004) includes about 3,300 residents. To avoid privacy concerns, Tulsa's database is restricted to suspected and actual gang members. In 2002, Denver officials were forced to drop a broader database after residents accused the department of compiling "spy files" against innocent people (Johnson 2004). The Denver database included names and information on people who were involved in such legal activities as lawful protests or demonstrations.

Gang suppression units utilize the "hit them as hard as we can" approach in their battle against street gangs. Police raid teams in gang suppression units are analogous to an enthusiastic football team hitting the field fired up for "battle." Among the more notable gang suppression units was the Los Angeles Police Department's (LAPD's) **Community Resources Against Street Hoodlums (CRASH)** unit. Created in the late 1970s, this antigang unit was a response to the growing street gang problem in Los Angeles. As described by former LAPD Chief of Police (1978–1992) Daryl Gates, CRASH consisted of a number of elite antigang units within the LAPD that were set up to suppress the increasing rate of gang violence and crime. CRASH officers were required to get to know gang members, their names, their friends, where they hung out, and the types of criminal activities that gang members participated in. Former CRASH officer Sergeant Brian Liddy stated:

> The primary mission of the CRASH unit is to gather intelligence on the criminal street gangs that exist within their geographic division and to monitor their activities. There are kind of two sides to it. There's the intelligence side, where you kind of got to know all these people by their nicknames, where they hang out, what kind of cars they drive. Then there's the crime suppression mode, where you're out trying to keep them from doing drive-bys and robberies and extortion, spray painting the buildings—the criminal end of their involvement (PBS, *Frontline* 2001).

As elite police officers, CRASH members were willing to work extra hard and were not afraid to mix it up with gang members and certainly were not intimidated by gangsters. A phrase commonly used by CRASH officers sums up their attitude: "intimidate those who intimidate."

The various CRASH units were assigned to monitor specific gangs throughout Los Angeles and to gather as much information as possible (e.g., asking gang members who they were currently feuding with, who was doing drive-bys on them, whether the Mexican Mafia was still "taxing" them) and ultimately suppressing their criminal activities. CRASH units would drive by a neighborhood to see who was spray painting apartments and other buildings. As discussed in Chapter 6, gang graffiti is not just "artwork" left behind by criminals, it tells a story about what has happened, or what will happen between rival gangs. It also serves as a marker of "claimed" territory. When a gang attempts to expand its territory, it will begin by spray painting graffiti on rival turf. The police officers in CRASH would, in effect, be tipped off about impending gang activity simply by being able to properly interpret gang graffiti. Information-gathering is a critical aspect of any suppression unit. However, relying on gang members for information presents some problems (they are criminals after all). Because gang members are not always the most trustworthy people, the police have to be careful not to act upon false information, or a false tip. Gang members also sometimes use their relationship with suppression units to serve their own needs by passing along information designed to harm their rivals.

Overall, the LAPD's CRASH units were very successful, citywide, in reducing gang-related crime. They were known on the streets as a quasi-gang that used the same brutal and sometimes illegal tactics as gangs. CRASH units relied heavily on sweeps as their primary tactic, and in 1988, LAPD Chief Gates initiated a CRASH operation known as **Operation Hammer** in South Central Los Angeles. "One thousand police officers swept through the area on a Friday night and again on Saturday, arresting likely gang members for a wide variety of offenses, including already-existing warrants, new traffic citations, curfew violations, gang-related behaviors, and observed criminal activities. All of those arrested (1,435 persons) were taken to a mobile booking operation adjacent to Memorial Coliseum" (Howell 2000, 22). Most of those arrested were later released without charges, but there were 60 felony arrests (which led to just 32 felony charges). In addition to the arrests, a great deal of information was added to the CRASH unit's data banks. Although the target area, South Central Los Angeles, is predominantly African-American, there were accusations that Operation Hammer was a racist suppression effort because 93% of those arrested were black. "The overall purpose was merely social control (of African-American youth) rather than a serious attempt at reducing crime" (Shelden et al. 2001, 244). The LAPD, predictably, stood by its belief that gang suppression units were necessary for citizen safety. Then-County Supervisor Kenneth Hahn believed that the gang problem was so serious that the National Guard should be sent into LA's gang neighborhoods to fight a "war" against gangs.

Accusations of corruption accompanied complaints of racism on the part of the LAPD and especially its CRASH units. The NAACP claimed that hundreds of complaints were filed against LAPD and CRASH. Among the accusations: police left gang suspects stranded on enemy turf and officers wrote over Crip graffiti with Blood graffiti and vice versa (Davis 1992). But the demise of the CRASH suppression unit finally occurred due to allegations of corruption in the Rampart District. The Rampart District has a notorious reputation in Los Angeles as one of the most violent areas anywhere in the country. In 1990, there were around 150 murders in the division; by 1997, the count was down to about 33 (PBS, *Frontline* 2001). The LAPD claimed the reason for the great reduction in violent crime in that district was due to CRASH. According to the former president of the LA Police Commission, Gerald Chaleff, the Rampart district has always done things "the Rampart Way" (PBS, *Frontline* 2001). The Rampart unit was in a building away from the main station, without supervision, because of space problems. These officers, sergeants and senior police alike, were used to doing whatever they wanted to. They got away with "questionable" behavior because of the population that they served—many people in that community were recent immigrants from Central and South America and more or less expected the police to be corrupt because that's the way it was in their home countries. Among the behaviors that were a part of the "Rampart Way" of doing things was their secret club and system of reward and recognition. They would give out placques to officers who shot gang members and they had their own tattoos and patches that they wore on their jackets. The tattoos and patches displayed a cowboy hat on a skull with aces and eights, which stood for the "dead man's" hand that Wild Bill Hickock had when he was shot playing poker. The placques also had shell casings engraved on them for the number of times the officer had hit the person he was shooting at. A special, distinctive placque was awarded for a fatal shooting. Members of the Rampart CRASH unit were known to use "drop guns"—guns recovered previously on the street, but never reported—as "planted" evidence against perpetrators they thought had guns but, as it turned out, did not. They did the same thing with drugs. Thus, if a CRASH officer wanted a gang member to go to prison but could not catch him in the act of committing gang crime, he would plant guns or narcotics on the member. It was also common to pay off informants with confiscated drugs that were never turned in to booking.

Ultimately, the worst scandal in LAPD history would ravage the Rampart unit and lead to its—and the rest of CRASH's—end. Former officer Rafael Perez of the Rampart Division admitted in court in 2000, as part of his plea bargain for drug charges in 1999, that he shot and framed an innocent man. Perez was caught while attempting to steal narcotics from an evidence storage facility and implicated other Rampart Division officers in a variety of abuses. The Rampart scandal led to the investigation of 70 current and former officers and the overturning of some 40 convictions. It is estimated that as many as 99 people may have been wrongly convicted based on false testimony by officers (Feldman 2000). In an attempt to institute changes, and facing political backlash from a number of organizations, LAPD Chief Bernard C. Parks disbanded all CRASH units effective March 12, 2000 (*LAPD Newsletter* 2000). As a result of the disbanding of CRASH, the computer database with files on more than 112,000 purported LA County gang members (62,000 of whom were identified by CRASH units) may now be completely compromised (O'Connor 2000). Many citizens of Los Angeles expressed a concern that without the CRASH units gang activity would escalate once again in the "City of Angels." However, it was clear that a city like Los Angeles, the street gang capital, could not go without a suppression unit, and indeed the CRASH units were replaced by Special Enforcement Units (SEU) to fight gang activity in Los Angeles.

Every large city in the United States has a gang suppression unit. In Baltimore, the police department created a **Violent Crimes Division** that has several units, two of which are the **Handgun Recovery Squad** and the **Youth Violence Strike Force**. The gang suppression units are deployed to specific, targeted areas. The Youth Strike Force works closely with the FBI and other agencies to apprehend and incarcerate violent gang members (Howell 2000). In St. Louis, Missouri, law enforcement officials have developed the Consent to Search and Seize protocols in conjunction with its **Firearm Suppression Program (FSP).** Once the unit receives information on a gang member, two officers visit the residence of the alleged member, speak with an adult resident, and request permission to search the home for illegal weapons. Residents are told that they will not be charged with the illegal possession of a firearm if they sign the Consent to Search and Seize form (Howell 2000, 22).

It is important to note that many city and county law enforcement agencies pool their resources with federal and state agencies, resulting in **multiagency initiatives**, to combat gangs and gang-related crime. Multiagency initiatives generally fall into one of two categories. "The most common type is Federal, State, and local law enforcement collaboration across jurisdictional boundaries. In other instances, crime control agencies (e.g., police, prosecutors, courts) collaborate in targeting gangs" (Howell 2000, 30).

Community Policing

"A major change in law enforcement has been to move from the traditional watchman policing and the professional legalistic policing models to community-oriented policing. Community-oriented policing emphasizes establishing and maintaining a cooperative relationship between police officers and the community" (Trojanowicz et al. 2001, 260). Throughout the United States, a number of communities have developed gang intervention strategies that attempt to incorporate both community facilities and the police. **Community policing** is the term applied to such an approach. "The increasing use of specialized police gang units as the principal form of police response to local gang problems coincided with the emergence of community-oriented policing in police departments across the country. Because the philosophy of community-oriented policing emphasizes despecialization and decentralization, whereas the very nature of gang units emphasizes specialization and centralization, a number of questions [arise]" (Webb and Katz 2003, 35–36). In other words, is the primary function and/or goal of community policing prevention or suppression? The very design, structure, and daily activities of community policing are contingent on this question. As one might imagine, there is a wide variety of community-policing programs. As MacDonald (2003, 102) explained:

> With almost as many definitions of "community policing" as there are police forces, hardly a department in the country doesn't claim to be doing it. But the core ideas are: an attention to local conditions, especially quality-of-life problems, rather than just the big felonies; an effort to solve the underlying causes of particular problems; working with local residents and with other government agencies to respond to crime and disorder. In the public's mind, community policing also taps nostalgia for the tough but friendly beat cop who knew everyone in the neighborhood and kept them in line with a sharp word.

The ideal of a beat cop in control of a few specific streets has long disappeared in the urban cities of America, but the hope of safer streets for all remains a consistent unifier of the various community-policing techniques.

"Strategically, community policing implements a range of programs such as foot patrol, bicycle patrol, citizen crime watch patrols as well as additional services that involve law enforcement officers" (Trojanowicz et al. 2001, 260). Ideally, community policing involves police officers becoming more involved in communities that are at a high risk for gang activity. It also involves "direct input from citizens and uses that input to identify community problems, prioritize those problems, and formulate responses to the problems (Webb and Katz 2003, 36). Unfortunately, one of the biggest problems associated with community policing is poor communication. In most cases, it seems that the communication between the two interested parties—community members and law enforcement—is lacking and uncooperative in application. In their evaluation of community-policing programs, Webb and Katz (2003, 36) found that "the lack of communication between citizens and the gang unit was particularly problematic when the gang unit attempted to carry out enforcement-oriented operations. In particular, we found that enforcement operations that are carried out without any citizen input or awareness, and often without input from other units in the agency, can create serious police–community relations problems." For example, a gang suppression unit in Las Vegas carried out a sweep without informing local community-policing leaders or the LV district commander of that neighborhood (Webb and Katz 2003).

Community policing emphasizes specific geographic areas such as neighborhoods and police beats. The police target the criminal activities and other social problems created by gangsters within this area. The idea behind this approach is the historic reality that gangs are turf-based. However, as police are aware, not all gangs (especially drug gangs) are tied to specific, limited geographic areas. Community policing is ultimately about the prevention of crime and disorder. Police officers are expected to stop gang activity before it happens (proactive policing), a task that is often difficult to accomplish, especially if members of the community do not fully cooperate by providing necessary information to the police to prevent criminal activities. Effective community policing must involve partnerships between the police and various community groups. Webb and Katz (2003) found that while police agencies may partner up with community groups, gang units seldom did this. "If the gang unit did partner, we found that it was typically with criminal justice personnel. Most of the gang units were not found to formally partner with community groups, local businesses, or other local or state agencies. The partnerships were typically established and maintained for the purpose of exchanging gang-related intelligence" (Webb and Katz 2003, 39). Webb and Katz also found little evidence that police gang units participated in problem-solving discussions with other members of the community-policing program.

There are many examples of community-policing programs. The Flint (Michigan) Police Department created **The Flint Neighborhood Foot Patrol Program** in 1979 as part of a greater initiative to integrate citizens into the policing of their neighborhood. Before 1979, all of the Flint police patrols were motorized. The program introduced 22 foot patrol officers assigned to 14 experimental areas, which included about 20% of the city's population. The basic goals of the Flint Neighborhood Foot Patrol were the following (Trojanowicz et al. 2001, 260):

1. To decrease the amount of actual or perceived criminal activity.

2. To increase the citizen's perception of personal safety.

3. To deliver to Flint residents a type of law enforcement service consistent with the community needs and the ideas of modern police practice.

4. To increase a community awareness of crime and problems and methods of increasing law enforcement's ability to deal with actual or potential criminal activity effectively.

5. To develop citizen volunteer action in support of, and under the direction of, the police department, aimed at various target crimes.

6. To eliminate citizen apathy about reporting crime to police.

7. To increase protection for women, children, and the aged.

Foot patrols provide local citizenry with the perception, as well as the reality (ideally), that the police care about the problems that they face on a daily basis. Through interaction, the citizens and police begin to develop a degree of intimacy with each other; which in turn leads to an effective cooperative relationship. "Evaluation research results showed that community residents felt that the Flint foot patrol officers were more effective in handling juvenile-related problems than were motor patrol officers. Further, the foot patrol officers were able to organize and support numerous neighborhood associations throughout the city, and these associations in turn play a key role in directing police efforts to work with juveniles" (Trojanowicz et al. 2001, 261).

In 1996, former NYPD police commissioner Howard Safir established the **Goal-Oriented Neighborhood Policing** program. Safir (2003, 3) stated, "The strategies that were implemented in this program were many and involved special units, task forces, and multi-agency partnerships. With these strategies in place, and a total commitment to fighting crime, the NYPD turned the city around." The basic premise of the Goal-Oriented Neighborhood Policy was to get police officers more involved with local neighborhoods. "To address the behavior of the police officer when interacting in the community, the NYPD adopted a policy of Courtesy, Professionalism, and Respect (CPR). With CPR we fostered respect for the public, and discipline, integrity, and professionalism among police officers" (Safir 2003, 4). Safir assigned officers from the Internal Affairs Bureau (IAB) and Quality Assurance Division (QAD) to monitor NYPD officers to make sure that they were fulfilling the CPR model. Civilians were encouraged to register violation complaints against officers who did not abide by the CPR principles. Under the Giuliani administration, the community-policing officers were expected to enforce and abide by strategic crime-fighting goals (Safir 2003, 7):

- Getting guns off the street
- Curbing youth violence on the streets and in the schools
- Driving drug dealers out of the city
- Breaking the cycle of domestic violence
- Reclaiming public spaces
- Reducing auto-related crime
- Reclaiming the roads of the city
- Courtesy, Professionalism, and Respect
- Bringing fugitives to justice
- Rooting out corruption

These strategies were created by focus groups, police officers, precinct commanders, community members, and an analysis of the many social problems that New York City was facing.

In Dallas, Texas, the **Office of Community Oriented Policing Services (COPS)** established five gang-related programs as part of a community-policing program. Three main suppression strategies were employed by Dallas gang units: saturation patrols/high-visibility patrols in target areas, aggressive curfew enforcement, and aggressive enforcement of truancy laws and regulations. Gang unit officers teamed with community-policing officers to carry out these strategies. Community evaluators examined weekly and monthly police reports (e.g., documented overtime-funded activities) to make sure that the police were in compliance with community expectations (Howell 2000). COPS initiatives have been used by a variety of communities across the country. For example, in Inglewood (CA), Seattle (WA), and Milwaukee (WI), COPS initiatives were used to reduce handgun violence; and in Salinas (CA), a COPS initiative targeted gang members under age 25 (Howell 2000).

The state of Illinois, through the Youth Services Department, has set up the **Gang Crime Prevention Center (GCPC)**, which is dedicated to involving all citizens in the fight against street gangs and the conditions that contribute to their formation and growth. The GCPC utilizes community resources, law enforcement resources, and other means to eliminate and control gangs throughout the state. Among the many programs established by the Youth Services Department is the Cook County Sheriff's **Police and Children Together (PACT) Camp**. The PACT program was created to address the lack of positive role models and recreational activities for vulnerable youth, which sometimes results in youth involvement with delinquent friends, drugs, or violence. The camps are designed to put youth and law enforcement personnel together in a cooperative setting that will ultimately strengthen bonds between youth and police and at the same time provide recreational activities that are fun, healthy, and "community positive." Each PACT Camp must have the following (Cook County Sheriff's Youth Services Department 1999):

1. At least one police-related activity.

2. Police officers serving as officer counselors and facilitating transportation for the campers.

3. At least one community-service project.

4. At least one team-building activity that involves police officers on the team (not as activity leaders).

5. Structured, daily physical activities that youths can do at home (probably exercises).

6. A graduation ceremony at the conclusion.

7. The presence of the chief for at least a portion of the camp.

The PACT camp is an annual event and the Youth Services Department hopes to create spin-off programs.

Perhaps the best-known community-policing organization is the Guardian Angels. Their trademark red berets make them easily identifiable by law-abiding citizens and criminals alike. The Guardian Angels were founded by Curtis Sliwa in 1979. At that time, Sliwa was a McDonald's night manager in a crime-ridden area of the Bronx.

Fed up with the crime in his neighborhood, Sliwa formed a voluntary, weapon-free patrol of 13 members who patrolled subways and city streets in an effort to rid the community of criminals. Once criticized as vigilantes, the Guardian Angels are now an acclaimed example of a successful community-policing group. The Guardian Angels do not merely protect the innocent from criminals—they live by a motto established by Sliwa: "Empower people to help themselves, build self-esteem and confidence, arm them with responsibility and you tap into the greatest source of lasting good possible" (GuardianAngels.org 2004). The Angels have grown from their initial foot patrols to the launching of CyberAngels (1998), "the Internet's largest cyber safety program" (GuardianAngels.org 2004). Today, the Angels have undertaken many school-based initiatives in an effort to empower people to help themselves.

Community-policing programs appear to have some success in dealing with youth gangs and gang-related problems. But as with all gang programs, extensive, formal evaluation is often lacking.

Judicial and Legislative Suppression Efforts

Keeping youths out of gangs begins with individual choice—deciding whether to join a gang or not. The parents and/or legal guardians are the primary agents of socialization that is designed to keep kids out of gangs and/or committing other acts of delinquency. The schools implement many programs that are also designed to keep students out of gangs. Despite all of these efforts at gang prevention, however, youths still turn to gangs. Inevitably, they come in contact with the police and their gang suppression activities. Assisting the police in their "war" against gangs are the courts and legislative bodies. It is the responsibility of the court to prosecute criminals and send them to detention centers or prison. The legislative body attempts to write laws that will further assist the police and their efforts at suppression.

JUDICIAL SUPPRESSION EFFORTS Judicial efforts include such strategies as the following:

- Injunctions—the banning of gang members from certain areas or congregating in public.
- Curfews—attempts to keep youths off the streets late at night and therefore away from gang and criminal activities.
- Truancy laws—efforts to keep youths in school.
- Banning certain attire—articles of clothing typically associated with gangs. This is often very controversial because one of the most common items banned is the six-pointed star worn by some gangs (e.g., the Gangster Disciples) but also by Jewish people.
- Banning gang colors—especially do-rags that indicate gang allegiance.
- Housing—housing authorities are authorized by HUD to evict gang members caught possessing or using guns (National Crime Prevention Council 1996).

- Prosecution—punishing gang members by sending them to detention centers, jail, or prison.

- Nuisance abatement laws—efforts to reduce gang or juvenile activities that cause harm to members of the community (e.g., banning the drinking of alcohol on sidewalks and in parks, noise limitations on stereos—especially car stereos).

- Loitering restrictions—efforts to stop gang members from hanging out together in public places even if they are not presently committing criminal acts.

Injunctions against gangs are one of the favorite judicial suppression efforts. They make use of loitering restrictions by banning gangsters from "hanging out" with each other in public places. Although there is no official agency responsible for tracking the use of injunctions against street gangs, according to Maxson and associates (2003), "the first reported use of a civil injunction for gang abatement was in Santa Ana, California, in 1980, although site abatements for other disorder problems like drugs or pornography were not uncommon. The Santa Ana city attorney obtained an injunction prohibiting youths from gathering and partying at a known gang hangout." From that point on, injunctions have been used routinely in a number of jurisdictions in Southern California. For the most part, these injunctions escaped public attention or interest, but periodically debates over the legality of specific injunctions become sensationalized in the media by political activists and attention-seekers. For example, in 1987 a widely publicized injunction was issued against the Playboy Gangster Crips. The American Civil Liberties Union (ACLU) lodged a court complaint against the legality of this injunction. "The challenge was partly successful in that an attorney was appointed to represent the gang and only illegal behaviors were included in the injunction in December 1987" (Maxson et al. 2003, 249). The ACLU would continue to play "watchdog" over future injunctions, especially after receiving numerous complaints from citizens concerned about the basic civil right to congregate, peacefully, in public. Most citizens support injunctions because they are generally successful in curtailing gang activities in targeted areas.

In order to continue using injunctions, district attorney's offices are careful with their wording. In 1992, the Burbank City Attorney's Office obtained an injunction against 34 members of the Barrio Elmwood Rifa gang. This was the first injunction to constrain gang members from associating with one another. It prohibited them from standing, sitting, walking, driving, gathering, or appearing anywhere in public view of each other (Castorena 1998). Prohibiting gang members from public association has remained a staple of court-ordered injunctions. For example, in 1992, Chicago officials adopted the **Gang Congregation Ordinance**, which was essentially an **antiloitering law** targeting street gangs. The ordinance dictates that police officers who observe a person they believe to be a criminal street gang member loitering in any public place with one or more other suspected gang members are to disperse and remove from the area such suspects who are standing around "with no apparent purpose." Any person who does not comply with this order is in violation of the ordinance. In 1993, a Jesus Morales and other individuals charged with violating the Chicago ordinance petitioned Cook County Circuit Court to dismiss the charges, claiming that the ordinance was unconstitutional and violated their rights under the First, Fourth, and Fourteenth Amendments to the Constitution. The court agreed and allowed a motion for dismissal of the charges. The city appealed all the way to the U.S. Supreme Court (losing each step of the way), which found that the ordinance was unconstitutional. The Supreme Court, in a 6–3 decision, ruled that the city's 1992 antiloitering ordinance, which resulted in 45,000 arrests in the three years it was enforced, violated the rights of the defendants because it failed to give citizens adequate notice of what was forbidden (Carelli 1999). In other words, this antiloitering statute was unconstitutional because it was overly broad and vague; it did not even offer a definition of a gang.

Meanwhile, in Southern California, at least 30 gang injunctions were issued from 1993 to 2000. In 1993, the LA County district attorney was granted an injunction banning the **Blythe Street Gang** from congregating in public areas. This Hispanic gang, with more than 500 members, had terrorized a formerly quiet San Fernando Valley neighborhood and turned it into an occupied zone. In 1997, the California Supreme Court ruled that this court injunction was an acceptable gang suppression tactic (Howell 2000). In July 1997, a court-ordered injunction was issued against the notorious Los Angeles **18th Street Gang**. "In a tough initiative to curb the mayhem of Los Angeles' most notorious gang—18th Street—a Superior Court judge on Friday barred members of one of the group's cliques from associating with each other in a terrorized southwest Los Angeles neighborhood. Judge Alan G. Buckner approved a preliminary injunction that carries unprecedented provisions in Los Angeles' long and frustrating war on gangs. The most significant and controversial: a ban on three or more gang members congregating, standing, sitting, walking, driving or appearing in public together anywhere in a 17-block area of Jefferson Park" (Rosenzwig and Gold 1997, A1). The injunction specifically targeted 18 members of one set of the 18th Street Gang, barring 3 or more of the 18 from associating in public view at any time and including prohibitions related to graffiti, blocking sidewalks and harassing residents, and acting as lookouts to warn against the approach of police. A month later, a new injunction with the same provisions was directed against all the sets of this gang found in the Pico-Union areas west of downtown (near the LA Convention Center), comprising more than 300 members (Krikorian and Connell 1997). But despite these injunctions, the gang continues to exist and flourish. In an attempt to dismantle the 18th Street Gang, in 2004 the Los Angeles city attorney's office won a permanent injunction against it that bars members from recruiting young people. The injunction covers gang members around Wilshire Boulevard in the mid-city area. Also in 2004, Los Angeles city attorney Rocky Delgadillo successfully received court approval for an injunction against the **Rolling 60s** gang in South Los Angeles to prevent members from driving together into a rival gang's territory (Garrison 2004). (It is interesting to note that city officials in Los Angeles no longer use "South-Central Los Angeles" to refer to that specific area of the city, because of the term's historically negative connotation. This crime-ridden area of the city is now called South Los Angeles, but city officials are naïve, at best, if they think renaming an area of a city will change its character. After all, "a rose by any other name, is still a rose." Los Angeles officials need to spend more time and effort improving the socioeconomic conditions of South-Central Los Angeles than on convincing residents that the area now called South Los Angeles has a better image.)

The use of injunctions remains controversial. In Southern California, law enforcement agencies have been fairly successful in implementing injunctions against gangs;

however, in other areas of the county (e.g., Chicago) injunctions have been shot down as unconstitutional. Unlike the broad Chicago ordinance that was struck down by the U.S. Supreme Court, the injunctions in Los Angeles names specific gang members and accuses them of being involved in criminal activity. Furthermore, the Los Angeles injunctions apply only to the gang's neighborhood, not an unrestricted geographical area. Citizens in embattled communities that are confronted by the lawlessness of street gangs remain the strongest proponents of injunctions, as they see and feel the benefits immediately. Furthermore, law enforcement agencies that have used injunctions typically view them as successful. Unfortunately, injunctions are often little more than quick fixes to a complicated problem that cannot be solved by simply banning the association of gang members. On the other hand, many communities need a quick fix to the gang problem in their neighborhoods.

Juvenile curfew ordinances are another important tactic in judicial gang suppression efforts. A large number of U.S. cities have issued curfews in an attempt to reduce the amount of youth gang criminal activity as well as youth victimization. Although all ordinances are not the same, generally speaking local officials determine what hours youths should not be allowed on the streets without adult supervision. In Buffalo, youths younger than 17 may not loiter, congregate, wander, or play in or upon any public place on weekdays (Sunday–Thursday) from 11 P.M. to 5 A.M. and weekends (Friday–Saturday) from 12 midnight to 5 A.M. Parents (or guardians) are held responsible for youths who violate curfew and may be fined up to $200 (Buffalo Police Department 2003). In Long Beach, California, the curfew is applied to youths from 10 P.M. to 6 A.M. and is directed at gang members. Washington, D.C. bars youths under 17 from being in public places if unaccompanied by a parent or guardian between 11 P.M. and 6 A.M. Breaking the law can result in 25 hours of community service for youth offenders and fines of up to $500 for parents who allow children to disobey the curfew (*New York Times* 1999).

Many jurisdictions report a reduction in crime after instituting a curfew. The Dallas police reported a drop in juvenile victimization (17.7%) and juvenile arrests (14.6%) from the year prior to the curfew during the hours of curfew enforcement. Statistics from the Phoenix police showed that 21% of all curfew violators were gang members and that there was a 10% drop in juvenile arrests for violent crimes after implementing an aggressive curfew program (Fritsch et al. 2003). An analysis of crime statistics in Detroit (Hunt and Weiner 1977) showed that although the crime rate decreased 6% during curfew hours (compared to the year earlier), it increased 13% during the afternoon. Just as there are legal concerns about the constitutionality of injunctions, there are those who wonder whether curfew ordinances infringe on the rights of individuals. A federal appeals court ruled in 1999 that teenagers do not have an unrestricted right to roam the streets late at night and that youth curfews are constitutional.

Truancy is often regarded as a minor offense; some call it a **status offense** (relatively minor offenses that may serve as precursors to more serious forms of delinquency). "Truancy can lead youth to substance and alcohol abuse or violence. Studies have revealed that there is a relationship between substance abuse and truancy" (Trojanowicz et al. 2001, 29). Truancy refers to unexcused absences by youths from school. Mandatory education laws require that youths attend school, but, of course, many times kids will skip out. There is no national data on truancy, but many cities indicate that truancy is a significant problem. "For instance, Pittsburgh reports that on an average day, approximately 3,500 students (12 percent of the total student population) are absent. Of these absences, almost 70 percent are unexcused. On an average day, Philadelphia reports almost 2,500 unexcused absences and Milwaukee reports approximately 4,000 unexcused absences" (Trojanowicz et al. 2001, 178). The concern with truancy is—what are kids doing if they are not at school and not at home being supervised by an adult? The answer usually entails some act of delinquency on the part of the truant. Truancy is often the first indicator that a juvenile is in trouble or on the way to trouble. As obvious as it may seem that truancy leads to delinquency, "the impact of aggressive truancy enforcement on crime rates remains essentially unevaluated" (Fritsch et al. 2003, 271).

Prosecution is a critical element in gang suppression efforts. The prosecutor is supposed to act in the best interests of the state (or "the people"). As the first line of defense against crime, law enforcement officers arrest people that they suspect of criminal activity. After an arrest is made there is little else (beyond offering testimony at trial) that the officer can do to assure that suspects are prosecuted and incarcerated for their crimes. It is the prosecutor's job to present enough evidence to find the accused guilty of a crime. The prosecutor, then, is the second line of defense, or "the regulator within the criminal justice system" (Shelden et al. 2001, 253). There are times when prosecutors may feel the evidence presented to them (by the police) is not substantial enough to go to court to seek a conviction. Strength of evidence is just one variable in a prosecutor's decision to proceed with a court case, however. Other factors may include special circumstances (e.g., a motorist who plows his car into a group of people because he suffered a heart attack while driving the car), the severity of the offense (the more serious offenses are the most likely to lead to prosecution), and public sentiment.

An interesting example of how public sentiment may sway a prosecutor's decision to go to court involves an incident that took place in Los Angeles. Graffiti scars the city of Los Angeles, and its residents have no tolerance for taggers and certainly do not view graffiti as some sort of "urban art" (in contrast, New York City commissions graffiti "artists" to paint murals). In 1995, William Masters confronted two taggers and asked them to stop defacing the property (support columns under a freeway) they were spray painting. The taggers refused, confronted Masters, and Masters took out a gun and fired at both of them. Masters freely confessed to killing one man and injuring the other. On the surface, this is an "airtight" case for any prosecutor to win. However, the LA public treated Masters like a hero, and radio call-in shows were dominated by citizens praising Masters for taking a "bite out of crime"—albeit, vigilante-style. (New York City once had its own public-favorite vigilante in Bernhard Goetz, the "Subway Shooter.") Masters went so far as to brag, "Where are you going to find 12 citizens to convict me?" (Estrich 1995, 11A). Not in Los Angeles. The district attorney's office announced that Masters would not be prosecuted, realizing that public sentiment was clearly on Masters' side.

There are still other conditions under which prosecutors may choose not to prosecute a particular case. LaFave and Israel (1992) have categorized five of them:

1. when the victim expresses a desire that the accused not be prosecuted (e.g., they may feel sorry for the offender or just wish to move on with their lives without dragging out the incident in the courts)

2. when the costs are too high for a local jurisdiction to cover, for example, a high-profile case that may last for months or years and the district attorney's office literally cannot afford the case

3. when prosecution would result in undue harm to an offender (e.g., an elderly person or a very ill person)

4. when the accused is capable of helping out in other cases ("copping an out-of-court plea")

5. when amends can be made in ways other than incarceration (e.g., paying restitution)

Shelden and associates point out one additional important factor to remember when examining the role of prosecutors in suppression efforts: "Unlike law enforcement, which is policy driven (i.e., creating policies that conform to legislative activity, local government mandates, and prosecutor-established standards), the prosecutor is often guided by political realities or ambitions. The prosecutor is usually an elected public official and is frequently provided with access to an assortment of resources capable of promoting a desired public image that is politically marketable" (2001, 255). Thus, the prosecutor may not always be working in the best interest of the people (the state), and it is also possible for a prosecutor to carry out a personal vendetta against individuals. On the other hand, prosecutors have the discretion to give deserving individuals second chances, and they have the freedom to look into the individual circumstances that led up to the criminal act.

The court is the legal foundation of the criminal justice system. The court is presumed to consist of an independent judge free from bias who runs trials based on preexisting legal norms and rules that do not change on a case-by-case basis, due process, and (generally) a jury of peers. The court is the setting of legal procedures where objectivity is supposed to reign. Ideally, if the police make a clean and accurate arrest of a suspect, the prosecutor does a good job in presenting the case, and the judge oversees the proceedings objectively, the perpetrator, if guilty, will be given a sentence of some sort; and if innocent, will be freed. The courts are in a strong position to assist suppression efforts against gangs. They provide the injunctions and establish the curfews that police officers need to fight the war on the streets. The judge, like the prosecutor, attained his or her position, as a rule, through an election. Consequently, this position is very political and a judge's personal bias, subjectivity, and political ambition may interfere with the objectivity of the judicial proceedings.

It is important to remember that many gang members are still youths. Consequently, many of them are tried in juvenile court or family court. The legal basis for juvenile court can be traced back to the concept of *parens patriae* (a Latin phrase that literally means "the parent of the country" and refers to the belief that the state has both the right and duty to direct and protect those of its citizens who need help, especially the young and mentally challenged). The basic idea is that young people are too immature to understand the meaning of their behaviors. In other words, they cannot, or should not, be held accountable for certain actions. Many people who work with gangs will state that gang members are very aware of what they are doing, even in the early teen years. Juvenile status has been a loophole that has allowed a great number of juvenile gang members to get away with less severe punishments for crimes. There is a movement among many legislatures to modify these legal restrictions.

LEGISLATIVE SUPPRESSION EFFORTS As previously stated, the police must create policies that accommodate current law. In their effort to suppress gang activity they must "play the hand that they were dealt." Arresting people for committing crimes against various laws is their greatest contribution to suppression efforts. Even prosecutors and judges with personal ambition for higher office must still work within the letter of the law. Thus, all three elements responsible for suppressing gang activity are dependent on legislators and the laws that they create in the fight against crime. Legislative bodies respond to demands from law enforcement and the general public, who elected them and who are the people that legislators represent in performing their jobs.

In regard to gang suppression, legislative bodies have worked diligently to create laws that are constitutional, enforceable, and yet do not interfere with individual civil rights guaranteed by the U.S. Constitution. Along with the creation of new laws, legislators may modify existing ones. Often the bills they introduce are not passed. For example, in 2001, legislation addressing the issue of adding "thrill" killings and gang-initiation slayings to the list of crimes eligible for the death penalty under New York's capital-punishment law was introduced in the New York State Senate. Thrill killing was described in Bill S.5409, Section 6, paragraph xiv, as "the defendant committed the *killing for the pleasure of it*." According to State Senator Michael F. Nozzolio (2004), the measure was not voted on during the 2001–2002 legislative session and has not been reintroduced since. An example of legislation modified for gang-related purposes are the "aiding and abetting" laws. Some jurisdictions may charge gang leaders involved in criminal enterprises, such as selling drugs, with aiding and abetting even if they are not actually caught selling drugs. In addition, gang members who ride along with others who commit a crime may be found guilty of aiding and abetting even if they never left the car to participate in the criminal act (Howell 2000).

A number of laws have been passed by legislative bodies that target gang-related activities. A few examples are provided here. In an effort to curtail gang graffiti in New York State, legislators passed **New York 125.60**. This law forbids any person from putting graffiti (defined as "the etching, painting, covering, drawing upon or otherwise placing of a mark upon public or private property with intent to damage such property") of any type on any building without the express permission of the owner or operator of said property. **New York 145.65** makes the possession of graffiti tools a class B misdemeanor. Graffiti tools are described as "any tool, instrument, article, substance, solution or other compound designed or commonly used to etch, paint, cover, draw upon or otherwise mark upon a piece of property for which that person has no permission or authority." In an effort to address gang assault, New York State passed **New York S 120.06** (gang assault in the second degree) and **New York S 120.07** (gang assault in the first degree). "A person is guilty of gang assault in the second degree when, with intent to cause physical injury to another person and when aided by two or more other persons actually present, he causes serious physical injury to such person or to a third person (New York S 120.06)." "A person is guilty of gang assault in the first degree when, with intent to cause serious physical injury to another person and when aided by two or more persons actually present, he causes serious physical injury to such person or to a third person" (New York S 120.07).

In the state of California, legislators passed **California 13825.2**, which established the California Gang, Crime, and Violence Prevention Partnership Program, a program administered by the Department of Justice for the purposes of reducing gang, criminal activity, and youth violence in communities with a high incidence of gang violence. **California 14000** established the Community Law Enforcement and Recovery (CLEAR) Demonstration Project, a multiagency gang intervention program under the joint jurisdiction of the LA County Sheriff's Department, the LA County District Attorney's office, the LA County Probation Department, and the LAPD. Among the primary roles of the district attorney under CLEAR is the preparation and prosecution of civil injunctions against gang activities occurring within targeted areas. Law enforcement and probation officials are to share information with each other as well as the DA's office. **California 14005** authorized an independent evaluation of CLEAR.

The District of Columbia passed legislation establishing a juvenile curfew. The Council of the District of Columbia (known as the Council) has determined that persons under the age of 17 years are particularly susceptible, due to their lack of maturity and experience, to participating in unlawful and gang-related activities and to becoming victims of older perpetrators of crime. To protect minors from each other and other persons, legislators enacted **District of Columbia 2-1541**, a curfew for those under the age of 17. The Council also passed legislation making it unlawful for a person to congregate in groups of two or more persons in public space on public property within the perimeter of a drug-free zone (**District of Columbia 48-1004**).

In an effort to fight gang intimidation, the state of Florida passed the Street Terrorism Enforcement and Prevention Act of 1990 (**Florida 874**). In brief, the state legislature established that every person has a legal right to be free from, and protected from, fear, intimidation, and physical harm caused by the activities of criminal street gangs and their members (**Florida 874.02**). Any person found to be victimized by gang intimidation has the right to pursue a civil case against the gang (**Florida 874.06**). Florida legislators consider gangs to be terrorist groups that represent a "clear and present danger" to citizens. It is the intent of the legislature, through the Street Terrorism act, to eradicate the terror created by criminal street gangs and their members by providing enhanced penalties and eliminating the patterns, profits, instrumentation, and property facilitating criminal street gang activity, including criminal street gang recruitment. The state of Illinois, in an attempt to protect witnesses to gang-related crimes from intimidation and retaliation, established the Gang Crime Witness Protection Fund (**725 ILCS 172/5-20**).

In addition to the creation of new laws, a few of which have just been described, legislators may also consider appropriate penalties to be attached to a violation. "Innovative penalty enhancement provisions that complement substantive criminal code provisions have been developed for use against gang members. They provide enhanced punishment for crimes that are often gang related, although they are not limited in application to gang members. These laws not only enhance penalties against principals charged with offenses such as drug trafficking, homicide, assault with a weapon, robbery, home invasion, arson, extortion, and auto theft, but also against accomplices charged with such offenses as conspiracy to commit a crime and aiding and abetting overt criminal acts" (Howell 2000, 40). Although most new laws and revisions to existing laws have suppression as the main goal, a number of legislatures have enacted new youth gang prevention measures as well.

During the past decade, it has become fairly common for law enforcement agencies to apply The Racketeer Influenced and Corrupt Organizations Act (RICO) to street gangs. "Used most often as a Federal prosecutorial weapon against high-ranking criminal group members, RICO has been used against youth and adult gang members by 17 percent of local prosecutors in large counties and less than 10 percent of prosecutors in small counties" (Howell 2000, 40). Prosecutors have learned that traditional approaches to fighting gangs have failed, and they view federal racketeering violations as a more suitable offense with which to charge gangs. According to Regoli and Hewitt (2003, 322):

> The RICO Act was signed into law in 1970 and was used for nearly two decades to fight the Mafia and other organized-crime groups. Today, however, prosecutors are turning to the RICO laws as a weapon against entrenched youth gangs partly because these laws allow prosecutors to charge gang members for simply being part of a criminal enterprise. This means that the more insulated and protected higher-level leaders of gangs can be prosecuted for the criminal activities of street-level members.

As an example of how this works, Syracuse law enforcement officials used RICO legislation in their battle against the Boot Camp gang. A great deal of the recent youth gang violence that has plagued Syracuse is the result of Boot Camp's drug enterprise. Homicide, gun dealing, violence, and drug trafficking were trademark criminal acts committed by Boot Camp. Prosecutors reasoned that bringing these thugs up on RICO charges would eventually lead to the strictest and harshest penalties allowed by law. Under RICO, a person can be found guilty of any charge that anyone in the group is accused of, regardless of whether these individuals were directly involved in the criminal acts or not. In the Syracuse case, three former Boot Camp members were arrested on RICO violations, which introduced the concept that even *former* gang members could be arrested under RICO. The Syracuse Partnership to Reduce Juvenile Gun Violence and the newly formed Families Against Injustice argued that it is not constitutional to include former gang members in RICO dragnets. Defense attorneys for the Boot Camp gang members took another tack— they did not deny the criminal activities of their defendants but argued that Boot Camp was nothing more than a group of guys who committed crimes independently. Defense attorneys also stated that Boot Camp members only hung out together to protect themselves from rival gangs. Boot Camp defendants admitted to committing a number of crimes, including murder, during the 2004 RICO hearings but insisted that they did not report to anyone (e.g., alleged gang leader Karo Brown). The importance of this is that in any RICO case against gang members, prosecutors must prove that the gang worked in unison as a criminal enterprise. As stated earlier (in Chapter 6), Karo Brown was ultimately found guilty of violating the RICO Act. The federal jury believed that Brown did run the violent street gang Boot Camp as a criminal business.

Regoli and Hewitt (2003) point out that in addition to RICO, gang suppression efforts have also included using the **Street Terrorism Enforcement and Prevention (STEP)** acts, based on the RICO model, and the **safe school zone** laws. "STEP Acts use a pattern of specified crimes as the basis for increasing sentences of youths convicted of gang-related crimes and mandating the forfeiture of a street gang's assets"

(Regoli and Hewitt 2003, 322). Because these acts make participation in a criminal street gang illegal, prosecutors avoid violating constitutional rights of free association. "By keeping precise records pertaining to gang incidents, the police assist prosecutors in targeting gang participants" (Regoli and Hewitt 2003, 323). Some states have enacted safe school zone laws that increase the penalties for certain weapons violations that occur within 1,000 feet of a school, public housing property, or a public park. "Violations include possessing a silencer or machine gun or carrying a pistol, revolver, stun gun or taser, firearm, or ballistic knife when hooded, robed, or masked" (Regoli and Hewitt 2003, 323). It should be noted that the Supreme Court deemed unconstitutional a federal safe school zone law that prohibits the mere possession of a gun within 1,000 feet of a school.

Local governments and jurisdictions have adapted existing laws and created new ones to combat the growing presence of gangs. When laws are created, civilians are expected to abide by them, police officers are expected to enforce them, prosecutors are supposed to present a case for conviction, and the courts are to serve as objective viewers of the whole process. The fact that some laws fail to produce the intended results and other laws are not looked upon favorably by a segment of the population is another problem altogether.

GANG TREATMENT PROGRAMS

Gang prevention programs have not been successful in their attempt to divert all youths away from gangs. In fact, the number of gang members continually increases. Suppression efforts to punish gang members and attempts to "scare" youth away from gangs have also failed to stop the increase. As a result, gangs exist throughout America. A number of agencies take a different approach to gang intervention—they attempt to treat the problem of gangbanging behavior. These professionals hope to rehabilitate gang members so that they can reenter conventional society. Gang treatment advocates look for alternatives to court processing for juvenile offenders in the hope that they can still be "rescued" from a life of gangism; they apply specific methods of treatment to rehabilitate gang members; and create programs for gang members in prison and ex-convicts who need to find a way to conform to conventional society.

Alternatives to Court Processing

Alternatives to court processing involves diversion—processing juveniles through non-court institutions. Without this diversion, juveniles would typically proceed to an adjudicatory, or fact-finding, hearing (Trojanowicz et al. 2001). A number of professionals are in a position to divert youths away from formal court action, including police officers and probation staff. Police officers "give a break" to many juvenile delinquents, who eventually grow out of their delinquent ways and become productive members of society. The discretion used by police officers, although flawed at times, can help "save" the lives of juveniles who were simply enjoying adolescent fun that, technically, violated the law. **Diversion**, then, is one of the most important and commonly used alternatives to court processing. "Diversion can be either *unconditional* or *conditional*.

Unconditional diversion is when the juvenile will attend school, stay out of trouble, and not reappear before the court for a specific period of time. *Conditional diversion* is when the juvenile is diverted from the system, but he or she is required to comply with various conditions. These conditions can include attending lectures, individual or group psychotherapy, alcohol and substance abuse treatment, and vocational or educational classes" (Trojanowicz et al. 2001, 264).

In 1970, the **Sacramento Diversion Project** was created. It was a program designed to help keep runaways and troubled youths out of jail. These juveniles would attend a meeting where police and social workers would attempt to convince the youths to call their parents (or guardians) so that they could avoid formal detention. Follow-up counseling sessions were established between professionals and the family on a volunteer basis. Two years later, additional minor offenses were covered by the diversion program. Many youths were successfully diverted ("treated") away from criminal proceedings, and the success of the Sacramento Diversion Project led many other communities to duplicate this alternative to court processing.

Probation is another common diversion tactic designed to keep certain youths (as well as adults) out of jail. Probation can be both informal (when compliance is voluntary) and formal (mandatory compliance in lieu of formal adjudication). In 1996, slightly more than half of probation cases were informal (Snyder and Sickmund 1999). There are a wide variety of probation programs. "The specific administration of the probation program depends upon the state and the jurisdiction. Although in many states probation is a part of the court—a juvenile court, probate court, or some other court jurisdiction—one probation department may be quite different from another. In most states, juvenile courts administer probation services, while in other states there is a variation" (Trojanowicz et al. 2001, 278). Probation involves the offender checking in with a probation officer at a specified time and place. In some cases, accounting for one's actions may be more severe and include **electronic monitoring**. Offenders under house arrest generally are fitted with electronic monitoring devices, usually an ankle attachment. Probation is an excellent diversionary tool for deserving offenders because it allows them an opportunity to remain in the community. If their behavior is positive, and they meet all the requirements of probation, they are free at the end of a designated period of time without having served jail time.

Gang members in treatment programs often have already been incarcerated. In the hope of keeping them out of trouble after release, many are placed on **parole**. Parole is a type of "aftercare" and is similar to probation, except for the fact that parolees have been incarcerated. When comparing these different populations, it is not surprising that the treatment success rate of parolees is much lower than those of probationers (Trojanowicz et al. 2001). Parole is granted when some governing body (e.g., a prison review board) determines that the violator has met community and rehabilitative objectives. The treatment aspect is handled by trained officers (who, unfortunately, are greatly overworked). Parole and probation officers have three functions to perform (Trojanowicz et al. 2001):

1. They must maintain surveillance of the offender. Continuous association reminds the offender of his (her) community obligations and of the threat of incarceration.

2. They must make the offender aware of the community services available to assist the offender in their rehabilitation.

3. They must counsel the offender and family and make them understand the conditions that led to criminal problems in the first place so as to eliminate the underlying causes of delinquency.

There are numerous types of parole and probation treatment programs and the current trend is to rely on these diversion tactics. As with most programs, the effectiveness of parole and probation in diverting youths from further gang activity is difficult to ascertain. The heavy caseloads that most officers carry make the treatment aspect of probation and parole secondary to the surveillance demands.

Restitution and community service is another common diversion treatment option available to offenders. "In instances where the offenses committed by juveniles involve property damage, property loss, or personal injuries to victims, restitution programs are increasingly being used as a method of holding the juvenile offenders responsible for their actions" (Kratcoski and Kratcoski 1996, 312). Delinquent youths, especially gang members, commonly deface property, especially with graffiti. Restitution programs have been designed to help youths pay for the damage they caused. One option involves working at specific job sites chosen by the court for which the offender does not receive a salary; instead, the money is taken by the court for payment to the victim. Community service programs are less expensive to operate than restitution programs and involve far less paperwork for administrators. They provide some of the same benefits, including the development of a feeling of personal responsibility and good work habits, as restitution programs. In addition, the community benefits from the work provided by the offender (Kratcoski and Kratcoski 1996).

A more severe diversionary tactic is to assign juvenile offenders to specialized **"boot camps."** This alternative to court processing is modeled after military boot camps where young men are put through rigorous training activities. The modified version of juvenile boot camps includes rigorous physical exercise, but with a more important, ultimate goal of building youths' self-esteem and confidence through hard work. The rehabilitative aspect of the boot camps attempts to reduce future criminal activity by changing the offender's attitudes and behavior (Trojanowicz et al. 2001). Juvenile boot camps are utilized by youths who would otherwise be confined in a facility. Youths selected for boot camps are more hard-core than those who might receive probation and yet are viewed as "treatable," but only under more extreme forms of diversion. Advocates of boot camps argue that the incarceration period is shorter than regular incarceration and therefore saves taxpayer money. Additionally, it is believed that many of these youths may disassociate themselves from the gang after successfully completing the program. Opponents argue that military-style training, in which officers yell and scream at youths, is hardly an effective diversionary treatment.

Juvenile boot camps were also inspired by Colorado's **Outward Bound** or **Wilderness Training** program. Outward Bound programs engage youths in rigorous physical work in forestry camps. Interestingly, the forestry camps for juvenile offenders were developed in the 1930s in the Los Angeles County Forestry Department. The juvenile offenders helped clear brush, learned about conservation, worked on road construction, did farm work, and so on. Wilderness Programs attempt to help build the self-esteem of troubled youths by involving them in such physical activities as rock climbing, rappelling, canoeing, backpacking, hiking, cave exploring, and so on. The effectiveness of wilderness programs remains unclear, with some more successful than others (Trojanowicz et al. 2001).

Methods of Treatment

Professionals have many methods of treatment available to help gang members leave the gang. Because of the great number of treatments and methods of implementing them, discussion here will be very limited and selective.

One treatment approach involves **transactional analysis**, which can be used both individually and in groups. This approach is primarily concerned with evaluating and interpreting interpersonal relationships and the dynamic transactions between the gang member (client) and the environment. The therapist examines clients' demeanor, gestures, vocabulary, and voice to gain insights into why they behave the way they do. This treatment appears to be "fun" because it involves playing games, by which the therapist learns a great deal about the client. Ultimately, the treatment attempts to teach clients to learn how to act appropriately in a group setting.

Cognitive therapies involve confronting and challenging the offenders' irrational thoughts and behavioral patterns. The offender is taught to take responsibility for his or her own actions as well as emotions. The therapist attempts to demonstrate to the gang member how his or her behavior is overly emotional and not rational—from a societal standpoint. In order to "correct" the irrational behavior of gang members (or other offenders), therapists employ cognitive skills development exercises. Particular emphasis is placed on developing decision-making skills, moral education, and replacing aggressive behavior. The cognitive therapy approach attempts to teach the client to think through a situation before taking any action (Trojanowicz et al. 2001, 340).

Vocational training is an atypical treatment approach in that it does not address the interpersonal dynamics of human behavior or spend a large time on diagnosis. Vocational training provides the client with vocational counseling in order to increase the client's knowledge of career choices and how to address job specifications and qualification requirements (Trojanowicz et al. 2001). Vocational training is a diversion method; it keeps offenders busy with jobs and career aspirations after successful training, in which they are taught job and computer skills. Job placement is key to the success of vocational training as an effective diversion method.

Behavior therapy, better known as **behavior modification**, is based on principles of learning theory as well as of experimental psychology (Trojanowicz et al. 2001). This form of therapy attempts to modify the undesired behaviors of juvenile offenders through a series of therapeutic sessions. Behavior modification therapists believe that just about any behavior can be modified, especially if the client is striving to change. The client goes through a series of "baby steps" toward the desired goal. Punishments and rewards are used as reinforcers. Positive behavior is rewarded; negative behavior is punished using a point system. The punishments for gang members need to be far more severe, because they are more adapted to violence than most nongang members. In general, behavior modification programs are most effective for those who want to change their behavior (e.g., someone who is afraid of heights and wants to overcome the fear) and less so for those who are forced into therapy (as are most gang members). Additionally, behavior modification treatments have positive results while the client is in the program, but the modified behavior usually reverts once the client is out of the program.

In addition to this very brief review of treatment methods, some other options include behavioral contracts, crisis intervention (discussed earlier in this chapter), and psychotherapy.

Prison Treatment Programs

The great influx of gangs into the prison setting has led prison officials to create programs that attempt to break the individual's alliance to the gang. This is a necessary undertaking, as most imprisoned gang members will eventually be released back into the community. Once again, there are numerous examples of prison treatment programs, and they have the same evaluative problems as the prevention and suppression strategies described throughout this chapter.

Among the more interesting prison treatment programs is the gang-busting program at the **Connecticut Garner Correctional Institution**. The goal of the Connecticut program is to build trust, and even friendships, among gangsters who might otherwise stab each other. Prison officials put rival gang members together in a prison gym and have them engage in activities where each other's safety is in the hands of a rival. One exercise involves a gang member dangling from a rope wrapped around his waist and looped over a metal rafter. Whether he falls to the hardwood floor below or is lowered slowly and safely depends on the rival gang member who is holding the rope. Prison officials hope that through these activities rival gang members will develop a trust in each other that will last outside prison. The Garner program treats gang affiliation as an addiction and uses a 12-step process, implemented over five months, designed to sever gang ties among inmates forever. Inmates who fail to participate in the program or refuse to renounce their gang ties after the program are separated from the rest of the prison population (*Syracuse Post Standard* 1997). With an estimated 20% of inmates in the nation's prisons gang members, the Garner program is being looked at closely by other states.

Jim Brown, former NFL great and Hall of Fame running back for the famed Cleveland Browns, has had his share of run-ins with the law. Retiring after nine short years, Brown left Cleveland for Hollywood to make movies and further increase his fame, but he never forgot about the people who were less fortunate. Jim Brown formed the **Black Economic Union** to help finance new black businesses (Terry 1997), and he is the founder and president of the **Amer-I-can** program, which helps inmates, ex-convicts, gang members, and troubled youths to manage their lives better. Most of the skills taught in the Amer-I-can program are job skills, such as how to dress for a job, face a prospective employer, and communicate effectively. The Amer-I-can program is driven by two basic principles: everyone must take responsibility for their behavior and, most importantly, no one is cursed from birth. Brown has risked his life for the program, acting as mediator for rival gangs in his own home. One night, Brown's chief of staff was shot 11 times by a gang that wanted Brown's program to fail. Brown's program has not failed. As of 1997, it has trained 17,000 inmates in California and more than 4,000 in New Jersey. The Amer-I-can program is taught in 24 schools in Ohio. Amer-I-can personnel are now training police officers how to handle gangs more effectively.

SUMMARY

This chapter discussed various gang intervention strategies. The two primary general strategies are gang prevention and gang suppression. Prevention strategies are divided into three categories: community prevention programs; prevention programs involving families, schools, and local business; and nationally based prevention strategies. It is their commitment to finding ways to keep youths out of gangs in the first place that links the three approaches. After-school programs that teach conflict-management skills and job-training skills are very popular prevention strategies. In addition, curfews are often implemented as a means of denying juveniles the opportunity to act delinquently. Ultimately, the goal is to safeguard the community against gang crime while also offering at-risk youths alternatives to gang life and assisting in their prosocial development. Prevention strategies reinforce the core principle of Travis Hirschi's social bond theory, namely, that all must form a bond with society in order to feel that they have a stake in what happens in the society. Attachment, commitment, involvement, and belief in society are all critical elements of gang prevention.

Although suppression strategies are ongoing and despite many high-quality prevention programs, the fact remains that the number of gangs and gang members increases annually, and citizens in many neighborhoods throughout the country are subjected to the violence and intimidation of gangs. Many police agencies have established specialized gang suppression units. Some units (e.g., the LAPD's CRASH unit) have crossed the line of legality in pursuit of eliminating gangs from their streets. Many communities have established community policing programs, which involve local citizens with law enforcement efforts to combat gangs. Courts have used all sorts of techniques to assist the police, including allowing the enactment of injunctions, nuisance abatements, loitering restrictions, curfews, truancy laws, and banning gang clothing and colors in schools. Recently, prosecutors have turned to federal laws, such as RICO, to levy the harshest penalties possible against gang members. Although many agencies have reported success with their programs, it is important to note that "the generalizability of any evaluation of a gang suppression strategy is at best difficult, at worst impossible. One specific problem with evaluation of gang intervention strategies is that police, prosecutor, and legislative definitions of gangs, gang-related crime, and gang members differ widely (Fritsch et al. 2003, 275).

Because of the overall ineffectiveness of prevention and suppression strategies in keeping youths out of gangs, a number of treatment programs have been created to help gang members leave the gang. A number of alternatives to court processing (probation, parole, restitution and community service, and boot camps) have been established to help youths avoid prosecution in the criminal justice system. Trained therapists and counselors also use a number of treatment methods to attempt to divert young people from gangs. Additionally, because of the large number of gang members in prison, a number of correctional facilities have created prison treatment programs designed to sever inmate ties with gangs.

Despite all these efforts, as old gang members are taken off the streets, either through prevention or suppression methods, new gang members have come in to take their place. It would appear that social policy makers are missing the main point: What most young people want is a future, or at least hope of a future. All the job training programs in the world are useless if American industry continues to abandon its citizens and moves its operations overseas. Job opportunities are needed, first and foremost, to keep at-risk juveniles out of the gangs.

CHAPTER TEN

Implications for the Future

The gang world is extremely violent and complex. One's perception of gangs is generally shaped by the level of contact with gangs. The vast majority of Americans have little or no direct contact and therefore tend to view gang members merely as punks and criminals who need to be locked up, and this limited view is often distorted by popular media portrayals of gangbangers. The people whose lives are daily affected by direct contact with gangs come to view America's street gangs as intimidating thugs. Law enforcement officers on the whole view gang members simply as criminals who need to be incarcerated. Gang researchers generally come to the realization that the development and maintenance of gangs in society is very much intertwined with the socioeconomic conditions that lead individuals to turn to gangs in the first place. For most gang members, the gang is a refuge from a world filled with disenchantment and perceived hopelessness. This brief summary is intended to emphasize the complexity of gangism and to help the reader understand the implications of gangs for the future.

A REVIEW

The difficulty of reaching a true understanding of gangs and gang-related behavior is illustrated in Chapter 1, "What is a Gang?" The fact that there is no agreed-upon definition of a gang (this includes both law enforcement and gang researchers) is highly problematic, for social research always starts with defining the problem and establishing its parameters. Consequently, the chapter described a number of definitions, including the author's, and the parameters of this book—a focus on street gangs (especially youth gangs). In addition, it described a number of non-street gangs, including motorcycle gangs, organized crime, the KKK, Skinheads, and prison gangs.

Chapter 2 provided a rather extensive history of gangs, an important topic because many people believe that street gangs are a recent phenomenon, whereas history demonstrate that delinquent youth groups, or gangs, have existed for centuries. Youth street gangs as a legitimate social problem first arose in New York City in the early 1800s with the formation of the Forty Thieves of the Five Points region of the city. A review of the history of gangs reveals how disadvantaged ethnic and racial groups tended to dominate gangs. As America's first urban ethnic minority group, the Irish dominated the gang world in the mid-1800s, for example. Victims of prejudice and discrimination in their homeland (as a result of England's brutal rule in Ireland), many fled Ireland and the potato famine of the mid-1800s—which was really an English attempt at genocide of the Irish. When the Irish arrived in the United States, they were victimized once again, this time by the prevailing Anglo-Saxon culture. The Irish were neither Anglo nor Saxon and were poor and undereducated, and they congregated in ethnic communities, taking pride in the one thing they did own—their neighborhood. The young Irish-Americans felt it necessary to protect their turf from outsiders who disapproved of their very existence. As the Irish slowly became assimilated into the surrounding culture, other ethnic groups took their place as victims of racial and ethnic prejudice and mistreatment. This pattern continued throughout the twentieth century and still exists at the beginning of the third millennium. History, clearly, does repeat itself. It seems an inevitable human trait that diverse people cannot live together harmoniously, especially when there are limited social and natural resources.

One of the most intriguing questions regarding gangs is why they exist. Chapters 3 and 4 attempt to address this rather simple question that involves relatively complicated answers. Chapter 3 offers a great number of theoretical explanations, including biological, psychological, and sociological theories. Chapter 4 offers different explanations of why gangs exist and persist in society. Instead of theoretical constructs, the focus in this chapter is on socioeconomic explanations. Among these factors are the shifting labor market, the development of an underclass, poverty, the feminization of poverty (an important variable when considering the fact that a great number of gang members come from single-parent families headed by an economically poor woman), the breakdown of the nuclear family (especially in regard to "missing" fathers), and poor levels of educational attainment. It has become clear to many researchers, including this author, that the most fundamental explanation for the escalation of gangs in the past two decades is economic realities. The lack of job opportunities is threatening to shake the very foundation of American sociey. The first warning sign of this truth is gangs and the realization that many youths honestly perceive the gang as their best hope of getting ahead in society, or at least maintaining an existence. Another very important consideration is the realization that many individuals, youths and adults, find the deviant lifestyle preferable to the conventional one. Legitimate society has its "thrill-seekers," people who need to live on the edge in order to feel alive. Well, many gang members have this same attitude; they join the gang simply because they find that the criminal and violent lifestyle is exciting and thrilling. They experience a "rush" of excitement and genuinely enjoy the gangbanging lifestyle. Removing these individuals from the gang will be the most difficult of all, because they are not looking for a job—they are looking for kicks and thrills.

Any comprehensive review of gangs must include a discussion on gang structure and process. Chapter 5 addresses these issues by examining the organizational component of gangs. Some gangs are so structured that they resemble the military, whereas others are loosely confederated groups of youths and young adults who view the gang as a temporary aspect of life. Other factors such as the processes of joining a gang, initiations, leadership, belief systems, leaving the gang, and the code of the streets reveal the sociological makeup of gangs. Especially important to gangs is symbolism: the use of graffiti, hand signals, gang colors, and clothing. Graffiti is a primary means of communication among gang members; it also provides law enforcement officials a written account of what is going on in the streets (e.g., what gangs are at war with each other, what gang is attempting to enlarge its territory, and so on).

Chapter 6 describes yet another facet of gangs, namely, that gangs vary a great deal by size. Many neighborhoods have local street gangs whose members are all youths from the neighborhood and that have no affiliation to larger regional and national gangs. These local gangs often disappear after a short period of time. Regional gangs are much larger than local gangs and are generally involved in some sort of criminal enterprise. They use their territory to set up illegal activities such as selling drugs and fencing stolen merchandise. The most dangerous gangs, generally speaking, are the super-sized gangs, or nation coalition gangs. Nation gangs include the Crips, Bloods, Folks, and People. They have set up cells throughout the country and maintain a loose confederation among the sets. This chapter also describes gang activity in the New York State cities of Syracuse, Rochester, and Buffalo (including some of the author's original research).

It is also interesting to note that more and more women are joining gangs. Female gangs are discussed in Chapter 7. Topics covered in this chapter include reasons why females join the gang, recruitment, initiation, affiliation to male gangs, criminal activities, relationships with males and schools, pregnancy, and family relationships. It appears that females, for the most part, join a gang for the same reasons as their male counterparts, although a distinguishing feature is the fact that a great number of female gang members were victimized, or witness victimization, in the home. They turn to the gang looking for a family substitute.

The primary reason the general public is concerned about gangs is because of their criminal activities. Chapter 8 describes the various types of criminal activities that gang members participate in as well as some statistical information. Among the criminal activities that gang members engage in are drug use, sale and distribution; violent assaults; and homicide. Gang members also participate in robbery, burglary/breaking and entering, larceny/theft, motor vehicle theft, extortion, forcible rape, and witness intimidation. Citizens are worried about being victimized by gang-related criminal activities, and for good reason, although they are more likely to be victimized by crimes such as robbery, theft, and witness intimidation and it is rival gang members who are more likely to be victims of the violent crimes perpetrated by gang members. Gang members participate in criminal activities for the same reason as criminal nongang members—economics. However, it is also true that because of the "rush" experienced in gangbanging, some gang members engage in violent and nonviolent crime because they find it exciting.

Regardless of why gang members engage in criminal activities, a number of officials have responded to their negative impact on society. Many social institutions are involved in diverting youths from gangs and other institutions are responsible for punishing gangsters. Chapter 9, "Gang Prevention, Suppression, and Treatment," addresses the various intervention strategies used. Prevention efforts, spearheaded by community programs and the schools, are designed to divert youths from joining the gang by creating social programs that provide job skills training and better educational opportunities. Suppression methods are employed by law enforcement and the courts. Their main focus is to punish and incarcerate gang members. Treatment programs have also been established to help break gang members' ties with the gang so that they can become productive members of society.

The evidence presented throughout this book indicates that the gang problem in American society is escalating. Gangs are nearly everywhere—they can be found in a wide variety of settings, including rural, suburban, and urban areas, on Native-American reservations, and in prisons. According to the National Alliance of Gang Investigators Association (NAGIA), gang members have now infiltrated a wide variety of social institutions that will allow them to continue to profit from their criminal enterprises. Gangs are found in the **workplace**, a distinct departure from the settings for their previous criminal activity. For example, when Hollywood movie executives attempt to make "authentic" street-based movies, they often turn to Suspect Entertainment, a company comprised of former Latino gang members. "They offer script consultations, graffiti artists, low-rider rentals and plenty of actors who come pre-equipped with gangster-standard goatees, shaved heads and tattoos" (Hernu 2004). (Members of Suspect Entertainment have appeared in such movies as *Training Day* and *S.W.A.T.*) Some gangs are moving from the streets to the corporate world, where they can potentially obtain larger profits from low-risk crimes like money laundering and product theft. The National Football League (NFL) banned the wearing of do-rags (bandanas and/or stocking caps) because the league considered the extra headwear too closely related to gang symbolism. A player may wear a skullcap in team colors or some other covering under their helmets if a doctor finds a medical necessity, such as a scalp condition (Weisman 2001).

Gangs are also found in the **military** and represent a potential security risk for many soldiers and citizens. Although the Secretary of the Army's Task Force on Extremist Activities 1996 investigation found little evidence of a widespread presence, it concluded that gangs do represent a security risk in the military. Gang members may join the military to learn military tactics they can bring back to the streets, and in some cases they have been found to be involved in drug trafficking and arms trafficking while serving in the armed forces. Gang members who enter the military often lie about their past criminal records, further increasing the risk they represent. Among the proactive measures used by the military to identify gang members is to conduct mandatory tattoo checks at reception centers.

A very disturbing trend is the increasing presence of gang members in the ranks of **law enforcement agencies** across the country. A survey conducted by the National Gang Crime Research Center of convicted gang members in 17 states revealed that gang members were also police officers in more than half of the states (NAGIA 2002). "The threat that gang members in law enforcement represent is multi-fold as these individuals are capable of jeopardizing cases under investigation, placing other officers in danger, exposing witnesses of gang-related crimes to intimidation or death, and compromising law enforcement tactics and sources of information" (NAGIA 2002, 9).

Gang members have also infiltrated other social institutions. They have in the past made some inroads in the world of **politics**. This influence was first noted in New York City in the era of Tammany Hall, whose corrupt political officials hired gang members to intimidate would-be voters. In contemporary America it would be difficult for gangs to have this same influence; however, if gang members were to register to vote and voted as a block, they could have a significant influence on local-level politics. Gangs—the Conservation Vice Lords, for example—have always been involved in local politics and some attempt to elect their own candidates. In New York City, the Almighty Latin King Nation is involved in voter registration, distributes campaign fliers for favorite candidates, and has been accused of intimidating voters into favoring its chosen candidates (NAGIA 2002). The corruption inherent in politics makes this social institution an attractive environment for business-savvy gang leaders, who could easily take advantage of money-laundering opportunities through monetary contributions to candidates.

Gangs are also on the **Internet**. Many gangs communicate with each other, just like conventional citizens, through e-mail, sometimes coding their messages. Gangs have also established their own websites. Rather sophisticated gang homepage websites have links to "sound-off" pages, "RIP" sections dedicated to fallen members, photos and bios of gang members, and graffiti and audio messages and music. The Internet is being increasingly used for criminal activities and has proven to be a tool for drug trafficking (NAGIA 2002). In Garland, Texas (a Dallas suburb), rival gang members organized a gang rumble by using the Internet. The March 3, 2004 brawl was preceded by gang members trading insults in a profanity-laced chat room. They decided to fight for real and set the time and place over the Internet. Nearly three dozen gangsters were arrested after this Internet-facilitated melee occurred (*Syracuse Post Standard* 2004).

Street gangs have become such a permanent fixture in American culture that it is time to recognize them as a social institution. "Of course, gangs may fade as another transient social form, culturally rejected and replaced by some other, as yet unenvisioned, structure of adolescence. This seems unlikely, however. The future of gangs may be uncertain, but recurring social crises in the coming decades are likely to ensure that gangs will be an important part of the future" (Fagan 2004, 255). There are many other social institutions, however, that are attempting to block the growing presence of street gangs, including the family, the local community, schools, law enforcement, and the entire judicial system. Attacking the disease of gangism must begin with intervention programs directed at very young children, especially at-risk youths. It is important that parents, school officials, and community leaders (who include law enforcement and politicians) learn to identify warning signs that youths may be turning toward gang life. Trump (1998) lists the following gang identifiers:

- the sudden use of *graffiti*, unusual signs, symbols, or writing, on walls, notebooks, class assignments, or gang "literature" books (referred to by this author and other gang researchers as "bibles")
- the use of *colors* or significant types or styles of *clothing*
- *tattoos* of the gang variety
- *suspicious bruises or injuries*, which may be the result of an initiation or actual gangbanging activity
- unusual *hand signals and handshakes* used when greeting others
- *language* that involves uncommon terms or phrases
- sudden, or erratic, changes in *behavior*

When a youth suddenly displays multiple warning signs, there is a high likelihood that he or she may be becoming involved in gang activity. According to The National Drug Intelligence Center (1995) there are other, less subtle ways of determining whether someone is a gang member or not.

- In some cases the individual will admit membership in a gang.
- Law enforcement officials may identify an individual as a gang member.
- Individuals who reside in, or frequent, a particular gang area and adopt the gang style of dress and mannerism.
- The youth is involved in violent and criminal behavior with a group of cohorts.

The effectiveness of law enforcement efforts to combat gangs is contingent on legislative tools (laws) that allow the police to apprehend and arrest gang members. Although brief attention was given to some of the legislative efforts designed to fight gangs in Chapter 9, it is important to reintroduce the topic of legislation here, as there are many recent and pending laws designed to combat the further growth of gangs in the present and the future.

RECENT AND PENDING LEGISLATION TO COMBAT GANGS

Many students (and nonstudents alike) ask me, "Why don't they just make it illegal to be a gang member?," the idea being that police could arrest gang members *before* they commit crimes. This overly simplistic question, which ignores the problems of properly defining what group of people constitute a gang as well as the legal rights of citizens to peacefully assemble in public, has not been ignored by legislators. Many laws have been recently passed (or are pending) that virtually make it illegal to be a gang member.

Gang Participation

In 1999, Omaha, Nebraska legislators passed Ordinance No. 34926 as part of its Municipal Code. Sec.18-81 (Declaration of nuisance; notice to abate) states that "any private place or premises within the city which is used as the site of a juvenile gathering is hereby declared to be a public nuisance. No person shall maintain any such nuisance." The police are given authority to abate the nuisance. In Arizona (Arizona 13-2308), assisting in a criminal syndicate is a class 4 felony. If the criminal syndicate is a street gang, such offenses may become class 3 or 2 felonies. California law (186.22) states that "any person who actively participates in any criminal street gang with knowledge that its members engage in or have engaged in a pattern of criminal gang activity, and who willfully promotes, furthers, or assists in any felonious criminal conduct by members of that gang, shall be punished by imprisonment in a county jail for a period not to exceed one year, or by imprisonment in the state prison for 16 months, or two or three years." Georgia law (16-15-4) makes it illegal for any person employed by or associated with a criminal street gang to conduct or participate in a pattern of criminal gang activity. It is also illegal to encourage, solicit, or coerce another person to participate in a criminal street gang. Iowa legislation (723A.2) states that any person who commits a criminal act for the benefit of a criminal street gang is guilty of a class D felony. Louisiana (15:1403), Minnesota (609.229), and Missouri (578.423) state laws make it illegal for any person to participate in a pattern of criminal gang activity.

Weapons

A number of laws have been enacted that deal with specific areas of gang activity. One of the most important of these is the use of weapons by gang members. Arizona law (Arizona 13-3102) states that a person is guilty of "misconduct involving a weapon" if a person knowingly discharges a firearm "at an occupied structure in order to assist, promote or further the interests of a criminal street gang, a criminal syndicate or racketeering enterprise." California law 186.22(a) gives law enforcement the right to take any firearm or ammunition that may be used with the firearm, for the purpose of criminal street gang use. In Mississippi (Mississippi 97-3-110), law enforcement has the right to seize firearms and motor vehicles (from juveniles) when they are used in conjunction with a drive-by shooting or bombing. Missouri law 578.435 allows law enforcement to confiscate any "weapon" (defined in section 571.010) that is owned or possessed by a member of a criminal street gang for the purposes of committing a crime. In Georgia, specific types of weapons (machine guns, sawed-off shotguns, and firearms equipped with a silencer) are forbidden (Georgia 16-11-160) in conjunction with and participation in criminal gang activity defined in Code Section 16-15-4. Any person who violates this code is guilty of a felony and is subject to a 10-year prison term (which would run consecutively with any other sentence the person has received). In Washington state (9.41.225), the use of a machine gun is considered a felony. This legislation is aimed primarily at gang members and other dangerous criminals.

Drive-By Shooting

One of the most effective means of intimidation used by gang members is the drive-by shooting. Drive-by shootings are not done only by gang members and therefore most legislation aimed at curtailing drive-by shootings is not limited to gang members. Nearly all states have some sort of legislation on record designed to punish those who engage in drive-by shootings. Arkansas law 5-74-107 states that it is illegal to discharge a firearm from a vehicle. Arizona law 13-1209 stipulates that persons who commit a drive-by shooting by intentionally discharging a weapon must surrender their driver's license. In Alaska (11.61.190) a person is guilty of the crime of "misconduct involving weapons in the first degree" when participating in a drive-by shooting. California law 12035(c) states that "any person who willfully and maliciously discharges a firearm from a motor vehicle at another person other than an occupant of a motor vehicle is guilty of a felony punishable by imprisonment in state prison for three, five, or seven years." New Mexico law 30-3-8 stipulates that shooting at or from a motor vehicle results in felony offenses. If the shooter injures another person, they are guilty of a third-degree felony; if great bodily harm is caused, the infraction increases to a second-degree felony. Discharging a firearm in Rhode Island (11-47-51.1) will result in imprisonment for not less than 10 years nor more than 20 years and will be accompanied by a fine of not less than $50,000.

Threats and Intimidation

Gang members may threaten and intimidate youths into joining their gang. There are a wide variety of laws on recruitment, threats, and intimidation violations on record with many more in the works. In Alaska such gang members would be in violation of Alaska Sec. 11.61.160, "recruiting a gang member in the first degree." A person is guilty of this crime if he or she threatens force against a person or property to induce a person to join in a criminal street gang or to commit a crime on behalf of a criminal street gang. A gang member may be found guilty of "recruiting a gang member in the second degree" in Alaska (11.61.165) if the recruiter is 18 years of age or older and the recruited is under age 18. In Arizona (13-1202), a person is guilty of "threatening or intimidating" by word or conduct to cause physical injury to another person or damage the property of another in conjunction with a criminal street gang or criminal syndicate or a racketeering enterprise. Indiana law 35-45-9-4 stipulates that a person is guilty of "gang intimidation," a class C felony, when threatening another person who refuses to join a criminal gang or who has withdrawn from a criminal gang. In New Hampshire, a person is guilty of criminal threatening when "(a) by physical conduct, the person purposely places or attempts to place another in fear of imminent bodily injury or physical contact; or (b) the person places any object or graffiti on the property of another with a purpose to coerce or terrorize any person" (New Hampshire 631-4).

Curfew

Ideally, children are in school during the daytime and off the streets at night. Keeping children busy in positive and enriching extracurricular activities is important in helping the youth of America avoid gangs. It is generally believed that it is in the best interest of youths to keep them off the streets and away from contact with deviant and criminal others. Truancy and curfew laws have existed for a long time in the United States. Truancy laws are more easily accepted by society—everyone recognizes that children need to be in school during the academic year. Curfew laws are more controversial because they may be applied in a variety of ways, including restrictions on adult, law-abiding citizens. Some curfews require that people show some sort of ID card—potentially violating civil rights.

Many local jurisdictions throughout the United States have curfew laws. It would be pointless to review a great number of them; however, a few examples are provided here. In 1999, the city of Los Angeles passed curfew restrictions for minors: "It is unlawful for any minor under the age of eighteen to be present in or upon any public street, avenue, highway, road, curb area, alley, park, playground, or other public ground, public place, or public building, place of amusement or eating place, vacant lot or unsupervised place between the hours of 10:00 P.M. on any day and sunrise of the immediately following day" (California Chapter IV, Sec. 45.03). A number of exemptions are allowed (accompanied by an adult or guardian, going or coming directly from or to their place of employment, medical appointment, etc.). The city of Los Angeles also has a daytime curfew prohibiting juvenile loitering between the hours of 8:30 A.M. and 1:30 P.M. (Sec. 45.04). Any minor who is subject to compulsory education or to compulsory continuing education is not allowed in any public place during school hours while school is in session. Los Angeles County has a nighttime curfew for minors (13.56.010) similar to that of the city of Los Angeles. Before taking an enforcement action, a law enforcement officer is obligated to ask the apparent offender's age and reason for being present in a "public place" during curfew hours (13.56.030). Parents and guardians may be held accountable for the minor's curfew violation (13.56.060).

Other cities have less stringent curfew requirements. For example, in 1999, Minneapolis, Minnesota adopted a curfew (395.20) for any person under 15 years of age between the hours of 10:00 P.M. and 4:00 A.M. daily (11:00 P.M. on Fridays and Saturdays). In 1996, St. Louis, Missouri established a curfew for juveniles (15.110.020) under the age of 17 between the hours of 11:59 P.M. and 5:00 A.M. Reno, Nevada established its curfew in 1999 and applies it to persons under the age of 18 (Sec. 8.16.010). The city of Las Vegas also applies its curfew to persons under the age of 18 (Sec. 10.54.010). In 1999, curfew violators in Oklahoma City, Oklahoma became guilty of a criminal offense if they were found in any public place during curfew hours (Sec. 30-424). As of 1999, curfew violators in Houston, Texas were guilty of a miscellaneous offense (Sec. 28-171); furthermore, "it shall be unlawful for the parent or guardian having legal custody of a minor to knowingly allow or permit the minor to be in violation of the curfew imposed in section 28-172(a) of this Code" (Sec. 28-172).

The primary reasons for curfews are the safety of youth and the protection of innocent citizens. If youths are off the streets and under proper adult supervision, they are less likely to become involved in criminal activity, including gang activity. Daytime curfews, or truancy laws, are designed to keep kids in school so that they may gain a proper education and achieve success in society as adults.

Gangs and Schools

School administrators are faced with many problems; providing a quality education in a safe environment ranks as their primary responsibility and potentially most challenging problem. Georgia law (20-8-6) requires that all educational facilities that employ campus policemen (including institutions of the university system of Georgia) report to the Georgia Bureau of Investigation and to the local law enforcement agency incidents of criminal gang activity occurring on or adjacent to the campus of the educational facility. Indiana state law (20-10.1-27-8) established the antigang counseling pilot program to provide financial assistance to participating schools. Students and parents are informed on the extent to which criminal gang activity exists within the schools.

Many school districts throughout the country believe that establishing a dress code policy is a good way of providing a positive learning environment. This idea is based on the assumption that most gangs are identified by specific colors and styles of clothing. Iowa law (279.58) gives the board of directors of a school district the right to adopt a dress code policy that prohibits students from wearing gang-related or other specific apparel deemed inappropriate. Nevada law 392.4635 allows the board of trustees of each school district the right to forbid "(a) a pupil from wearing any clothing or carrying any symbol on school property that denotes membership in or an affiliation with a criminal gang; and (b) any activity that encourages participation in a criminal gang or facilitates illegal acts of a criminal gang." School officials have the right to suspend or expel any student found in violation of this policy. California law (35183) declares that California children have the right to an effective public school education free from the threat of violence; "gang-related apparel" is deemed hazardous to the health and safety of the school environment. Section 7 of this law encourages school districts to establish a school dress uniform as a means of establishing a "coming together feeling" among members of the student body.

In addition to dress codes, many states have empowered school districts with the authority to combat gangs in a variety of other ways. Utah law 53A-11-902 establishes conduct and discipline policies and procedures. Section 7 of this law establishes "specific provisions for preventing and responding to gang-related activities in the school, on school grounds, on school vehicles, or in connection with school-related activities or events." Washington law (148-120-100) prohibits gang activity on school grounds. Claiming membership in, association with, affiliation with, or participation in a gang or gang-related activities at school or during school-related functions is not allowed in any way.

Nuisance Abatement

Gangs represent a much larger problem off school campuses than they do on them. The schools do not want gangbangers on their premises, residents don't want them in their neighborhoods, and legislators don't want them on public grounds. In 1999, Dade County (Miami), Florida enacted Ord. No. 99-43, Nuisance Abatement. Section 2-98.4 declares that "any places or premises which are used as the site of the unlawful sale or delivery of controlled substances, prostitution, youth and street gang activity, gambling, illegal sale or consumption of alcoholic beverages, or lewd or lascivious behavior may be a public nuisance that adversely affects the public health, safety, morals, and welfare." Also in 1999, the city of Miami enacted its own public nuisance code legislation (Ord. No. 11797). Section 46-1 set the parameters as "any building, place or premises located in the city which has been used on three or more occasions, documented by substantiated incidences, as the site of the unlawful sale or delivery of controlled substances" or any other criminal act (as defined by Florida law) "within a six-month period from the date of the first substantiated incident, at the same location, is declared an unlawful public nuisance." In 1999, Houston, Texas passed nuisance abatement legislation (Ord. No. 99-1201) in an attempt to increase the quality of life of its residents as well as to fight criminal activity by both gang members and non-gang members. Reno, Nevada (Chapter 8.22, Sec. 8.22.020) has passed nuisance abatement ordinances as a means of keeping its community, including property, buildings, and premises within its limits, safe and as aesthetically pleasing as possible by forbidding a number of criminal activities, especially the use of graffiti by gang members.

Graffiti

All graffiti represents an attack on property and on society as a whole. Graffiti, one of the worst eyesores in a community, is despised by all law-abiding citizens. A great deal of graffiti is gang-related. Many legislative bodies have passed laws and ordinances against the use of graffiti, especially by gang members. A few examples of these ordinances are described here. In 1997, Anchorage, Alaska passed legislation (8.05.375) with the intent of preventing graffiti and promoting its eradication. Anchorage legislators believed that graffiti adversely affects the community by lowering property values and compromises the security of the community. Graffiti is defined as "any inscription, symbol, design or configuration of letters or numbers written, drawn, etched, marked, painted, stained, stuck on or adhered to any surface on public or private property without the express permission of the owner of such property, including but not limited to trees, signs, poles, fixtures, utility boxes, walls, paths, walks, streets, underpasses, overpasses, bridges, trestles, buildings or any other structures or surfaces." Implements that create graffiti, such as aerosol paint containers, markers, and gum labels (stickers, decals, posters, etc.), are also banned if they are used for the purpose of creating graffiti. In Honolulu, Hawaii, it is illegal for an adult to furnish, in any manner, a minor with any graffiti implement (Sec. 40-11-2). Denver, Colorado outlawed the possession of graffiti materials by minors in 1995 (Sec. 24-66), "It shall be unlawful for any person under the age of eighteen (18) years to possess any can of spray paint, broad tipped marker pen, glass cutting tool, or glass etching tool or instrument." Clearwater, Florida forbids graffiti (Sec. 20.05): "It shall be a violation of this section for any person to paint, draw, or otherwise apply graffiti to any wall, post, column, or other building or structure, or to a tree, or other exterior surface, publicly or privately owned, within the City of Clearwater (Ord. No. 5492-93). Graffiti is not allowed in Minneapolis, Minnesota. In 1998, Minneapolis passed legislation (Ord. No. 98-Or-045) stating that "no person shall willfully or wantonly damage, mutilate or deface any exterior surface of any structure or building on any private or public property by placing theron any marking, carving or graffiti." As of June 1999, Omaha, Nebraska also forbade graffiti (Ord. No. 34926). Legislators in Omaha viewed graffiti as a "blighting factor, which not only depreciates the value of the property which has been the target of such malicious vandalism, but also depreciates the value of the adjacent and surrounding properties, and in so doing negatively impacts upon the entire community" (Sec. 18-60). Also in 1999 the city of Charlotte, North Carolina prohibited graffiti (Ord. No. 1345, Sec. 10-17) as did Oklahoma City, Oklahoma (35-142). Oklahoma City especially targeted gang-related graffiti, stating that gang graffiti serves as "a catalyst for gang-related criminal violence within the City" (35-142).

Further examples of graffiti ordinances can be found in Los Angeles and the surrounding area. Los Angeles County forbids the application of graffiti and the possession of graffiti implements: "It is unlawful for any person to apply graffiti to any trees or structures including, but not limited to, buildings, walls, fences, poles, and signs" (Sec. 13.12.030). Furthermore, "it is unlawful for any person under the age of eighteen years to have in his or her possession any graffiti implement while on any school property, grounds, facilities, buildings, or structures, or in areas immediately adjacent to these specific locations upon public property, or upon private property without prior written consent of the owner or occupant of such private property" (Sec. 13.12.040). Adults are also prohibited from possessing "any graffiti implement while in or upon any public facility, park, playground, swimming pool, recreational facility, or other public building owned or operated by the county. . . ." (Sec. 13.12.050). The city of Los Angeles amended its Municipal Code in 1999 (Chapter IX), stating that business owners are responsible for keeping their property clean of accumulations of trash, debris, and so on. Early legislation (1996) had already stipulated that business owners must clean their property of graffiti, as it is "unlawful for the owner or person in control to allow to exist any graffiti on a building or fence when such graffiti, as defined in Section 49.84 of the Los Angeles Municipal Code, is visible from a public street or alley. It shall also be unlawful if such owner or person refuses to consent to the removal of the graffiti by the City after being notified by the Department that the City wishes to remove the graffiti" (Sec. 91.8904.1).

Thus, local jurisdictions throughout the country have passed legislation to combat the scourge of graffiti. In many cases, the state has stepped in to pass laws making graffiti illegal. In New York (145.60) it is illegal for any "person to make graffiti of any type on any building, public or private, or any other property real or personal owned by any person, firm, corporation or any public or instrumentality, without the express permission of the owner or the operator of said property." Possessing graffiti instruments is also forbidden (145.65). In 2002, California (Penal Code 594) declared that "every person who maliciously commits any of the following acts with respect to any real or personal property not his or her own, in cases other than those specified by state law, is guilty of vandalism: (1) Defaces with graffiti or other inscribed material. (2) Damages. (3) Destroys." The phrase "graffiti or other inscribed material" includes "any unauthorized inscription, word, figure, mark, or design, that is written, marked, etched, scratched, drawn, or painted on real or personal property" (California Penal Code 594(e)). One well-written federal law could make graffiti illegal throughout the nation and make such an offense subject to federal law.

Gang Databases

A great deal of legislation is written to aid law enforcement agencies and prosecutors in their fight against criminals and gangs. Colorado established the Colorado Bureau of Investigation, which has as a primary responsibility "to develop and maintain a computerized data base for tracking gangs and gang members both within the state and among the various states." Florida passed a law (985.08) authorizing the creation of information systems for the purpose of establishing a statewide criminal gang database. Tennessee law (38-6-102) establishes a centralized system of data collection on criminal gang activity. Texas (61.02) and Virginia (16.1-299.2) are among the other states that established such gang databases.

Expert Testimony

It is common in many types of criminal cases to call on "expert testimony" to enhance one's chances of gaining a favorable court decision. A number of states now recognize certain individuals as "gang experts" whose courtroom testimony is to be valued and regarded significant. In Alaska, it is admissible to call in a gang expert to testify on a variety of gang activities, including "common characteristics of persons who are members of the criminal street gang or criminal street gangs; rivalries between specific criminal street gangs; common practices and operations of the criminal street gang" (Alaska 12.45.037). Nevada state law (193.168) allows expert testimony in such cases as those concerning "characteristics of persons who are members of criminal gangs; specific rivalries between criminal gangs . . . terminology used by members of criminal gangs, codes of conduct, including criminal conduct, of particular gangs; and, the types of crimes that are likely to be committed by a particular criminal gang or criminal gangs in general."

Probation and Parole

The courts may choose to set probation and parole conditions that require the parolee to stay away from certain individuals. For example, in Illinois the court may set as a condition of probation or of conditional discharge that the minor "refrain from having any contact, directly or indirectly, with certain specified persons or particular types of persons, including but not limited to members of street gangs and drug users or dealers" (Illinois 805-24). Conditions of continuance under supervision may be extended to known street gang members and drug users or dealers (Illinois 805-19). In Nevada, the parole board may prohibit association with members of criminal gangs as a condition of parole: "The board may, as a condition of releasing a prisoner on parole, prohibit the prisoner from associating with the members of a criminal gang" (Nevada 213.1263).

Gang Prevention and Effective Deterrence Act of 2004

Some people argue that there are already plenty of laws to prosecute gangs and that the problem is, rather, having the proper *resources* to combat gangs. To that end, Senators Orrin G. Hatch (R-Utah) and Dianne Feinstein (D-California) proposed the Gang Prevention and Effective Deterrence Act of 2004 (S.1735), originally introduced in 2003 under the same name. This bill would authorize the expenditure of $650 million, $450 million of which would be used to support federal, state and local law enforcement efforts against violent gangs and $200 million of which would be used for intervention and prevention programs for at-risk youths. This bill would also "enhance" a number of existing gang and violent crime penalties. For example, Sec. 106 would transform the murder-for-hire statute (18 USC 1958) into a *felony*-for-hire offense and significantly increase the applicable penalties. Sec. 104 amends the Travel Act (18 USC 1952) by adding conspiracies to the list of crimes regarding "travel to promote certain offenses" and significantly increasing penalties, including a new death penalty. Section 205 expands the right of law enforcement to use wiretaps. Hatch and Feinstein argue that it is imperative that this legislation be passed because of the great number of gang members. They cite figures (similar to those used in this book) from the latest available National Youth Gang Survey, which estimates there are more than 25,000 gangs and over 750,000 gang members active in more than 3,000 jurisdictions across the United States. In 2004, the Senate Judiciary Committee considered but did not pass the Gang Prevention and Effective Deterrence Act, and it was reintroduced in 2005.

Some have criticized the proposed Gang Prevention and Effective Deterrence Act as a political tool to further the careers of Senators Hatch and Feinstein. Other critics are concerned that the act continues a dangerous trend toward the federalization of local crime and the substitution of federal resources for state resources. (Note that when the Constitution was first enacted, it recognized only three federal crimes—piracy, treason, and counterfeiting—there are now more than 3,000 federal crimes, 40% of them having been adopted since 1970.) For example, Section 201 would effectively turn all double homicides that involve interstate travel into a federal crime. Section 206 would raise any offense to a felony that "by its nature, involves a substantial risk for physical force or injury against the person or property of another." Of course, the very nature of crime implies "substantial risk" to a person. Some critics believe that what is needed is more police officers on the streets to decrease gang participation; community advocates and gang rehabilitation counselors stress the need for after-school programs.

SUMMARY

Ultimately, legislative efforts must combine with socioeconomic efforts to steer at-risk youths away from gangs. As argued throughout this book, the key issue is economics, specifically, the creation and maintenance of well-paying jobs. "The future of gangs is tied to the future of urban crises in social control, social structure, labor markets, and cultural processes in a rapidly changing political and economic context" (Fagan 2004, 255). Thus, society needs to provide jobs for people; jobs, in turn, provide hope. Hope helps to establish the critical bonds that individuals need to feel a part of society and therefore have a vested interest in its maintenance and smooth operation. Sociologists and economists, however, claim that under capitalism there will always be the "haves" and the "have-nots"—it is inevitable. In order to encourage people to work hard, the highest-paying jobs are generally the most difficult to attain. High-paying jobs, then, are a reward for those who strive to be productive members of society. In other words, it is up to individual motivation, hard work, and, often, luck.

Many times, however, individuals do work hard, go to school, and find a job only to have it taken away because the company moves overseas in order to make greater profits. It is the greed of wealthy capitalists that is ruining American society, not capitalism, although it may be argued that the materialism and selfishness of this era have led to the growth of the deviant and criminal subculture. This reasoning is in line with Merton's theory of anomie (see Chapter 3). Merton suggested that blocking the opportunities to achieve desired goals leads to deviant means of attaining success—which is often measured materialistically. Feelings of hopelessness also contribute to a deviant and gang lifestyle. Clearly, business leaders and politicians need to address the issue of job creation. The federal government should refuse to conduct business with any American corporation that abandons the United States for cheaper labor costs overseas. This is just one strategy; it is up to social and legislative leaders to come up with many more policies designed to keep America strong for all its citizens—after all, it is not just gang members who need good jobs.

Another important approach to curtailing gang activity involves the legalization of recreational drugs. The so-called War on Drugs has failed miserably. Because of the economic deprivation brought about by the failure of government and business to provide adequate, well-paying jobs, many people see the selling of drugs as a means of making money. This should be a wake-up call for all "leaders" of U.S. society. The legalization of street drugs (especially marijuana and cocaine) would obviously eliminate a large proportion of crime. When drugs are legal, the black market disappears, and the lure of selling drugs for money disappears with it. Furthermore, the small percentage of people who steal property and rob innocent victims in order to pay for the high cost of illegal drugs would no longer have to commit such crimes. A significant number of nonviolent drug offenders could also be released from incarceration, which would dramatically reduce taxpayer costs. The legalization of drugs would also free police officers to perform more important duties. Furthermore, studies have consistently shown that in countries where recreational drugs are legal, both crime and drug usage decrease. In other words, the entire society benefits from the legalization of recreational drugs, and the number of gang members would also decrease dramatically.

Minch Lewis, Syracuse city auditor, is one governmental leader willing to publicly recommend the decriminalization of drugs in order to reduce the crime associated with the sale of illegal substances. According to Lewis, "the Syracuse Police Department is spending an inordinate amount of time and money addressing the drug problem in the city, but would be more effective if its focus changed" (Weibezahl 2003, B5). Most proponents of the legalization, or decriminalization, of recreational drug use also recommend regulation (e.g., selling marijuana in a fashion similar to the way that tobacco is sold and regulated) and treatment for addicts. The bottom line is simple—just as Prohibition failed miserably, because people like to drink alcohol, making recreational drug use, sale, and distribution illegal is not going to stop their occurrence. What we have instead directly fuels the black market, criminality, and the senseless incarceration of many otherwise law-abiding citizens.

Another important step to take in the war against gangs (and crime in general) is stricter gun control. According to the Justice Department's Bureau of Justice Statistics, there were more than 350,000 incidents of gun violence, including 9,369 homicides, committed in 2002. Gun control is a sticky issue. The Constitution (Second Amendment) guarantees that "a well regulated Militia" (the armed services) has the right to bear arms. Nowhere does the Constitution guarantee that any individual who wants a gun can, in fact, possess one. As the saying goes, "guns don't kill people, people with guns kill." Gang members are often better armed than the law enforcement officers who are responsible for repressing criminal activity.

This argument over gun control is an old one, and most people have strong feelings about it. However, something that all law-abiding citizens agree on is that gun running and trafficking of illegal guns to militant groups is wrong. But inevitably criminals find a way around any legislation passed to curtail gun sales to them. Among the "unforeseen" problems associated with gun trafficking involves an incident that occurred near the end of 2003. Federal prosecutors reported that they broke up a weapons-trafficking ring in which Ohio college students allegedly bought handguns that were then funneled to a violent New Jersey street gang. According to federal prosecutors, current and former students at Wilberforce University in Xenia, Ohio went to the Hole in the Wall store, filled out federal background checks, and falsely claimed that they were the actual purchasers, when in fact they purchased the guns for gang members in exchange for unspecified amounts of money. Attorney General John Ashcroft stated, "the charges were the latest example of the Justice Department's nationwide crackdown on gun crime, which he said has resulted in a 24 percent increase in weapons prosecutions in 2003 compared with 2002" (*Syracuse Post Standard* 2003, A4). Ashcroft also mentioned that several other "straw buyer" rings had been broken up in North Carolina, South Carolina, and Arkansas. The ease with which criminals can attain guns, both legally and illegally, is scary to law-abiding citizens, and many feel the need to possess a gun in order to protect themselves. And thus the circle of violence continues.

It is very important that intervention and prevention programs continue. They have not kept everyone out of gangs, but intervention and diversion programs may have saved potentially millions of other youths from turning to gangs, so it is critical that funding continues. Intervention programs also depend on well-meaning individuals who truly possess a desire to make American society a better one in which to live. School intervention programs are of particular importance. Many students today live in constant fear of violence, and this violence is no longer limited to the "bully" in the school. There are still individual bullies, but at many schools the bullies are gangs. The constant threat of gang violence and the high-profile, Columbine-style (Littleton, Colorado) incidents of school shootings have led to the development and implementation of safe-school plans. Many schools have banned the wearing of alleged gang-related colors on school campuses. Unfortunately, it is difficult to ascertain whether such policies have any appreciable effect on the levels of school violence. Furthermore:

> Youth gang intervention is a very formidable enterprise. Because we lack a clear understanding of why and how youth gangs form, preventing their formation is problematic. Gang interventions rarely are based on theoretical assumptions. This lack of knowledge impedes efforts to disrupt existing gangs and divert youth from them. Gangs dissolve and disappear for reasons that are poorly understood. In some cities, youths who join gangs leave them within about 1 year. Yet we do not understand why. Future youth gang research must address the formation of gangs, disruptive forces, and factors that account for diversion of youths from gangs (Howell 2004, 318).

This book has been written with the hope that it would add to the general knowledge of gangs and gang formation. It has placed particular attention on theoretical explanations of why youths join a gang and has also focused on the socioeconomic factors (e.g., the "rush" aspect of gang behavior) that lead to gang formation. The growing presence of street gangs in nearly all social institutions is an alarming reality. Their increased involvement in criminal activity, especially drug sale and distribution, has made the problem of street gangs in the United States even more alarming. And the problem doesn't stop at our borders—the process of globalization includes the globalization of gangs. Street gangs exist in such countries as Russia and Japan, something that once would have been considered improbable.

In this discussion of stemming the increasing tide of individuals who are turning to gangs, two factors stand out. First, to combat the growth of gangs, the socioeconomic conditions that lead to gang formation must be addressed. In Los Angeles, an organization called Homeboy Industries provides jobs to gang members. The director of this organization is Father Gregory Boyle, who has adopted the motto "Nothing stops a bullet like a job," the implication, of course, being that if policy makers are serious about stopping the gang warfare that plagues America, they must find/create adequate-paying jobs for youth (and jobs for adults, for that matter). Second, a large percentage of youths in America does not belong to gangs, even in "troubled" neighborhoods and family environments. Joining a gang, despite the pressures one might feel from peers, is still a choice. Personal responsibility to "do the right thing" (stay out of a gang) cannot be passed off to, and blamed on, society.

REFERENCES

Albanese, Jay. 2002. *Criminal Justice*, 2nd edition. Boston: Allyn and Bacon.

Alonso, Alejandro. 2002. "18th Street Gang in Los Angeles County." Available: http://www. streetgangs.com/18thstreet.html.

Althaus, Dudley. 1995. "Why Migration Will Play a Major Role in the Future of the U.S. Southwest." *Houston Chronicle*, Dec.14.

Anderson, David C. 1995. *Crime and the Politics of Hysteria: How the Willie Horton Story Changed American Justice*. New York: Times Books.

Anderson, Elijah. 1999. *Code of the Street: Decency, Violence, and the Moral Life of the Inner City*. New York: Norton & Company.

Anderson, Mark, and Mark Jenkins. 2001. *Dance of Days*. New York: Soft Skull Press.

Anti-Defamation League. 2005. "The Five Percenter." Available: http://www.adl.org/hate_symbols/Five_Percenters.asp.

Archer, John. 1991. "The Influence of Testosterone on Human Aggression." *British Journal of Psychology* 82(1):1–28.

Asbury, Herbert. 2002. "The Gangs of New York" in *Gangs*. Ed. Sean Donohue. New York: Thunder's Mouth Press. (Originally published in 1927 by Knopf.)

Associated Press. 1998. "Injunction Targets Hollywood Gang." Available: http://www.streetgangs. com/topics/1998/041498.html.

Bandura, Albert, and Richard Walters. 1963. *Social Learning and Personality Development*. New York: Holt, Rinehart and Winston.

Barger, Ralph "Sonny." 2001. *Hell's Angels*. New York: Perennial.

Bartollas, Clemens, and Stuart J. Miller. 2001. *Juvenile Justice in America*, 3rd ed. Upper Saddle River, NJ: Prentice Hall.

Becker, Howard. 1963. *Outsiders: Studies in the Sociology of Deviance*. New York: Free Press.

Belknap, Joanne. 2001. *The Invisible Woman: Gender, Crime and Justice*, 2nd ed. Belmont, CA: Wadsworth.

Berry, Bonnie. 1998. "Criminal Criminologist Newsletter." Available: http://www.sun.soci.niu.edu.

Berry, Wallace B. 1997. "He Shows Gang Members a Way out of Violence." *Parade Magazine*, January 26:7.

Best, Joel, and David F. Luckenbill. 1994. *Organizing Deviance*, 2nd ed. Englewood Cliffs, NJ: Prentice Hall.

Bing, Leon. 2001. "Do or Die," in *Gangs*. Ed. Sean Donohue. New York: Thunder's Mouth Press.

———. 2001. "Homegirls." *Rolling Stone*, April 12:76–86.

Black Panther Party. 1999. "The FBI's War on the Black Panther Party's Southern California Chapter." Available: http://www.itsabouttimebbp.com/Chapter_History/FBI_War_LA_Chapter.html.

Bilchik, Shay. 1998. "Youth Gangs: An Overview." *Journal Justice Bulletin: Office of Juvenile Justice and Delinquency Prevention*.

Billings Gazette. 1995. "Nuke Photos of Students Off Limits," January 21:1A.

Bjerregard, B. and C. Smith. 1993. "Gender Differences in Gang Participation, Delinquency and Substance Abuse." *Journal of Quantitative Criminology* 4:329–355.

Black Guerilla Family. 2003. "Activity of the Black Guerilla Family." Available: http://www. knowgangs.com/gang_resources/black_guerilla_family/bgf_001.htm.

Blazak, Randal Evan. 1995. *The Suburbanization of Hate: An Ethnographic Study of Skinheads Subculture*. PhD diss., Ann Arbor, MI: UMI Dissertation Services.

Block, Carolyn R., and Richard Block. 1993. "Street Gang Crime in Chicago." Washington, D.C.: National Institute of Justice, U.S. Department of Justice. Research in Brief.

Booth, Martin. 1999. *The Dragon Syndicates: The Global Phenomenon of the Triads*. New York: Oxford.

Borges, Jorge Luis. 2002. "Monk Eastman, Purveyor of Iniquities" in *Gangs*. Ed. Sean Donohue. New York: Thunder's Mouth Press.

Bracken, Michael B., and Stanislav K. Kasl. 1975. "First and Repeat Abortions: A Study of Decision-Making and Delay." *Journal of Biosocial Science* 7:374–491.

Buffalo News. 1999. "Gang Members Indicted in Drug and Murder Case," March 5:B4.

Buffalo News. 2002. "Canadian Police Arrest 27 in Crackdown on Biker Gangs," June 6:A3.

Buffalo News. 2002. "41 Members of Gang Arrested on Various Charges," October 31:A8.

Buffalo News. 2003. "Gang-Assault Sentence Handed Down," May 18:C3.

Buffalo Police Department. 2003. "The Curfew Ordinance." Available: http://www.city-Buffalo. com/police.

Burch, J., and C. Kane. 1999. *Implementing the OJJDP Comprehensive Gang Model*. Fact Sheet. Washington, DC: US Department of Justice, Office of Justice Programs, Office of Juvenile Justice and Delinquency Prevention.

Bynum, Timothy S., and Sean P. Varano. 2003. "The Anti-Gang Initiative in Detroit," in *Policing Gangs and Youth Violence*. Ed. Scott H. Decker. Belmont CA: Wadsworth.

Campbell, Anne. 1984. *The Girls in the Gang*. New York: Basic Blackwell.

———. 1987. "Self Definition by Rejection: The Case of Girl Gangs," in *Female Gangs in America*. Ed. Meda Chesney-Lind and John M. Hagedorn. Chicago, IL: Lake View Press.

———. 1991. *The Girls in the Gang*, 2nd ed. New York: Basic Blackwell.

———. 1993. *Men, Women, and Aggression*. New York: Basic.

Campo-Flores, Arian. 2003. "Gangland's New Face: The South Sees a Surge in Violence by Latino Groups." *Newsweek*, December 8.

Carelli, Richard. 1999. "Chicago Anti-Loitering Law Against Gangs Struck Down." *Buffalo News*, June 10:A1.

Carlson, Peter. 2003. "Tupac's Mother Quite Radical Herself." *Syracuse Post-Standard*, October 20:D4.

Carter, Chelsea J. 1999. "One Time Miscreants Turn Talents Elsewhere by Making Legitimate Art Out of American Graffiti." *Buffalo News*, January 10:A13.

———. 2004. "Why Did the 91-year-old Man Rob Banks?" *Syracuse Post-Standard*, March 28:A13.

Cartwright, Duncan. 2002. *Psychoanalysis, Violence, and Rage-Type Murder*. New York: Brunnel-Routledge.

Case, Dick. 2002. "Life on the Streets, Guns & Gangs: More Violent, Brazen." *Syracuse Post-Standard*, June 9:A1.

———. 2003. "New Yorkers Need Guts to Clean Albany Slate." *Syracuse Post-Standard*, October 11:B1.

Castorena, Deanne. 1998. *The History of the Gang Injunction in California.* Los Angeles: Los Angeles Police Department Hardcore Gang Division.

Century, Douglas. 2004. "Big Trouble in Little China." *Blender*, April: 82–88.

Chambliss, William. 1964. "A Sociological Analysis of the Law of Vagrancy." *Social Problems* 12:67–77.

———. 1993. "State Organized Crime," in *Making Law: The State, the Law and Structural Contradictions.* Bloomington, IN: Indiana University Press.

———. 1998. *On the Take*, 2nd ed. Bloomington, IN: Indiana University Press.

Chambliss, William, and Robert Seidman. 1971. *Law, Order, and Power.* Reading, MA: Addison-Wesley.

Champion, Dean John. 2004. *The Juvenile Justice System*, 4th ed. Upper Saddle River, NJ: Prentice Hall.

Cheektowaga Times. 2003. "Police are Alerted to Gang's Agenda," December 18:1. Available: http://www.cheektowatimes.com/News/2003/1218/Front_Page/004.html.

Chesney-Lind, Meda. 1997. *The Female Offender: Girls, Women, and Crime.* Thousand Oaks, CA: Sage.

Chesney-Lind, Meda, and Randall G. Shelden. 2004. *Girls, Delinquency and Juvenile Justice*, 3rd ed. Belmont, CA: Wadsworth.

Chin, K. 1986. *Chinese Triad Societies, Tongs, Organized Crime, and Street Gangs in Asia and the United States.* Ann Arbor, MI: University Microfilms International.

Chin, Ko-Lin. 1990. *Chinese Subculture and Criminality: Non-traditional Crime Groups in America.* Westport, CT: Greenwood.

———. 1996. *Chinatown Gangs: Extortion, Enterprise, and Ethnicity.* New York: Oxford.

Cloward, Richard. 1959. "Illegitimate Means, Anomie, and Deviant Behavior." *American Sociological Review* 24:164–176.

Cloward, Richard, and Lloyd Ohlin. 1960. *Delinquency and Opportunity: A Theory of Delinquent Gangs.* New York: Free Press.

Coakley, Jay. 2001. *Sport in Society*, 7th ed. Boston: McGraw Hill.

Cohen, Albert. 1955. *Delinquent Boys: The Culture of the Gang.* New York: Free Press.

Cohen, Rich. 2002. "Tough Jews" in *Gangs.* Ed. Sean Donohue. New York: Thunder's Mouth Press.

Cohen, Stanley. 1980. *Folk Devils and Moral Panics: The Creation of the Gang.* Glencoe, IL: Free Press.

Coldren, James R., and Daniel F. Higgins. 2003. "Evaluating Nuisance Abatement at Gang and Drug Houses in Chicago," in *Policing Gangs and Youth Violence.* Ed. Scott H. Decker. Belmont, CA: Wadsworth.

Colorado Department of Natural Resources. 2003. "Help Catch a Thief and Preserve the Future of Hunting." Available: http://www.dnr.state.co.us/news/press.

Cook County Sheriff's Youth Services Department. 1999. "Police and Children Together (PACT) Camp." Available: http://www.cookcountysheriff.org/youthsvcs/special_projects/pact.html.

Cooley, Charles. 1909. *Social Organization*. New York: Scribner.

Covey, Herbert C., Scott Menard, and Robert J. Franzese. 1992. *Juvenile Gangs*. Springfield, IL: Charles C. Thomas.

Cressey, Donald. 1969. *Theft of the Nation*. New York: Harper Row.

Crip History. 2003. "Crib History." Available: http://www.36rovals.8m.com/crip.

Curran, Daniel, and Claire Renzetti. 1994. *Theories of Crime*. Boston: Allyn and Bacon.

Curry, G. David. 1998. "Female Gang Involvement." *Journal of Research in Crime and Delinquency* 35(1):100–118.

Curry, G. David, and Scott H. Decker. 2003. *Confronting Gangs: Crime and Community*, 2nd ed. Los Angeles: Roxbury.

Daniels, Douglas Henry. 1997. "Los Angeles Zoot: Race 'Riot,' the Pachuco, and Black Music Culture." *The Journal of Negro History* 82(2), Spring:201–220.

Danitz, Tiffany. 1998. "The Gangs Behind Bars." *Insight on the News*. Available: http://www.findarticles.com.

Dannen, Fredric. 2002. "Bo Ying," in *Gangs*. Ed. Sean Donohue. New York: Thunder's Mouth Press.

Davis, M. 1992. *City of Quartz*. New York: Vintage Books.

Davis, N. 1999. *Youth Crisis*. Westport, CT: Praeger.

Davis, Roger H. 1995. "Cruising for Trouble: Gang-Related Drive-by Shootings." *The FBI Enforcement Bulletin* 64(1):16–23.

Decker, Scott H. 2004. "Legitimating Drug Use," in *Understanding Contemporary Gangs In America*. Ed. Rebecca D. Petersen. Upper Saddle River, NJ: Prentice Hall.

Decker, Scott H., ed. 2003. *Policing Gangs and Youth Violence*. Belmont, CA: Wadsworth.

Decker, Scott H., and Barrik van Winkle. 1996. *Life in the Gang: Family, Friends, and Violence*. New York: Cambridge University Press.

Decker, Scott H., and G. David Curry. 2002. "Gangs," in *Encyclopedia of Crime and Punishment*, Vol. 2. Thousand Oaks, CA: Sage.

———. 2003. "Suppression Without Prevention, Prevention Without Suppression," in *Policing Gangs and Youth Violence*. Ed. Scott H. Decker. Belmont, CA: Wadsworth.

Decker, Scott H., and Barrik Van Winkle. 1996. *Life in the Gang: Family, Friends, and Violence*. New York: Cambridge University Press.

Delaney, Tim. 2001. *Community, Sport, and Leisure*. Auburn, NY: Legend Books.

———. 2004. "The Russian Mafia in the United States," in *Social Diseases: Mafia, Terrorism and Totalitarianism*. Ed. Tim Delaney, Valerii Kuvakin, and Tim Madigan. Moscow, Russia: Russian Humanist Society Press.

———. 2004. *Classical Social Theory: Investigation and Application*. Upper Saddle River, NJ: Prentice Hall.

———. 2005. *Contemporary Social Theory: Investigation and Application*. Upper Saddle River, NJ: Prentice Hall.

Delaney, Tim, and Allene Wilcox. 2002. "Sports and the Role of the Media," in *Values, Society & Evolution*. Ed. Tim Delaney. Auburn, NY: Legend Books.

Deschenes, Elizabeth Piper, and Finn-Aage Esbensen. 2001. "Violence Among Girls: Does Gang Membership Make a Difference," in *Female Gangs in America*. Ed. Meda Chesney-Lind and John M. Hagedorn. Chicago: Lake View Press.

Donahue, Sean. 2001. *Gangs: Stories of Life and Death from the Streets*. New York: Thunder's Mouth Press.

Dowdy, Zachary R. 2004. "Patchwork of Gang Violence." *Newsday.com*, October 14. Available: http://www.newsday.com.

Duffy, Lori. 1996. "Expert Says Gangs Offer Acceptance." *Syracuse Post-Standard*, November 7:A16.

———. 1996. "Shootings Spark Concerns about Role of Latin Kings." *Syracuse Post-Standard*, November 7:A1.

Esbensen, Finn-Aage. 2000. "Preventing Adolescent Gang Involvement." Office of Juvenile Justice and Delinquency Prevention (OJJDP). September.

Esbensen, Finn-Aage, Elizabeth Piper Deschenes, and L. Thomas Winfree Jr. 2004. "Differences Between Gang Girls and Gang Boys," in *Understanding Contemporary Gangs in America*. Ed. Rebecca D. Petersen. Upper Saddle River, NJ: Prentice Hall.

Esbensen, Finn-Aage, and D. W. Osgood. 1997. "National Evaluation of G.R.E.A.T." Washington, DC: US Department of Justice, National Institute of Justice.

Elsner, Alan. 2003. "Gang Violence Rising on Indian Reservation in S.D." *USA Today*, December 23:13A.

Empey, Lamar. 1982. *American Delinquency*, rev. ed. Lexington, MA: D. C. Heath.

Encyclopedia Americana—International Edition. 1998. Danbury, CT: Grolier.

English, T. J. 1995. *Born To Kill*. New York: William Morrow and Company.

Erickson, Maynard. 1971. "The Group Context of Delinquent Behavior." *Social Problems* 19:114–129.

Ernst, Tom. 2002. "Program Seeks to Deter Growth of Gangs." *Buffalo News*, March 22: B3.

Estrich, Susan. 1995. "Public Cheers Killer as Justice Fails." *USA Today*, February 9: 11A.

Ewen, R. B. 1988. *An Introduction to Theories of Personality*. Hillsdale, NJ: Lawrence Erlbaum Associates.

Fagan, Jeffrey. 1996. "Gangs, Drugs, and Neighborhood Change," in *Gangs in America*, 2nd ed. Ed. C. R. Huff. Thousand Oaks, CA: Sage.

———. 2004. "Gangs, Drugs, and Neighborhood Change," in *Understanding Contemporary Gangs in America*. Ed. Rebecca D. Petersen. Upper Saddle River, NJ: Prentice Hall.

Farley, John. 1998. *Sociology*, 4th ed. Upper Saddle River, NJ: Prentice Hall.

Farley, Reynolds, Sheldon Danziger, and Harry J. Holzer. 2000. *Detroit Divided*. New York: Russell Sage Foundation.

Feldman, Charles. 2000. "Anti-Gang Units a Casualty of Los Angeles Police Scandal," March 13. Available: http://www.cnn.com.

Feldman, Steven R., Anthony Liguori, Michael Kucenic, Stephen R. Rapp, Alan B. Fleischer, Jr., Wei Lang, and Mandeep Kaur. 2004. "Ultraviolet Exposure is a Reinforcing Stimulus in Frequent Indoor Tanners." *Journal of the American Academy of Dermatology* 51(1): 45–51.

Female Gangs. 2003. *Female Gang Member Relationships*. Available: http://www.uic.edu/orgs/kbc/Hagedorn/girlgangs.html.

Finckenauer, James. 2002. "Crime and Criminals," in *Encyclopedia of Crime and Punishment*, Vol. 3. Thousand Oaks, CA: Sage.

Fink, Arthur E. 1938. *Causes of Crime*. New York: A. S. Barnes.

Finnegan, William. 2002. "Cold New World: Growing up in a Harder Country," in *Gangs*. Ed. Sean Donahue. New York: Thunder's Mouth Press.

Fiore, Faye. 1997. "Professor Compares a Violent Tribe to Gangs." *Los Angeles Times*, November 30:A1.

Flanigan, Patrick. 2003A. "Cops Come Down hard on Gang." *Rochester Democrat and Chronicle*, December 22:1A.

———. 2003B. "Neighborhood Mum on Gang." *Rochester Democrat and Chronicle*, December 23:1A.

Flowers, R. Barri. 1995. *Female Crime, Criminals and Cellmates: An Exploration of Female Criminality and Delinquency*. Jefferson, NC: McFarland & Company.

Fong, Robert S. 1990. "The Organizational Structure of Prison Gangs: A Texas Case Study." *Federal Probation* 54(1):36–43.

———. 1991. "The Detection of Prison Gang Development: An Empirical Assessment." *Federal Probation* 55(1):66–69.

Fontana, Andrea. 1973. "Labeling Theory Reconsidered," in *Outsiders: Studies in the Sociology of Deviance*. Ed. Howard Becker. New York: Free Press.

Foster, Janet. 1990. *Crime and Community in the City*. New York: Routledge.

Fox, James, and Jack Levin. 2002. "Mass Murder" in *Encyclopedia of Crime and Punishment*. Thousand Oaks, CA: Sage.

Fried, Albert. 1980. *The Rise and Fall of the Jewish Gangster in America*. New York: Holt, Rinehart and Winston.

Fritsch, Eric J., Tory J. Caeti, and Robert W. Taylor. 2003. "Gang Suppression Through Saturation Patrol and Aggressive Curfew and Truancy Enforcement," in *Policing Gangs and Youth Violence*. Ed. Scott H. Decker. Belmont, CA: Wadsworth.

Garrison, Jessica. 2004. "L.A.'s 18th Street Gang is Hit with Injunction Forbidding Recruiting." *Los Angeles Times*, July 3:B7.

Gearty, Robert, and Bill Hutchinson. 2001. "Sweeping up Street Gang Bloods, Bloodettes, Indicted." *Daily News*, 7.

George, John, and Laird Wilcox. 1996. *American Extremists*. Amherst, NY: Prometheus Books.

Glynn, Matt. 2002. "Dude, Where's My Car?" *Buffalo News*, February 19:B6.

Goldentyer, Debra. 1994. *Gangs*. Austin, TX: Steck-Vaughn.

Goldstein, Arnold P. 1991. *Delinquent Gangs: A Psychological Perspective*. Champaign, IL: Research Press.

Grann, David. 2004. "The Brand: How the Aryan Brotherhood Became the Most Murderous Prison Gang in America." *The New Yorker*, February 16, 23: 157–171.

Grennan, Sean, Marjie T. Britz, Jeffrey Rush, and Thomas Barker. 2000. *Gangs: An International Approach*. Upper Saddle River, NJ: Prentice Hall.

Groves, B. M., B. Zuckerman, S. Marans, and D. J. Cohen. 1993. "Silent Victims: Children Who Witness Violence." *Journal of the American Medical Association* 269:262–264.

GuardianAngels.org. 2004. "Welcome to GuardianAngels.org." Available: http://www.outta-sites.com/clients/guardianangels/webie.

Gurr, T. A. 1989. *Violence in America: Protest and Rebellion*. Newbury Park, CA: Sage.

Hagan, F. 1983. "The Organized Crime Continuum: A Further Specification of a New Conceptual Model." *Criminal Justice Review* 8:52–57.

Hagedorn, J. M. 1988. *People and Folks: Gangs, Crime and the Underclass in a Rustbelt City.* Chicago: Lake View Press.

———. 1991. "Gangs, Neighborhoods, and Public Policy." *Social Problems* 38:529–542.

———. 1994. "Neighborhoods, Markets and Gang Drug Organization." *Journal of Research in Crime and Delinquency* 31:264–294.

Hamm, Mark. 1994. *American Skinheads.* Westport, CT: Praeger.

Harper, G., and L. Robinson. 1999. "Pathways to Risk Among Inner-City African American Adolescent Females: The Influence of Gang Membership." *American Journal of Community Psychology* 27:383–404.

Harris, Julie Aitken, Rushton J. Phillippe, Elizabeth Hampson, and Douglas N. Jackson. 1996. "Salivary Testosterone and Self-Report Aggressive and Pro-Social Personality Characteristics in Men and Women." *Aggressive Behavior* 22: 321–331.

Harris, M. G. 1988. *Cholas: Latino Girls and Gangs.* New York: AMS Press.

———. 1997. "Cholas, Mexican-American Girls, and Gangs," in *Gangs and Gang Behavior.* Ed. G. Larry Mays. Chicago: Nelson-Hall.

Hay, D., P. Linebaugh, J. Rule, E. P. Thompson, and C. Winslow, eds. 1975. *Albion's Fatal Tree: Crime and Society in Eighteenth-Century England.* New York: Pantheon.

Hayden, Tom. 2004. *Street Wars: Gangs and the Future of Violence.* New York: The New Press.

Healy, Patrick. 2004. "U.S. Indicts 30 in L.I. Gangs Crimes, Including 5 Murders." *The New York Times*, February 5:B8.

Henderson, Eric, Stephen J. Kunitz, and Jerrold E. Levy. 2004. "The Origins of Navajo Youth Gangs," in *Understanding Contemporary Gangs in America.* Ed. Rebecca D. Petersen. Upper Saddle River, NJ: Prentice Hall.

Herbeck, Dan. 2000. "Fear Strikes Home." *Buffalo News*, July 17:A1.

Hernu, Piers. 2004. "Guns and Popcorn." *FHN*, May:99–102.

Hewitt, John, and Randall Stokes. 1975. "Disclaimers." *American Sociological Review* 40(1):1–11.

Hickey, Eric, ed. 2003. "The Zoot Suit Riots," in *Encyclopedia of Murder & Violent Crime.* Thousand Oaks, CA: Sage.

Hirschi, Travis. 1969. *Causes of Delinquency.* Berkeley: University of California Press.

Hirschi, Travis, and Rodney Stark. 1969. "Hellfire and Delinquency." *Social Problems* 17:202–213.

Howell, James C. 1998. *Youth Gangs: An Overview.* Office of Juvenile Justice and Delinquency Prevention. Washington, DC: U.S. Department of Justice.

———. 2000. *Youth Gang Programs and Strategies.* Washington, DC: U.S. Department of Justice.

———. 2004. "Youth Gang Homicides," in *Understanding Contemporary Gangs in America.* Ed. Rebecca D. Petersen. Upper Saddle River, NJ: Prentice Hall.

———. 2004. "Promising Programs for Youth Gang Violence Prevention and Intervention," in *Understanding Contemporary Gangs in America.* Ed. Rebecca D. Petersen. Upper Saddle River, NJ: Prentice Hall.

Howell, James C., and Scott H. Decker. 1999 (January). "The Youth Gangs, Drugs, And Violence Connection," in *OJJDP Juvenile Justice Bulletin.* Washington, DC: U.S. Department of Justice.

————. 1999 (December). "Youth Gang Drug Trafficking," in *OJJDP Juvenile Justice Bulletin.* Washington, DC: U.S. Department of Justice.

Huff, C. R. 1989. "Youth Gangs and Public Policy." *Crime and Delinquency* 35:524–537.

————. 1990. *Gangs in America.* Newbury Park, CA: Sage

————. 1993. "Gangs in the United States," in *The Gang Intervention Handbook.* Ed. H. Goldstein and C. R. Huff. Champaign, IL: Research Press.

Huizinga, D. 1997. "Gangs and The Volume of Crime." Paper presented at the annual Meeting of the Western Society of Criminology, Honolulu, HI.

Hunt, A. L., and K. Weiner. 1977. "The Impact of a Juvenile Curfew: Suppression and Displacement Patterns of Juvenile Offenses." *Journal of Police Science and Administration* 5(4):407–412.

Hunt, Geoffrey, Kathleen MacKenzie, and Karen Joe-Laidler. 2004. "I'm Calling My Mom," in *Understanding Contemporary Gangs in America.* Ed. Rebecca D. Petersen. Upper Saddle River, NJ: Prentice Hall.

Huston, Peter. 1995. *Tongs, Gangs, and Triads: Chinese Crime Groups in North America.* Boulder, CO: Paladin.

Hutson, H. R., D. Anglin, N. Kyriacou, J. Hart, and K. Spears. 1995. "The Epidemic of Gang-related Homicides in Los Angeles County from 1979 through 1994." *Journal of the American Medical Association* 274:1031–1036.

Hutson, H. R., D. Anglin, and M. J. Pratts. 1994. "Adolescents and Children Injured or Killed in Drive-by Shootings in Los Angeles." *New England Journal of Medicine* 330(5):324–327.

Illinois State Police. 2002. "Violence Education Gang Awareness." Available: http://www.isp. state.il.us/crime/vega/htm.

Interagency Task Force. 2003. *Girls and Gangs.* Available: http://www.faculty.smsu.edu/m/ mku096/nogangs/Girls/girls%20and%20gangs.html.

Ivins, Molly. 2003. "Drug Policy Totally out of Line." *Buffalo News*, July 18:C11.

Jackson, R., and W. D. McBride. 1992. *Understanding Street Gangs.* Placerville, CA: Copperhouse.

Jamison, Michael. 2000. "Hell's Angels." *Organized Crime in America.* Belmont, CA: Wadsworth.

Jankowski, Martin Sanchez. 1991. *Islands in the Street: Gangs and American Urban Society.* Berkeley: University of California Press.

Jenkins, Morris. 1995. "Fear of the 'Gangsta': Policy Responses to Gang Activity in the City of Boston." PhD diss., Northeastern University, Department of Law, Policy, and Society.

Joe, K., and Meda Chesney-Lind. 1995. "Just Every Mother's Angel: An Analysis of Gender and Ethnic Variations in Youth Gang Membership." *Gender and Society* 9:408–431.

Johnson, Kevin. 2004. "Mean Streets Once Again: Gang Activity Surging." *USA Today*, July 21:1A, 2A.

Johnson, Marilynn S. 2003. *Street Justice: A History of Police Violence in New York City.* Boston: Beacon.

Johnson, Paula B., and David O. Sears. 1971. "Black Invisibility, the Press, and the Los Angeles Riot." *The American Journal of Sociology* 76(4, Jan.):698–721.

Juvenile Justice Bulletin. 1999 (Dec.). "Youth Gang Drug Trafficking." Washington, D.C. Department of Justice/Office of Juvenile Justice and Delinquency Prevention.

Katz, Charles M., Edward R. Maguire, and Dennis Roncek. 2000. "A Macro-Level Analysis of the Creation of Specialized Police Gang Units: An Examination of Rational, Social Threat, and Resource Dependency Perspectives." Unpublished manuscript.

Katz, Jack. 1988. *Seductions of Crime*. New York: Basic.

Kavieff, Paul. 2000. *The Purple Gang*. Fort Lee, NJ: Barricade Books.

Keene, J. 1989. "Asian Organized Crime." *FBI Law Enforcement Bulletin* 58(10): 12–17.

Keiser, R. Lincoln. 1969. *The Vice Lords*. New York: Rinehart and Winston.

Kelleher, Jennifer Sinco, and John Moreno Gonzales. 2004. "West Coast Gang Built Up and East." *Newsday.com*. Available: http://www.newsday.com/news/local/longisland/ny-liprim.

Kennedy, Kelly. 1998. "Straight Edge: Is it a Gang or a Brotherhood." *Salt Lake City Tribune*, January 31.

Kenney, Dennis J., and James O. Finckenauer. 1995. *Organized Crime in America*. Belmont, CA: Wadsworth.

Kessler, Robert E., and Andrew Smith. 2004. "Police: Gang Paired in Nassau." *Newsday.com*, October 13. Available: http://www.newsday.com.

Keyes, Cheryl. 2002. *Rap Music and Street Consciousness*. Urbana, IL: University of Illinois Press.

Kitchen, D. B. 1995. *Sisters in the Hood*. PhD diss., Western Michigan University.

Kitwana, Bakari. 2002. *The Hip Hop Generation: Young Blacks and the Crisis in African-American Culture*. New York: Basic Books.

Klein, Malcolm. 1971. *Street Gangs and Street Workers*. Englewood Cliffs, NJ: Prentice Hall.

———. 1995. *The American Street Gang*. New York: Oxford University Press.

Klein, Malcolm, and Cheryl L. Maxson. 1989. "Street Gang Violence," in *Violent Crimes, Violent Criminals*. Ed. N. Weiner. Beverly Hills, CA: Sage.

Klein, Malcolm, Cheryl L. Maxson, and L. C. Cunningham. 1991. "'Crack,' Street Gangs, and Violence." *Criminology* 29(4): 623–650.

Klinteberg, Britt. 1989. "Aggressiveness and Hyperactive Behavior as Related to Adrenaline Excretion." *The European Journal of Personality*. Available: http://www.search.epnet.com/direct.asp?an=12061706&db=pbh.

Knight, Nick. 1982. *Skinhead*. New York: Omnibus.

Knox, George W. 2001. "Female Gangs: A Focus on Research." *OJJDP Juvenile Justice Bulletin*.

Kodluboy, Donald W. 1996. "Asian Youth Gangs: Basic Issues for Educators." *National Alliance of Gang Investigators Associations*. Available: http://www.nagia.org/asian_youth_gangs1.htm.

Korem, Dan. 1994. *Suburban Gangs*. Richardson, TX: International Focus Press.

Kotulak, Ronald. 2003. "Poverty, Malnutrition Can Lower a Child's IQ Score," *Syracuse Post-Standard* (originally published in the *Chicago Tribune*), December 9:E1.

Kratcoski, Peter, and Lucille Dunn Kratcoski. 1996. *Juvenile Delinquency*, 4th ed. Upper Saddle River, NJ: Prentice Hall.

Krikorian, Greg. 1997. "Study Ranks Joblessness Top Factor in Gang Toll." *Los Angeles Times*, October 28:B1.

Krikorian, Greg, and Rich Connell. 1997. "Wide Injunction Sought Against 18th Street Gang." *Los Angeles Times*, August 4:A1.

Krikorian, Michael. 1997. "Violent Gang Is a Stain on a Proud Ethnic Community." *Los Angeles Times*, August 17:B1.

Krisberg, Barry. 1975. *The Gang and the Community*. San Francisco: R&E Research Associates.

Kulkus, Emily. 2003. "A Look at Carousel's Curfew, Six Months Later." *Syracuse Post-Standard*, December 20:A6.

LaFave, W. R., and J. H. Israel. 1992. *Criminal Procedure*, 2nd ed. St. Paul, MN: West.

Laidler, K. A., and G. Hunt. 1997. "Violence and Social Organization in Female Gangs." *Social Justice* 24:148–169.

LAPD Newsletter. 2000 (Apr). "CRASH Units Replaced by New Special Units." XLVI(IV).

Lardner, James, and Thomas Reppetto. 2000. *NYPD: A City and Its Police*. New York: Henry Holt and Company.

Lauderback, D., J. Hansen, and D. Waldorf. 1992. "Sisters Are Doin' It for Themselves': A Black Female Gang in San Francisco," *The Gang Journal* 1:57–72.

Lavigne, Y. 1993. *Good Guy, Bad Guy*. Toronto: Random House.

Lee, Yueh Ting. 1993. "Ingroup Preference and Homogeneity Among African and Chinese American Students." *Journal of Social Psychology* 133:225–235.

Lemann, Nicholas. 1991. "The Other Underclass." *The Atlantic Monthly*. Available: http://www.theatlantic.com/politics/poverty/othurnd.htm.

Lemert, Edwin M. 1951. *Social Pathology*. New York: McGraw Hill.

Levin, Brian. 2005. "Radical Religion in Prison." Available: http://www.splcenter.org/intel/intelreport/article.

Lindberg, Richard. 2003. "Spotlight on Asian Organized Crime." Available: http://www.nasiangangs.htm.

Lombroso, Cesare. 1911. *Crime: Its Causes and Remedies*. Trans. H. P. Horton. Boston: Little, Brown (originally published 1876).

Lyman, Michael D., and Gary W. Potter. 2000. *Organized Crime*, 2nd ed. Upper Saddle River, NJ: Prentice Hall.

MacDonald, Heather. 2003. *Are Cops Racist?* Chicago: Ivan R. Dee.

Main, Frank, and Carlos Sadovi. 2002. "Gangs Channel River of Drug Cash from Streets to Shops, Studios—even Vegas." *Chicago Sun Times*, April 7:6A–9A.

Maltz, M. 1985. "Towards Defining Organized Crime," in *The Politics and Economics of Organized Crime*. Ed. H. Alexander and G. Calden. Lexington, MA: D. C. Heath.

Mark, Gregory Yee. 2004. "Oakland Chinatown's First Youth Gang: The Suey Sing Boys," in *Understanding Contemporary Gangs in America*. Ed. Rebecca D. Petersen. Upper Saddle River, NJ: Prentice Hall.

Marshall, George. 1994. *Spirit of '69: A Skinhead Bible*. Scotland: S. T. Publishing.

Martin, Constance. 2000. *Endocrine Physiology*. New York: Oxford University Press.

Martinez, Pila. 1999. "Novel Attempt to Curb Prison Gang Violence." *Christian Science Monitor* 91(164):2.

Marx, Gary, and Teresa Puente. 1999. "Latin Kings Find New Trade." *Chicago Tribune*, September 18.

Maslow, A. 1951. *Motivation and Personality*. New York: Harper & Row.

Matza, David. 1964. *Delinquency and Drift*. Englewood Cliffs, NJ: Prentice Hall.

Maxson, C. L. 1998. "Gang Homicide," in *Studying and Preventing Homicide*. Ed. D. Smith and M. Zahn. Thousand Oaks, CA: Sage.

Maxson, C. L., and Malcolm Klein. 1989. "Street Gang Violence," in *Pathways to Criminal Violence*. Ed. N. A. Weiner and M. E. Wolfgang. Newbury Park, CA: Sage.

Maxson, Cherly L., Karen Hennigan, and David C. Sloan. 2003. "For the Sake of the Neighborhood?" in *Policing Gangs and Youth Violence*. Ed. Scott H. Decker. Belmont, CA: Wadsworth.

Mazon, Mauricio. 1984. *The Zoot-Suit Riots*. Austin, TX: University of Texas Press.

McCorkle, R., and T. Miethe. 1998. "The Political and Organizational Response to Gangs: An Examination of a Moral Panic." *Justice Quarterly* 15:41–64.

———. 2002. *Panic: Rhetoric and Reality in the War on Street Gangs*. Upper Saddle River, NJ: Prentice Hall.

McCrary, Gregg O., and Katherine Ramsland. 2003. *The Unknown Darkness: Profiling the Predators Among Us*. New York: William Morrow.

McDevitt, Jack, Anthony A. Braga, Dana Nurge, and Michael Buerger. 2002. "Boston's Youth Violence Prevention Program," in *Policing Gangs and Youth Violence*. Ed. Scott H. Decker. Belmont, CA: Wadsworth.

McDevitt, Jack, Jack Levin, and Susan Bennett. 2002. "Hate Crime Offenders: An Expanded Typology." *Journal of Social Issues* 58(2):303–318.

McGarrell, Edmund F., and Steven Chermak. 2003. "Problem Solving to Reduce Gang and Drug-Related Violence in Indianapolis," in *Policing Gangs and Youth Violence*. Ed. Scott H. Decker. Belmont, CA: Wadsworth.

McPhee, Michele. 2003. "Asian Eagles Ganging Up." *Daily News*, November 24:10.

Merton, Robert K. 1968. *Social Theory and Social Structure*. Glencoe, IL: Free Press.

Michel, Lou. 2002. "Homicide Upsurge." *Buffalo News*, January 2:A6.

Mieczkowski, Thomas. 1986. "Geeking Up and Throwing Down: Heroin Street Life in Detroit." *Criminology* 24:645–666.

Miller, J. 2001. *One of the Guys: Girls, Gangs, and Gender*. New York: Oxford University Press.

Miller, Walter B. 1957. "The Impact of a Community Group Work Program on Delinquent Corner Groups." *Social Science Review* 41(4):390–406.

———. 1958. "Lower Class Culture as a Generating Milieu of Gang Delinquency." *Journal of Social Issues* 14(3):5–19.

———. 1959. "Preventive Work with Street-Corner Groups: Boston Delinquency Project." *Annals of the American Academy of Political and Social Science* 322:97–106.

———. 1962. "The Impact of a 'Total Community' Delinquency Control Project." *Social Problems* 10:168–191.

———. 1966. "Violent Crimes in City Gangs." *Annals of the American Academy of Political and Social Science* 364:96–112.

———. 1973. "The Molls." *Society* 11:32–35.

———. 1975. *Violence by Youth Gangs and Youth Gangs as a Crime Problem in Major Cities*. Washington, DC: U.S. Department of Justice.

———. 1982. *Crime by Youth Gangs and Groups in the United States*. Washington, DC: National Institute of Juvenile Justice and Delinquency Prevention, U.S. Department of Justice.

Moore, Jack B. 1993. *Skinheads Shaved for Battle*. Bowling Green, OH: Bowling Green State University Popular Press.

Moore, Joan W. 1991. *Going Down to the Barrio*. Philadelphia: Temple University Press.

―――. 1993. "Gangs, Drugs, and Violence," in *Gangs: The Origins and Impact of Contemporary Youth Gangs in the United States*. Albany, NY: SUNY Press.

Moore, Joan W., and John Hagedorn. 2001. "Female Gangs: A Focus on Research." *OJJDP Juvenile Justice Bulletin*.

Mulvaney, Jim. 1993. "'Skinhead' Founder Renounces His Ties." *Las Vegas Review-Journal* August 1.

Myers, David G. 1998. *Psychology*, 5th ed. Holland, MI: Worth.

1997 National Youth Gang Survey. 1999 (Dec.). U.S. Department of Justice, OJJDP.

National Advisory Committee on Criminal Justice Standards and Goals. 1976. *Organized Crime, Report of the Task Force on Organized Crime*. Washington, DC: Law Enforcement Assistance Administration.

National Alliance of Gang Investigators Associations. 2002. "The National Gang Threat." Available: http://www.nagia.org.

National Center for Neighborhood Enterprise. 1999. *Violence-Free Zone Initiatives: Models of Successful Grassroots Youth Intervention*. Washington, DC: National Center for Neighborhood Enterprise.

Nawojczyk, Steve. 1997. "Street Gang Dynamics." Available: http://www.gangwar.com/dynamics.

New York Post. 2003. "2 Arrested in Gang Sex Rite," May 21:22.

Newswire. 2002. "Controversial Detroit Rapper Now Offering Extreme Kidnapping Adventure to Hardcore Thrill Seekers." October 21 (Article A93091592).

Nisbet, Robert. 1969. *The Quest for Community*. New York: Oxford University Press.

Nozzolio, Michael F. 2004. Personal mail correspondence dated January 26, 2004.

Nye, F. I. 1958. *Family Relationships and Delinquent Behavior*. New York: Wiley.

NYPD and Department of Correction. 2001. As reported in the *Daily News*, April 8:5.

Office of Juvenile Justice and Delinquency Prevention (OJJDP). 2000. "1998 National Youth Gang Survey." Washington, D.C.: U.S. Department of Justice.

―――. 2001. "1999 National Youth Gang Survey." Washington, D.C.: U.S. Department of Justice.

―――. 2004 (April). "OJJDP Fact Sheet." U.S. Department of Justice.

O'Brien, John. 2003. "2 Gang Members enter RICO Pleas." *Syracuse Post-Standard*, November 5:B5.

―――. 2003. "Boot Camp Fugitives Caught in Connecticut." *Syracuse Post-Standard*, October 29:A1.

―――. 2003. "How Boot Camp Ruled a Gang." *Syracuse Post-Standard*, September 3:A1.

―――. 2004a. "'Gang' was Forbidden Word for Police." *Syracuse Post-Standard*, July 20: A1, A8.

―――. 2004b. "'I Wanted a Name. I Wanted to be a Gangster.'" *Syracuse Post-Standard*, July 25:A1, A16.

―――. 2004c. "Evidence Shows Little Boot Camp Opulence." *Syracuse Post-Standard*, August 2: A1, A8.

O'Brien, John, and Maureen Sieh. 2003. "Jail Keeps List of Inmates Who Say They're in Gangs." *Syracuse Post-Standard*, October 11:A1.

———. 2003. "Alleged Gang Members Hired to Work with Kids." *Syracuse Post-Standard*, December 7:A1.

O'Brien, Margaret. 1999. "At Least 16,000 Girls in Chicago's Gangs More Violent Than Some Believe, Reports Say." *Chicago Tribune*, September 17:5

O'Connor, Anne-Marie. 1997. "Tijuana Gunman May Have Mexican American Mafia Tie." *Los Angeles Times*, November 29.

———. 2000. "Massive Gang Member List Now Clouded by Rampart." *Los Angeles Times*, March 25:A1.

O'Hara, Jim. 2003. "Gang-Related Cases Moving Quickly in Court." *Syracuse Post-Standard*. May 19:A1.

Oliveiri, Chad. 2004. "The Mess We're in: State of the City." *City*, March 10–16:8.

O'Neill, Terry. 2002. "Biker Gangs—Stronger than Ever." *Report* (Alberta) 29(4):18–22.

O'Shaughnessy, Patrice. 2001. "NYPD Beefs up Units to Fight Growing Menace." *Daily News*, April 8:3, 5.

Outlaws, Mobsters & Crooks: From the Old West to the Internet. 1998. "Belle Starr." Available: http://www.galenet.com/servlet/BioRC.

Padilla, Felix. 1992. *The Gang as an American Enterprise*. New Brunswick, NJ: Rutgers University Press.

Papadimitriou, Dimitri. 1998. "Employment Policy, Community Development, and the Underclass." Available: http://www.ideas.repec.org/p/wpa/wuwpma/9802016.html.

Parade Magazine. 2003. "Thieves' Favorites," August 17:14.

Parade Magazine. 2003. "Gangs Terrorize France," April 28:9.

PBS—*American Experience*. 2002. "Timeline: Zoot Suit Riots." Available: http://www.pbs.org.

PBS—*Frontline*. 2001. "LAPD Blues: CRASH Culture." Available: http://www.pbs.org/wgbh/pages/frontline/shows/lapd/scandal/crashculture.html.

Pearce, Diana. 1978 (Feb.). "The Feminization of Poverty: Women, Work, and Welfare." *Urban and Social Change Review*, 30.

Pearson, G. 1983. *Hooligan: A History of Reportable Fears*. New York: Schocken Books.

Pendolino, Amanda. 2002. "Teens Speak out on the Galleria's New Escort Policy." *Buffalo News*, July 31:2.

Perez, Luis. 2004. "Program Redirects the Unruly." *Syracuse Post-Standard*, January 4:B8.

Pope, Carl E., and Rick Lovell. 2004. "Gang Prevention and Intervention Strategies of the Boys and Girls Clubs of America," in *Understanding Contemporary Gangs in America*. Ed. Rebecca D. Petersen. Upper Saddle River, NJ: Prentice Hall.

Perkins, U. E. 1987. *Explosion of Chicago's Black Street Gangs: 1900 to the Present*. Chicago: Third World Press.

Petersen, Rebecca. 2004. *Understanding Contemporary Gangs in America*. Upper Saddle River, NJ: Prentice Hall.

Port Washington News. 1998. "Port Police Arrest 8 MS-13 Gang Members," March 6.

Portillos, Edwardo Luis. 1997. "Women, Men and Gangs: The Social Construction of Gender in the Barrio," in *Female Gangs in America*. Eds. Meda Chesney-Lind and John M. Hagedorn. Chicago: Lake View Press.

Posner, Gerald L. 1988. *Warlords of Crime: Chinese Societies—The New Mafia*. New York: McGraw-Hill.

Powell, Robert Andrew. 2003. *We Own This Game*. New York: Atlantic Monthly Press.

Quicker, John. 1983. *Home Girls*. San Diego, CA: International Universities Press.

Quinney, Richard A. 1970. *The Social Reality of Crime*. Boston: Little, Brown and Company.

———. 1977. *Class, State, and Crime: On the Theory and Practice of Criminal Justice*. New York: David McKay.

———. 1991. *Journey to a Far Place: Autobiographical Reflections*. Philadelphia: Temple University Press.

Quinney, Richard A., and J. Wildeman. 1991. *The Problem of Crime: A Peace and Social Justice Perspective*, 3rd ed. Mountain View, CA: Mayfield.

Ramos, George. 1997. "3 More Sentenced to Life in Mexican Mafia Case." *Los Angeles Times*, September 4:B3.

Raum, Tom. 1999. "United States Tabbed as World's Largest Supplier of Weapons." *Buffalo News*, August 7:A3.

Reardon, David C. 1993. "Abortion and the Feminization of Poverty." Available: http://www.afterabortion.org/poverty.html.

Reckless, W. C. 1961. "A New Theory of Delinquency and Crime." *Federal Probation* 25:42–46.

———. 1973. *The Crime Problem*, 5th ed. Englewood Cliffs, NJ: Prentice Hall.

Regoli, Robert M., and John D. Hewitt. 2003. *Delinquency in Society*, 5th ed. Boston: McGraw-Hill.

Reiner, I. 1992. *Gangs, Crime and Violence in Los Angeles: Findings and Proposals from the District Attorney's Office*. Arlington, VA: National Youth Gang Information Center.

Reiss, Albert. 1951. "Delinquency as the Failure of Personal and Social Controls." *American Sociological Review* 16:196–207.

Richardson, John H. 1997. "Secrets of the Kings." *New York*, February 17.

Robarchek, Clayton, and Carole Robarchek. 1997. *Waorani: The Contents of Violence and War*. New York: Harcourt Brace.

Roosens, Eugene E. 1989. *Creating Ethnicity*. London: Sage.

Rosenzweig, David, and Meta Gold. 1997. "Sweeping Order to Limit Activity of 18th Street Gang." *Los Angeles Times*, July 12:A1.

Roth, Melissa. 1998. "Posse Paraphernalia." *George Magazine*, March.

Rozanski, Lauren. 2003. An unpublished manuscript of interviews with members of the Mara Salvatrucha Gang.

Ryan, John, and William M. Wentworth. 1999. *Media and Society*. Boston: Allyn and Bacon.

Safir, Howard. 2003. *Security: Policing Your Homeland, Your City*. New York: St. Martin's Press.

Sahagun, Louis. 1997. "Tribes Struggle with Violent-Crime Wave." *Los Angeles Times*, November 9:A18.

Sampson, Robert J., and Byron W. Groves. 1989. "Community Structure and Crime: Testing Social Disorganization Theory." *American Journal of Sociology* 94:774–802.

Sanders, William B. 1970. *Juvenile Offenders for a Thousand Years*. Chapel Hill: University of North Carolina Press.

———. 1994. *Gangbangers and Drive-by's: Grounded Culture and Juvenile Gang Violence*. Hawthorne, NY: Aldine DeGryter.

Savelli, Lou. 2000. "Introduction to East Coast Gangs." *National Alliance of Gang Investigators Associations*. Available: http://www.nagia.org.

Schlesinger, Arthur M. 1992. *The Disuniting of America*. New York: W. W. Norton.

Schmalleger, Frank. 2004. *Criminology Today*, 3rd ed. Upper Saddle River, NJ: Prentice Hall.

Schneider, Eric C. 1999. *Vampire, Dragons, and Egyptian Kings: Youth Gangs in Postwar New York*. Princeton, NJ: Princeton University Press.

Schumer, Charles E. 2003. Press Release. November 26. Available: http://www.senate.gov/~schumer/schumer.

Scott, Marvin B., and Stanford M. Lyman. 1968. "Accounts." *American Sociological Review* 33(Feb.):46–62.

Selcraig, Bruce. 1999. "Into the Heart of Darkness." *U.S. News & World Report* 126(9):18–21.

Shakur, Sanyika. 2003. "Monster: The Autobiography of an L.A. Gang Member," in *Gangs*. Ed. Sean Donohue. New York: Thunder's Mouth Press.

Shelden, Randall G., Sharon K. Tracy, and William B. Brown. 2001. *Youth Gangs in American Society*. Belmont, CA: Wadsworth.

Sheldon, William. 1949. *The Varieties of Delinquent Youth*. New York: Harper.

Shibutani, Tamotsu. 1955. "Reference Groups as Perspectives." *American Journal of Sociology* 6:562–569.

Shoemaker, Donald. 2000. *Theories of Delinquency*. New York: Oxford University Press.

Short, James F., Jr. 1974. "Collective Behavior, Crime, and Delinquency," in *Handbook of Criminology*. Ed. Daniel Glaser. Chicago: Rand McNally

Short, James. 1990. "New Wine in Old Bottles? Change and Continuity in American Gangs," in *Gangs in America*. Ed. C. Rondal Huff. Newbury Park, CA: Sage.

Siegel, Larry J. 1995. *Criminology: Theories, Patterns, and Typologies*, 5th ed. Minneapolis/St. Paul: West Publishing.

Siegel, Larry J., Brandon C. Welsh, and Joseph J. Senna. 2003. *Juvenile Delinquency*, 8th ed. Belmont, CA: Wadsworth.

Sieh, Maureen. 2003. "Police, Residents Talk About Gangs." *Syracuse Post-Standard*, July, 29:A1.

Sikes, Gini. 2001. "8 Ball Chicks: A Year in the Violent World of Girl Gangsters," in *Gangs*. Ed. Sean Donahue. New York: Thunder's Mouth Press. (Originally published in 1997 by Anchor Books/Doubleday.)

Simon, David R., and Frank E. Hagan. 1999. *White-Collar Deviance*. Boston: Allyn and Bacon.

Sitkoff, Harvard. 1971. "Racial Militancy and Interracial Violence in the Second World War." *The Journal of American History* 58(3, Dec.):661–681.

Snyder, Howard N., and Melissa Sickmund. 1999 (Sept.). *Juvenile Offenders and Victims: 1999 National Report*. Washington, DC: Office of Juvenile Justice and Delinquency Prevention.

Solotaroff, Ivan. 2002. "Gangsta Life, Gangster Death," in *Gangs*. Ed. Sean Donohue. New York: Thunder's Mouth Press.

Southern Poverty Center. 2002. "A Hundred Years of Terror." Available: http://www.iupui.edu/~aao/kkk.

Spencer, William. 1987. "Self-work in Social Interaction: Negotiating Role-Identities." *Social Psychology Quarterly* 50(2):131–142.

Spergel, Irving. 1990. "Youth Gangs: Continuity and Change," in *Crime and Justice: A Review of Research*, Vol. 12. Ed. Michael Tonry and Norval Morris. Chicago: University of Chicago Press.

————. 1995. *The Youth Gang Problem: A Community Approach*. New York: Oxford University Press.

Spergel, Irving, and G. Curry. 1990. "Strategies and Perceived Agency Effectiveness in Dealing with the Young Gang Problem," in *Gangs in America*. Ed. C. Ronald Huff. Newbury Park, CA: Sage.

————. 1993. "The National Youth Gang Survey: A Research and Development Process," in *The Gang Intervention Handbook*. Ed. Arnold P. Goldstein and C. Ronald Huff. Champaign, IL: Research Press.

Spunt, Barry. 2002. "Gangs," in *Encyclopedia of Crime and Punishment*, Vol. 2. Thousand Oaks, CA: Sage.

Stamford, Bryant. 1987 (Dec.). "The Adrenaline Rush." *The Physician and Sports Medicine* 15(12):184.

Stranhan, Thomas. 1991. "Women Increasingly Receive Public Assistance as Abortion is Repeated," *Association for Inter-disciplinary Research in Values and Social Change Newsletter* 4(2):3–7.

Sutherland, Edwin. 1939. *Principles of Criminology*, 3rd ed. Philadelphia: Lippincott.

————. 1947. *Principles of Criminology*, 4th ed. Philadelphia: Lippincott.

Sutherland, Edwin, and Donald R. Cressey. 1978. *Criminology*, 10th ed. Philadelphia: Lippincott.

Sykes, Gresham, and David Matza. 1957. "Techniques of Neutralization: A Theory of Delinquency." *American Sociological Review* 22:664–670.

Syracuse Post-Standard. 1997. "Program Tries to Sever Gang Ties," March 17:A1.

————. 1997. "War and Peace Between the Gangs of Syracuse," December 12:A1.

————. 2003a. "Census Survey Shows More People Fall Below Poverty Line," September 3:A3.

————. 2003b. "Ohio Dealer, N.J. Gang Members Indicted in Firearms Conspiracy," December 12:A4.

————. 2004a. "Census Forecasts Fast Growth for Minorities," March 18:A12.

————. 2004b. "Gangs Organize Rumble by Using the Internet," May 13:A5.

————. 2004c. "Deportations and Arrests Follow Probe of Gang," November 18:A12.

————. 2004d. "Teens Charged After Boy Dies in Initiation Fight," September 17:A6.

————. 2004e. "Haiti Beset by Gangs After Storm," September 29:A12.

————. 2004f. "Man Sentenced 25 Years to Life for Killing Witness," September 14:A4.

————. 2005. "White Supremacist Prison Gang Members Indicted," January 6:A11.

Tannenbaum, Frank. 1938. *Crime and the Community*. Boston: Ginn.

Taylor, Carl S. 1989/1990. *Dangerous Society*. East Lansing, MI: Michigan State University Press.

————. 1990. "Gang Imperialism," in *Gangs in America*. Ed. C. R. Huff. Newbury Park, CA: Sage.

————. 1993. *Girls, Gangs, Women, and Drugs*. East Lansing: Michigan State University Press.

Taylor, Diane. 2001. "Girl-Gang Princess. . . At 18 Months Old." *The Mirror*, 23:15.

The Age. 2003. "Part-time Work Spawns Rural Underclass," April 25. Available: http://www.theage.com.au/articles/2003/04/25/1050777401309.html.

The Citizen. 2004. "The Lawless West?: Rural Idaho Grapples with Gang Violence," October 29:B6.

The Crime Encyclopdia. 1998. "The World's Most Notorious Outlaws, Mobsters, and Crooks." Detroit: UXL.

Thio, Alex. 2003. *Sociology*. Boston: Allyn & Bacon.

Thomas, Vanessa. 2004. "Meaner Streets." *Buffalo News*, August 22.

Thomas, Vanessa, and T. J. Pignataro. 2003. "Shooting Season." *Buffalo News*, July 25:A1.

Thompkins, Douglas E. 2004. "School Violence," in *Understanding Contemporary Gangs in America*. Ed. Rebecca D. Petersen. Upper Saddle River, NJ: Prentice Hall.

Thompson, Carol Y., Robert L. Young, and Ronald Burns. 2003. "Representing Gangs in The News: Media Construction of Criminal Gangs," in *Readings in Juvenile Delinquency and Juvenile Justice*. Ed. Thomas C. Calhoun and Constance L. Chapple. Upper Saddle River, NJ: Prentice Hall.

Thompson, D. W., and L. A. Jason. 1988. "Street Gangs and Preventive Interventions." *Criminal Justice and Behavior*, 15:323–333.

Thompson, Ginger. 2004. "Gangs Confound Law." *Syracuse Post-Standard* (originally appearing in the *New York Times*), September 26:A4.

Thompson, Hunter S. 1999. *Hell's Angels, a Strange and Terrible Saga*. New York: Random House.

Thorton, William E., and Lydia Voight. 1992. *Delinquency and Justice*, 3rd ed. New York: McGraw-Hill.

Thrasher, Frederic. 1962/1927. *The Gang*. Chicago: University of Chicago Press.

Tifft, Austin T. 1964. "The Coming Redefinitions of Crime: An Anarchist Perspective." *Social Problems* 26:392–402.

Tonry, Michael, and Mark H. Moore. 1998. *Youth Violence*. Chicago: University of Chicago Press.

Totten, Mark D. 2001. *Guys, Gangs, & Girlfriend Abuse*. Orchard Park, NY: Broadview.

Trojanowicz, Robert C., Merry Morash, and Pamela J. Schram. 2001. *Juvenile Delinquency*, 6th ed. Upper Saddle River, NJ: Prentice Hall.

Trump, Kenneth S. 1996. "Gangs and School Safety," in *Schools, Violence and Society*. Ed. Allan M. Hoffman. Westport, CT: Praeger.

———. 1998. *Practical School Security: Basic Guidelines for Safe and Secure Schools*. Thousand Oaks, CA: Corwin Press/Sage Publications.

Turner, Ralph H., and Samuel J. Surace. 1956. "Zoot-Suitors and Mexicans: Symbols in Crowd Behavior." *American Journal of Sociology* 62(1, Jul.):14–20.

Tyre, Peg. 1997. "New York Turns up the Heat on Crips, Bloods." *CNN Interactive*, August 27.

Tyson, Ann Scott. 1997. "Prison Threat: Gangs Grab More Power." *Christian Science Monitor* 89(160).

U.S. Census Bureau. 2003. "Poverty: 2002 Highlights." Last revised on September 26, 2003. Available: http://www.census.gov.

Vergano, Dan. 2002. "The 'Gangs' All Here, on a New York Tour." *USA Today*, December 3:8D.

Verhovek, Sam Howe. 1997. "As Texas Executions Mount, They Grow Routine." *New York Times*, May 25:A1 and A6.

Vigil, James D. 1988. *Barrio Gangs*. Austin, TX: University of Texas Press.

———. 1988. "Group Processes and Street Identity: Adolescent Chicano Gang Members." *Ethos* 16:421–445.

————. 1990. "Cholos and Gangs: Culture Change and Street Youths in Los Angeles," in *Gangs in America*. Ed. C. R. Huff. Newbury Park, CA: Sage.

————. 1997. "Origins of Mexican American Gangs: Learning from Gangs." *The Mexican American Experience, Eric Digest*. Available: http://www.ed.gov.databases/ERIC_Digests.

Vigil, James D., and J. M. Long. 1990. "Emic and Etic Perspectives on Gang Culture: The Chicano Case," in *Gangs in America*. Ed. C. R. Huff. Newbury Park, CA: Sage.

Vold, G. B. 1958. *Theoretical Criminology*, 2nd ed. New York: Oxford University Press.

Wade, Carole, and Carol Tavris. 2002. "Hormones and Emotions," in *Psychology*, 7th ed. Upper Saddle River, NJ: Prentice Hall.

Walker-Barnes, Chanequa J., and Craig A. Mason. 2001. "Perceptions of Risk Factors for Female Gang Involvement Among African American and Hispanic Woman." *Youth and Society* 32(3):303–336.

Warren, Jennifer, and Dan Morian. 2003. "Crips Target of Prison Lockdown." *Los Angeles Times*, July 1:B1.

Webb, Vincent J., and Charles M. Katz. 2003. "Policing Gangs in an Era of Community Policing," in *Policing Gangs and Youth Violence*. Ed. Scott H. Decker. Belmont, CA: Wadsworth.

Weibezahl, Sue. 2002. "Gang Violence Task Force Hits the Streets." *Syracuse Post-Standard*, June 9:A8.

————. 2003. "Police Say It's Working, but Some Residents are Disagreeing." *Syracuse Post-Standard*, May 19:A1.

————. 2003. "Street Violence, Killings, Sweep Upstate Big Cities." *Syracuse Post-Standard*, August 3:A1.

————. 2003. "Auditor: Anti-Drug Tactics Flawed." *Syracuse Post-Standard*, December 30:B5.

Weiser, Benjamin. 2003. "Founder of East Coast Bloods is Given 50 Years." *New York Times*, April 15:2D.

Weisheit, Ralph A., and L. Edward Wells. 2004. "Youth Gangs in Rural America." *NIJ Journal* 5:2–6.

Weisman, Larry. 2002. "Do-rags Formally Fall Out of Fashion with NFL." *USA Today*, March 29:1C.

Welling, Dale A. 1994. "Experts Unite to Combat Street and Prison Gang Activities." *Corrections Today* 56(5):148–149.

Williams, Frank P., and Marilyn D. McShane. 1994. *Criminological Theory*. Englewood Cliffs, NJ: Prentice Hall.

Wilson, William. 1987. *The Truly Disadvantaged*. Chicago: University of Chicago Press.

————. 1996. *When Work Disappears: The World of the New Urban Poor*. New York: Vintage Books.

Wolf, Daniel R. 1991. *Rebels*. Toronto: University of Toronto Press.

Yablonsky, Lewis. 1959. "The Delinquent Gang as a Near-Group." *Social Problems* 7:108–117.

————. 1997. *Gangsters: Fifty Years of Madness, Drugs, and Death on the Streets of America*. New York: New York University Press.

Youth Gangs and Juvenile Violence. 2003. "Indicators of Gang Membership." The Office of the Attorney General, State of Arkansas.

INDEX